"This is a rigorous, thoughtful and comprehensive book. It offers educators, at every level of instruction and engagement, a clear and useful guide. This is an innovative contribution to classroom practice and pedagogical theory."

Ron Scapp, *Professor of Humanities and Teacher Education at College of Mount Saint Vincent, New York, USA*

ENVIRONMENTAL LIBERATION EDUCATION

Environmental Liberation Education offers an easy-to-use, culturally responsive, and student-centered teaching approach to academic engagement and systemic change. It explains social-emotional tools and inquiry practices to discuss, reflect, and act for superdiverse student success, happiness, and global citizenship in a challenging, biodiverse world.

The book presents three Transformative Tools: Diversity Circles to organize, Multicultural Mindfulness to process, and Approach-in-Dimension to assess. The Tools show educators at all levels across disciplines how to reduce bias and make sustainability decisions daily. They empower teachers to develop peace for academic concentration in busy classrooms through a holistic understanding of body, mind, culture, and environment. The book offers a range of classroom-based and professional development exercises for critical consciousness, including mindfulness practices, transformative journal worksheets, cultural actions, and a self-survey to establish a baseline for hands-on diversity, well-being, and sustainability competencies.

Synthesizing multicultural and environmental education through mindfulness practices, *Environmental Liberation Education* is an invaluable resource for educators-in-training and practicing teachers.

Micaela Rubalcava is Professor of Education at Truckee Meadows Community College, USA, where she co-founded the award-winning Faculty for Radical Empowerment and Enlightenment (FREE). This book is inspired by Fulbright research in Chile and grounded in smalltown mountain sensibility from Quincy, California, where she and her life partner raised three children.

ENVIRONMENTAL LIBERATION EDUCATION

Diversity, Mindfulness, and Sustainability Tools for Teachers and Students

Micaela Rubalcava

Designed cover image: AlexMax / Getty images

First published 2025
by Routledge
605 Third Avenue, New York, NY 10158

and by Routledge
4 Park Square, Milton Park, Abingdon, Oxon, OX14 4RN

Routledge is an imprint of the Taylor & Francis Group, an informa business

© 2025 Micaela Rubalcava

The right of Micaela Rubalcava to be identified as author of this work has been asserted in accordance with sections 77 and 78 of the Copyright, Designs and Patents Act 1988.

The Open Access version of this book, available at www.taylorfrancis.com, has been made available under a Creative Commons Attribution-Non Commercial-No Derivatives (CC-BY-NC-ND) 4.0 license.

Any third party material in this book is not included in the OA Creative Commons license, unless indicated otherwise in a credit line to the material. Please direct any permissions enquiries to the original rightsholder.

The electronic version of this book was funded to publish Open Access through Taylor & Francis' Pledge to Open, a collaborative funding open access books initiative. The full list of pledging institutions can be found on the Taylor & Francis Pledge to Open webpage.

Trademark notice: Product or corporate names may be trademarks or registered trademarks, and are used only for identification and explanation without intent to infringe.

ISBN: 978-1-032-42891-8 (hbk)
ISBN: 978-1-032-42888-8 (pbk)
ISBN: 978-1-003-36475-7 (ebk)

DOI: 10.4324/9781003364757

Typeset in Galliard
by SPi Technologies India Pvt Ltd (Straive)

CONTENTS

Annotated Table of Contents — ix

    Introduction – How to Read This Book — 1

PART I
Big-Picture Transformation in the Real World — 19

  1 Culture-Conscious Listening and Global Praxis for Big-Picture Change — 21

  2 Transformative Teachers Now — 50

  3 Bias, Antibias, and Culture Competence — 90

  4 Structural Competence for Teachers — 125

PART II
Three Transformative Tools — 161

  5 Tool #1 – Diversity Circles — 163

  6 Tool #2 – Multicultural Mindfulness — 216

  7 Tool #3 – Approach-in-Dimension — 252

PART III
Multicultural Mindfulness for a Sustainable World — 289

8 Environmental Liberation Education — 291

Glossary — *326*
References — *339*
Index — *351*

ANNOTATED TABLE OF CONTENTS

Introduction: How to Read This Book

Explain how to:

- Integrate multicultural, mindfulness, and environmental education best practices into subject requirements and academic routines.
- Apply holistic student success, teacher empowerment, and knowledge development practices to hourly and daily education.
- Implement Three Transformative Tools.
- Develop your transformative teaching journey with Multicultural Mindfulness Activities and Transformative Breathwork and Journals provided in each chapter.
- Relate cultural identity terms to a global framework.
- Use the Glossary to reference terms of art about the emerging field of Environmental Liberation Education.

Provide:

- *Culture Survey* to personalize your diversity baseline.
- Summary of research methods, areas, data collection, coding, and analysis.
- Multicultural Mindfulness Activity to get started: *Diversity Circle Now*.

PART I
Big-Picture Transformation In The Real World

Chapter 1
Culture-Conscious Listening and Global Praxis for Big-Picture Change

Explain how to:

- Develop diversity as a source of solutions rather than view it as a problem.
- Use Culture-Conscious Listening for inclusive academic concentration.
- Apply Global Praxis to uplift academic engagement with sustainability outcomes.
- Experiment with transformative practices for big-picture change with Environmental Liberation Education.

Provide:

- Two Multicultural Mindfulness Activities and a journal question: *Split-Second Conflict Resolution*, *Culture-Conscious Listening*, and *What's a Transformative Teacher?*

Chapter 2
Transformative Teachers Now

Explain how:

- Good teachers are key to diverse student success.
- Systemic bias and unsustainable procedures fail students and teachers.
- Mindfulness is transformative.
- Transformative teachers help reform broken systems.
- Transformative teaching is easy and joyful.

Provide:

- Two Multicultural Mindfulness Activities and one journal question: *Un-biasing the Mind*, *Inclusive Academic Concentration*, and *How is Global Praxis a Verb and Environmental Humanization a Noun?*

Chapter 3
Bias, Antibias, and Culture Competence

Explain how:

- Educators choose bias or antibias hourly and daily.
- Ten forms of bias pose barriers to inclusive student success, knowledge accuracy, and sustainability systems.
- Well-intentioned educators unconsciously stereotype, favor, and exclude cultures.
- Multicultural Mindfulness develops culture competence for antibias decisions.
- Transformative teachers strengthen antibias decisions by applying structural competency to academic space, time, materials, and learning environments.

Provide:

- Two Multicultural Mindfulness Activities and one journal question: *Reducing Arm's-Length Bias, 4-Rs Antibias Practice*, and *How do Anglo-conformity and White Supremacy Impact My Classroom?*

Chapter 4
Structural Competence for Teachers

Explain how:

- Education is vital to economic-social systems and teachers are central to education.
- The substructure-superstructure model helps teachers visualize structural competence.
- Structural competence empowers teachers as change agents for cultural inclusion.
- Transformative teachers use structural competence to facilitate student-centered academic engagement, professional efficacy, and holistic humanization through education.
- Transformative teachers develop structural competence with Three Transformative Tools to advance culturally responsive holistic education for global citizenship and participation in a green economy.
- Education in Chile and Finland provides systemic reform lessons to learn from failure and success to develop Environmental Liberation Education.

Provide:

- Two Multicultural Mindfulness Activities and one journal question: *Structural Competence Imagination, Choice Education versus Equity Education*, and *What's Culture-Conscious Listening for Equity?*

PART II
Three Transformative Tools

Chapter 5
Tool #1 – Diversity Circles

Explain how Diversity Circles are inclusion learning communities to:

- Structure cross-cultural social-emotional trust during change for equity and sustainability in academic routines.
- Collaborate for holistic student success and teacher empowerment in a globalized world.
- Integrate cultures in phases with flexible strategies incorporating ethnic studies, diverse ways of knowing, community practices, and ecological activities into subjects.
- Organize diverse people for Environmental Liberation Education to develop Multicultural Mindfulness peace with big-picture Approach-in-Dimension design and assessment to meet requirements.

Provide:

- Two Multicultural Mindfulness Activities and one journal question: *Five Diversity Circle Projects, Diversity Circle Recipe*, and *How do Diversity Circles reconcile the oppressor–oppressed conflict?*

Chapter 6
Tool #2 – Multicultural Mindfulness

Explain how Multicultural Mindfulness is an inclusive peace process to

- Apply holistic curriculum and knowledge development to big-picture change.
- Nurture cultural inclusion and diversity belonging in academic concentration.
- Integrate body-mind-culture-environment activities into subjects for student and teacher reconciliation and humanization.
- Use backwards design to engage subjects with culturally responsive systemic questions.
- Prompt reflective liberation and sustainability action to link subjects to human superdiversity in Earth biodiversity.
- Develop inward calm to address fear of change and outward compassion to resolve creative tension non-defensively.
- Collaborate on joyful justice projects to integrate academics into global citizenship and a sustainability economy.

Provide:

- Two Multicultural Mindfulness Activities and one journal question: *Shaping Space for Interbeing*, *Drive-All-Blames-Into-One*, and *What's Multicultural Mindfulness?*

Chapter 7
Tool #3 – Approach-in-Dimension

Explain how the Approach-in-Dimension is a philosophy of education rubric to

- Determine a transparent approach to humanization through academic design and evaluation, adaptable to professional passion, subject requirements, and site cultures.
- Analyze six ideological *approaches* to five education *dimensions* for holistic planning and assessment.
- Change assimilation and segregation education with activities for holistic and integrated student success, educator empowerment, and accurate knowledge for a sustainable world.
- Collect cultural data and achievement results about progress, stasis, or setbacks from academic engagement changes.
- Compare philosophical intentions to data and results to guide decisions about space, time, materials, and learning environments.

Provide:

- Two Multicultural Mindfulness Activities and one journal question: *Healthy Multicultural Identity Quest*, *Superdiverse Biodiverse Me Turtle*, and *What's the Approach-in-Dimension?*

PART III
Multicultural Mindfulness for a Sustainable World

Chapter 8
Environmental Liberation Education

Explain how Environmental Liberation Education is holistic action-reflection to:

- Reduce bias, assimilation, segregation, and environmental destruction in education by integrating multicultural, mindfulness, and sustainability into academic activities.
- Empower educators and students by engaging core content with critical consciousness circles indoors and outdoors, on site and off, through big picture themes.
- Motivate subject engagement with local and global systems questions, cultural practices and stories, and scientific data through problem-solving projects.
- Apply Three Transformative Tools to structure, process, and assess academic engagement for inclusive humanization in a superdiverse-biodiverse world.

Provide:

- Fresh examples showing the fun and ease of Environmental Liberation Education.
- Two Multicultural Mindfulness Activities and one journal question: *Nonverbal Communication Toothpick Game, Environmental Liberation Education Made Easy*, and *What's Environmental Liberation Education?*

Glossary
References
Index

INTRODUCTION

How to Read This Book

Guiding Purpose

Explain how to

- Integrate multicultural, mindfulness, and environmental education best practices into subject requirements and academic routines.
- Apply holistic student success, teacher empowerment, and knowledge development practices to hourly and daily education.
- Implement Three Transformative Tools.
- Develop your transformative teaching journey with Multicultural Mindfulness Activities and Transformative Breathwork and Journals provided in each chapter.
- Relate cultural identity terms to a global framework.
- Use the Glossary to reference terms of art about the emerging field of Environmental Liberation Education.

Provide a

- *Culture Survey* to personalize your diversity baseline.
- Summary of research methods, areas, data collection, coding, and analysis.
- Multicultural Mindfulness Activity to get started: *Diversity Circle Now*.

Why Transformative Teaching Now?

In *Why We Can't Wait*, Dr. Martin Luther King, Jr. described the "mythical concept of time" about the deferral of justice for African Americans.[1] Today, this concept pertains to *all* life on a planet suffering from climate change. We're all out of time. This book offers Three Transformative Tools to grow compassionate collaborations for culturally responsive change with humanization questions and joyful justice practices. It describes an empowerment approach to transformative teaching – Environmental Liberation Education – to replace mainstream exclusions with diversity experiences. Environmental Liberation Education integrates subjects into multicultural, mindfulness, and sustainability circle activities, indoors and outdoors, on site and off. This book explores the intersection of biodiversity and cultural diversity. It describes action-reflection for holistic student success, teacher empowerment, and eco-friendly academics during our teachable moment.

The Diversity Circles tool organizes for inclusion. It gathers cross-cultural collaborations for academic action-reflection to make prosocial change. This alliance-building tool develops culturally responsive learning communities to integrate sustainability activities into routines. The Multicultural Mindfulness tool provides a process for peace. It is a set of well-being practices. It includes procedures for holistic academic concentration, diversity belonging, and environmental consciousness. The Approach-in-Dimension tool is design and assessment for holism. This big-picture matrix helps educators define humanity in education with transparent reference points about diversity and change in subjects and students in classrooms, labs, and meeting rooms and across sites.

This book explains how to integrate arts and sciences into body-mind-culture-environment activities during "hourly and daily" education, not as a distraction to requirements but to deepen student engagement and professional development.[2] Transformative teaching is activating subjects with humanization questions and circle projects about cultures, mindfulness, and nature. Transformative teaching is reducing over-standardized, stratified, and environmentally alienating procedures by implementing social emotional academic learning in real time. Transformative teachers increase multicultural and ecological unity events. Transformative teachers link academics to the environment through culture to learn how to respond to change and make change. We heal broken systems with culturally creative environmental experiences to practice education as freedom.[3]

Environmental Liberation Education is an approach to transformative teaching that connects subjects to local and global intergenerational relationships. This approach strengthens curriculum, outcomes, knowledge, communications, and site interactions with sustainability values. It develops cultural, structural, and ecological competence through mindfulness during routines. It assists subject planning and assessment with critical consciousness for the green "new economy."[4] Environmental Liberation Education reimagines academics with action-reflection circles for Earth stewardship. It uses backwards design,[5] asking: How do we reconceive this requirement with open-mindedness? How do we invigorate this classroom, lab, meeting room, or site activity with diversity and sustainability questions? How do we interpret this subject for multicultural global citizenship?

This book welcomes teachers and students of all identities and demographic backgrounds into egalitarianism. We each come from different cultural standpoints within systemic racism and environmental alienation. We have regional experiences in globalization and climate crises. We have personal proclivities, assorted areas of expertise, and distinct work to do, but prosocial healing is collective. As we develop intersectional identities in community, we connect academics to sustainability in context. Our transformative decisions repair divisions with antibias-antiracist changes for shared purpose through climate justice projects to reduce consumption and reuse, recycle, and restore Earth holistically.

Transformative teaching is applying "joyful and just" activities hourly and daily.[6] It is mindfulness of the universe while meeting social-emotional academic needs with cultural responsiveness. It is de-stressing education with respect for sun, land, sky, and water. It is exercising

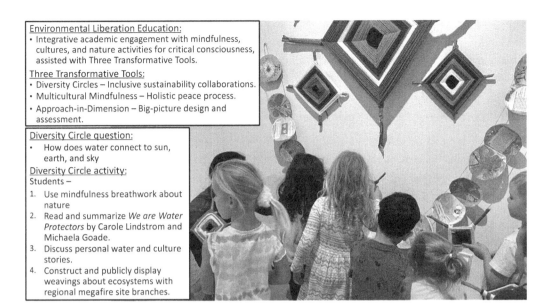

FIGURE I.1 Environmental Liberation Education in action. Photo by Tim Ill.

academic freedom to deepen the humanization goals that motivate teachers and students.[7] Rather than being overwhelmed by systemic divisions or stymied by fear, we use peace precepts for gratitude and to work through creative tension during change. We uplift academic expectations with a integrated sense of humanity to engage subjects with cultures, mindfulness, and nature now.

What's Sustainability?

Sustainability is intergenerational stewardship for balance in cultural, economic, and environmental systems. "The practice of sustainability recognizes how these issues are interconnected and requires a systems approach and an acknowledgement of complexity."[8] Multicultural Mindfulness is a cornerstone to this systems approach for educators. Multicultural Mindfulness is a peacegiving, culturally responsive process. Educators use Multicultural Mindfulness to reduce conflict during sustainability changes to education space, time, materials, and learning environments.

> Intergenerational equity is a notion that views the human community as a partnership among all generations. Each generation has the right to inherit the same diversity in natural and cultural resources enjoyed by previous generations and to equitable access to the use and benefits of these resources. [T]he present generation is a custodian of the planet for future generations.[9]

Sustainability is our motivation. Transformative teachers facilitate diverse students into culture-conscious subject engagement for well-being now, mindful of future generations. We do more than follow requirements. We *reinterpret* mandates and *apply* holistic decisions to reduce the dehumanizing and unsustainable systems that undermine academic concentration.

4 Introduction

Multicultural Mindfulness humanizes classrooms by removing cultural barriers to teaching and learning and by increasing equity experiences through universal design. Educator mindfulness *of* human superdiversity in Earth's biodiversity reshapes curriculum, instruction, and assessment toward liberating outcomes.

Three Transformative Tools for Environmental Liberation Education

This book is for busy education students, teachers, scholars, and administrators, preschool through higher education. Three Transformative Tools – Diversity Circles, Multicultural Mindfulness, and Approach-in-Dimension – form a healing path. Each tool is explained with examples and models. Together, the tools support transformative teaching through Environmental Liberation Education. Diversity Circles form the *structure*. Multicultural Mindfulness is the *process* for the structure. The Approach-in-Dimension *plans* and *evaluates* process outcomes to develop structural change. We use Three Transformative Tools to reduce environmental alienation and social-economic stratifications reproduced through mainstream education that largely serves the global extraction-consumption economy. These tools develop cultural methods for diverse student success through justice and ecological activities before "the human race disappears."[10]

How This Book is Different

This book explains how to strengthen culture competence with structural competence. It develops critical consciousness to challenge *systemic* bias. Rather than intermittently add more prepackaged solutions, this book supports your professional capacity to collaborate on liberation. This book explains that structural racism impacts everything at school, operating beneath "race-neutral" policies and "color-blind" wishes.[11] We start with pragmatic compassion for everyone caught in assimilation and segregation systems. Transformative teachers perceive routines with a cultural lens. We see diversity in classrooms, labs, hallways, meeting rooms, auditoriums, cafeterias, and grounds and in interactions between schools and communities. We also spot inequities so we can apply non-defensive analysis moment by moment and make decisions for holistic change.

This book illustrates how transformative classrooms are unlike mainstream classrooms. Otherwise known as "banking education," mainstream classrooms deliver curriculum standardized into commoditization.[12] Banking education is the opposite of liberation education. *Transformative* classrooms spend less time in top-down activities and more time in

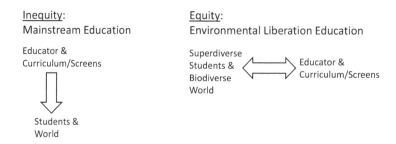

FIGURE I.2 Top-down Inequity versus Horizontal Equity graphic. Created by the author.

student-centered sensory circles with real-world experiences. Transformative classrooms learn required content, yes, but we do so with big-picture questions and cultures, mindfulness, and nature activities, indoors and outdoors. We respect diverse ways of knowing and grow social-emotional integration experiences *during* academic engagement.

Happily, part of the teacher job description is to make decisions about education space, time, materials, and learning environments. *Transformative* teachers use this academic freedom to change divisive policies with cultural action. We reduce vertical screen and lecture procedures and increase horizontal hands-on integrations. We facilitate circle openers and diversify core content with intersectional project teams. We close sessions with culturally responsive reflections.[13] We welcome different languages. We scaffold application, analysis, synthesis, and evaluation experiences into knowledge and comprehension objectives framed by sustainability.

We regulate academic freedom with collaborative scientific peer review. We gather diversity information from culture surveys and apply action research to evolving materials. Transformative teachers balance mainstream textbooks and unit packages with diverse funds of knowledge from community resources, ethnic studies, women's studies, and other identity studies.[14] Librarians help us curate diversity, mindfulness, and sustainability themes. We refresh cross-cultural connections, rotating perspectives in community participation with diverse guest speakers and field trips for equity experiences. We globalize curriculum, instruction, and assessment with multimodal environmental education.

Whether your classroom or program runs vertically or like the horizontal relationship graphic above, this book is for you.[15]

Establish Your Diversity Baseline

The Multicultural Mindfulness tool for Environmental Liberation Education facilitates a holistic process with three mindfulness principles: impermanence, interbeing, and emptiness.[16] Briefly, this means that transformative teachers respond to change inclusively with an open mind. We apply Multicultural Mindfulness peace practices to everyday routines. We use Multicultural Mindfulness before, during, and after core academic engagement activities. These practices are personal *and* collective (e.g., breathwork, body-mind-culture-environment integration exercises, and healing reflections). One reflection is to take a culture survey to establish a reference point for transformation.

Culture surveys come in many forms. The survey below helps to personalize a diversity baseline to apply Multicultural Mindfulness with an "unbounded clarity of mind."[17] This survey elicits a reference for your equity, inclusion, and sustainability progress. You reflect on your cultural story and social norms in your profession. You consider humanity in your most important subjects and how you respond to cultural perspectives in curriculum and requirements. Feel free to adapt this survey to use with your own students or colleagues. There are no wrong answers. Please use a journal to write self-survey answers.

Journal

Designate a journal for reading notes and journal exercises in each chapter. Your journal can be a simple notebook for your preferred note-taking style. Or it could be an artsy booklet you make. *Hand*writing translates theory into personal meaning. Handwriting documents data and creates cultural artifacts for developing ideas. Adapt your journal to modality preferences. Consider variation, such as outlining, scribbling, printing, calligraphy, cursive, illustrating, doodling, diagramming, collaging, and coloring. Try journaling outdoors or indoors with background aromas or music, alone or with others, and with cultural and nature objects nearby, integrating body, mind, culture, and environment into holistic reflection.

Survey Answers

Brainstorm answers fairly quickly. It should take about 20 minutes, with about one minute for each prompt. If you're a student, answer from your most recent school experiences. If you're an employed aide, teacher, or professor, answer about your most recent classroom or research experiences. If you're an administrator, answer about your program. Write heartfelt responses, reflecting on bias and culture. Notice assumptions that unconsciously influence routine decisions that may, as research suggests, end up ranking students and content into cultural tiers.[18]

Your answers also establish a diversity *success* baseline. You describe inclusion practices you already use. You explain how you engage cultures in your curriculum, outcomes, knowledge, communications, and interactions. You consider how you document and share diversity successes. You reflect on best practices that develop knowledge for skillful participation in a challenging world.

Culture Survey

In a global context

1 Define "culture" in your own words.
2 Describe your students' "diversity."
3 Describe your "diversity."
4 Compare and contrast "diversity," "equity," and "inclusion."
5 (a) Define "mindfulness." (b) Describe your go-to mindfulness practices.
6 (a) Define "sustainability." (b) Describe your go-to sustainability practices.
7 Describe how you support inclusive academic success in core content and how you engage with diversity on campus.
8 Describe your equity, mindfulness, and/or sustainability collaborations for your most important subjects or programs.
9 Describe how you facilitate curriculum engagement through diverse perspectives.
10 Describe how you research, create, and disseminate new multicultural, mindfulness, and/or sustainability knowledge in your field of expertise.
11 Describe how you identify and reduce your own unconscious bias habits.
12 Describe how you connect academic *routines* to multicultural, mindfulness, and/or sustainability experiences.
13 (a) Rate your culture competence and (b) rate your structural competence, using a scale of 1 (nonexistent) to 10 (actively fluent).
14 Describe your go-to non-defensive communication methods when the going gets rough.
15 Name a colleague to invite to form a (or join an existing) Diversity Circle: An education learning community of two or more participants, as diverse as possible, engaged in peace-giving holistic change.

Book Activities and Organization

This book is designed to deepen culture competence with structural competence. It describes how to apply transformative tools to best practices that connect your subject expertise and campus conditions to sustainability experiences *with* students and colleagues now.

Multicultural Mindfulness Activities

Each chapter describes activities to involve you in the Multicultural Mindfulness process. They present hands-on exercises for holistic change. Some of these action-reflection exercises are breathwork practices, and others are lesson plans for classroom or professional development activities, ranging from a few minutes to about an hour, with minimal materials. They emerged from community college action research, but they're adaptable to any curriculum or program at any education level.[19] They aim to help you reduce bias habits from unconscious stereotypes. They support you to work *with* student and colleague cultures with inclusion concepts in the subjects you teach and research, relating what you do to mindfulness of diversity, equity, and sustainability.

Transformative Breathwork and Journal

At the end of each chapter, use the Transformative Breathwork and Journal to put you inside this book's imaginary Diversity Circle. You are invited to reflect *with* me, the author, and with the transformative educators cited in this book. After breathwork, you are encouraged to read a journal passage prompt and write a reflection on core concepts that apply to you, such as how to "un-standardize" or "detrack" your classroom or committees and how to plan, implement, and evaluate multicultural, mindfulness, and sustainability education in core content.[20]

Chapter Organization and Glossary

The chapters are organized into the following categories – Context, Theory and Practice, Application, Examples, Conclusion, and Transformative Breathwork and Journal, with interspersed Multicultural Mindfulness Activities. Chapter 8 is different; it concludes the book with three synthesis sections, offering fresh insights about transformative teaching with Environmental Liberation Education. The glossary briefly defines key terms that appear in each chapter, noting where in the book to find detailed explanations.

Cultural Identity Terms

Issues surrounding cultural terms, categorization, and identity politics, such as whether to capitalize Black and White, and the growing use of the term "Latinx," are complicated and fraught with controversy. Entire books have been written about the construction of human categories.[21] This book strives for a culturally sustaining approach, mindful of how superdiversity in biodiversity shapes humanity, enmeshed in shifting racialized systems involving globalization and mass migration. This book recognizes that though many people wish for a colorblind society, race persists as a "primary" or "central axis" culture category in most contexts because of centuries of economic and social structures that have cumulatively damaged or privileged groups on the basis of race.[22] Thus, depending on context, this book variously uses "Native American," "American Indian," and "Indigenous"; "Asian American"; "Hispanic" and "Latinx"; "African American" and "Black"; and "European American" and "White"; however, other categories and self-identifications are also recognized. Following the style guidelines of the American Psychological Association, this book capitalizes these terms, including Black and White.

Summary of Research Methods, Areas, Data Collection, Coding, and Analysis

Mixed-Methods Action Research

The research methodology, data collection, and data analysis that inform this book developed from two decades of literature review and case study of teacher education. Case notes were developed into premises, theories, and action-reflection procedures discussed below, resulting in Three Transformative Tools – Diversity Circles, Multicultural Mindfulness, and Approach-in-Dimension – for Environmental Liberation Education.

This book employs "mixed methods" action research to combine grounded theory, critical theory, case study, narrative, and visual inquiry. Research techniques for comparative inductive and deductive analysis were applied to coding education literature, national and international documents, student survey responses, case journaling in natural settings, curriculum studies, visual information, and notes about experiential phenomena and physical artifacts. The research weaves together about 300 works about education, focusing on multicultural education, liberation education, mindfulness education, and environmental education, as well as works with examples about education systems in three countries: the United States, Chile, and Finland.

The research integrates data from multiple sources to relate teacher and teacher training experiences, student outcomes, curriculum designs, and knowledge development to a definition of academic achievement that encompasses diversity and humanization criteria. It examines recurrent words, factors, patterns, and statistics, using a spiral method for action research.[23] Initially, open coding was used by taking extensive comprehension notes to recognize significant pieces of data. Then, in multiple reviews, the ideas, attitudes, phrases, and trends that reappeared in the data were reassessed with narrative structure to give meaning to discovery. The mixed-methods action research was integrated into criteria advanced by diverse educator-activists, primarily James A. Banks, Edward Clark, John B. Diamond, Roxanne Dunbar-Ortiz, Paulo Freire, Thich Nhat Hanh, bell hooks, Amanda E. Lewis, Martin Luther King, Jr., Sandra Nieto, Christine E. Sleeter, Ronald Takaki, and Cecilia Vicuña.

Three Research Areas

This book synthesizes three areas for adaptability to educators of all identities and demographic backgrounds in different fields of expertise and levels of education. The first area investigates culture conflict and integration in education, examining systemic bias-versus-antibias curriculum, mindfulness programs, and unsustainable routines-versus-sustainability activities. This area is about understanding *what* to transform. The second area analyzes the impact of multicultural education on mainstream education. This area examines ethnic studies, multicultural education, and Minority-Serving Institutions to survey diversity innovations involving students and teachers to understand *who* transforms. The third area analyzes education in global context, comparing US education with international examples about private-versus-public and liberation education, illustrating pros and cons. This area is about *how* to transform institutions in systems.

These three areas inform core practices explained in this book, such as Culture-Conscious Listening and Global Praxis in the Multicultural Mindfulness tool. The three areas examine racial ideologies in bias patterns in education that harm student outcomes and environmental health. They show how to integrate structural competence into culture competence during subject engagement *with* students and colleagues to connect inclusion education to world healing. The three areas strengthen the humanization goals that motivate teachers, establishing what, who, and how to change mainstream procedures with awareness of superdiversity *in* biodiversity.

Collection, Coding, and Analysis

Research collection, coding, and analysis cover the following Environmental Liberation Education criteria, theories, and topics, punctuated by international illustrations of education reform:

1. Paulo Freire's liberation education theory of humanization praxis with "*conscientização*" (critical consciousness) and Cecilia Vicuña's feminist environmental arts education theory of "*espaciotiempo*" (spacetime), with topics such as resisting "banking education" with culture circles, and using structural analysis for cultural action with coding hinged themes, such as mothers with children, to change systems.[24]
2. James A. Banks's multicultural education and reform theories, with topics such as additive, contributions, transformative, and social action, and how to reduce prejudice, construct knowledge inclusively, enact culturally relevant pedagogy, integrate ethnic studies content, and diversify school social systems.[25]
3. Dr. Martin Luther King, Jr.'s explanation of nonviolent direct action, with topics such as evidence collection, negotiation, self-purification, and direct action; this is reinterpreted by bell hooks with concepts about intersectional feminist transformative education.[26]
4. Environmental education reform focusing on the works of Edward Clark and Phil Gang, with topics such as "ecological systems," "humanity-through-nature," restorative ecology, and big-picture questions and designs.[27]
5. Mindfulness education, culturally responsive education, and international education reform, with topics such as the three mindfulness principles of "interbeing," "impermanence," and "emptiness" and basic practices such as "five mindfulness trainings" and "*Tonglen*" breathwork, from Thich Nhat Hanh and Chögyam Trungpa. Other criteria, theories, and topics include Social Emotional Learning (SEL), multiple intelligences, cognitive range, equity education, antibias-antiracist change, Culturally Relevant Education (CRE), learning communities, and race-class-gender interdisciplinary curriculum transformation.[28]

Global Examples

Global examples about transformative teaching give texture to Environmental Liberation Education criteria, theories, and topics. Examples of success – such as Finland's universal public education system, operated flexibly by highly qualified teachers with student-centered designs – model how to integrate academics equitably and humanize sustainably. Other examples demonstrate how to change unfortunate conditions marked by segregation and unsustainability, like liberation education used to repair distressed systems in Brazil and Chile. Global examples illustrate how pliable education elements – space, time, materials, and learning environments – can be maneuvered by teachers to facilitate a holistic philosophy of humanity, such as by applying the Environmental Liberation Education approach to transformative teaching.

Research with Mindfulness

The book's research develops holistic transformative criteria, theories, and topics by applying mindfulness to antibias-antiracist strategies for change toward sustainability unity. Mindfulness is peace now. It is compassionate awareness to develop the art and science of calm cultural and environmental listening. It is the reflective process of present-moment belonging. Mindfulness integrates. It makes connections between unlike categories, such as joining the liberation education, multicultural education, nonviolent direct action, environmental education, and public education fields synthesized in this book. Mindfulness involves being present with suffering and healing to "open our mind so the light of concentration will reveal what is there and liberate what is there." Mindfulness empowers *nonviolent* structural change for a better world.[29]

Antibias-antiracist theory involves taking action and expressing ideas against racism.[30] This isn't only opposing explicit racism; it's also resisting mainstream norms that enforce racism subtly. This starts with concentration on barriers to cultural respect. At school, this is listening for "race-neutral" language and "the rhetoric of broadening equality" that mask systemic inequities and obstruct cross-cultural respect. It's perceiving unconscious biases in hourly and daily academics that perpetuate structural racism. Mindful antibias-antiracist practitioners attempt to calmly recognize hypocrisies in routines, revealing how "the *ostensive aspect* (the ideal of the routine)" often contradicts "the *performative aspect* (the routine as practiced)."[31]

Antibias-antiracist practices identify how *de facto* segregation and racialized patterns pit poor White Americans against poor people of color. They interrupt the steady beat of discrimination networking through modern US bureaucracies – otherwise known as "'new racism,' 'color-blind' racism, 'laissez-faire racism,' 'symbolic racism,' 'racial apathy,' or 'averse racism.'" Antibias-antiracist theory proposes that transformation toward unity occurs when people on location *apply* diversity activities to uproot "practices that maintain racial inequality" and abuse Earth.[32] Antibias-antiracist educators protect the integrity of ethnic studies and multicultural education while *integrating* equity policies for culturally responsive inclusion experiences across the curriculum.[33]

Mindfulness nourishes true happiness.[34] Mindfulness *of* the "humanity-*through*-nature" paradigm gives antibias-antiracist education environmental purpose.[35] Mindfulness brings in thousands of years of metacognition about holistic well-being. Mindfulness reveals the violent human causes of global warming and peaceful solutions "to liberate what is there."[36] It develops *intergenerational* environmental consciousness. Mindfulness integrates body, mind, culture, and environment into knowledge to grow ecosystems with interbeing, impermanence, and emptiness values. Mindfulness *of* history, such as awareness of "hunter-gatherer" and "agricultural age" systems, shows alternatives to "mechanistic industrial age" consciousness absorbed in racialized extraction, commoditization,

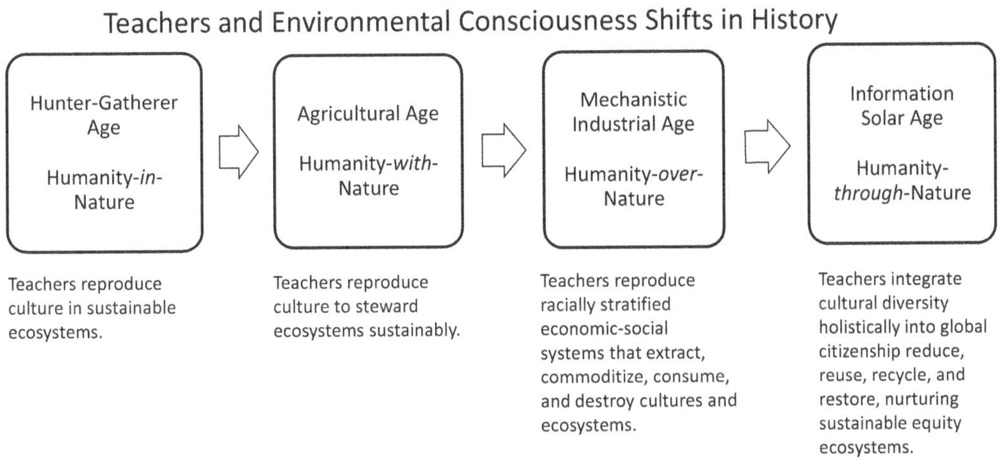

Teachers and Environmental Consciousness Shifts in History

Hunter-Gatherer Age	Agricultural Age	Mechanistic Industrial Age	Information Solar Age
Humanity-*in*-Nature	Humanity-*with*-Nature	Humanity-*over*-Nature	Humanity-*through*-Nature
Teachers reproduce culture in sustainable ecosystems.	Teachers reproduce culture to steward ecosystems sustainably.	Teachers reproduce racially stratified economic-social systems that extract, commoditize, consume, and destroy cultures and ecosystems.	Teachers integrate cultural diversity holistically into global citizenship reduce, reuse, recycle, and restore, nurturing sustainable equity ecosystems.

FIGURE I.3 Environmental Consciousness historical flowchart. Created by the author.

and consumption patterns. Awareness of consciousness differences empowers everyday educators to make decisions for cultural action to reduce, reuse, recycle, and restore ecology *during* subject engagement, depicted in the flowchart above.[37]

Environmental Liberation Education

The Environmental Liberation Education approach that emerged from research describes mindfulness practices to transform suffering at school through joyful justice action-reflection routines. It's a philosophy of education for environmental consciousness to develop knowledge holistically and graduate students inclusively into the "information solar age" with global citizenship skills, such as sustainability proficiencies and cross-cultural collaboration competencies.

Structure

Transformative teachers *with* colleagues *and* students treat academic content as a medium for systemic change through holistic education. Collaboration for change has been used in US education learning communities for decades, and it embodies the culture circle model of global liberation education.[38] This book also investigates the *sangha* structure, a time-honored social unit for mindfulness education. The *sangha* models holistic well-being and compassion cooperation. *Sangha* circles have been practiced globally since 566 BCE.[39] The mindfulness *sangha* is a community of practice for body-mind-culture health and "work for the benefit of others."[40] *Sanghas* meet regularly to share knowledge and accountability during the continual transformation of self and society toward reconciliation. Consistent action-reflection in a community of care helps "to realize liberation, peace, and joy" through three principles for generosity: interbeing, impermanence, and emptiness.[41] *Sangha* collaboration principles and structural integrity reinforce the education learning communities and cultures circles that define Diversity Circles for Environmental Liberation Education.

Process

One *sangha* method is the basis for the 4-Rs Antibias Practice in the Multicultural Mindfulness toolbox, explained in Chapter 3.[42] Like all Multicultural Mindfulness practices, it is a process method. First, educators *recognize* alienation experiences from oppression systems, such as education segregation, racialized tracking, and assimilation curriculum, all of which narrow academic achievement and ignore the project of integrated environmental education for all. Second, educators *refrain* from perpetuating the inequities and environmental damages we recognize. Third, educators take *restorative action* for critical consciousness to connect education to real-world healing. Fourth, transformative educators *resolve* to remain proactive with holistic change, refusing to be overwhelmed by the systemic scale. We act and reflect to design, implement, redesign, and reimplement academic activities to reduce, reuse, recycle, and restore compassionately and equitably.

One illustration of such resolve is the work of bilingual special educator Juliana Urtubey – 2021 National Teacher of the Year – who demonstrates how to commit to "joyful and just" education. Urtubey shows how to take the professional leap from ignoring or being overwhelmed by injustice, to instead *recognize* the challenges of teaching in a segregated Title I school. She *refrains* from caving to the negativity of dilapidated buildings, discouraged colleagues, and at-risk students deflated by systemic inequities. She takes *restorative action* by collaborating on environmental projects through diversity teams. She creates school-community gardens and murals to integrate science, math, arts, and social studies standards into regional cultural stories expressed through garden artwork, planting motifs, and sustainability projects, such as farmers' market and butterfly and bee plots. The multicultural teams she organizes *resolve* to remain in committees for long-term equity and sustainability practices.[43]

Design and Assessment

The Approach-in-Dimension is a design and assessment tool based on the multicultural education scholarship of James A. Banks. Banks wrote about two models. One is about four *approaches*, and the other is about five *dimensions*.[44] The Approach-in-Dimension reconceives Banks's models by synthesizing them, inserting "Mainstream" at the start and "Environmental Liberation Education" at the end, resulting in *six* approaches to five dimensions. Different from checklists about diversity outcomes, the Approach-in-Dimension *integrates* Banks's work into a philosophical map. By choosing a philosophical destination for curriculum, learning outcomes, knowledge, communications, and site interactions, the Approach-in-Dimension supports teachers to more accurately guide the cumulative effect of the about 1,500 decisions we make daily.[45]

Everyday teachers become transformative teachers when we reflect on disciplinary best practices as well as political ideologies in routines.[46] The Approach-in-Dimension matrix invites teachers to select from the wide array of best practices that exist for student interactions, subject development, and academic evaluation. With clarity of purpose, we make decisions with mindfulness. For example, the partially filled Approach-in-Dimension chart below shows a range of philosophies for one education dimension – site interactions – about a project.[47] It shows how each of the six education philosophies differently arrange space, time, materials, and the learning environment for the project. Determining a

FIGURE I.4 Garden-Mural Approach-in-Dimension Example graphic. Created by the author.

philosophy about humanity is an exercise of academic freedom. It's like choosing a brand. Transformative teachers tailor philosophical decisions to subject expertise, requirements, and site conditions. Then, as we develop best practices through professional collaboration and assessment reflection, we are supported to change designs when we find that outcomes don't match philosophical intentions.

Three Transformative Tools

In summary, mixed-methods action research was used to gather, code, and analyze literature, documents, surveys, case study notes, curriculum studies, visuals, and artifacts about multicultural, mindfulness, and sustainability education, with global examples. The book's research developed topics, criteria, and theories that evolved into Three Transformative Tools for Environmental Liberation Education. These tools support everyday teachers to make hourly and daily decisions to change mainstream routines from exclusion patterns and unsustainable outcomes into inclusion and sustainability experiences. The three tools assist collaborations to create equity pathways for inclusive student success, preparing students holistically for skillful participation in a superdiverse-biodiverse world.

Transformative teachers work in teams. Two or more participants form a Diversity Circle, providing a trust-building home base for calm action-reflection about holistic education. Participants use Multicultural Mindfulness compassion to infuse subject engagement with body-mind-culture-environment integration activities. The Approach-in-Dimension tool guides academic design and evaluation with big-picture clarity. Its rubric outlines six approaches in five dimensions to assist educators to determine humanization criteria to guide antibias decisions.

As a labor of love, transformative teachers counteract inequity systems by shaping equity ecosystems in classrooms, labs, and meeting rooms and across sites. We orient diverse students to a sustainability economy using reduce, reuse, recycle, and restore materials and routines during subject engagement. We deepened social emotional academic learning with multicultural imagination and critical consciousness projects. We roll up our sleeves to reconcile divides, uplifting expectations with cultural and Earth well-being experiences now.

MULTICULTURAL MINDFULNESS ACTIVITY

Diversity Circle Now

Outcome

- Grow a Diversity Circle.
- Experiment with Culture-Conscious Listening.

Key Concepts

- **Breathwork**: Conscious breathing for body-mind well-being and academic concentration.
- **Culture-Conscious Listening**: A five-step Multicultural Mindfulness practice about diversity: Culture-Conscious Breath, Pleasant Eye Contact, Compassionate Support, Brief Summary, and Antibias Question.
- **Diversity Circle**: Humanization learning community for holistic change with two or more participants, as diverse as possible. Your circle integrates critical consciousness into subject action-reflection with cultural, mindfulness, and environmental practices. Your circle assesses outcomes with inclusion, equity, and sustainability criteria for local and global healing.

Resources

- Journal, pencil, an example or symbol of nature, a place to meet indoors or outdoors.

Big-Picture Question

- How do we support diverse student success now?

Start

- **Invite** a colleague to discuss student diversity and the cultures that shape a subject.

At the First Meeting

- **Discuss** what Culture-Conscious Listening might be.
- **Apply** what you think Culture-Conscious Listening is without worrying about details (it's explained in Chapter 1). Don't be concerned about listening "correctly," just notice culture at your meeting. Try the first step – Culture-Conscious Breath – a reflective inhale-exhale about culture: "What biases are here?" "What cultures are in my heart?" or "What cultures are here?"

- **Each describe** nature in or near your meeting, discussing how nature relates to, or is alienated from, your academic routines, speculating about how different cultures interact with the example of nature you observe.
- **Each tell** a personal cultural story from lived experience or about the cultures in your classroom, lab, or meeting rooms or across campus.
- **Journal** *Antibias Questions* that emerge. Write questions about diversity or inclusion, such as "What other cultures do we need to understand in this topic?" "What stereotypes do we need to challenge?" "How do we relate this topic to big-picture systems?" or "What diverse perspectives guide this topic to social justice *and* sustainability?"
- **Journal** about *assumptions* that surfaced about cultures.
- **Schedule** another meeting.

Middle

- After the first meeting, **apply** one cultural story, assumption, or Antibias Question that surfaced to a classroom, lab, or meeting room activity.
- **Confirm** that your activity engages a required subject. You're bringing diversity into core content. Also, seek an opportunity for students or colleagues to pose culture questions related to the content.

Closing

At the second meeting, using Culture-Conscious Listening:

- **Discuss** what happened during your diversity activity, such as a question about culture or bias, an antibias insight, or a subject diversification.
- **Each describe** your recollection of nature in or near the location of your activity, discussing how nature related to it or was absent.
- **Plan** the next diversity activity you will soon try, but this next time, integrate a nature or sustainability experience, such as going outdoors or bringing nature indoors. Again, your experiment should activate required subject engagement.
- **Determine** more meetings to:
  - Take and discuss the *Culture Survey* above.
  - Read a diversity, mindfulness, or sustainability resource, book club–style.
  - Develop Culture-Conscious Listening competency while doing diversity-sustainability activities.
- **Remember**, transformation is as much about breaking personal bias and destruction habits as it is about changing systems. As you grow culture competence to reduce racism and sexism, you also increase sustainability experiences with holistic academic routines. You realize that big-picture education motivates academic concentration and professional development. Once your commitment to liberation begins, culture-conscious questions personalize Multicultural Mindfulness. You discover that because you are part of structural solutions through academic inclusion, you're not at the mercy of systemic racism and global warming. You collaborate non-defensively for restorative action. You apply compassion to decisions for intergenerational culture change. You embrace diversity as an hourly and daily *solution* rather than see it as a problem.

Notes

1 King (1964), 85.
2 Lewis and Diamond (2015), xix.
3 hooks (1994).
4 Reece (2022), 40.
5 Sleeter and Carmona (2017).
6 Urtubey (2023, June 20).
7 Rubalcava (2005); Fried (2001).
8 Block (2016).
9 Summers and Smith (2014).
10 Hanh and Weare (2017), xiv.
11 Lewis and Diamond (2015), xix, 145.
12 Freire (1985), 59.
13 Madden-Dent and Oliver (2021).
14 Banks (2003); Cuauhtin, Zavala, Sleeter and Au (2019); Fiol-Matta and Chamberlain (1994); Hu-DeHart (1993); Sleeter and Zavala (2020).
15 Freire (1985), 80.
16 Hanh (all); Hanh and Weare (2017); Trungpa (1993).
17 Trungpa (1993), 223.
18 Lewis and Diamond (2015).
19 Action research about Multicultural Mindfulness was conducted at Truckee Meadows Community College, a Hispanic-Serving Institution and one of the first community college teacher training programs in the US. The author was hired to establish the program in 1999. The research engaged interactive field experience classrooms, cafeterias, themed outdoor education collaborations, and education courses, including special education, involving preschool through college students and educators.
20 Lewis and Diamond (2015), 177; Sleeter and Carmona (2017), title.
21 Barrera (1979); DiAngelo (all); Gordon (1964, 1991); Kendi (2019); Lewis and Diamond (2015); Omi and Winant (1986); Takaki (all); West (1993).
22 Lewis and Diamond (2015), 11; Omi and Winant (1986), 61.
23 Menter, Eliot, Hulme, Lewin and Lowden (2011); Putman and Rock (2018).
24 Freire (1985), 19, 59; Vicuña (2017, July 7), 22.
25 Banks (all).
26 King (1964); hooks (1994).
27 Clark (1991), 44; Gang (1991), 79.
28 Bloom (1974); Emdin (2016); Fiol-Matta and Chamberlain (1994); Gardner (1983); Gay (2000); Geri and MacGregor (1999, January); Hanh (all); Kendi (2019); Ladson-Billings (1995); Madden-Dent and Oliver (2021); Roberts and Pruitt (2009); Smith, MacGregor, Matthews, Gabelnick (2004); Trungpa (1993).
29 Hanh (2008), 80; Hanh (all); Hanh and Weare (2017).
30 Kendi (2019).
31 Lewis and Diamond (2015), 13.
32 Lewis and Diamond (2015), 8, 169.
33 Banks (2003); Cuauhtin, Zavala, Sleeter and Au (2019); Hu-DeHart (1993); Kendi (2019); Sleeter and Zavala (2020).
34 Hanh (all); Hanh and Weare (2017).
35 Gang (1991), 79.
36 Hanh (2008), 80.
37 Gang (1991), 79.
38 Freire (1985); Geri and MacGregor (1999, January); Lardner (2018, July 9–12); Maher (2005); National Association (2023); Roberts and Pruitt (2009); Smith, MacGregor, Matthews and Gabelnick (2004); Vescio, Ross and Adams (2008, January); Lardner (2018, July 9–12).
39 Buswell (2004), 933.
40 Trungpa (1993), 215.

41 Hanh (2006), 9.
42 Hanh (all); Hanh and Weare (2017).
43 Urtubey (2023, June 20).
44 Banks (1988, 1993).
45 Goldberg and Houser (2017, July 19).
46 Darling-Hammond (all).
47 Banks (1988, 1993); Urtubey (2023, June 20).

PART I
Big-Picture Transformation in the Real World

1
CULTURE-CONSCIOUS LISTENING AND GLOBAL PRAXIS FOR BIG-PICTURE CHANGE

Guiding Purpose

Explain how to

- Develop diversity as a source of solutions rather than view it as a problem.
- Use Culture-Conscious Listening for inclusive academic concentration.
- Apply Global Praxis to uplift academic engagement with sustainability outcomes.
- Experiment with transformative practices for big-picture change with Environmental Liberation Education.

Provide

- Two Multicultural Mindfulness Activities and a journal question: *Split-Second Conflict Resolution*, *Culture-Conscious Listening*, and *What's a Transformative Teacher?*

Context

Unrest in Santiago

One crisp winter afternoon, I slipped away from my team to explore Santiago city streets on my own. Soon I'm trotting shoulder to shoulder, apace with crosswalk crowds of quick-moving Chileans forming human wedges against rushing cars. Rounding a corner, out of breath from the group jog, I face an angry mob.

The young protesters, some shirtless in body paint, display a fierce illustration of years of community activism, school shutdowns, and social strife, violent and nonviolent. Protest leaders perch atop a large horse statue, clinging to its rider, José de San Martín, the victor whose valiant efforts decolonized Chile from Spain in 1818. I make global connections. Chile is a long narrow country that stretches almost twice as far as my home state, California. But Chile's thinner, like a frayed ribbon disintegrating westward. Its diverse landscape is vulnerable to human impact. I see events in our common economic and political timeline that produced climate change: conquest, colonization, genocide, forced labor, liberation, industrialization, and globalization.

DOI: 10.4324/9781003364757-3
This chapter has been made available under a CC-BY-NC-ND license.

This land feels familiar. California has similar diverse biomes and cultures. We have geographic dramas with prodigious mountain chains overlooking the Pacific Ocean. I recognize the social climate, having been a child in Northern California living on the same Oakland street as a Black Panther Party headquarters during the civil rights era. I recall the Indigenous occupation of Alcatraz Island in the San Francisco Bay and participating in street marches to grocery stores to boycott grapes for primarily Mexican, Asian, and Native American farm workers' rights and to restrict pesticides. I feel like I know this topography and its cultural unrest.

Liberation from colonialism didn't stop dehumanization or ecological destruction. The freedom fought for by people like José de San Martín didn't prevent Chile's absorption into the global extraction-consumption economy. It didn't avoid the reckless "mechanistic-industrial" system these bare-chested protestors oppose.[1] These youth cry for equality and sustainability. They fight corporate voraciousness and authoritarian government. They demand public institutions to meet universal human needs – clean air, drinkable water, sustainable food, secure housing, cultural authenticity, quality education, and sustainable livelihoods.[2] They seek Global Praxis – action and reflection for world healing – and a few years later they get what they're looking for when, in 2021, their own celebrated student activist compatriot, Gabriel Boric, becomes Chile's new president.[3]

During the volatility before me, I use Culture-Conscious Listening - breathwork for calm reflection to perceive cultures with compassion. I make cross-cultural connections, observing Chilean demonstrators waving red, white, and blue single-star flags that blend with their painted bodies. I know this motif from US flag colors, which contrasts with Indigenous flag colors, like the vibrant yellow, green, red, blue, black, and white flag colors of Chile's Mapuche peoples, or the rainbow of colors of diverse Indigenous nation flags in the land now called California. These activists are like courageous protesters back home – civil rights participants back in the day and more recent collaborators with the Standing Rock Sioux Tribe to protect water and Black Lives Matter participants for social justice. These are change-makers vocalize metrically with the crowd.[4] Their chants reverberate eons of collective struggles: "Free and Equal Schooling!," "Free Wallmapu!," and "We're not Afraid!"[5]

Snowcapped Andes

The Chilean dissenters are watched by alert military police in olive-green uniforms, armed with guns and chemical hoses. Some sit in tanks produced by the global military-industrial complex that arms terrorists and dictators and guards dehumanizing and environmentally harmful commerce all over the world. Demonstrators and police here are dwarfed by the magnificent but smog-obscured, snowcapped Andes. This is the highland home of a millennium of diverse Indigenous communities who integrated civilization through *quipus*, a mathematical knotting system for scientific, economic, and cultural communication.[6] However, at the moment, this mountain range divides, a geo-political boundary separating Chile from Argentina, Bolivia, and Peru.

This demonstration is small compared with many in Chile, but I carry its panoramic tableau in my mind's eye when I join my team. Before I enter the restaurant, I glance up to admire the serrated edges of the great peaks framing Santiago, one sliver in the longest continental mountain range on the planet. It's a precious source of Earth's snow and water in a vibrant geography that sculpted irreplaceable Indigenous stewardship practices and traditional ways of knowing. Such ecological wisdom and cultural practices are now sorely needed to stop global warming from centuries of abuse in the post-colonial "mechanistic industrial age."[7]

And this is what lingers: the tarnish of air pollution fouling these beautiful mountains and Indigenous homelands. This image – impressive Andean heights over outraged Chilean youth – is punctuated in my memory by dirty skies. Soon I'm inside, seated next to the guest of honor, US Deputy Cultural Attaché Teresa Ball, during the Fulbright Scholar Luncheon that brought this book into being.

Listen First

Decades before as his student, I read Ronald Takaki's *A Different Mirror: A History of Multicultural America* about the democratic imperative of "a more inclusive multicultural context."[8] Takaki argues that US egalitarianism is corrupted by violent displacements and domination systems – colonial land stealing, Indigenous genocide, Black chattel slavery, lynching of people of color, inhumane labor conditions for the poor of all backgrounds, bureaucratized cultural rankings and exclusions, and environmentally damaging industries. We're not a democracy until we repair racialized inequities and unsustainable systems. That's why professionals who operate institutions, like educators, are key to structural transformation.

This insight crystallized for me in Santiago. I was in the same city where, more than half a century before, exiled Brazilian liberation educator Paulo Freire wrote *Pedagogy of the Oppressed*, the worn dog-eared copy of which I carried in the book bag at my feet. Freire explains a literacy program wherein the oppressed co-create "generative" themes with transformative teachers in "culture circles" for "*conscientização*" (critical consciousness) through humanization actions. Participants listen, share evidence, develop themes, code, dialogue, act, and transform. This is "reflection and action upon the world in order to transform it," empowering learners with holistic education to change inequity systems.[9]

Freire's program was so successful – 20,000 culture circles bringing the poor (many Afro-Brazilian descendants of enslaved peoples) to literacy in 45 days – that he was imprisoned and exiled. He continued his work in Chilean *barrios* while he wrote his book. His concept was that healing starts with listening – *cultural* listening for problem-posing – to engage subjects with emotional storytelling and community data while solving real-world problems.[10]

Collaboration for Integrative Change

Santiago hosts our team of 16 race-, class-, and gender-diverse US educators in a Fulbright-Hays Seminars Abroad Program. We're at the geometrical midpoint in this nation's most densely populated region, inside its government nucleus. In this moment, we form our own culture circle. We're multicultural educators investigating themes about student success and knowledge in a globalized world. In our circle, we observe how Chile's "living codes" express the same neoliberal dictums that dehumanize systems in the United States.[11] Using a big-picture lens about human superdiversity in Earth's biodiversity, we ask, "What does Chile teach about how to change dehumanizing systems in US education?"

Evidence from Chile informs the Three Transformative Tools for Environmental Liberation Education presented in this book. These tools empower teachers to collaborate for integrative change, addressing the academic side of the sustainability equation. Transformative teachers strengthen subject engagement with culturally responsive social-emotional learning during routines. We facilitate critical consciousness circles to motivate students with "natural awe" activities. We advance holistic education to reconceptualize subjects to develop a joyful and just green "new economy" and Earth stewardship.[12]

MULTICULTURAL MINDFULNESS ACTIVITY

Split-Second Conflict Resolution

Outcome

- Apply split-second conflict resolution.

Key Concept

- **4-Rs Antibias Practice:** Based on Thich Nhat Hanh's mindfulness writings about conflict: *Recognize*, *Refrain*, *Restorative Action*, and *Resolve*.

Resources

- Journal, pencil, an example or symbol of nature, a place to meet indoors or outdoors.

Big-Picture Question

- How do we reduce bias on the spot?

Start

In whole group circle:

- **Individually write** journal header – *One-Minute Conflict Resolution*.
- **Read**:

4-Rs Antibias Practice Summary

During active conflict, practitioners breathe to:

1. **Recognize** dehumanization due to systemic bias and segregation.
2. **Refrain** from making biased or divisive decisions, such as racialized ability-grouping, punishing from assumptions, ignoring disinformation, and permitting Anglo-conformist curriculum.
3. **Take Restorative Action**, such as to facilitate non-defensive listening, multicultural story sharing, antibias questions, stereotype investigation, and inclusive sustainability activities.
4. **Resolve** to prevent bias, such as participation in peace spaces, culture compassion projects, and multicultural reconciliation meetings.

  - **Journal** simple phrases (as if explaining to a child) for *Recognize*, *Refrain*, *Restorative Action*, and *Resolve*.
  - **Discuss** phrase definitions (e.g., Refrain: Be kind always).

Middle

In whole group circle:

- **Journal** a conflict you've recently experienced on campus that didn't go well. Review what happened in your mind's eye. Give the conflict a name, such as "Bullying."

- **Read aloud** each of the following four explanations, one at a time, **breathing** after each for one-minute breath cycles:

    1 **Recognize** a bias provocation in the conflict you named, such as yelling, spewing lies, hallway gossip, mocking laughter, exclusion whispering, eye-rolling, racist language, fighting words, hypocritical denial, colorblind ignorance, and cultural avoidance behaviors. Think: What was your defensive reaction during the provocation?
    2 **Refrain** by visualizing yourself abstaining from the reaction that failed you during the conflict. Imagine handling the bias provocation calmly. Think: What mindfulness practice can I use next time I feel provoked? For instance, "Tell the offending [person] that *you – not* the target – are offended and bothered by the behavior and that [the behavior] must stop."[13]
    3 **Take Restorative Action** such as by applying nonviolent communication protocols. Facilitating feelings acknowledgements, facts summaries, and antibias questions. Think: What restorative action can I take to draw attention away from the target of bias? What non-defensive descriptions explain the conflict's range of emotions and interpretations?
    4 **Resolve** the conflict with a follow-up meeting for amends and reconciliation. Think: What healing activities engender cross-cultural respect and trust between the parties?

- **Journal** an answer:

    1 How does mindfulness breathwork replace conflict anxiety with peace and prompt non-defensive antibias action?

Closing

In whole group circle:

- **Brainstorm** "Resolve Meeting Protocols" and decide on a symbol or example of nature for ambience at the Resolve Meeting. For example:

    Resolve Meeting Protocols
    *Nature item: A talking stick

    1 **Agreement with Incident Summary** – Each person finds a point of agreement and summarizes Incident facts.
    2 **Contradictions Observation** – Each person describes words versus tone and behavior.
    3 **Motives Perception** – Each person hypothesizes about underlying causes and motives.
    4 **Emotions Scan** – Each person accounts for past and present emotions regarding the conflict. How was I feeling then? How am I feeling now?
    5 **Amends-Making and Receiving** – Each person forgives and is forgiven for misdeeds, committing to change behavior and pose antibias-antiracist questions to invite compassion into the relationship, such as "How may we support each other in stopping this behavior? How may I support you in building goodwill and friendship?"[14]

Theory and Practice

How Do We Change Unsustainable Systems?

Facilitating inclusive student success and humanization knowledge in the midst of dehumanizing global systems means activating this teachable moment. As educators collaborate on antibias-antiracist ecology projects during academic routines, we center diversity in sustainability. Sustainability is intergenerational stewardship of cultural, economic, and environmental equity systems for holistic well-being. It's "the integration of environmental health, social equity and economic vitality in order to create thriving, healthy, diverse and resilient communities for this generation and generations to come."[15] Unbalanced inequity systems are unsustainable. However, accelerating climate change prompts action now, such as integrating multicultural, mindfulness, and environmental activities into education.

Three Transformative Tools

Think of the Three Transformative Tools as a resource kit for diversity belonging. This kit is for teachers and student teachers of all backgrounds, identities, disciplines, and education levels. We are all needed in multicultural-multiracial alliances to reconceptualize academics holistically for sustainability:

1. *Diversity Circles* (Chapter 5) form a transformative home base. They're the social structure for trust between two or more participants, as diverse as possible, to develop critical consciousness for joyful justice education. They're liberation culture circles – part education learning community and part mindfulness *sangha*. In seven types and five phases with three strategies, participants act and reflect on cultural and environmental stories, data, and questions about systems to connect academics to local and global healing.[16]
2. *Multicultural Mindfulness* (Chapter 6) is calm compassion. It's an array of reflective peace practices to integrate body, mind, culture, and environment into academic concentration and professional development. It grows awareness of ecology, change, and spaciousness in diversity through breathwork, research, journaling, dialogue, and generous actions during everyday routines. It is education activities for sustainable eating and exercise, emotional regulation during communication, cultural well-being practices, community actions, and big-picture restorative justice.[17]
3. *Approach-in-Dimension* (Chapter 7) is a guide for teachers to apply academic freedom to subject design and evaluation. It is a matrix for defining activities with a clear-eyed philosophy of humanity for curriculum, learning outcomes, knowledge development, communications, and site interactions. This is a planning and assessment map with diversity, equity, inclusion, and sustainability criteria.[18]

Superdiversity in Biodiversity

The three tools replace assimilation divisions with Environmental Liberation Education unity *through* diversity. The changes that collaborators make support inclusive student success in the context of human superdiversity and Earth's biodiversity.

The complexity of the changes ushered in by transnational population flows and the accompanying impact on language use emanating from new communication technologies, movement of goods and capital, transnational contact and recontact, and new and return migration have moved [education] to a new critical examination of previously unquestioned issues. New discourses... examine *superdiversity*.[19]

Environmental Liberation Education addresses superdiversity and biodiversity experiences that impact school. It helps educators resist systemic segregation from the global extraction-consumption economy. It advances holistic education through cultures, mindfulness, and nature activities indoors and outdoors to engage students in subjects to prepare for green economic participation and global citizenship.

What Are Transformative Teachers?

Transformative teachers are everyday educators who collaborate for holistic change with humanization questions and sustainability activities during inclusive academic routines. We're antibias-antiracist professionals who insert culturally responsive eco-friendly questions into this academic moment. We reduce standardized Anglo-conformist education and make room for diverse ways of knowing, "multiple intelligences," and a range of educational objectives.[20] We motivate students by diversifying resources and integrating community supports into hourly and daily education, facilitating social-emotional academic activities assessed with the big-picture criteria we choose.

Rather than caving to unconscious bias by deferring to over-standardization – or dividing students (often unintentionally) according to systemic inequities – transformative teachers balance vertical interactions with horizontal relationships. We reduce dehumanization patterns and increase human connections to cultures in nature on site and off. Transformative teachers replace "systems of domination" with curiosity about equity ecosystems.[21] We develop culture competence with structural competence, meeting requirements with arts and sciences holism while making systemic changes for a livable world.

"Untamable Mane of Hair"

This book began during a lunch in Santiago, Chile. I'm seated next to Attaché Ball. We discuss Chile and the United States as we spoon pickled *pebre* onto *pan amasado* from the colorful woven basket we share in the upstairs banquet hall at Divertimento Chileno. This historic restaurant at the edge of the Parque Del Cerro San Cristóbal is a stone's throw away from the home of Nobel Prize–winning poet, Pablo Neruda. It's a tourist destination, a whimsical, blue abode that Neruda named "La Chascona" ("untamable mane of hair").

I can't hide a shudder when Attaché Ball's *congrio granado* arrives. I flash on an image in Neruda's poem, *Nothing but Death*, "as though we lived falling out of the skin into the soul," because what I see on her plate is a peeled snake.[22] But Deputy Ball smiles with satisfaction. The eel enters on a bright green bed of garlic sautéed spinach. She lifts her fork and knife, cutting a bite and explains how the US Embassy is busy with a visit by the Donald Trump administration. Vice President Mike Pence will be in Santiago in a few days.

Ms. Ball tactfully represses embarrassment over hosting the Trump administration because, I surmise, she is a career diplomat representing the overall picture of US democracy during her appointment in Chile. She is on a global journey that her Twitter account describes as "the road less traveled by" in a life that started as a "Girl from Appalachia."

Attaché Ball explains she's not a fan of the flipped seasons between the two countries. Season reversals between the US and Chile extend extreme weather events, complicating family vacations. Deputy Ball narrows her concentration, looking as if she's about to slap a mosquito on her arm. She explains how her family was unable to spend the previous holidays in the US because wildfires and flood events overlapped for months. When she looks to me for understanding, I nod and commiserate. Yes, yes, these catastrophes appear everywhere now. We had a flood where I live in rural Northern California that shut down my commute to Reno, Nevada. Yearly wildfires force evacuations, raze buildings, and kill people, blackening and decimating towns with names like Paradise and Greenville.

Climate Crises

We go back to our meals, quietly noting how these serial climate crises hurl a final ultimatum at the human condition. Planetary annihilation of our own doing requires immediate restorative action of our own making. But it's all happening at a scale that seems too large to tackle. In that moment together, talking animatedly with pre-Covid-19 abandon, the prospect of solving climate problems appears remote. The everyday sacrifices that sustainability demands feel too annoying and futile for the bits of destruction that intermittently disrupt our routines.

A few years later, however, we'll both be smacked with global hardships that afflict even the privileged. Our lived experiences, though easier than many, will suffer pandemic morbidity augmented by scary politics. We'll become defensive, hiding behind computer screens when we can, guarding scarce resources. We'll lose sight of cultural compassion, distracted by fear, disinformation, corruption, and violence. We'll wonder how science could be sidelined, yet we'll hope for environmental and public health policies to save the planet.

Deputy Ball sips her fizzy drink and whispers behind a shielding hand that she affirmatively does *not* like Santiago, the capital city of her Embassy office. The area is inundated with stagnant air pollution, and she has asthma. She explains that she didn't like the russet smoke that congealed in the city the previous summer when Chile was ravished by wildfires crowning so hot, and blazing so wide, that specialty firefighters with sophisticated equipment flew in to help from overseas. And the great Mapocho River – dividing the city in half, flowing from pristine springs high in the Andes down to the Pacific Ocean – turns, on occasion, the anemic color of stale coffee mixed with artificial creamer.

We sigh together, agreeing that Chile's polymorphous topography and distinctive flora and fauna, though distant geographically from the United States, connect ecologically through sea currents and the interlaced climate. Governments in both countries are politically guilty of enabling under-regulated enterprises that destroy natural resources and biota for corporate gain. We both understand the science that explains what we must do, and more importantly what our children need, to restore clean air, drinkable water, and healthy agriculture in interconnected lands and oceans.

Pisco Sours and Broken Education

Attaché Ball lowers her voice again to get to her main point with me as a professor of education: Her most pressing disaffection with Chile is its education system. She tells me it had been wrecked by privatization. Contrary to the choice theory that some policymakers assert, which alleges efficiency and opportunity through market competition, privatization in Chile had long-lasting poor results: school segregation widened, academic standards lowered, fields of study shut down, student debt inflated dramatically, teachers de-professionalized, and school stress increased.[23]

Ball explains that lately her stay-at-home husband greets her with a *pisco sour* in hand and parental anxiety creasing his brow. He vents about his latest efforts to get their two-year-old daughter into a proper playgroup. Pre-preschool playgroups are competitive and expensive in Santiago. Any playgroup worth its muster has a wait list and charges tuition. If their toddler does not get into a reputable playgroup to prepare her developing brain with pre-literacy skills, she won't qualify for the academic preschool on which Deputy Ball's husband has set his sights. If their toddler does not get into a selective preschool, then she won't matriculate into the exclusive kindergarten and elementary programs he wants, and she won't be admitted into the elite university-bound track worthy of a diplomat's family.

Environmental Liberation Education

This book expands liberation education with mindfulness and environmental education in a globalized world. It supports teachers and students in healing education from the grassroots. Environmental Liberation Education transforms suffering from dehumanization systems by integrating academics into big-picture problem-solving. It helps to reduce defensiveness from different standpoints simultaneously – oppressed *and* oppressors – by allowing the oppressed to lead liberation.[24]

Liberation theory asserts that education is pivotal in the network of institutions that either dehumanize or humanize. Liberation theory uses the substructure-superstructure model. It explains that education, given its intergenerational function in the social superstructure, reproduces the patterns of the economic substructure that funds it, which in global corporate capitalism is stratified. However, liberation educators recognize inequities at school, and make proactive hourly and daily decisions to integrate social systems through justice designs for curriculum, outcomes, knowledge, communications, and interactions.

Transformative teachers facilitate critical consciousness circles *with* students.[25] We understand that race, socially constructed and enforced through violence and bureaucracy, must be addressed. Centuries of *racialization* through economic-social systems push unjust and unsustainable cycles.[26] As *transformative* teachers we facilitate culture-conscious change. We redesign status quo space, time, materials, and learning environments to emancipate classrooms with Multicultural Mindfulness peace.

Culture Clash

Liberation education theory explains that apart from external economic-social structures, teachers are the single most influential factor inside education to diverse student success. We're more impactful than facilities, administrators, materials, and programming because we engage curriculum with students face to face almost every day. However, about 80% of teachers in the United States are White and undertrained in diversity education. Yet, across the nation, about 50% of students are of color.[27] Our classrooms enroll culturally and racially diverse students who are inequitably ranked in segregated districts.[28]

This is a long-standing culture clash. Mostly White teachers unintentionally make implicit bias decisions that reinforce racialized tracks, tiers, and segregation. Unconsciously, teachers are part of what excludes some students and cultural perspectives from education.[29] Such dissonance not only undermines diverse student attainment and the richness of plurality but weakens teachers.[30] Enrollments in credential programs are down, and job turnover is high: up to 50% of educators leave the profession during the first five years of employment.[31]

Therefore, transformative teachers are essential. We come from every demographic background. Armed with culture competence deepened by structural competence, we strengthen professionalism from different standpoints toward a common cause. We use social-emotional learning to include students in academics, connecting subjects to cultures in the environment. We resist assimilation and segregation systems fracturing education by guiding *intergenerational* change to connect classrooms to cultures in the world.

Why Culture-Conscious Listening?

As these insights developed in Chile, I knew my primarily European American academic colleagues back home, for the most part, are *not* liberation educators. Most are sparingly versed in multicultural education, lacking in culture competence, and deficient in structural competence beyond its theory. I myself had grown complacent despite the excellent ethnic studies training I got at UC Berkeley. I had to admit that I was no longer regularly *activating* the critical consciousness culture circles that started off my career in the 1990s at De Anza College in Cupertino, California. I was a Chicano Studies professor working with Latinx students, and we integrated academics into antibias-antiracist projects for change. One student-led activity was a mass checkout of library books using golf carts to remove library resources to illustrate what a mainstream library looks like to Latinx students. Student activists wanted to show the cultural neglect of "normal" assimilationist holdings. Our activism changed administrators' minds, resulting in the procurement of 1,000 Latinx resources for the central campus library.[32] But other than Faculty for Radical Empowerment and Enlightenment (FREE) (discussed below), I hadn't done anything similar for almost 20 years.

I therefore returned from my research in Chile contemplating how to again engage activism, but this time mindful of environmentalism. We needed modern tools informed by old-school theory to dismantle bias. I researched what it means to bring equity and sustainability into academics in the "information solar age."[33] I wanted to help integrate diversity and ecology into my courses, unit sequencing, textbook choices, assignment rubrics, unit discussions with students (40% of whom are Latinx in my program), and projects with colleagues (80% of whom are White). I used site routines and transformative activities already in motion – such as the Bee Campus USA garden and other diversity-sustainability collaborations with campus leaders such as Cecilia Vigil and Yevonne Allen – as footholds for change.[34] I applied academic freedom to classroom space, time, materials, and learning environments, collaborating with peers to activate superdiversity-biodiversity themes to connect education to the real world.

In the spirit of making "connection before correction," I listened for student and teacher cultures about how to design and engage curriculum with diversity integration.[35] I asked, How do educators disrupt systemic racism's "widespread set of ideas/stereotypes" in routines?[36] Using action research, I combined reconciliation listening,[37] antibias-antiracist[38] change strategies, and mindfulness praxis[39] to develop five steps to Culture-Conscious Listening with the help of students and colleagues: Culture-Conscious Breath, Pleasant Eye Contact, Compassionate Support, Brief Summary, and Antibias Question (explained below). As the practice emerged, I observed that Culture-Conscious Listening not only respects diversity, providing information for culture competence, but also is a way to develop social-emotional academic learning to engage *systems* to reduce racism and increase sustainability solutions.

As a core Multicultural Mindfulness practice, the five steps intervene in unconscious bias decisions. The steps interrupt mainstream stereotypes that feed alienation and segregation patterns by encouraging holistic responses "here and now."[40] They help participants consider colorblind bias reactions that rank and divide. They train in the value of diversity. The steps nurture culturally responsive classroom, lab, and meeting room interactions. They attend to nonverbal communication as well as cross-cultural storytelling and evidence-gathering. Culture-Conscious Listening contextualizes equity in diversity, which is a central purpose of Environmental Liberation Education.[41]

Why Compassion Breathwork?

But Culture-Conscious Listening is not easy in our world of disinformation, culture conflict, and structural inequities. Compassion is a cornerstone to changing dehumanizing systems, and it needs nurturing. While some defensiveness is necessary for survival, hyper-defensiveness from systemic inequities diminishes compassion and fans social stress. When we react to assumptions out of anxiety before considering evidence, defensiveness unintentionally reinforces systemic bias by sowing injustice into everyday interactions, such as when we favor, dismiss, or lash out.[42] In racialized systems, defensiveness reacts to assumptions and stereotypes about physical traits and outward appearances. Compassion, however, tempers rote judgments with open-mindedness. One way to nurture compassion is with body-mind breathwork to address fear directly. This is why antibias breathwork is the first step of Culture-Conscious Listening.

Breathwork softens the emotionality of bias often pulsing from the brain's amygdalae. Breathing makes space for cultural interpretations from prefrontal cortex and hippocampus exchanges. A helpful practice is nose breathing deep into the lower belly to activate the vagus nerve of the parasympathetic nervous system. This relieves stress. Breathwork soothes the amygdalae, which are two jumpy almond-shaped organs in the brain. Breathwork calls off these two fearful watchdogs that bark with fight, freeze, and flight stress.[43]

Breathwork pacifies bias feelings by de-escalating agitation and inviting reflection. Conscious breathing allows the thinking brain to moderate perceptions of words, tones, and nonverbal communication with awareness of different cultural experiences and language norms. It nourishes the forward-facing compassion center of the mind, allowing information from the hippocampus to energize problem-solving.[44] Non-defensive breathwork, especially when conducted in or with nature, prompts feelings of "interdependent" belonging to motivate compassionate action. Breathwork and collaborating with others for "the reverential treatment of nature" reduce defensive behaviors otherwise triggered by the divisive inequity systems to which people have become inured.[45]

Five Steps to Culture-Conscious Listening

1. *Culture-Conscious Breath:* The listener pauses to breath early in the interaction to calm fight, freeze, and flight body-mind stressors. This supports non-defensive reflection about cultures and assumptions.
2. *Pleasant Eye Contact:* The listener uses culturally respectful body language to encourage the talker to speak freely.
3. *Compassionate Support:* The listener patiently maintains considerate body language throughout the communication to nurture non-defensive perceptions.
4. *Brief Summary:* The listener affirms the talker's story by stating a point of agreement and offers an outline of facts, perspectives, and themes, with observations of the speaker's tone. The listener asks: Is the summary accurate?
5. *Antibias Question:* The listener poses a welcoming question to invite cultural diversity and healing into transformative action.

When conducted at school, these steps train multicultural awareness *during* academics. They activate the "third ear" or "third eye" of culture consciousness to perceive segregation.[46] Participants drop armored reactions to diverse people caught up in racist systems, looking for inclusion windows.

Culture-Conscious Listening nurtures diversity with non-defensive culture competence. Transformative teachers and superdiverse students together "practice being vulnerable in the classroom, being wholly present in mind, body, and spirit."[47] We look for diverse ways of knowing to make inclusion decisions about school space, time, materials, and learning environments. We spot contradictory emotions in ourselves and others about cultures in

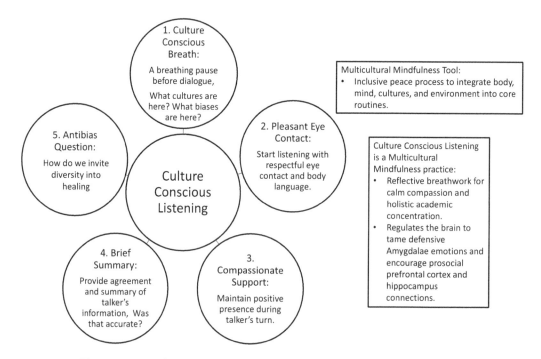

FIGURE 1.1 Five steps to Culture-Conscious Listening graphic. Created by the author.

curriculum, and we look for social misperceptions. We learn "to teach in a manner that respects and cares for the souls of our students" and colleagues.[48] As we grow holism experiences, we interrupt systemic racism, classism, and sexism and make room for cross-cultural understanding through subject engagement.[49]

MULTICULTURAL MINDFULNESS ACTIVITY

Culture-Conscious Listening

Outcome

- Implement the Culture-Conscious Breath.

Key Concepts

- **Breathwork:** Conscious breathing for body-mind well-being now.
- **Culture:** Shared artifacts, practices, and beliefs of any group interacting in systems.
- **Culture-Conscious Breath:** The listener breaths reflectively to relieve fight, freeze, and flight stressors and open holistic awareness about cultures: "What biases are here?" "What cultures open my heart?"
- **Culture Competence:** Antibias-antiracist strategies deepened with cross-cultural compassion and unity skills applied to hourly and daily decisions.
- **Culture-Conscious Listening:** Five steps to welcome diversity: Culture-Conscious Breath, Pleasant Eye Contact, Compassionate Support, Brief Summary, and Antibias Question.

Resources

- **Breathwork Bell**, an example or symbol of nature, a place to meet indoors or outdoors.

Big-Picture Question

- How do we uplift culture competence with compassion and joy?

Start

During established classroom, lab, or meeting room routine:

- **Ring** a breathwork bell for activity transition.
- **Announce:** "We're developing mindfulness for academic concentration, making body-mind connections to calm anxiety and engage the subject with an open mind."
- **Explain:** "Breathwork calms brain sensors to bring peace to strong emotions, prompt reflection, and soothe the urge to run with fear, freeze in confusion, or lash out in anger.
    A best practice is to nose-inhale into your lower belly, then a mouth-exhale through a relaxed smile. I'll ring the bell four times, during which we will do Box Breathing – Breath-in 1-2-3-4, hold 1-2-3-4. Breath-out 1-2-3-4, hold 1-2-3-4."
- **Decide** if you want everyone to sit, stand, or lie down.
- **Model** a deep breath cycle with one hand on your heart and the other on your belly to show breathing movement and counting.

In whole group circle:

- **Box Breathe** together as you ring the bell four times.

Middle

- If you haven't done so previously, define *culture*.
- **Instruct**: "Everyone will do four breath cycles again, but this time replacing counting with a *gatha*: 'Breathing in, I know I'm cultural. Breathing out, I know others are cultural.'"
- **Implement** *gatha* breathing with four more rings of the bell.

Closing

- After the last ring dissipates, **discuss** a question:

  1 How do you feel right now after doing the culture-conscious breath step (calm, clear, relaxed, happy, tense, anxious, numb, annoyed, etc.)?
  2 How easy or hard was it to keep your mind on your breath?
  3 What did you feel as you acknowledged cultures (happy, wise, generous, curious, bored, confused, etc.)?
  4 What ideas came to you about your own culture(s) and the cultures of others?
  5 How do cultures relate to nature in our region?
  6 How do cultures and nature relate to our subject topic?

Application

Some US institutions have been able to implement social justice policies. Social justice policies invest in institutional opportunities for low-income families and children, such as Head Start for early childhood education, Medicaid for the poor, Medicare for the elderly, and the GI Bill. These programs help meet basic needs *through* the social superstructure, opening access to economic substructure participation. These applications provide transformative teaching models.[50]

Desegregated Head Start – Reducing Pre-prejudice

Head Start for preschoolers illustrates a social justice application that mitigates education exclusions with free early childhood curriculum for holistic academic engagement. Head Start began in the US in the 1960s with a mission to socialize diverse children living in poverty with high-quality health, nutrition, social services, and education. It uses "whole child" practices informed by "a deep understanding" of how children with "serious socioeconomic disadvantages" learn. Head Start supports academic concentration by addressing the physiological, safety, and belonging needs of enrolled children. Its evolution from a cultural deficit to a cultural assets model displays its own program evolution from an Additive approach to Social Action (see Chapter 7).[51] Head Start shifted over decades as its educators advanced in culture and structural competence from professional development, learning how to make cultural empowerment decisions, connecting school to the real world.[52]

Culture-Conscious Listening and Global Praxis   35

FIGURE 1.2   The author, seated third from the left, circa 1965. Photo by Marden VanWinkle.

My own Head Start experience is a starting point in my transformative journey. In 1965, I attended one of the first Head Start programs, at the Mayfield School on the land that is now called Palo Alto, California.[53] Our Mayfield class photograph (I'm seated third from left) displays a desegregated Student Cohort Diversity Circle guided by a mixed-race teacher team. We're 19 three- and four-year-old children, animated and multiracial, laughing shoulder to shoulder. We're gender-balanced African American, European American, Latinx, Indigenous, and Asian Pacific American students. Our teachers present racial diversity as well. Our "multi-cultural pre-kindergarten project" is funded by Title I, using an "Art in the Child's Life" curriculum to develop "expression of self-identity." Our class showcases how transformative teachers facilitate social-emotional academic learning with diverse students through culturally responsive activities connected to world healing.[54]

Rather than spending my early childhood days isolated in low-income housing with the adversities (emotional, physical, and sexual abuse and uncertain nutrition) of my young single mother's poverty, I enjoyed the nourishing space that Head Start offered for academic engagement *with* diversity. My Head Start teacher team modeled desegregation while engaging multiple intelligences. They designed activities from an "Experience-Centered Language Program for Early Skill Building and Remediation."[55] While "remediation" is now understood as a cultural deficit term, the "*performative*" implementation I experienced can be characterized as assets-based. My multicultural teachers socialized multiracial students *together* in circle learning with cultural materials to nurture our diversity.[56]

This transformative teacher team integrated multi-sensory manipulatives "to stimulate multimodal learning avenues: visual, auditory, kinesthetic, olfactory."[57] They supported children to develop "communicative skills" and pre-literacy language as components of "social competency" and "social mobility" skills.[58] Circle activities – standing to explain handheld identity objects to a diverse audience with imaginative cultural voices – generate academic vocabulary holistically. Such desegregated activities counteract pre-prejudice ideas in

FIGURE 1.3 Culture-Conscious Listening photo of the author. Photo by Marden VanWinkle.

developing youth. Culturally responsive academics support children to make social-emotional connections between self, communities, and environment.

Beyond balancing phonics with whole language for integrated literacy development, these transformative teachers activated outdoor education. During my Head Start enrollment, we took outdoor field trips to explore diverse community cultures and nature in sensory-rich settings, such as botanical parks and marshlands, as well as inside public institutions, such as museums and libraries. The Head Start program at Mayfield School shows antibias-antiracist methods and holistic education for "content integration" and "an equity pedagogy" toward "prejudice reduction" during academics. It models inclusive learning environments for culturally responsive social-emotional curriculum and the "knowledge construction process." Thus, desegregation activities for multicultural *academic* engagement invite belonging in an "empowering school culture."[59]

How Is Telling Your Cultural Story Transformative?

My Head Start experience illustrates how transformative teachers support cultural story and healthy multicultural identity development. Cultural stories personalize culturally responsive education.[60] A Healthy Multicultural Identity Quest (Chapter 7) reframes the hero[ine]'s journey with the following plotline: Departure, Resistance, Initial Allies of Support, Obstacles, Reciprocal Allies, Soul-Search for Purpose, Reluctance to Transform, Reconciliation, and Return Home with Multicultural Belonging.

My own cultural story, like everyone else's, displays setbacks and breakthroughs in antibias-antiracist environmental consciousness. My journey began with a *Departure* from a White/Latinx culture-clashing home and, after some *Resistance*, was followed by events with multicultural-multiracial *Initial Allies of Support* in the Head Start program described above.

Next, I interacted with *Reciprocal Allies* – diverse peoples where I lived and urban schooling experiences – to help me overcome *Obstacles*, such as a series of adverse childhood experiences due to poverty.

My *Soul-Search for Purpose* was energized by the social and political climate of Northern California in an epoch of civil rights activism. In San Francisco and Oakland, I was part of street dance performances and artists collaboratives. I participated in protests initiated by Cesar Chavez and Delores Huerta down the street from where I lived. My first neighborhood best friend was a girl in a Black Panther household, whose organization provided a free school breakfast program from which I benefited. On the flip side, I profited from the White privilege of my European American mother. At the same time, she didn't teach me to be a culture-conscious Chicana-Mestiza applying Tecuexe community practices or speaking Nahua to respect my Ute-Aztec lineage from lands that are now called central-south Mexico.

After Head Start and early elementary public schooling, my peer-diversity experiences were scaffolded throughout the schools I attended during multiple moves. Fortunately, unlike many US school children, I had key teachers who conveyed high expectations and multicultural values over years, extending a scaffolding for culture competence and positive achievement outcomes.[61] Nonetheless, quite a few of my public school teachers were White and ill trained in how to integrate diverse students into culturally relevant academics.

In college, I had a wonderful set of diverse antibias-antiracist teachers. At UC Berkeley, I took classes from African American, African, Chicano, Chicana, Native American, and Asian Pacific American instructors, including transformative ethnic studies professor Ronald Takaki, whose scholarship informs this book. Furthermore, some of the world's most progressive thinkers of the time spoke on campus or protested the University of California's investments in South Africa with anti-apartheid demonstrations of the mid-1980s. This diversity of transformative professors, thinkers, and activists culminated when I attended a culture circle facilitated by Paulo Freire at Berkeley's Dwinelle Hall, during which he demonstrated liberation education. Later, in 1990, I heard Nelson Mandela speak at the Oakland Coliseum about truth and reconciliation for universal human rights, shortly after his release from 27 years in prison in South Africa.

Nelson Mandela, Paulo Freire, and educators of color at UC Berkeley were, of course, interspersed with White educators who taught much of my higher education. Nonetheless, my diverse teachers instructed, in no uncertain terms, that education is political. They taught that White supremacy and White superiority beliefs perpetuate systemic racism and antidemocratic policies and practices throughout US institutions. In our critical consciousness circles, these transformative educators taught that democracy cannot be realized without *equity* in diversity and that, until systemic inequities are structurally replaced with inclusion solutions, corporatism and wealth gaps will derail democracy. They taught me to call out colorblind Anglo-conformist exclusions and push for equity experiences in public education to support the economic and civic inclusion of all peoples.

How to Spot One's Own Bias

As the author of a book addressing systemic bias, it's important to model how to spot one's own bias during a Healthy Multicultural Identity Quest. Bias is the baggage one brings to cultural *Departure* events and it's the self-justifying *Resistance* and fear one feels about honest self-reflection. It's one of the defensiveness *Obstacles* that must be faced and overcome during the *Soul-Search for Purpose* for *Reconciliation*. Bias is a snare in the *Reluctance to Transform*. Bias triggers big emotions, unmindful speech, and conflict actions. However, consistent reflection on one's lived intersectional experiences shines a light on cultural conditioning to remind us to practice hourly and daily compassion.

In my case, I'm a bi-racial Chicana with early childhood experiences with my father, Roberto Rubalcava, who was a youth radical in the ethnic studies movement that started in various locations, including in San Jose, California, where I was born in an apartment to my teen European American mother, Marden VanWinkle. Roberto's education was influenced by Latin American liberation movements, including from his trip to Cuba to meet with Fidel Castro. My interactions with Roberto were limited primarily to the first few years of my life, but these experiences seeded my Chicana-Mestiza critical consciousness. When I found out much later that the largest part of my ethnicity is descended from enslaved Tecuexe, Uto-Aztec peoples in the land now called Los Altos de Jalisco, Guadalajara, Mexico, I realized that my mixed identity was itself subject to the global caste system.

All along, I've taken advantage of the unearned benefits of White privilege from my light brown skin tone. I've assimilated, in many ways, into the European American identity of my mother, who was my caretaker. I competed hard to achieve in the assimilation curriculum I received in most of my public school classrooms. However, even as I assimilated, I also experienced prejudice against my somewhat Mexican appearance and Chicana-Mestiza self-determination.

What's Antibias-Antiracist Environmental Consciousness?

Antibias-antiracist environmental consciousness emerges by reflecting on intergenerational violence and nonviolence to expose unhealthy and healthy practices and events. This holistic consciousness unifies diverse identities through *Reciprocal Allies*. Friendships during my own journey involve diversity and curiosity about how to develop antibias-antiracist concepts into unity actions. I was lucky to learn from liberation educators who facilitated culture circle inquiry led by diverse students. I engaged in mindfulness circles and retreats in my neighborhoods and also with Pema Chödrön and Thich Nhat Hanh. I participated in committees with students and educators of color, such as Precious Hall and Yuli Chavez Camarena, whose transformative leadership and scholarship grew my culture consciousness. I learned how to balance scientific research with action research using *multiple* sources for diverse perspectives, cultural ways of knowing, and fields of study about a topic. Using comparative evidence in case studies, I learned how to apply critical consciousness to data analysis. I used an *intersectional* structural lens to develop and disseminate findings, translating diversity reflection into social action for liberation experiences.

My identity quest continues as a seasoned educator, expanding with environmental consciousness. For almost a quarter of a century, I have commuted from my Northern California mountain home (a region that has suffered the decimation of *two* towns from mega fires to date) to work in neighboring Nevada, the country's driest state. During these decades, I have observed the impact of superdiverse humans on biodiverse nature.

Just down the canyon from my home in Quincy was Paradise, a town where my own children played high school soccer on a field that no longer exists due to the 2018 Camp Fire, the deadliest and most destructive wildfire in California history, killing 86 people, many of whom were disabled, elderly, and poor.[62] Even closer, with flames I could see from my porch, was the 2021 Dixie Fire, "the first wildfire in history to burn clear across the Sierra

Nevada Mountains," destroying a million acres and leveling Greenville, our neighboring town.[63] Fatefully, Greenville's first European American occupants had violently displaced most of the Mountain Maidu living in the area to impose logging industry and privatized real-estate onto communal land. In 1850, "Indian lodges were numerous in [Indian] Valley and villages probably edged the entire valley." However, within a few decades, White invaders seized land and passed acts to legalize "indentured servitude [effective slavery]" and deny "self-representation" by Indigenous peoples, thereby fracturing and expunging thousands of years of interconnected Maidu cultural practices integrated into biodiversity. Maidu sustainability practices had protected regional water and applied cultural fires to thriving forest stewardship.[64]

However, dam construction and forest clear-cutting by European Americans to serve the White-dominated capitalist economy weakened ecosystems' resilience. The Dixie Fire tore through the Greenville Rancheria, a place where 162 Indigenous peoples were living in 2021. In a graphic illustration of the intersection of environment and culture, the Dixie Fire razed Rancheria medical and dental facilities, the tribal office with all its Indigenous historical documents, and its environmental and fire office.[65]

Employed in Reno, I was similarly confronted by assimilation and dehumanization projects that resulted in pollution and the devastation of Numu (Northern Paiute), Wašiw (Washoe), Newe (Western Shoshone), and Nuwu (Southern Paiute) tribal stewardship practices on the precious inland Truckee Meadows watershed – the namesake of Truckee Meadows Community College (TMCC) where I work. This watershed is unique in that it starts in Lake Tahoe and flows not into the Pacific Ocean like most large western rivers but to Pyramid Lake, the heart of the Pyramid Lake Paiute Tribe Reservation. Toxins and water degradation from decades of non-Indigenous industrialization in the region contaminate the very community whose cultural practices kept it clean.[66]

Because I apply my Healthy Multicultural Identity Quest insights to professional practice, education students in my courses collaborate with regional environmental and cultural organizations on culturally responsive outdoor education, such as *Earth Day Every Day* and watershed activities, with regional elementary school children.[67] My students co-lead culture circles, involving children in critical consciousness academics "to make a positive impact on the community in regards to waste, noxious weeds, and the local watershed." We join with other transformative educators, such as in sustainability events and pollinator garden activities with native species and Indigenous practices, to expand our repertoire of culturally respectful environmental activities. Moreover, my students write case studies about academic projects with Indigenous plants and medicines. For instance, one Native American student designed and facilitated a series of lessons with Toza, Big Sage, and other plants with story sharing and elder participation for culturally responsive social-emotional academic learning. This Newe-Numa teacher credential student expresses antibias-antiracist environmental consciousness:

> Newe-Numa (Shoshone Paiute) beliefs start with Earth. Everything on Earth has life, has spirit, and is all connected. Humans have a spirit which is connected to plants, animals, water. With these connections, children from diverse backgrounds and abilities have a stronger sense of who they are. These connections guide children, give them strength, and hope to continue their lives on the 'red road.' Red road is living a humble life demonstrating that we are all different, but can still have values, ethics, and respect for all walks of life, not just humans. Teaching with plants helps children become interactive with lessons. Plants create an environment rich in cultural kindness and peer connections.[68]

> Diversity Circles Tool:
> - Inclusive collaborations to apply Multicultural Mindfulness to big picture academic activities designed and evaluated with Approach-in-Dimension humanization criteria.

> Diversity Circle question:
> - How do we protect Earth?
> - How do we steward it equitably, respectfully, and sustainably?
>
> Diversity Circle activity:
> - Student Cogen Diversity Circle designs Earth Day stations: Solar System Parachute, Sustainability Mural, Earth Action Book Club, Nature Poetry Slam.

FIGURE 1.4 Students engaging the Diversity Circles tool. Photo by the author and Fe (fee) Danger.

Two Bookends – Culture-Conscious Listening and Global Praxis

Culture-Conscious Listening gathers cross-cultural information about suffering and healing to guide Global Praxis activities that connect academics to real-world liberation. My Fulbright experience in Chile made me realize late in my career that I wasn't doing enough with social justice education. Despite my best intentions to value diversity, I wasn't taking big-picture actions to create space for inclusion and sustainability. I also knew I couldn't expect comprehensive policy from above for systemic change anytime soon. So I had to do what I could in my context. I wanted to use my nook in my corner of academia at a Hispanic-Serving Institution (HSI) to experiment with mainstream education change. I started collaborating anew with culture consciousness action. While Culture-Conscious Listening is the start of liberation action, it needs real-world culmination. For that we have Global Praxis.

Multicultural Mindfulness begins with Culture-Conscious Listening and peaks with Global Praxis to flank Environmental Liberation Education. Culture-Conscious Listening is hourly and daily antibias compassion. Global Praxis is applying compassion to community healing events. While Culture-Conscious Listening collects cultural data, witnesses community stories, and poses inclusion questions, Global Praxis is hands-on. Together, they engage subjects with multiple modalities and cognitive levels through cultures, mindfulness, and nature activities, indoors and outdoors.

> There is an Anishinaabe prophecy that speaks of two roads: One road is a natural path. It leads to global peace and unity that embraces the sacred relationship between humanity and all living things. On this path, all order of creation – mineral, plant, animal, and human – are relatives deserving of respect and care. We are instructed to use our voices to speak for those who have not been given a voice.[69]

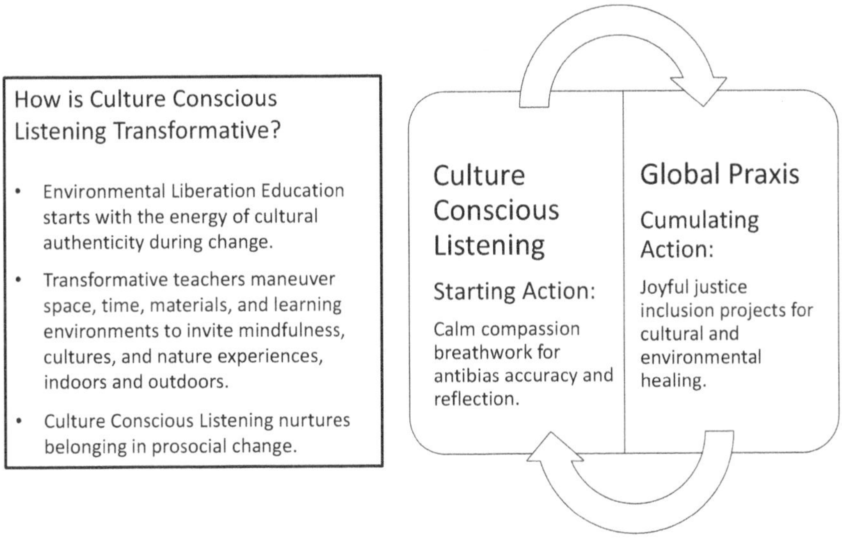

How is Culture Conscious Listening Transformative?

- Environmental Liberation Education starts with the energy of cultural authenticity during change.
- Transformative teachers maneuver space, time, materials, and learning environments to invite mindfulness, cultures, and nature experiences, indoors and outdoors.
- Culture Conscious Listening nurtures belonging in prosocial change.

Culture Conscious Listening

Starting Action:

Calm compassion breathwork for antibias accuracy and reflection.

Global Praxis

Cumulating Action:

Joyful justice inclusion projects for cultural and environmental healing.

FIGURE 1.5 Culture-Conscious Listening-Global Praxis graphic. Created by the author.

Culture-Conscious Listening elicits community voices for "natural path" nonviolent communication that "embraces the sacred relationship between humanity and all living things." Global Praxis integrates cross-cultural information from labs and field experiences for interactive "respect and care."[70] These two core practices resist "humanity-*over*-nature" academics and advance "a transformative approach to global studies" through core content. They activate education through an intersectional race-class-gender lens "viewed from the perspectives of ethnic groups within several nations" simultaneously.[71] These two big-picture practices help educators and students activate the Three Transformative Tools for Environmental Liberation Education for inclusive world healing experiences. For instance, the two practices integrate into three Diversity Circle tool curriculum strategies – Sharing, Circle Questions, and Global Praxis – explained in Chapters 5 and 6. Diversity Circle strategies systematize Environmental Liberation Education changes to mainstream academics with holism activities, such as when teachers and students conduct Healthy Multicultural Identity Quests to identify with "humanity-*through*-nature" during subject engagement.[72]

Examples

Classroom and Campus

Classroom and campus examples illustrate how to apply transformative practices to various education levels, programs, and locations. Examples in this book come from action research conducted at the HSI where I teach, such as Culture-Conscious Listening and Global Praxis described above. These practices show how Minority-Serving Institutions (MSIs) drive diversity transformation in higher education. MSIs have relatively desegregated student bodies and federal funding, hiring comparatively more diversity-minded professionals than at Predominantly White Institutions (PWIs).[73]

For instance, I collaborate with colleagues in various Diversity Circles to support students with social-economic experiences that pose barriers to academic success. We experiment to revise requirements with diversity, mindfulness, and sustainability criteria. When assessed with philosophical rubrics, such as provided by the Approach-in-Dimension, we find, all too often, outcomes that fall short of holistic humanization. We find evidence of disengagement and alienation despite best intentions. Poor results prompt improvement with culture surveys and action research involving ethnic studies, women's studies, mindfulness education, and environmental education. As we grow structural and culture competence, we integrate different perspectives, modalities, and sustainability experiences into evolving academic activities.[74]

Classroom Examples

In Academic Faculty Diversity Circles, colleagues and I assess and revise our courses for more inclusive and sustainable space, time, materials, and learning environments. Most of the changes I make are with my face-to-face courses:

- *Student-led Activities:* Over half of my face-to-face class meetings are given over to student- and community-led academic circles with cultures, mindfulness, and nature, indoors and outdoors.
- *Outdoor Education:* We go outside relatively often, for a few minutes or more in most sessions. We take field trips for culturally creative subject engagement, developed with intergenerational action-reflection circles.
- *Curriculum Diversification:* We revise classroom welcome statements, assignment rubrics, reading requirements, and project groups to feature mixed-groups, interdisciplinary, and hands-on culturally relevant activities. We use our classroom library for students to co-create curriculum from a growing mix of multilingual, multicultural, environmental, and mindfulness resources.
- *Multicultural Mindfulness:* When I enter the classroom, I take my own Culture-Conscious Breath for holistic academic concentration to recognize student cultures and facilitate diversity, mindfulness, and sustainability content and activities during class. I open most meetings with whole-class circle breathwork, using a chime or rain stick with body-mind-culture-environment prompts. We use very little screen time to open space for face-to-face listening, trust-building discussions, and Global Praxis events.[75]

Campus Example

Outside the classroom, another transformative example happens annually in our evolving Laboratory Diversity Circle – Faculty for Radical Empowerment and Enlightenment (FREE) – which has been in continuous operation since I co-founded it with Julia Hammett in 2003. FREE is student-centered, integrating scheduled classes across campus into a yearly academic theme. Involving about 200 students and 10 cross-disciplinary faculty yearly, FREE experiments with holistic academics. For example, one project theme – "Whole Campus Book Club for Belonging: Diverse Indigenous Perspectives" – involved a cross-section of faculty, staff, and students from various classes and departments. Participants selected and read books by Indigenous authors to expand academic engagement with authentic cultural voices. One goal was to develop academic accuracy in historical time lines and literature analysis by integrating multiple perspectives to observe how intergenerational trauma and liberation experiences are often ignored topics in mainstream education. The project defined how diverse communities and cultural ways of knowing resist oppression locally, as well as exist apart from the trauma cycles of domination systems through living humanization and cultural thriving regionally.

Participants engaged in book club discussions facilitated by business, history, and English teachers, identity board displays, and student-led time-line activities. In one activity – *Mapping US History: Indigenous Perspectives* – diverse students posted a 24-foot time line on an auditorium wall, headed with the question: "When US history starts here, who belongs?" Using data summaries from *An Indigenous Peoples' History of the United States* by Roxanne Dunbar-Ortiz and from the edition for young people adapted by Jean Mendoza and Debbie Reese, time-line participants wrote answers onto notes at ten time-line points, starting 4 million years ago and going to 2022. Participants listed demographic changes in the US at each date, naming who appeared to "belong" at the time.

This belonging theme evolved into a new 2022–23 FREE theme, "The Year of Sustainability," a project that infused sustainability activities across two institutional prongs: campus infrastructure and campus community. Engaging over 280 projects to reduce, recycle, and renew indoors and outdoors, the theme developed student-centered activities to change academic curriculum, knowledge development, and grounds with Earth health experiences. A theme goal was to involve as many students, staff, and faculty in at least one sustainability event somewhere on campus. This evolved into the 2023–24 FREE theme, "Seventh Generation," involving participants to look backwards and forwards three generations for holistic stewardship action. Participants refreshed existing sustainability projects inspired by a 200-year vision, asking, "What needs to change for lasting wellness that respects regional Indigenous ways of knowing?" For instance, in a 2024 event involving about 300 participants, one culture, science, technology, engineering, arts, and math (C-STEAM) project integrated math, biology, geology, and education classes into "turtle island" earth activities with living tortoises and problem sets about hexagonal sustainability factors in rocks and computations. Inspired by the hexagonal shape of turtle scutes, this project resulted in the installation of a land acknowledgement plaque in a campus pollinator garden with an "Honoring the lands of the Great Basin Tribes Ceremony" involving tribal drumming, singing, and dancing. Michelle McCauley, from the Pyramid Lake Paiute Tribe, explains regional stewardship of the Cui-ui fish: "We want to maintain the fish in our lakes. That means ensuring no water outsourcing from the Truckee River to farming lands and those who are not the original protectors. Sustainability is a new term to me. I've always called it 'taking care of the land.'" The plaque states: "These lands continue to be a gathering place for the Indigenous Peoples and we honor them".[76]

Conclusion

What Can Teachers Do?

After Attaché Ball put down her fork, the waiter came to clear plates. The luncheon in Santiago that inspired this book was concluding. When we stood to leave, we looked at each other, reflecting on our discussion about world systems, broken education, and climate crises, dropping our shoulders, sighing, as if to ask, "What can we do?" Environmental Liberation Education shows there's *a lot* teachers can do to empower our profession and support diverse students through culturally responsive academic engagement. When we use Culture-Conscious Listening and Global Praxis, we liberate. We relate subjects to living cultures in the real world.

Transformative teachers are listeners, motivators, and doers. As listeners, we breath to calm bias and cultivate cultural and sustainability awareness. As motivators, we communicate empathy through culturally respectful inquiry. We are patient as we facilitate cross-cultural compassion activities. As doers, we express positive reinforcement and facilitate multicultural activities for diversity belonging in healing. As change makers, we ask big-picture questions and collaborate on inclusive restorative projects *during* academic engagement.

Dr. Martin Luther King, Jr. declared that the deadline for systemic justice was up in 1963. He focused on healing injustices suffered by people of color. Thirty years later, transformative scholar Ronald Takaki described the need for "a more inclusive multicultural context":

> This broader and comparative approach opens the possibility of understanding and appreciating our racial and cultural diversity – Native Americans as well as peoples from different 'points of departure' such as England, Africa, Ireland, Mexico, Asia, and Russia. This is the story of our coming together to create a new society.[77]

This "coming together" has, unfortunately, been filled with violence and oppression. The jury's out about Takaki's optimism for a new society in a land of systemic dehumanization. Time's up for *all* life on a planet beset with climate change. However, Dr. King's work provides hope. He describes how to collaborate to collect "the facts to determine whether injustices exist." He explains skillful "negotiation" to respect diverse perspectives. He shows how to grow trust through multicultural alliances with "self-purification" circle exercises for nonviolent "direct action."[78] Dr. King's steps inform the Three Transformative Tools presented in this book to strengthen education *with* diversity. These tools encourage inclusive student success and develop humanizing knowledge by organizing, processing, and assessing change.

The systemic inequities that afflict education won't heal through wishful thinking. Underregulated for-profit extraction-consumption productions segregate and destroy through economic-social trauma cycles. However, *transformative* teachers collectivize to *apply* holism on the spot. Unified by the "global-ecocentric paradigm," we enact well-being designs *during* hourly and daily requirements.[79] We revolutionize locally with antibias-antiracist environmental consciousness, liberating mainstream routines with multicultural, mindfulness, and environmental circle activities.

In *Be Free Where You Are*, Thich Nhat Hanh explains to prison inmates that mindfulness is freedom. Mindfulness is "to be truly present in the moment." Mindfulness practices reduce aggression, arrogance, envy, delusion, and grasping habits. Mindfulness cultivates "joy" experiences regardless of conditions, including incarceration.[80] Dr. King, who collaborated with Thich Nhat Hanh in freedom projects, demonstrates how mindfulness motivates cultural healing in bad circumstances. Dr. King took thoughtful action while "confined…alone in a narrow jail cell." Responding to Alabama clergymen detractors, in "the margins of the newspaper in which [their] statement appeared while I was in jail," Dr. King observed how "the dark clouds of racial prejudice" awaken "urgency of the moment and sensed need for powerful action antidotes to combat the disease of segregation." Dr. King explained how the seeds of justice wouldn't be planted or tended by status quo operators. Mainstream educators are anesthetized by hierarchical cultural conditioning to stand by norms with colorblind indifference, but justice practices and the fair rule of law come from the "sensed need" of the oppressed to take action *with* committed allies.[81]

Many students and educators of color suffer at school from race, class, and gender judgments, misplaced anger, false accusations, and defensive hypocrisies from "the dark clouds of racial prejudice" in divisive procedures marked by "increased surveillance, restricted freedom of movement, and suspicions about intentions."[82] However, the "sensed need" for equity experiences motivates projects for true happiness through the value of diversity.[83] Transformative teachers support marginalized peoples to take the "'status of a full partner in social interaction.'"[84] Antibias-antiracist teaming for unity offsets assimilation exclusions with inclusion actions. Our diversity practices are *transformative* because we rearrange top-down arrangements with circle interactions and undo ranking schedules with culturally responsive activities. We invite multicultural community supports into classrooms and outdoor education. We diversify classroom libraries, take cultural field trips, showcase multilingual speakers, and prioritize cultural mentoring.[85] Our efforts improve academic concentration by reducing social stress to meet the human need to belong with culturally responsive holism solutions in the environment we share.[86]

The Three Transformative Tools are not prescriptions. They're support to what you already do. They develop critical consciousness for open-minded academic space, time, materials, and learning environments. They offer best practices to deal with a world of suffering. Think of the tools as aids to *recognize* how students struggle and how knowledge is warped by the dominant culture and its unsustainable inequity systems. These are instruments to *refrain* from overreacting with unconscious bias. They support *restorative action* to insert joyful justice events into subject development. They assist *resolve* to collaborate to connect requirements to cultures, mindfulness, and nature, indoors and outdoors.

Welcome to Our Diversity Circle

Diversity Circle collaborations of two or more participants are evolving homerooms for systemic transformation. We start with Culture-Conscious Listening to hear one another and to welcome our diverse identities, ideologies, and areas of expertise as we translate lived cultural pain into "powerful action antidotes." Then we apply what we learn to hands-on Global Praxis, enacted in labs and field experiences.[87] Our circles are like neighborhood watches, patrolling and refurbishing the cracked foundation of US education with joists for inclusion and equity. Our work integrates multicultural, mindfulness, and sustainability activities into subjects to support holistic student success for a livable world.

Think of this book as its own Diversity Circle. We swap cultural stories, pose big-picture questions, and share peace practices. We try Multicultural Mindfulness Activities. Our Diversity Circle develops liberation theory with social-emotional curiosity about stewardship. We're multicultural, gender-balanced, and intersectional. We work through class conflicts with patience and nonviolence. Our circle is you, your colleagues, students, me, and the global educators in this book. At the end of each chapter, a breathwork and journal question puts you inside our imaginary Diversity Circle. Please reflect through journaling and challenge yourself to take liberation action: *How am I teaching to transform today?*

TRANSFORMATIVE BREATHWORK AND JOURNAL

Journal Question: *What's a Transformative Teacher?*

> Mindfulness…means to be truly present in the moment. When you eat, you know what you are eating. When you walk, you know that you are walking. The opposite of mindfulness is forgetfulness. You eat but you don't know that you are eating, because your mind is elsewhere. When you bring your mind back to what is happening in the here and now, that is mindfulness.[88]
>
> –Thich Nhat Hanh

Breathwork

Wherever you are, take a mindful moment to relax. Use a timer chime if you like. Close or lid your eyes, taking several slow deep breaths, smiling slightly, noticing sensations: smells, sounds, touch, taste, and sight (if your eyes are open).

Now breathe while internally reciting the **gatha** below:

Breathing in, I calm my body.
Breathing out, I smile.
Dwelling in the present moment,
I know this is a **transformative** moment.[89]

Then:

Breathing in **What's a Transformative Teacher?**
Breathing out openness.

Repeat for as long as you like, or until the timer chimes.

Journal

Imagine we're in a Diversity Circle with the transformative practitioners cited in this book. We want to support superdiverse student success in a biodiverse world. Read our answers below. Reflect on your meditation. Briefly answer the journal question above in a way that's meaningful to you.

Paulo Freire

Transformative teachers are:

- Liberation educators who facilitate culture circles for academic self-determination and critical consciousness with real-world action.
- Collaborators in culturally responsive humanization education.
- Student-centered practitioners who integrate subjects into community stories, data, themes, and questions to code and decode economic-social contradictions for praxis solutions.[90]

George I. Sanchez

A transformative teacher is:

- "The advance agent of a new social order."
- A highly qualified educator who helps desegregate by resisting White supremacy and supporting academic self-determination.
- A facilitator of student cultural assets in academic development.
- An antiracist-antibias practitioner with high academic expectations.[91]

Liz Kleinrock

Transformative teachers focus on:

- Student critical consciousness to understand the purpose of education and how to use education to empower rather than to harm.

- Engaging diversity to co-create equity and inclusion experiences *with* students by destigmatizing taboo subjects.
- Social and emotional development of diverse students to support intersectional identity development through academic engagement.[92]

Gloria Ladson-Billings

Transformative teachers use:

- Culturally Relevant Education (CRE) – concrete experiences, dialogue strategies, caring practices, and personal accountability.
- Best practices for inclusion to develop diverse student success, cultural competence, and critical consciousness.[93]

Micaela Rubalcava

Transformative teachers are:

- Collaborators for holistic academics with cultures, mindfulness, and nature circle activities, indoors and outdoors, on site and off.
- Facilitators of integrative subject engagement with big-picture questions and multi-modal culturally responsive sustainability projects.
- Open-minded practitioners of every background who change assimilation and segregation space, time, materials, and learning environments with Environmental Liberation Education or a similar unity approach.

Notes

1 Gang (1991), 79.
2 Antonio Campaña 2017 Fulbright interview/seminar, in Rubalcava (2001–2024).
3 Malinowski (2022, January 13).
4 Lindstrom (2020); Teller (2016).
5 Antonio Campaña 2017 Fulbright interview/seminar, in Rubalcava (2001–2024).
6 Vicuña (2017, July 7).
7 Gang (1991), 79, Reece (2022).
8 Takaki (1993), "Author's Note".
9 Freire (1985), 69, 19, 36, 101.
10 Aubrey and Riley (2016); Diaz (2018); Freire (1985), 36; hooks (1994).
11 Freire (1985), 103; Emdin (2016), 175.
12 Keltner (2023), 14; Reece (2022), 40.
13 Englander (2016), 27.
14 Englander (2016), 27.
15 Block (2016).
16 Freire (1985); Geri and MacGregor (1999, January); Hanh (all); Lardner (2018, July 9–12); Maher (2005); National Association (2023); Roberts and Pruitt (2009); Smith, MacGregor, Matthews and Gabelnick (2004); Trungpa (1993); Vescio, Ross and Adams (2008, January).
17 Hanh (all); Hanh and Weare (2017); Trungpa (1993).
18 Banks (1988, 1993).
19 Valdés (2016), 79.

20 Bloom (1974); Gardner (1983).
21 hooks (1994), 21; Doll, Brehm and Zucker (2014).
22 Neruda (2023, September 6).
23 Arveseth (2014); César Peña 2017 Fulbright interview/seminar, in Rubalcava (2001–2024).
24 Freire (1985).
25 Freire (1985); hooks (1994); Nieto (2013); Valenzuela (2016).
26 Alexander (2010); Barrera (1979); Kendi (2019); Ladson-Billings and Tate (2006); Rothstein (all).
27 Ingersoll (2015); Ingersoll and Smith (2003); Sleeter (all).
28 Ewing and Hannah-Jones (2018, November 29); Frankenberg, Garces and Hopkins (2016); Rothstein (all); Walter (2019, May 16).
29 Lewis and Diamond (2015).
30 Deruy (2017); Ellison and Freedberg (2015, May 21); Gray and Taie (2015); Guin (2004); Pabon, Sanderson and Kharem (2011); Partelow, Spong, Brown and Johnson (2017, September 14); Sleeter (2001, 2011); Terada (2019, February 4); Quinlan (2016, May 6); Barnes, Crowe and Schaefer (2007).
31 Ingersoll (2015); Ingersoll and Smith (2003).
32 Rubalcava (2001–2024).
33 Gang (1991), 79.
34 Elena Bubnova: February 14, 2018 email to the author, in Rubalcava (2001–2024); Cecilia Vigil: 2022–23 emails to the author in Rubalcava (2001–2024).
35 Kleinrock (2021).
36 Lewis and Diamond (2015), 58.
37 Ellison (1998); Tutu and Tutu (2014); Verschelden (2017).
38 Chang and Ifill (2018, April 19); Derman-Sparks (1989); Eberhardt (2019); Kendi (2019); Lewis and Diamond (2015); Nordell (2021).
39 Hanh and Weare (2017); Madden-Dent and Oliver (2021); Rechtschaffen (2016).
40 Hanh (2002a), 59.
41 Rubalcava (2001–2024).
42 Eberhardt (2019).
43 Damasio (1994); Eberhardt (2019); Keltner (2023); LeDoux (1996); Verschelden (2017); Whalen and Phelps (2009).
44 Damasio (1994); Eberhardt (2019); Keltner (2023); LeDoux (1996); Verschelden (2017); Whalen and Phelps (2009).
45 Keltner (2023), 137–138; Vedantam (2023, March 13 and 14).
46 Madison (2013, 2018, 2020).
47 hooks (1994), 21.
48 hooks (1994), 13.
49 Eberhardt (2019); Ellison (1998); Hanh (all); Hanh and Weare (2017); Trungpa (1993); Tutu and Tutu (2014); Verschelden (2017).
50 Oakes and Lipton (2007); Spring (all).
51 Banks (1988).
52 National Head Start Association (2019).
53 National Head Start Association (2019).
54 Schoorl (2008); Rubalcava (1965a).
55 Rubalcava (1965b, 1965a).
56 Lewis and Diamond (2015), 13.
57 Rubalcava (1965a, 1965b).
58 Rubalcava (1965a, 1965b).
59 Banks (1993), 5–7.
60 Urtubey (2023, June 20).
61 Barnett (2020, May 6); Heckman (2020); Nevada (2010).
62 Bizjak, Yoon-Hendricks, Reese and Sullivan (2018, December 4).
63 Lonas (2021, August 19); Hernández (2021, August 4).
64 Middleton (2018), 187.
65 Brannon (2021, August 6); Middleton (2018).
66 Keep (2019–2020).
67 Bullard and Xin (2012).

68 Keep (2019–2020); Rubalcava (1965a, 1965b); Cecilia Vigil: 2022–23 emails to the author, in Rubalcava (2001–2024).
69 Lindstrom (2020).
70 Lindstrom (2020).
71 Gang (1991), 79; Banks (2003), 23.
72 Gang (1991), 79.
73 Blake (2018, March); Espinoza, Turk and Taylor (2017); Li and Carroll (2007); Petchauer and Mawhinney (2017); Gasman, Samayoa and Ginsberg (2016).
74 Rubalcava (2001–2024).
75 Rubalcava (2001–2024).
76 Rubalcava (2001–2024); Truckee (2018 and 2024).
77 Takaki (1993), "Author's Note".
78 King (1964), 78.
79 Gang (1991), 78.
80 Hanh (2002a), 50–51.
81 King (1964), 76, 89, 95.
82 Lewis and Diamond (2015), 78, quoting Nancy Fraser.
83 King (1964), 89; Hanh (all); Hanh and Weare (2017).
84 King (1964), 89.
85 Gay (2000); Ladson-Billings (1995); Sleeter and Carmona (2017); Sleeter (2001, 2011); Sleeter and Zavala (2020); Valenzuela (2016).
86 Hanh and Weare (2017).
87 King (1964), 98.
88 (2002a), 50.
89 Hanh (2008), 36.
90 Freire (1985).
91 Au, Brown and Calderón (2016), 109.
92 Kleinrock (2021).
93 Ladson-Billings (1995).

2
TRANSFORMATIVE TEACHERS NOW

Guiding Purpose

Explain how

- Good teachers are key to diverse student success.
- Systemic bias and unsustainable procedures fail students and teachers.
- Mindfulness is transformative.
- Transformative teachers help reform broken systems.
- Transformative teaching is easy and fun.

Provide

- Two Multicultural Mindfulness Activities and one journal question: *Un-biasing the Mind, Inclusive Academic Concentration*, and *How is Global Praxis a Verb and Environmental Humanization a Noun?*

Context

How Do Teachers Impact Education?

Apart from socio-economic status, teachers are the most important factor to student success.[1] Especially with at-risk students, teachers have more impact on academic achievement than other aspects of education, such as facilities, administrators, or curriculum. We're important because we make up to "1,500 decisions" a day. While actively teaching, we make about seven decisions per minute.[2] We make academic determinations throughout education routines. "Teachers engage in complex decision-making before, during, and after a lesson is taught."[3] Teachers impact knowledge development and student academic engagement "hourly and daily" as we judge behaviors and manage relationships while constructing and delivering subjects for engagement.[4]

DOI: 10.4324/9781003364757-4

This chapter has been made available under a CC-BY-NC-ND license.

These are cultural decisions. The materials teachers feature and the learning outcomes we expect convey cultural perspectives. When we highlight or remove content, impart or omit subject themes, and input or exclude evaluation data, we're making determinations that either compassionately respond to or alienate cultures. The same goes for how teachers communicate and facilitate socialization and emotional intelligence.[5] We favor certain cultural values and languages, and this devalues other cultures. We separate or unite identity groups during academic activities, and this segregates or integrates during subject engagement.

Teachers make judgments about cultures and ideologies when we guide knowledge development during classroom discussions, lab experiments, research projects, and collegial collaborations. Knowledge activities shape disciplines and offer arts and sciences breakthroughs about subjects. Teachers design and select themes and activities informed by subject expertise. Teachers decide how to arrange education space and time to sequence academic practices. Our management decisions develop positive or negative social-emotional interactions through subjects. We sanction or exclude voices and choose modalities and cognitive levels for academic activities. We determine what cultural artifacts, practices, and beliefs about knowledge to welcome or reject and what to censor, what is optional, and what to require. We routinize how content is received, by whom, where, when, how, and why.[6]

Teachers communicate high, middle, or low expectations to different learners variously. We emphasize skills for guided practice, making templates for collaborations and independence. Teachers assess student performance with formative and summative evaluations. We make countless determinations about academic events, big and small. Thus, everyday educators significantly influence student success and ideological development through a stream of cultural decisions about behaviors, relationships, environmental arrangements, and subjects that cumulate in humanization or dehumanization outcomes.[7]

Good Teachers and a Core Teacher Paradox

The humanization goals that motivate US teachers are holistic, but our system divides. About 80% of teachers are European American, coming to school not only culturally conditioned by Anglo-conformity but also without much multicultural education training. Yet teachers educate an increasingly diverse student body. Even the most experienced, effective, and highly qualified teachers are undermined by the paradox of wanting to humanize in a dehumanizing system. Teachers of all demographic backgrounds are inspired by humanization through subject knowledge and skills, but the profession does not adequately prepare for culture or structural competence to handle bias and unsustainable structures skillfully.[8]

We know that good teachers manage to apply best practices to humanize despite dehumanizing structures. Good teachers are passionate and highly qualified with subject expertise *and* persuasive communication skills. We're professionals who carefully plan, collaborate, convey, and assess curriculum, knowledge, and outcomes. The more experience we have, the better we become, improving efficacy with ongoing reflection and subject development. Many of us use humanization methods, such as inquiry circles, prompt-and-response sequences, motivation strategies, and problem-solving project themes and materials designed to fascinate. We engage content enthusiastically *with* students and colleagues setting up inviting academic routines and rigorous arts and sciences disciplinary norms for an ongoing flow of teachable moments.[9]

While most teachers are motivated to the profession by humanization goals, we work in an institution that is preoccupied with economic efficiency goals. The US economy produces commodities and services from extraction, mechanization, and cyber industries rooted in systemic inequities and dehumanization patterns. The pressure to assimilate youth and skew knowledge for a culturally tiered corporatized economy pushes US education into biased, segregated, and environmentally alienating routines.[10]

A core teacher paradox, then, is that motivational humanization goals – actualization, socialization, and citizenship – are integrative but US education is stymied by tiers. These tiers align with a stratified economy that separates people and funds institutions unequally. This economy and its corresponding territorial politics set up education to neglect holistic social-emotional academic learning. For example, industry-driven gun proliferation fuels violence and fear at school. Racially inflected for-profit interests oppose antibias-antiracist practices to shift academic requirements with equity criteria. Corporate capitalist obstacles prevent concerted environmental stewardship knowledge and skill development in core content or during education routines. Such obstructions come from profit systems dependent on racialized cheap labor, gender divides, and extractive resource production that destroys biodiversity.

Because the US economy was founded to segment, monopolize, and deplete without inclusive humanitarian regulations, social institutions and culture patterns alienate and over-standardize.[11] Meanwhile, the humanization that teachers and students cherish would thrive through inclusion activities *if* equity regulations were permitted to develop unity through diversity over time. While good teachers find ways to humanize despite unsustainable and stratifying policies and habits, much of our transformative work is limited to isolated classrooms, labs, meeting rooms, programs, and events. In sites otherwise dominated by individualism and race, class, gender divisions, unconsciously, many of us act defensively, perpetuating bias hourly and daily.[12]

Resolving the Paradox

Happily, good teachers – of any identity, area of subject expertise, and teaching level – become *transformative* when we collaborate in peace circles, as diverse as possible. We collectivize to respond to change as we facilitate egalitarian experiences while assuaging social and emotional anxieties from structural segmentations. We collaborate for benevolence, approaching social justice from a position of love. In the absence of effective equity policies from legislators, multicultural-multiracial grassroots alliances forge holism change now. Our alliances grow by forgiving one another's mistakes and setbacks even as we rejoice in cultural inclusion, equity, and sustainability moments as they occur. Transformative teachers reclaim the humanization goals that motivate our profession with *integrative culture-conscious* decisions about academic design, engagement, and assessment. Transformative teachers foster unifying antibias-antiracist academic experiences by involving diverse students in mixed project groups with cross-cultural subject materials about global problem-solving. We co-create *holistic* humanization outcomes through communities of care to develop democratic citizenship skills during academic engagement.

Teachers of color and White teachers rely on one another during model compassionate liberation teams. Operating from divergent yet intersectional cultural standpoints within systemic bias, we nurture collegiality by *integrating* classrooms, labs, meeting rooms, and sites with diversity best practices. Structural change is not without conflict. That's why we use non-defensive precepts to figure out how to reduce over-standardized requirements, pre-packaged products, tiered schedules, and vertical relationships. We courageously create interdisciplinary content with open-ended questions, experimenting with culture, mindfulness, and nature activities. We empower the profession and support diverse student success by strengthening humanization with Environmental Liberation Education. Transformative teachers develop healthy multicultural identities and Earth stewardship by engaging subjects with student-centered practices unified by the wide scope of superdiversity in biodiversity.

How Does Superdiversity Reconceptualize Humanization?

Superdiversity is a way of thinking about human diversity in a globalized world of uncertain resources during climate change. Superdiversity is the experience of eight billion (and growing) people on Earth navigating cross-cultural connections and clashes through migrations and crises entwined in economic-social systems that impact the planet. Superdiversity reconceptualizes the humanization goals that motivate teachers locally with global vision. We perceive humanity outside of the nation-state framework. We understand that students and knowledge are impacted by superdiversity in biodiversity, a big picture currently tarnished by global warming.[13]

Schools are microcosms in a world grappling with assimilation and segregation divisions and changing environmental conditions. Superdiversity reconceptualizes humanization by recognizing that cultural contradictions in education are accelerated and intensified by the "new communication technologies, movement of goods and capital, transnational contact and recontact, and new and return migration" of superdiversity.[14] Rather than xenophobic interpretations of cultures, separating cultures from Earth, or viewing global systems as removed from individuals, groups, classrooms, labs, meeting rooms, and sites, transformative teachers connect local academics to wide-vision humanization. Transformative teachers

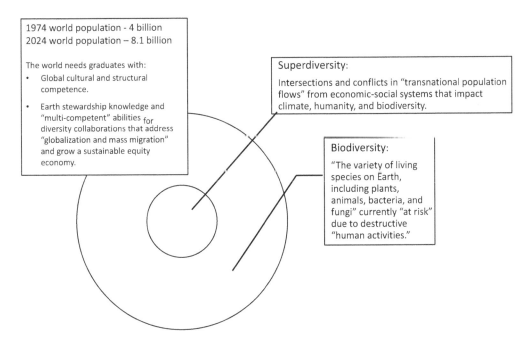

FIGURE 2.1 Superdiversity/Biodiversity graphic. Created by the author, citing Valdés (2016), 79.

change education space, time, materials, and learning environment procedures with mindfulness of intergenerational intersectional cultures and natural resources in a globalized world, depicted in Figure 2.1.[15]

What's Transformative Teaching Theory?

Transformative teaching theory is the art and science of holistic education change. It is social justice collaboration to shift how educators address assimilation and segregation from status quo and fear mindsets to inclusive growth mindsets. It is intervening in mainstream academic routines with equity and sustainability activities. Even the most effective US educators are part of an institutional network that dehumanizes communities of color and alienates people from the environment. Anglo-conformist education reproduces dehumanizing social-economic systems through racialized programs and achievement tracks and fields of study involved in global warming.[16] However, when transformative teachers make culture-conscious decisions to reshape subject engagement by integrating superdiverse students into social justice and green economy projects, we humanize from the ground up.

Transformative teaching theory is holistic action-reflection in curriculum, learning outcomes, knowledge development, school communications, and site interactions. Systemic equity progresses by integrating body, mind, culture, and environment into a *variety* of transformative activities throughout institutions. As a range of participants collaborate to reinterpret status quo procedures in the social superstructure, diversity inputs are strengthened to reshape the economic substructure. Through education's central role in the social superstructure, reform happens as *teachers* – who have authority over subject and student activities – team for culturally responsive liberation experiences.[17] Transformative teaching theory, thereby, uplifts the humanization goals that motivate education with local and global citizenship activities.

Transformative teaching theory synthesizes liberation education with multicultural, mindfulness, and environmental education. The Three Transformative Tools for Environmental Liberation Education facilitate best practices for this synthesis. The tools assist participants to be "co-investigators" of Anglo-conformist divisions.[18] They grow "critical consciousness" for integration through culture circles.[19] Transformative teachers *collectivize* to pry loose the stranglehold of an inequity economy that manufactures conflicts and global warming. We replace "mechanistic-industrial" content throughout sites with subject diversification, not to romanticize diversity but to facilitate a multicultural green economy. We change education with community empowerment and big-picture well-being experiences now.[20]

How *Does Transformative Teaching Reform?*

Transformative teaching reforms by framing diversity not as a problem but as a source of solutions to systemic challenges. Transformative teachers identify failing assimilation and segregation policies. We grow culture competence with structural competence to replace "a settler colony's national construction of itself" with academic activities for "multicultural, multiracial democracy."[21] We participate in Diversity Circles to nurture cross-cultural trust during routines. We apply Multicultural Mindfulness peace practices to conflict as we grow unity in diversity. We plan and evaluate change with the Approach-in-Dimension for philosophical clarity about challenging concepts – diversity, equity, inclusion, and sustainability – to more accurately guide humanization.

Transformative teaching reforms by activating academic freedom to replace exclusion space, time, materials, and learning environments with inclusive mindfulness and culture experiences featuring nature, indoors and outdoors – such as by doing the following:

- Reducing academic tiers and increasing mixed-group collaboration projects with sustainability themes.
- Limiting screens and increasing hands-on academics in the real world.
- Sequencing prompt-and-response progressions during subject engagement with multi-modal, multi-lingual, and multi-level cognitive activities.
- Integrating multicultural, mindfulness, and sustainability resources into core curriculum.
- Implementing inquiry projects with big-picture subject themes from student-generated questions and culture surveys.
- Involving diverse community supports in antibias-antiracist academic projects to reduce corporatism and materialism and increase body-mind-culture-environment co-generation.
- Organizing students to help design and implement requirements holistically.
- Using concrete experiences, dialogue strategies, caring practices, and personal accountability methods during subject development.[22]

When transformative teachers collaborate on universal design for culturally responsive student inclusion, everyone benefits.[23] When a few classrooms, labs, or meeting rooms nurture diversity, others pick up on inclusive sustainability joy. As specific locations improve, programs and departments adapt, influencing whole sites, districts, and systems. As education develops big-picture humanization activities, other institutions that interact with schools – law, police, social work, health services, libraries, and business – respond with holistic changes. When diverse graduates with body-mind-culture-environment skills enter the economy, for-profit systems adopt humanitarian regulations to accommodate diversity inputs. As the for-profit economy strengthens with diversity regulated for public good, it pays a living wage and makes healthful products to offer society. When social institutions are supported by an inclusive green economy, bureaucracies reproduce egalitarian sustainability experiences to give back to the economy. Thus, in full circle, education transformation advances systemic justice from a position of love.[24]

What *Does Transformative Teaching Reform?*

Structural goals and biases in US education have failed students and teachers. The primary goal of US education – economic efficiency – has been caught in substructure-superstructure inequity loops.[25] The loop starts as "schools educate future workers"; then "better workers increase productivity"; then "economic growth pays for investment in education"; and the loop closes with "investment in schools" to "educate future workers." This is education's assimilation succession. The cycle has been funneled through contradictory racialized yet ostensive colorblind policies, producing and reproducing segregated tiers of "better workers," managers, leaders, and corporations to grease the extraction-consumption-destruction economy, using education as its pipeline.[26]

In this pipeline, even highly qualified US educators are unable to accomplish "effective assimilation" for many.[27] Despite pockets of sustainability and equity programs, US education is a faulty social superstructure institution. It divides "young people" into stratified sites through biased enrollment and completion procedures, thereby failing and excluding some young people altogether while preparing tiered graduates for a segmented economy. Youth from privileged families get educated at "selective" sites "for the most selective jobs and positions" in US society. Poor youth may drop out altogether, while youth from middle- and lower-middle income families don't matriculate into college at nearly the same rate, and when they do enroll, they disproportionately attend under-funded institutions with open-door policies and lower standings in the "university/college ranking system," thereby acquiring less desirable occupations.[28]

Moreover, the system doesn't train a diverse teacher force for culture and structural competence to facilitate inclusion inside classrooms, labs, or meeting rooms. Mainstream educators – racially homogenized and over-bureaucratized – operate Eurocentric rules that emphasize lower-order knowledge for many rather than critical consciousness for all. Ironically, the systemic inequities that teachers reproduce undermine the humanization goals that motivate the profession. Moreover, segregation is intergenerational, a self-fulfilling prophesy that prevents equal, integrative participation in the first place.[29]

Transformative teaching helps to solve these problems by *recouping* the humanization goals we treasure. We counteract the contradiction of operating structures and biases that assimilate, segregate, and destroy. We confront dehumanization by overcoming our "very passive approach that allows patterns of social injustice to continue" through culturally responsive academic interactions *with* students.[30] We animate joyful justice *during* subject engagement. Transformative teaching helps reform inequity systems at the root of the global warming economy by integrating core content into interdisciplinary sustainability projects.

The Bias Obstacle to Transformative Teaching

Bias prevents prosocial change through ignorance and denial. The question isn't *whether* US educators – 80% of whom are European American and largely untrained in diversity education – are biased.[31] We are. Everybody's biased. The salient questions are

- How does Anglo-conformist bias obstruct me from our transformative teaching now?
- How can we reach out to participate in diversity collaborations to *reduce* bias decisions during everyday routines?
- How does my team *grow* culture competence with structural competence to *integrate* diverse students in high-expectation academic outcomes?

One-off diversity trainings, celebration events, or additive requirements do not answer these questions. An outsourced multicultural education workshop does not change systemic bias. Diversity committees that slightly revise curriculum do not transform curriculum with an intersectional race-class-gender paradigm. One ethnic studies class or a single diversity course mandate does not change mindsets. Rather, social justice change in education involves consistent antibias-antiracist decisions uplifted with the value of holism to reshape curriculum, learning outcomes, knowledge development, school communications, *and* site interactions.

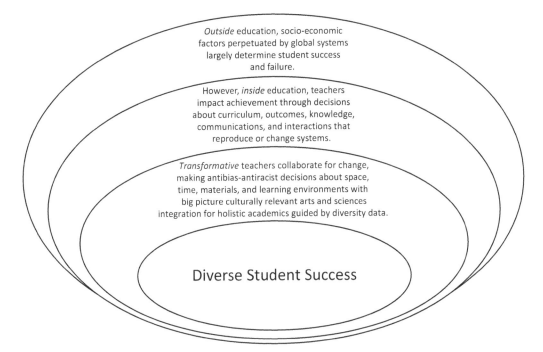

FIGURE 2.2 Student Success graphic. Created by the author.

Compassionate action-reflection identifies the myriad ways that bias dehumanizes to strengthen resolve during big-picture change. Transformative teachers detrack and un-standardize academics through inclusive sustainability activities, empowering the profession and students with a "global-ecocentric" mindset that clears bias obstacles, shown in Figure 2.2.[32]

How Do Transformative Teachers Reduce Bias?

As detailed in Chapter 3, bias in US education perpetuates the "recurring dream" of Anglo-conformity.[33] This is the dehumanizing myth that ranks cultures and alienates people from the environment. Portrayed as colorblind individualism in academic standards, Anglo-conformity at school limits the range of best practices in teachers' "repertoire of instructional strategies." Anglo-conformity, learned in childhood in segregated neighborhoods, is subsequently hardened by segregated schooling, including in teaching credential programs that enroll mostly White students and offer little diversity curriculum.[34]

The systemic bias that educators unconsciously habituate before entering the profession is solidified after hire while teaching at tiered sites. Anglo-conformist bias entrenches further because very few teachers participate in diversity professional development. Most US teacher professional development isn't integrated or holistic; rather it's intermittent, additive, and compartmentalized. Our trainings scarcely confront White superiority bias, individualism, or how the for-profit economy divides cultures and alienates people from the environment. Most trainings don't equip teachers with antibias-antiracist sustainability skills.[35] But our routines – individualistic high-stakes testing, delivering curriculum for extraction-consumption careers, sitting in rows and stations facing screens, using prefabricated curriculum products, and pushing students through racially tracked pipelines – reinforce bias habits throughout our careers.

While Anglo-conformity is pervasive and can feel overwhelming, the good news is that bias systems at school are maintained *or* changed through routines that *we* operate. While conducting routines, teachers *can* decide to participate in multicultural alliances to reshape space and time with culturally relevant materials and integrative designs. We *can* implement interdisciplinary multimodal knowledge and eco-friendly antibias-antiracist practices during academics.[36]

Why Do Transformative Teachers Develop Critical Consciousness?

This book proposes that everyday teachers become transformative by reconceptualizing the humanization goals that motivate our profession with "critical consciousness" activities.[37] Liberation education explains critical consciousness as part of humanization. It offers "*conscientização*" (as Paulo Freire termed it) developed in "culture circles" from academic action-reflection to solve economic, social, and political contradictions.[38] *Environmental* Liberation Education connects critical consciousness to Environmental Humanization goals, integrating subjects into local and global citizenship projects about superdiversity in biodiversity during climate change.

When critical consciousness is expanded by Environmental Humanization, teachers and students synthesize multicultural, mindfulness, *and* environmental education. This balances Western arts and sciences with diverse ways of knowing, such as by listening to Traditional Ecological Knowledge (TEK) (aka Native Ways of Knowing).[39] TEK deepens arts and sciences with longitudinal cultural-environmental data documented over thousands of years. These intergenerational stories and practices model how to center education on Earth stewardship.

> TEK is an Indigenous science of our relationship to the natural world, taking varying and local forms in five thousand or so Indigenous cultures around the world. It has evolved into a cultural belief system… through tens of thousands of hours of observing flora and fauna, weather systems, the power of plants, migration patterns of animals, and life cycles; compiling the data; testing hypotheses with empirical evidence and cultural input from elders; and transmission of knowledge through oral, religious, and pictorial traditions.[40]

TEK embodies three mindfulness principles – impermanence, interbeing, and spaciousness – about the universe. It inspires east, south, west, and north cultural journeys *as part of* core academic engagement through sun, earth, sky, and water themes. TEK involves Culture-Conscious Listening to Indigenous peoples about making reparations by giving land back and supporting communities of care to protect cultures connected to the environment in sustainable systems.[41] For instance, transformative teachers can apply the Haudenosaunee value of studying those who came before and those who aren't yet born but who will inherit the Earth.[42] Peace projects honoring diverse ways of knowing connect personal cultures to institutional and world systems, thereby guiding holistic change with critical consciousness, shown in the visual below.

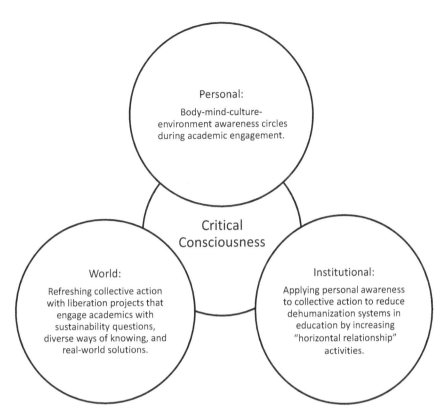

FIGURE 2.3 Critical Consciousness graphic. Created by the author.

Theory and Practice

How Has US Education Failed Students and Teachers?

Economic efficiency has been the main goal of US education since its beginnings, training and tracking generations of workers, managers, and leaders for civic engagement in a capitalist economy. The US teacher force was developed to meet this goal.[43] In the 1800s, the US teaching profession was primarily populated by European American females molded by bureaucratic training and management practices administered by European Americans. The Troy Female Seminary, established in 1821 by Emma Willard in New York, and Mount Holyoke, established in 1837 by Mary Lyon in Massachusetts, trained the first generation of teachers in the United States with "rigorous" standards. The objectives were to ensure quality and to accommodate interchangeable job rotations by the young female European American teachers who were affordable to neighborhoods. Paid 60% of what men were paid to teach, White females soon occupied the education career with a "professionalizing motherhood" version of feminism.[44]

Unfortunately, the cost-effectiveness that put European American female teachers in high demand also weakened academic freedom in curriculum and instruction. Early teacher training models were factory-like, standardizing practices and materials to accommodate the rapid turnover of short career cycles obliging marriage and family priorities. Moreover, the dominant professional culture of English-only values were directed primarily to European American students. These early educators and students engaged a Eurocentric curriculum in segregated top-down "banking education" units alienated from multicultural sustainability.[45]

Historically, US Education has mirrored the White-dominated mechanistic-industrial economy it serves: desks bolted in rows, close monitoring of student behaviors, homogenized hygiene and food services, English language learning, and Eurocentric curriculum. Traditionally, students were required to keep their hands still while memorizing content. The Anglo-conformist model obscured diversity in classrooms. Cultures that didn't readily assimilate were deemed deficient or excluded altogether.

The definition of "humanization" that motivated early teachers neglected diverse cultural and environmental holism. US public education was bureaucratized for White teachers to instruct poor White children about how to overcome perceived character shortcomings and develop industrial skills for factory labor. Some upward mobility opportunities were built in for the best and the brightest of these children to enroll in higher education to gain qualifications for high-status jobs and social positions. However, public education was part of a tiered system topped by selective private schools that developed enlightenment skills for managers and leaders to operate a racialized version of humanity. The system as a whole, steeped in traditions dating to "12th-century Europe" where knowledge was anchored in the Christian church, was dissociated from egalitarianism and naturalism.[46]

For instance, later, when authorized to instruct students of color also, teachers delivered Eurocentric curriculum and perpetuated the White-superiority versus cultural-deficiency paradigm. Teachers conveyed structural bias through "selection" and "processing" decisions about student behaviors – dress, movement, noise, language, articulation, and comportment – that withheld or offered academic resources unfairly.[47] Biased teacher decisions impacted students' sense of belonging in or disaffection from education. Teacher evaluations funneled students into racialized academic success or failure pipelines with divided programs and tracks that treated cultural diversity and environmental education as null or extra curriculum.

Horace Mann – the "father of the common school" – orchestrated free public education with professional teacher standards specifying assimilation.

> Horace Mann feared that growing crime rates, social class conflict, and the extension of suffrage would lead to violence and mob rule. Commonly held political values would curtail political violence and revolution. He envisioned public schools teaching common political values for the purpose of maintaining political order. For Mann, the important idea was that all children in society attend the same kind of school. This is what was meant by 'common.' It was a school common to all children.[48]

Mann explained in an 1840 lecture, "Characteristics of the Ideal Teacher," how female teachers must acquire subject matter knowledge, instructional skills, and an aptitude to manage the moral character and good behavior of students.[49] Teacher evaluations emphasized punctuality, regulations, and order. Humanization goals standardized segregation during this time in all areas of education: curriculum, outcomes, knowledge, communications, and social interactions. This Anglo-conformist version of humanization had the "best intentions," aiming for charity and upward mobility for children of the working class, but it was disinformed by White racism.[50]

The predominance of European American female teachers as conveyers of standardized Anglo-conformist knowledge to mostly European American children normalized Eurocentric literacy and the claim of White privilege as rungs in the ladder of success. US public education was asserted in rhetoric to be a "social mobility" model.[51] However, its results divided. Through education, communities of color and diverse ways of knowing have been marginalized or excluded as deficient, while White individuals and peoples who comport with Anglo-conformist materialism are understood as achievers.[52]

Currently, systemic bias, still transmitted by teachers, most of whom are White, manifests in paperwork-heavy high-stakes testing and assessment loops about lower-order objectives, with separate higher-order programs for the gifted and talented and college-bound. Unintentionally, educators track workers versus managers and leaders into tiers that largely match the socio-economic status to which they were born. For instance, science, technology, engineering, and mathematics (STEM) programs reproduce segregated outcomes, and African Americans and Latinx are underrepresented in STEM fields.[53] Moreover, while contemporary STEM curriculum develops higher-order cognition skills for analytical careers, its worth in the corporatized for-profit economy devalues social, philosophical, and creativity skills from arts, humanities, and social sciences by contrast.[54]

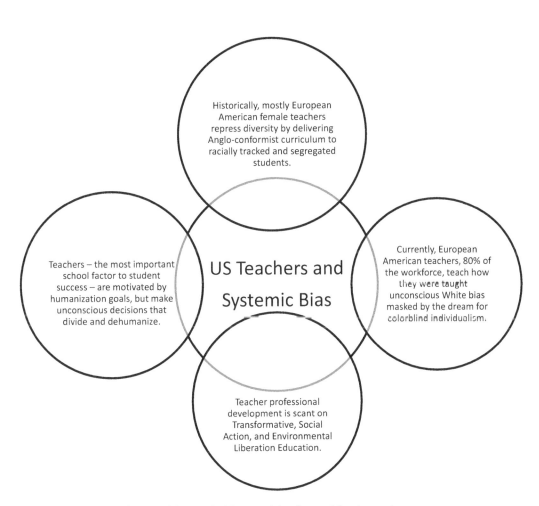

FIGURE 2.4 US Teachers and Systemic Bias graphic. Created by the author.

MULTICULTURAL MINDFULNESS ACTIVITY

Un-biasing the Mind

Outcome

- Create a visual for mindfulness *of* diversity for your antibias breathwork practice.
- Use your visual to uplift negative and neutral feelings about cultures with positive emotions.
- Journal about Multicultural Mindfulness.

Key Concepts

- **Alaya**: Home ground for unbiased goodness and non-defensive generosity from mindfulness.[55]
- **Culture**: Shared artifacts, practices, and beliefs of any group, impacted by human needs, power systems, and generational cycles.
- **Spacetime Superpower**: Academic freedom to maneuver classroom space, time, materials, and learning environments during the hourly and daily decisions that shape education.[56]

Resources

- Journal, pencil, basic classroom art supplies to make a poster, copy of Figure 2.5 (below), an example or symbol of nature, a place to meet indoors or outdoors.

Big-Picture Question

- What's big-picture diversity?

Start

Whole group circle while passing around Figure 2.5:

- **Read aloud and discuss** *Alaya* definition.
- **Discuss:** How does Figure 2.5 express *Alaya*?

In three diversified project teams:

- **Assign** one concept to each team – interbeing, impermanence, and emptiness – to define in a sentence.

Whole group circle:

- **Discuss** the definitions and brainstorm visual symbols for each.

Individually:

- **Research** or reflect on a definition of and find or create a visual symbol about (select one):
  1. Culture
  2. *Alaya*
  3. *No Mud, No Lotus*[57]
  4. Antibias theory

5 Change theory
6 Ecology and life cycles
7 Growth mindset[58]
8 The psychology of happiness

Middle

Whole group circle:

- **Discuss** participant visual symbols and the nature example or symbol.

Individually

- **Select** a symbol that personally inspires from those discussed for poster artwork (collage, paint, color, draw). Note: individual poster artwork and writing time can go for as little or as long as desired.
- **Write** a word or phrase that relates the artwork to mindfulness of diversity.

Closing

Together:

- **Stand** or **sit** to breath consciously while looking at one's completed poster, placed about 6 feet away. Breathe in through the nose, deep into the belly, and breathe out through a slightly smiling mouth, natural and relaxed, with a timer for a few minutes:

    a **Breathe in**, a specific negative feeling about a person.
    Breath out, uplifting that to a neutral feeling about a culture that person appears to represent.
    b **Breath in**, a specific neutral feeling about a person.
    Breathe out, uplifting that to a positive feeling about a culture that person appears to represent.
    c **Breathe in**, fear of diversity.
    Breathe out mindfulness of diversity.

Individually:

- **Journal** about one idea to change classroom space, time, materials, or the learning environment with cultural diversity during a required subject.
- **Hang** posters to use for future antibias breathwork for mindfulness of diversity.

Why Do Transformative Teachers Practice Mindfulness?

Consistent mindfulness, practiced in communities of care, help heal the body-mind nexus with well-being experiences massaged by interbeing, impermanence, and emptiness principles. Mindfulness alleviates anxiety and heals agitated behavior. It develops non-defensive emotional intelligence for academic concentration and professional development.[59] *Multicultural*

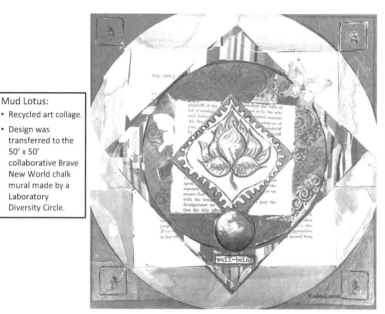

FIGURE 2.5 Mud Lotus artwork. Created by the author.

Mindfulness brings peace to cultural interpretations, bias triggers, and diversity fears in a world of culture clashes and adversities, such as military-industrial-complex violence, human-created climate crises, demographic shifts from resource scarcities, fundamentalism politics, and cyber disinformation. It supports a cross-cultural growth mindset[60] for open-minded calm to support holistic happiness.

Mindfulness fosters goodwill for nonviolent resistance to "common school" "rules" that portray diversity as deficiency. While we "are not responsible for what [our] ancestors did, [we] are responsible for the society [we] live in, which is a product of that past. Assuming this responsibility provides a means of survival and liberation."[61] Mindfulness assists healthy multicultural identity development with culture-assets education.[62] Mindfulness investigates "beyond boundaries," opening possibilities to redirect subjects to support a new green economy and multiracial democracy. As bell hooks explains:

> There is a serious crisis in education. Students often do not want to learn and teachers do not want to teach. More than ever before in the recent history of this nation, educators are compelled to confront the biases that have shaped teaching practices in our society and to create new ways of knowing, different strategies for the sharing of knowledge. We cannot address this crisis if progressive critical thinkers and social critics act as though teaching is not a subject worthy of our regard.... I celebrate teaching that enables transgressions – a movement against and beyond boundaries. It is that movement which makes education the practice of freedom.[63]

Because the Environmental Liberation Education approach to transformative teaching embraces mindfulness, it "enables transgressions" by nurturing trust during collaborations to develop "the practice of freedom." Evaluating diversity efforts with philosophical

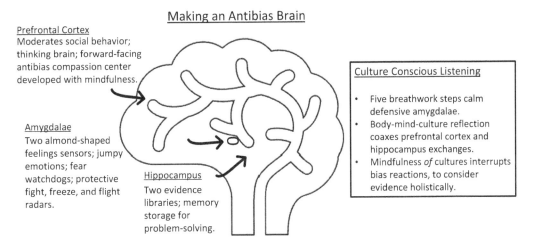

FIGURE 2.6   Making an Antibias Brain graphic. Created by the author.

transparency about what to change and why, transformative teachers engage academics through action-reflection dialectic. We use breathwork to heal aggression, desire, and fear on the spot. We ask culturally courageous questions, experiencing "new ways of knowing, different strategies for the sharing of knowledge."[64] We develop mindfulness love to reduce defensiveness from fear about economic-social contradictions while increasing liberation consciousness for humanization *through* the holism we cocreate.

The Bias Brain

Everyone is prone to territoriality. This comes from the defensive brain perceiving categories and limited resources. Almond-shaped amygdalae in our brains fan emotions from assumptions about boundaries. The amygdalae conduct ego-bias "productions"[65] from stereotypes palpitating with feelings: "We are not thinking machines that feel; rather, we are feeling machines that think."[66] The amygdalae are like fear, anger, and pleasure radars scanning the world.

Located deep in the temporal lobe, the amygdalae are built-in red-flag warning devices. They vibrate defensively in threatening or potentially painful situations. Their role is to alert the hypothalamus, the basic nervous system that triggers fight, freeze, and flight reactions during danger. They push the brain and body – quickening heart, sweaty palms, clenched stomach, stiffened neck, furrowed brow – to quick judgments from associations. They pulsate with fast-moving deductions, provoking self-protective decisions. The amygdalae form an emotional command center and must be mindfully regulated to allow the non-defensive, antibias parts of the brain to flow.[67]

The Antibias Brain

The prefrontal cortex, the thinking brain, moderates social behavior and, with its partner the hippocampus, forms the brain's antibias dynamic duo. The hippocampus on either side of the brain informs evidentiary responses in exchanges with the prefrontal cortex, which attends to cultural meaning and language. Together, they engage the antibias-antiracist steps involved in shifting color-stratified systems into culture-conscious egalitarianism. To take these courageous steps, practitioners swaddle the amygdalae in a blanket of calm with body-mind exercises, such as breathwork about culture and eye contact with nature. These practices galvanize antibias expectations about human interconnections through nature with prefrontal cortex-hippocampus synapse exchanges.[68]

Multicultural Mindfulness breathwork and interactions with nature nurture non-defensiveness in three brain aspects impacted by the amygdalae. First, mindfulness breathwork calms the primitive brain focused on survival. The practices slow heart rate and lower blood pressure to encourage body-mind well-being. Second, mindfulness practices bathe the emotional brain with visualizations to relax nerves in the limbic system. They offer antibias response alternatives to fear, anger, and pleasure reactions that, in the rush to avoid pain, skip to selective emotional memories that warp perception. Third, mindfulness practices for social-emotional metacognition exercise the outermost part of the brain involving the prefrontal cortex, enabling *thinking about thinking* to consider one's own biases.[69]

Many teachers haven't experienced much mindfulness education. Most of us haven't had comprehensive diversity training. We're under-versed in environmental education. As a profession, US teachers don't know how to integrate these three fields into daily practice. We don't routinely use body-mind holism strategies to develop culturally responsive academics. We don't connect classroom time-on-task to Earth's well-being. Instead, we unwittingly permit "guard dog" defensiveness from the amygdalae to get angry at, tune out, or hide from the world. "The amygdala activity can literally hijack other brain processes…there are way more neural connections from the amygdala to the cortex (thinking brain) than vice versa."[70] Transformative teachers, however, do our best to develop a repertoire of "wise owl" responses to replace anxiety about diversity in a globalized world.[71]

Multicultural Mindfulness practices aerate sweaty palms, untighten stomachs, release clenched jaws, relieve necks and shoulders, deepen shortened breaths, and soothe the racing heart. Understanding that body-mind-culture processes – such as jumping to conclusions in micro-seconds – are happening with everyone all the time helps each of us to patiently offer reciprocal support for one another's growth. We form circles to handle professional stress impaired by culture conflicts and resource scarcities. With breathwork, we invite inclusion experiences into our memory banks. We lower our heart rates and relax muscles to tame hypervigilant amygdalae. We slow the automaticity of reactions from assumptions, developing empathetic reflection about stereotypes for compassion responses. With breathwork, we replace aggression, confusion, and escapist habits with impermanence, interbeing, and emptiness consciousness to grow holistic sustainability by taking responsibility to reconcile and forgive.

Consciousness and the Brain

Ibram X. Kendi explains that racism is "terminal and curable," healed with a "reorientation of our consciousness" by people on the ground who implement inclusion decisions.[72] Inclusion experiences counteract the steady beat of for-profit systemic stratifications dividing education. Liberation consciousness grows through education when teachers use compassion activities during academic routines. The antibias that brain transformative teachers nurture connects body to mind while developing cultural and environmental well-being in real time.

Multicultural Mindfulness practices include three Diversity Circle strategies (described in Chapter 5) – Sharing, Circle Questions, and Global Praxis – for prosocial change:

1. *Sharing* – Participants circle to practice mindfulness and discuss culture and nature stories, materials, and data about required subjects, taking notes and doing activities, indoors with nature and outdoors.
2. *Circle Questions* – Diverse students pose big-picture questions, incorporating insights from Sharing and concurrent activities, labs, and field experiences.
3. *Global Praxis* – Discussions about Circle Questions prompt participants to refresh labs and field experiences with holistic healing activities, cogenerating stories, materials, and data for the next Sharing.

Multicultural Mindfulness nourishes the antibias brain with liberation consciousness. It develops resilience to deal with systemic crises, culture clashes, and climate disasters. Rather than succumbing defensively to economic-social trauma cycles that fuel school stress, transformative action-reflection de-stresses. During conflict, Multicultural Mindfulness invites nonviolent pause for participants to regroup to cultivate present-moment peace and welcome *diversity* into problem-solving. Inclusion consciousness reduces divisive fight, freeze, or flight habits by valuing diverse cultural ways of knowing during holistic action.

Shifting Consciousness with Culture-Conscious Listening

As explained in Chapter 1, Culture-Conscious Listening is a core Multicultural Mindfulness practice that pacifies the amygdalae with antibias breathwork. It helps teachers and students spot dehumanization events during systemic interactions. Calm reflection tempers bias habits and supports a growth mindset.[73] Culture-Conscious Listening starts with a deep breath into the bottom of the lungs, preferably through the nose, to nourish body-mind-culture-environment integration. Then, while listening with a relaxed smile, we ask inclusion questions:

- Is what I'm doing evidence-based, or am I reacting to assumptions?
- Am I compassionately aware of stereotypes from systems?
- What biases, especially my own, are here?
- What cultures and contexts don't I understand?
- What's a point of agreement?
- How do I shift defensiveness into openness for sustainable solutions?
- How do we act for holism?

MULTICULTURAL MINDFULNESS ACTIVITY

Inclusive Academic Concentration

Outcome

- Apply Culture-Conscious Listening to alleviate social anxiety.
- Develop culturally responsive academic concentration by taking turns as listener and talker about a subject.

Key Concepts

- **Breathwork:** Conscious breathing for body-mind wellness.
- **Culture:** Shared artifacts, practices, and beliefs of any group interacting in systems.
- **Culture-Conscious Listening:** Five steps to welcome diversity: Culture-Conscious Breath, Pleasant Eye Contact, Compassionate Support, Brief Summary, and Antibias Question.

Resources

- **Breathwork bell**, a board or sidewalk to write a question, an example or symbol of nature, a place to meet indoors or outdoors.

Big-Picture Question

- How do I reduce social anxiety and increase inclusive academic concentration?

Start

Whole group circle:

- **Review** the definition of culture (above).
- **Explain** that Culture-Conscious Listening is about compassion for reciprocal understanding. While it can be uncomfortable to listen for culture during academic engagement, participants report feeling "supported by the compassionate questions," perceiving one another "like it was for the first time." Discussing cultural awareness about the "same fears" and considering "different fears" about subjects support social-emotional academic learning. Inclusive academic concentration is developed with nonviolent communication.
- **Form** diversity partners with as much race, ethnicity, gender, class, and age heterogeneity as possible.
- **Ask** pairs to face one another, and ask one another about cultural preferences for eye contact, and then look respectfully into one another's eyes with welcoming smiles.
- **Explain:** We are going to do a two-minute Culture-Conscious Listening exercise. No one needs to fully understand Culture-Conscious Listening to try it.
- **Review:** Five Steps to Culture-Conscious Listening:

    1 *Culture-Conscious Breath* – Breathe for awareness of cultures and bias.
    2 *Pleasant Eye Contact* – Breathe to show respectful eye contact with a natural welcoming smile.
    3 *Compassionate Support* – Patiently maintain positive body language.
    4 *Brief Summary* – Express agreement about something in the talker's message. Outline what the talker said. Ask: Was that accurate?
    5 *Antibias Question* – Ask: What cultures model success in this topic? How do we apply cultural evidence to inclusive solutions?

Middle

- **Instruct** partners to take turns as listener and talker, two minutes each. One person talks at a time.

- **Explain** a guiding question. This is a compassion question about an academic topic. For example: What do you fear most about [topic]? What makes academic concentration hard about [topic]? What do you know about [topic]? What makes you curious about [topic]?
- **Instruct**:
    1. Each partner answers the guiding question.
    2. Before starting the first timer, both partners take a Culture-Conscious Breath for reflection: What cultures are here?
    3. One partner answers the guiding question for two minutes, talking stream-of-consciousness with stories and examples while the other listens, nodding with courteous eye contact and a smile.
    4. After two minutes, the listener describes a point of agreement, summarizes the talker's information, and asks: Was that accurate?
    5. Once the original speaker endorses or adjusts the summary, the listener asks an antibias question about the talker's message. For example: What cultures model success in this topic?
    6. Partners switch roles.

Closing

Whole group circle:

- **Discuss** one or more questions:
    1. What was the hardest part of the exchange?
    2. Do you feel connected to your partner? Why/Why not?
    3. What did you learn about your partner's cultural perspective about the topic?
    4. What did you learn about your own cultural perspective about the topic?
    5. What did you learn about inclusive academic concentration?
    6. Which listening step was the easiest? Most challenging?
    7. Does the topic feel relatable now? Why/Why not?

Application

What's Spacetime Superpower?[74]

Spacetime in Spanish, *espaciotiempo*, is a liberation concept developed by Cecilia Vicuña, a Chilean feminist poet and environmental arts educator. "We can simultaneously be time – and space – bound while completely free. I am constantly faced with that double capacity."[75] Vicuña compares inclusion with exclusion spacetime. Her work depicts freedom from oppression through multicultural-multiracial ecological connections, local and global, toward "the cosmic scale of *spacetime*."[76]

Spacetime *superpower* is an imagination-growing concept to empower teachers in real-time problem-solving. Spacetime superpower symbolizes transformative teaching solutions. It is applying academic freedom hourly and daily to decisions to energize cultural inclusion. It is shaping school spacetime with diversity materials and equity learning environments for holism events.[77] It is agency to replace unsustainable bias procedures and content with culturally responsive ecological activities. Transformative teachers deploy spacetime superpower to perceive divisions in over-standardized classroom layouts. It shines a light on alienation from top-down timetables. We *reform* curriculum and knowledge by rearranging classrooms, labs, meeting rooms, and sites to make room for humanizing sustainability experiences.

Education Students Demonstrate the Accessibility of Transformative Spacetime

Education students at Truckee Meadows Community College illustrate the ease of applying spacetime superpower. In one teacher preparation course, students are required to do 30 hours of field experience, conduct a one-hour team-teaching demonstration, and plan and reflect collaboratively throughout course meetings. Students act and reflect on field experiences in regional elementary schools to collaborate on culturally responsive sustainability activities. In evolving Diversity Circles, these students discuss how field experience and team-teaching demonstrations engage best practices for social-emotional academic learning.[78] They focus on Multicultural Mindfulness practices to develop their teacher spacetime superpower.

Using Environmental Liberation Education rubrics to reinterpret curriculum standards, the teams synthesize science, mathematics, the arts, and social studies. They reimagine education with multicultural inclusion and environmental consciousness activities. During the process, I, as the professor, become a "student," following team instructions. Using backwards design to engage subjects with big-picture questions, the teams co-create body-mind-culture-environment integration activities to meet requirements with multiple intelligences: linguistic, logical-mathematical, musical, spatial, bodily-kinesthetic, interpersonal, intrapersonal, naturalistic, and existential.[79] After each team demonstration, everyone reflects, assessing learning behaviors about topics with diversity and sustainability criteria to clarify what worked and what could be improved.

At the start of the semester, I describe spacetime superpower. I explain that mainstream education devours school spacetime with dehumanizing assimilation and segregation experiences. However, teachers are motivated to the profession to humanize, and knowledge is power. Teachers make hourly and daily decisions about students and knowledge development. Teachers make better decisions when we collaborate purposefully, kind of like a Marvel superhero team that has one another's backs while solving problems. We do prosocial work to de-stress academics and support inclusive academic concentration with culturally responsive curriculum and instruction. We help to heal suffering from bias systems by designing and implementing the joyful justice space, time, materials, and learning environments.

Then we do breathwork to develop our spacetime superpower, using such prompts as these:

1 *Space*: Breathing in, math worksheets about alienating topics done in rows; breathing out, math circles about culturally responsive environmental topics.
2 *Time*: Breathing in, standardized pop quizzes; breathing out, student-designed quizzes.
3 *Materials*: Breathing in, rote memorization of Eurocentric US history; breathing out, balancing textbooks with diverse cultural perspectives and multi-modal projects about US history.
4 *Learning Environment*: Breathing in, segregated and tracked programs always indoors; breathing out, integrated academics with outdoor experiences.

We discuss big-picture questions: How do we respect cultures? How do we integrate environmental education into routines? We focus on teacher agency to reshape school *space* with nature holism experiences, indoors and outdoors. We explore how teachers decide who sits and stands and where academic learning happens by rearranging furniture, designing inclusion stations, and adjusting partitions and lighting. We brainstorm diversity themes for classroom libraries and peace corners. We consider how to make multicultural walls, floors, ceilings, and windows with symbols and objects. We talk about how to feature nature and handmade materials for hands-on action-reflection on site and in parks and gardens. Thus, education students are quick to learn about spacetime superpower, integrating music and recycled art projects into science units, making seating changes and taking nature walks during math problem sets, doing theatrical book readings in multiple languages in unusual settings for language arts, and facilitating environmental mindfulness exercises for social studies, such as circle breathwork about history and environmental topics.

Reshaping Space with Flexible Seating

For example, one education student reported how her master teacher allowed her to rearrange furniture in a chaotic classroom characterized by student outbursts and low attendance. This student-teacher applied her superpower to reinterpret space with flexible seating to markedly improve academic concentration for the rest of the semester. This first-grade classroom was in a low-income school where some students had been getting weekly referrals and study hall detentions. One first grader had been suspended for threatening violence when he said he would see another student "in the graveyard." She explained that her assigned classroom was so stressed that most children didn't have the opportunity for basic academic concentration. Thus, neither the students who were physically removed from the classroom for poor behavior nor those remaining experienced productive academic engagement.[80]

This education student said she couldn't fathom how to insert diversity education into a classroom in such disarray. She understood that the students must crave multicultural knowledge because her culture consciousness observations revealed incongruence between home and school cultures. With her cultural eye, she saw daily spacetime *exclusions*. She didn't observe culturally responsive multiple intelligences activities, like those we practiced in our college classroom, such as with worldbeat music, multicultural art projects, or desegregated project groups. She wondered: How could this classroom handle more than back-to-the-basics structure? How could it fit in breathwork circles, multicultural physical education, or environmental education outdoors? She observed off-task behaviors and minimal academic engagement, and she couldn't figure out how to bring in Environmental Liberation Education.

However, because she had completed her team-teaching demonstration earlier, experimenting with inclusion spacetime design and having written a research paper about flexible seating, she asked her master teacher if she could try a rearrangement. She noticed that most off-task behaviors came from a few first graders who appeared incapable of sitting still, demanding constant deskwork monitoring. These children distracted others by fiddling, squirming, crisscrossing the room, and blurting noise and bad language. She also noticed that most students in the classroom sat in rows.

She interviewed the agitated first graders, asking them questions about comfort and belonging. They described they wanted to feel safe on something soft. She collaborated to construct two benches with cushions, which she brought into the classroom along with a large ball seat, accommodating the children whose behaviors were most disruptive. Other classmates, who were performing adequately in regular chair-single desks, remained in place.

The first-grade classroom learning environment changed immediately. For the rest of the semester, the master teacher didn't make a single referral, study hall, or suspension recommendation. The students who had previously been most unruly were able to complete academic work and contribute to an integrated classroom culture.

My student reported that inclusion spacetime is an "amazing" power. During reflection, new questions arose: Was the change because of the kinesthetics of pillows? Or was it the cultural inclusion from listening to students compassionately? Was the shift from the lovingly handmade benches constructed with natural materials? How about the rest of the class? How can *all* students in the classroom experience the benches and the ball equitably? How might getting outdoors expand flexible seating with the spaciousness of nature?

Reshaping Time and Materials with Love

Another illustration shows how to apply teacher spacetime superpower to *time* and *materials*. This education student conducted a one-month experiment of reading books with an agitated third grader for a few minutes during lunchtime. After four weeks, she observed that her student went from reading resistance to academic engagement during whole-class reading activities. She noticed that he was able to participate in the school's buddy reading program, which he'd previously avoided.

This teacher-in-training rewarded her student's reading engagement by bringing in "new" books into the existing classroom library. She resourced a used-books warehouse available to district teachers. She filled a box with books she selected for artful illustrations, emotional plotlines, inclusive characters, varied settings, and inviting tones with well-being and happiness themes. Thus, in a month, she expanded the classroom inclusion spacetime with academic nurturing of an at-risk student at lunchtime and by rewarding the whole class with holism books.

This education student smiled widely as she described diverse third graders rushing to form a line to read the "new" books she introduced as "Global Praxis" books. She explained to the children that Global Praxis is world love. She said she couldn't believe it when she later overheard these third graders using the term, "Global Praxis." Thus, one-on-one compassion time led to a classroom library space uplift with healing materials for all.

Education student anecdotes illustrate that transformative teaching is fun. Future teachers show how to activate academic freedom. They readily integrate diversity, mindfulness, and environmental education into requirements. They *act* from a position of love to integrate diverse students into academic engagement, and *reflect* on academic holism with cultural questions and evidence discussions to refresh and improve. They reduce Anglo-conformist exclusions by increasing inclusion and sustainability experiences during routines, such as with natural materials for flexible seating spaces, one-on-one reading time, recycled well-being materials, and nurturing a loving learning environments. Applying the spacetime superpower, the next generation of teachers transforms with Environmental Liberation Education.

Nurturing **Transformative** *Collaborations*

Teacher spacetime superpower is collaborative. We change the status quo with collective action-reflection, making decisions to deflect alienation routines and grow prosocial experiences. But developing cross-cultural trust and integrative humanization is multipronged. The Three Transformative Tools facilitate overlapping components of change. For example, one Multicultural Mindfulness practice – Antibias Communication Norms – is also the first Diversity Circles phase, and it provides Approach-in-Dimension humanization criteria to align transformative design with assessment. Antibias Communication Norms is active compassion with reciprocal respect through considerate noun and pronouns use, taking turns listening and speaking, and using big-picture critical thinking. Transformative communication involves deep listening to reduce bias and integrate cultures into inclusive academic engagement through communities of care.[81]

Chicana feminist Dolores Huerta and Chicano Cesar Chavez illustrate an antibias multicultural alliance for nonviolent social change. Through three decades of circle meetings for community understanding and big-picture solutions, they cogenerated regional projects to transform adverse environmental conditions for diverse farmworkers. Respectful of identities, they developed a multicultural network of community organizers, such as Filipino-American

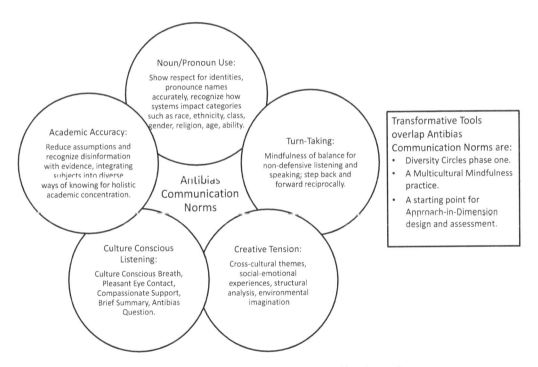

FIGURE 2.7 Antibias Communication Norms graphic. Created by the author.

activist Larry Dulay Itliong, mobilizing multiracial marches and labor strikes for humanization, including a 300-mile walk from Delano to Sacramento. They used Antibias Communication Norms practices with door-to-door voter registration campaigns, communicating in home languages on location among communities of color. They stood vigil with one another during policy-changing hunger strikes and hospital recovery from police brutality. They picketed pesticide-covered grapes outside grocery stores and other public spaces.

Over time, their collaboration for environmental transformation advanced global changes, visibly increasing Mexican American political participation in US institutions, including in education, such as with the development of Chicano Studies. Their actions marshalled environmental reforms, including pesticide restriction legislation and sustainable farming conditions. They advanced multiracial justice outcomes, such as procuring labor contracts, disability insurance, pensions for diverse agricultural workers, and strengthened home–school connections.[82]

The successful grassroots alliance between Huerta and Chavez is one of many, illustrating the power of the Community Supports Diversity Circle. When different kinds of Diversity Circles operate simultaneously, communicating respectfully about global questions, they intersect for cross-institutional systemic change.

Start a Diversity Circle now

Nobel Laureate Gabriela Mistral of Chile explains the urgency of present moment cultural action in *Su Nombre es Hoy* (His/Her/Your/Their Name is Today):

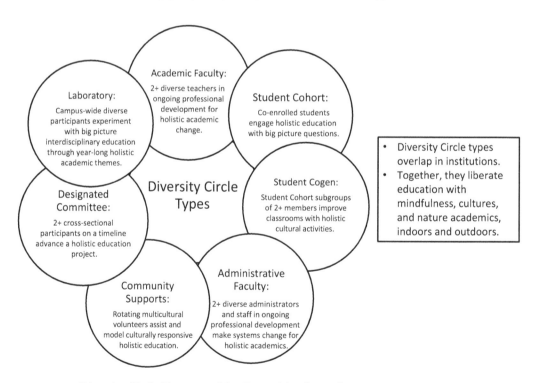

FIGURE 2.8 Diversity Circle Types graphic. Created by the author.

We are guilty of many errors and many faults, but our worst crime is abandoning children, neglecting the fountain of life. Many of the things we need can wait. The child cannot. Right now is the time bones are formed, blood is made, and senses are developed. To the child we cannot answer "Tomorrow," the child's name is today.[83]

Mistral implores cultural action *today* for intergenerational sustainability. One way to activate humanization now is to participate in a Diversity Circle by reaching out to a colleague for holistic change action with backwards design:

1 Pose a big-picture question that relates to your routines. For example:
   - How do your students interact with superdiversity and biodiversity?
   - How does climate change factor into your core content?
   - How do regional and global events provide teachable moments?
   - How do cultures relate to your discipline and research?
   - What philosophy of education guides your most-used best practices?

2 Imagine a happy ending. For example:
   - Equitable and excellent subject mastery to prepare students inclusively for a sustainability economy.
   - Meeting academic requirements with multicultural, mindfulness, and environmental projects.
   - Active community participation to integrate diverse ways of knowing into hands-on subject engagement.
   - Effective program and district desegregation and diversity hiring and retention procedures.
   - Culturally responsive openers and closures to relate subjects to current events.
   - Transparent humanization design and assessment.

3 Partners formulate one big picture question that applies to core activities of each partner.
4 Partners collaborate on one shared activity to engage a subject or routine requirement of each partner.
5 After the planning meeting, each partner does the activity.
6 After activity completion, partners meet to assess required subject or routine outcomes as well as a diversity or sustainability outcome.

Now you're off and running. When you meet next, try using Antibias Communication Norms (Figure 2.7) as you collaborate on another backwards design.

Example

Outdoor Education Program: Transformative Challenges and Breakthroughs

Transformative teachers relate local conditions to world healing. Some schools and campuses support transformative teachers with active diversity, equity, and sustainability programs. Such sites advance holistic inclusion projects, integrating cultures, mindfulness, and nature into academic engagement. But most sites conduct mainstream education, perpetuating divisive, alienating, and unsustainable experiences. Fracturing from bias systems persists through paradox, such as when well-meaning teachers, operating in bureaucracies dominated by the culture of individualism, are fearful of *collectivizing* cross-culturally for liberation. Many do not know how to change stratified systems by mixing student groups or diversifying curriculum with culture and environmental themes to reduce racialized tracking and environmental destruction.

The following example, however, shows transformative breakthroughs. Educators in a small mountain town in Northern California model how to change space, time, materials, and learning environments with sustainability questions. These transformative teachers reform mainstream education with interdisciplinary outdoor education to integrate public school students into holistic humanization experiences. The example also reveals areas for growth in culture consciousness and multicultural alliances to uplift the program from Social Action about sustainability to Environmental Liberation Education.

Northern California Watershed Program

In the Plumas Unified School District (PUSD), the "6th Grade Watershed Year is a capstone for elementary education and a catalyst for the secondary years that follow." The program engages students in integrated science, social studies, mathematics, language arts, and visual arts activities with a big-picture design for outdoor education about regional ecosystems. In 1988, collaborators secured watershed education funding, which has continued annually since. The program reinterprets state curriculum standards by incorporating the surrounding environment.[84]

The unit starts in early elementary school classrooms with hiking field trips to springs, creeks, rivers, lakes, and marsh ecosystems, culminating in a district-wide sixth-grade program that involves high school student chaperons and community mentors. Participants physically follow the county's watershed, travelling from Sierra Valley – the headwaters of the Feather River – down to the Pacific Ocean. "During the course of the year, students participate in more than a dozen field trip days as they explore what it means to be a 'Mountain Kid' and then follow their Feather River water drop from the source to the sea."[85]

Sixth-grade field trips in the PUSD involve students in academic reading and writing; photo and illustration note-taking, excursion charts; visual, sound, olfactory, touch, and taste observations; flora and fauna counts; forestry science projects; specimen laboratories; art projects; and data documentation and collection through environmental journaling with science questions.

The Sierra Valley starting point is an expansive intramountain valley of grasslands and sagebrush in a region of the homelands of Mountain Maidu, Paiute, and Washoe peoples, near where the Cascades meet the Sierras, close to the Nevada border. Sierra Valley is home to a variety of wild birds, some that migrate the planet, and some, once endangered, are now flourishing in its protected wetlands, including red-tailed hawks, peregrine falcons (the fastest animal in the world), and bald eagles. Deer and some elk live in the area, and antelopes run the valley floor at up to 55 miles per hour. After observing Sierra Valley plants and animals, such as sandhill cranes, long-billed curlews, and loggerhead shrikes, students participate in a series of field trips, following creeks and rivers for 250 miles to the San Francisco Bay, where one sixth-grade class spent a night in an underwater submarine.

Nature and Humans

Students examine interconnections between nature and humans. They investigate the sliver of public lands in a now-protected region that is surrounded by vast areas that lack cultural or environmental protection. Students investigate the history of salmon in the Oroville Dam area, once a centerpiece of Indigenous communities in the area now called Paradise, California, which was the site of the 2018 Camp Fire, fueled in large part from tinder conditions manufactured by the cultural domination and environmental malpractice of European American invaders. The Camp Fire killed 86 people in one fell swoop, many of whom were disabled, elderly, and poor.[86]

Students know about this horrific fire, and they relate observations about regional climate crisis events to the overall watershed where they live. Students document damage from the 2021 Dixie Fire that burned close to a million acres along parts of this watershed, razing communities, such as family homes in Indian Falls, the Greenville Rancheria, and the town of Greenville, where European Americans had violently dislodged Mountain Maidu peoples in the mid-1800s. European Americans took over the place now called Greenville to impose a logging town, dislodging and dehumanizing Indigenous peoples to feed the rapidly growing statewide appetite for hydropower and water for the growing European American–dominated cities downstream.[87]

This racist cultural invasion harmed Indigenous peoples with diseases and by destroying ecosystems that they had previously stewarded with cultural and spiritual ecological practices for thousands of years. For instance, European Americans imposed a guardianship legal system in which White peoples were appointed as guardians to control the affairs and assets of Native Americans (who were deemed incompetent to do it themselves), using laws distorted by racism to clear-cut, mine, and force flooding and damning. Unlike the sustainable cultural fires overseen by the Mountain Maidu and other tribes to keep Northern California forests and animals healthy, current mega-fires burn at such a high temperature that they obliterate remaining mountain spring and watershed habitats, Indigenous lands, sacred gathering places and cultural homes including tribal documents, records, and historical and living artifacts.[88]

Sustainability Questions

Students in the watershed program think critically about how human-caused climate change requires diligent human solutions. They ask sustainability questions: How does overlogging harm? What regional biodiversity can be protected and restored? What can forestry management do to help? How do we regulate energy distribution for public good *and* sustainability? PUSD educators describe "the sixth extinction," which, unlike the five other mass extinctions in Earth's history, is "man-made."[89] Students team for social-emotional learning, engaging visual, kinesthetic, naturalistic, and existential intelligences to deepen linguistic and logical-mathematical curriculum standards. They discuss feelings and journal to describe and analyze, mapping waterways, drawing geography, and formulating hypotheses about nature from hikes and outdoor games. As they camp, swim, and white-water raft down the Feather River, students activate full-range cognitive engagement.

The watershed program cogenerates environmental consciousness for ecosystem health. Students actively learn how the hotter, bigger wildfires they have personally witnessed ravaging coniferous old growth forests can inspire conservation practices. They examine the interrelationship of human superdiversity in Earth's biodiversity. As an example of intergenerational sustainability, high school students who mentor sixth graders during watershed events, and have themselves been through the program, apply ecosystem knowledge to senior projects with action-research to restore local lakes and waterways. Their projects include conserving and restoring the Sierra Nevada yellow-legged frog habitat, tracking and supporting gray wolves that have returned to the region, and fostering controlled and cultural burns for forest stewardship.

Culture Consciousness and Multicultural Alliance Shortcomings

However, while the program aligns with California curriculum standards, reshapes academics with Global Praxis, and integrates diverse students into outdoor education with big-picture questions, it doesn't explicitly nurture cross-cultural alliances for antibias-antiracist holism. Activating multicultural understanding about systemic racism, sexism, and class inequities develops environmental education into Environmental Liberation Education. For instance, the appendix time line in *Upstream: Trust Lands and Power on the Feather River* is culturally responsive material that provides a regional chart "to place both land and water decisions in Maidu country in the context of water resources development in the state and the nation, with a focus on tribal concerns."[90] While the Plumas County watershed program illustrates environmental education excellence, it doesn't use culture-conscious action-reflection about the impact of systemic racism on the region to make climate justice changes on the ground.

Opportunities for Cross-Cultural Growth

Most students served by PUSD are European American. Quincy, with about 5,000 inhabitants, is the most populous community in a county the size of Delaware. Quincy contains Plumas County's sole institution of higher learning, Feather River College (FRC), the smallest community college in California. Most of the residents of Quincy (approximately 77%), including its teachers, are White.[91] Without activating antibias-antiracist culture consciousness, the watershed program defers to Anglo-conformist bias and divisions by unconsciously reinforcing racialized segregation and systems in the region through education. However, this mountain area, like *everywhere* in the US, is rich with cultural diversity, living and historical, as well as bountiful cultural assets to empower multicultural-multiracial alliances to transform education through Environmental Liberation Education.

For instance, the watershed program could prioritize regional multiracial perspectives about lived experiences from stories, documents, and artifacts of local Native American, Latinx, and African American peoples. For instance, students could attend Maidu Summit organization public meetings to learn about water and forest stewardship practices from regional Indigenous peoples. They could attend visual and performing arts events featuring Maidu and other Indigenous cultures conducted by Indigenous peoples. One Greenville Maidu artist, Levi Mullen, says, "I want to focus on the universe and get people focusing outside themselves and all the things around us and try to connect it all together."[92] Watershed students could visit the Greenville Rancheria 30 miles from Quincy to listen to cultural stories and observe stewardship practices with native plant species and medicinal herbs of the Maidu communities that have lived in the area for at least 8,000 years before European Americans harmed the ecosystems with mines, dams, and de-forestation.[93]

Another local resource, FRC, enrolls a relatively racially diverse student body because its campus features a "strength in retaining and graduating underserved student populations." FRC hosts several sports programs that integrate multicultural-multiracial youth from across the nation and internationally. FRC implements "practices that improve success of underserved racially minoritized students." The college's "culture of openness and inclusivity" marks its academics as one of the top community colleges "in the country in enrolling and supporting associate degree completion for African-American/Black students."[94] Diverse community college students could guest-speak about lived experiences from watersheds and forests in other areas of the world. Cross-cultural and cross-regional perspectives deepen environmental education with liberation questions about diverse ways of knowing from rural, suburban, and urban human interactions with both declining and thriving waterways.

The region also has visual and performing arts events in local arts programs. Plumas Arts, an affiliate of the California Arts Council, hosts holistic experiences, such as when Spanish-Latinx muralist Rafael Blanco painted two outdoor murals featuring multicultural-multiracial people. The murals portray Latinx images to show how Latinx peoples comprise approximately 6% of Quincy's demographics. Plumas Arts Exhibits spotlight diverse artists, including works from inmates in the High Desert State Prison, 75 miles away in Lassen County, most of whom, owing to racist mass incarceration, are of color.

Another source of diverse racial perspectives to bring holism to the watershed program is to study the history of African American families in the region. The African American community experience in the area offers a counter-narrative to themes of rural US racism with an example of a time of partial desegregation. African Americans migrated to the area primarily from the South in the 1920s to work in the lumber industry. Much earlier than at most other US mills, they received pay equal to that of European American workers.

> By all accounts Quincy Lumber gave equal pay to its White and Black employees and many African American men worked in skilled positions nearly impossible to gain in the southern mills… where Black workers received on average about 50% of the pay of White employees for comparable jobs.[95]

African Americans currently comprise 8% of Quincy's population but, at points in the town's history, comprised 40% of the area's population, leading and participating in community groups such as the Starlight Missionary Baptist Church, a Masonic chapter, The Harlem Club, and a chapter in the Order of the Eastern Star.[96]

> Though segregated housing was the norm, little else was divided by race. After two years of resistance from White locals, African American children began attending local schools in 1940. Their presence generated for the time and place scenes of remarkable integration. In fact, by the Spring of 1954, a Black senior, John Clark, was elected student body president at Quincy High School.[97]

The mid-century African American experience in Quincy – a history little known today by many of the town's inhabitants, most of whom are White – is an instance of rural racial desegregation in an industry embroiled in watershed ecology: forestry millwork. Moreover, schools along waterways down to the San Francisco Bay Area enroll students of color, offering opportunities for multicultural-multiracial pen pal interactions and meet-and-greet sister-school gatherings to share cross-cultural water stories and data from different parts of state.

In summary, the PUSD watershed program, while excellent with a state-of-the-art sustainability curriculum, has room to develop with an inclusive antibias-antiracist paradigm to engage diverse perspectives into a holistic understanding how systemic inequities impact cultural action to protect and restore water and forest ecosystems. Big-picture multicultural education about the social and environmental consequences of for-profit extraction-consumption water, lumber, and energy industries develops inclusive sustainability activities.

Environmental Liberation Education Redesign

An Environmental Liberation Education redesign for the PUSD watershed program might investigate differences in access to clean water, healthy forests, organic local foods, pollution-free air, and ecologically safe and sound spaces across various Northern California communities. For example, expanding the program's customary visit to Pier 39 in San Francisco with a ferry ride to Alcatraz Island, students could answer the question: How has the Indigenous peoples' action of seizing Alcatraz for 18 months impacted California sustainability legislation?

Big-picture multicultural-multiracial questions develop environmental knowledge holistically. Curiosity about Alcatraz Island's occupation in 1969 leads to studying the thousands of years of Indigenous stewardship and hundreds of years of Indigenous resistance to White-dominated cultural and ecological destruction patterns. Curriculum opens up into enquiries about how environmental justice on Alcatraz Island is almost entirely neglected by California's content standards. Culturally responsive curriculum transformation generated by conducting a geological analysis of the island and comparing native plants and species there to that of Plumas County would involve students in systems healing. Students could review historical records to understand how Hopi men were unjustly imprisoned on Alcatraz in 1894 and how that compared with racist treatment of Mountain Maidu peoples. Students could learn that Alcatraz events energized feminist multiracial sustainability events throughout the US and compare that with feminist cultural actions of living Mountain Maidu peoples.[98]

Reforming environmental education with multicultural-multiracial consciousness transforms education with culturally responsive sustainability *collaborations* for inclusive "humanity-*through*-nature" action. Students learn about green *equity* vocations in regional economies by inviting culturally diverse community members to explain careers as wildfire specialists, naturalists, hydrologists, ecosystems engineers, conservation resource experts, forest managers, environmental lawyers, organic farmers, and environmental artists. An ecological and just economy involves a cross-cultural network of environmentally conscious professionals working together. Thus, multicultural-multiracial alliances have the capacity to shift Social Action efforts into Environmental Liberation Education, engaging academic standards with culturally responsive environmental stories, *equity* stewardship questions, and conservation and restoration activities that bridge local diversities with regional communities along this rich and extensive California watercourse, traversing inland mountains and transitional valleys to the Pacific Ocean.[99]

Conclusion

Transformative Teaching is Easy and Fun

Life on this planet is a work in progress, and education is the heartbeat of *intergenerational* sustainability. But today our schools are divided and unsafe. The teacher's job is complicated and stressful. Throughout US history, humanitarian change-makers have pushed for egalitarian policies to stop suffering from "manifest destiny," genocide, slavery, land-stealing, environmental destruction, and other toxic patterns that corrupt democracy and fuel global warming.[100] However, US institutions continue to network "consistently harmful spaces."[101] As bureaucratic operators, many teachers unintentionally perpetuate the inequity systems and racist ideologies behind corporate profits in the extraction-consumption economy that undercuts student inclusion and holistic knowledge.

US classrooms exist on Indigenous lands that have been harmed by "colonialist settler-state" designs, according to Dunbar-Ortiz.

> The decision to establish Carlisle and other off-reservation boarding schools was made by the US Office of Indian Affairs.... The stated goal was assimilation. Indigenous children were prohibited from speaking their mother tongues or practicing their religions, while being indoctrinated in Christianity. As in the Spanish missions in California, in the US boarding schools the children were beaten for speaking their own languages, among other infractions that expressed their humanity. Although stripped of the languages and skills of their communities, what they learned in boarding schools was useless for the purposes of effective assimilation, creating multiple lost generations of traumatized individuals.[102]

Schools are financed for assimilation into economic-social systems that operate cheap labor and natural resource depletion. They're funded to maintain largely materialistic commerce and class stratifications. Everyday educators work within a centuries-old substructure-superstructure context that, tragically, administers unsustainable bias routines to privilege a few and exclude many. This system dehumanizes.

The good news is that teachers are the most important factor to student success within education because of the many decisions we make hourly and daily. We're gatekeepers of culture change, which is worthy of mindfulness. When we collaborate to act and reflect with big-picture questions about US education, we *can* avoid past mistakes. We reduce bias by getting curious about how to change the assimilation and segregation structures established historically to privilege European Americans. We acknowledge that tiered schools have cycled generational trauma and environmentally destructive outcomes that harm us all. We see, as Timothy San Pedro suggests, that "safe" education needs to be redefined.

> Learning is not often safe as it involves such profound transformation. And what facilitates learning for one person is often unproductive or even harmful for another. The white centeredness of education is what has led to consistently harmful spaces for racially minoritized and Indigenous populations. Truth would involve reckoning with that history and the less than polite reality of learning. The danger with calls for safe spaces is that they are fueled more by logics of identity politics than learning and architectures of harm.[103]

Empowered by multiple perspectives, liberation education theory, and mindfulness best practices, transformative teachers collaborate *with* students and colleagues for holistic activities that honor living Indigenous and other stewardship cultures. It's a relief to *do* something humane about suffering. It's inspiring to cocreate multicultural-multiracial understanding for systemic healing. Teachers have the power to collaborate to reshape mainstream space, time, materials, and learning environments for inclusive student success and environmental well-being.

Education change involves applying prosocial events to academic engagement. Transformative examples abound. Two examples – teacher education students in Reno, Nevada and educators in a 6th Grade Watershed Year program in Plumas County, California – show how transformative teaching is easy and fun. These transformative participants apply academic freedom to shift routines. They model action-reflection to change *where*, *how*, and *when* students learn with flexible seating, multimodal outdoor education, and one-on-one nurturing. These educators demonstrate how to apply spacetime superpower to change materials, such as using recycled books and nature journals. They display how to expand learning environments by giving students choices, diversifying classroom libraries, and activating student-centered field trips with community supports. They model how holistic education for sustainability uplifts subject requirements.[104]

Transformative Teachers Are Inclusive

Transformative teachers span the planet. For instance, Chilean environmental arts educator Cecilia Vicuña has been practicing for five decades across the world. Vicuña began her environmental arts career in Santiago during the time that Paulo Freire developed liberation education there. Vicuña's environmental liberation practices build on Freire's culture circles, deepening critical consciousness with feminism. While Freire's work empowers disenfranchised learners with literacy developed through social action, Vicuña's work spotlights *ecological actions* with diverse women and children.

Vicuña's vibrant *obras* – from discarded wood, rocks, metal, and other found objects, along with multicolored wool and cotton weavings – show "the birth of the spring of water through the child whose death is the cascade that pours into the ocean from mountains through the cosmic scale of *spacetime*."[105] Vicuña's *precarios* (fragile beach sculptures or precarious things made of destructible objects) portray culture conflict and reconciliation. Her work offers "ephemeral site-specific performance and installations set in nature, streets, and museums [to] combine ritual and assemblage."[106] She shows how to broaden the humanization goals that motivate educators with superdiversity-biodiversity arts education. Vicuña demonstrates cultural participation on "the imaginary scale of space across the Americas that unites the body to the galaxy."[107]

Similarly, Gloria Ladson-Billings and Christopher Emdin inspire transformation. They model US civil rights methods: investigation of injustices, negotiation, self-purification, and direct action. As transformative African American educators, they show how culturally relevant student-centered liberation education reduces racist events in US classrooms. Their examples explain the clash of primarily European American teachers – conditioned to White bias – versus the need for equity academics. They show how cultural action fortifies the "psychic space" that students inhabit – body-mind-culture-environment – with critical consciousness.[108]

Likewise, Vietnamese mindfulness educator Thich Nhat Hanh, featured throughout this book, demonstrates change through compassion. He shows social action from compassionate listening and explains the details of cultural-emotional empathy practices. Hanh encourages teachers to think big about humanization with consistent mindfulness of interbeing, impermanence, and emptiness. He outlines hourly and daily methods – mindful consumption, mindful speech, family responsibility, acts of generosity, and peace service – for education routines.[109]

Another transformative educator, African American feminist bell hooks, makes pedagogical connections between Thich Nhat Hanh and Freire, describing both as liberation educators who emphasized "'whole' human beings, striving not just for knowledge in books, but knowledge about how to live in the world." She explains that Hanh and Freire model "self-actualization" through "progressive, holistic education, 'engaged pedagogy' [that] is more demanding than conventional critical or feminist pedagogy [because it] emphasizes well-being."

> Freire's work affirmed that education can only be liberatory when everyone claims knowledge as a field in which we all labor. That notion of mutual labor was affirmed by Thich Nhat Hanh's philosophy of engaged Buddhism, the focus on practice in conjunction with contemplation. His philosophy was similar to Freire's emphasis on 'praxis' – action and reflection upon the world in order to change it.[110]

Similarly, Indigenous educator Ned Blackhawk models how to apply academic accuracy to transformation. Blackhawk explains how centering historical time lines on Indigenous experiences offers a long view to develop holistic knowledge. He asserts that action-research about dehumanization leads to cultural stewardship solutions and practices that heal intergenerational racism, sexism, and classism.

Blackhawk describes how rapid US economic growth fueling Earth's destruction – from westward expansion to globalization – extracts, pollutes, divides, and kills in a land dominated by Europeans. This Eurocentric trajectory broke dramatically from the sustainable human–environment balance of hunting, gathering, trading, cultivating, and domesticating that diverse Indigenous peoples have practiced on these lands for thousands of years. What followed was the violent institutionalization of cheap and slave labor of Indigenous peoples and Africans and other people of color to operate for-profit extraction industries, such as mining, dams, big agriculture, and consumer manufacturing. These industries propelled the US to economic world power status with production practices that, ironically, destroy the land where people must live.[111]

This chain of systemic racism – conquest, imperialism, colonialism, and authoritarianism – comes from land-sequestering and the genocide, servitude, segregation, and mass incarceration of people of color.

> In North America, European ships began capturing Native peoples as early as the 1490s off the Northeastern coastline.... and Native peoples there were forced into slavery. They mined, harvested cotton and sugar, and died in large numbers. European slavery did eventually [become] overwhelmingly tied to African slavery, but [enslavement] isn't a 19th-century story exclusively.... The Spanish conquest of the Caribbean, Mexico, and subsequent explorations into the Southeast and Southwest now form essential beginnings for understanding the cataclysmic rupture brought by European colonialism, in which Indigenous slavery became one of the driving motivations for conquest as well as one of the most profitable forms of colonization.[112]

Blackhawk's culture consciousness about US history illustrates that without direct intervention, mainstream institutions are destined to reproduce unsustainably dehumanizing systems for years to come. For instance, US public education established in the 1800s for economic efficiency is marked by assimilation and exclusions at sites so dehumanizing that many Indigenous children tried to run away from, were abused at, and died in boarding schools, separated from their families in horrible conditions.[113] Cruelty in the name of education is the crux of Native American detachment at school. Eurocentric extraction-consumption patterns rapidly devastated ecosystems and cultures in the crosshairs of industry. Thus, Blackhawk shows that when transformative educators reflect mindfully about diverse perspectives for truth in history, we work diligently not to repeat it.

In summary, transformative teachers are everywhere. We don't have to look far for healing. Our next-door colleague can be a Diversity Circle collaborator. When we team with diversity, we model cultural inclusion and how to cocreate academic integration. Everyone has a stake in antibias unity. When teachers of color and White teachers work together, our activities reform failing systems by reducing exclusion patterns through holism events. Our communities of care apply the brain science of mindfulness for calm in social-emotional academic learning activities. We use peace precepts to work through the conflicts of change, developing reciprocal healthy multicultural identities during evolving collaborations.

Liberation action-reflection *during* subject engagement reduces dehumanizing and dividing assimilation habits. When educators reflect *with* students on superdiversity in biodiversity, we develop Environmental Liberation Education. We apply critical consciousness inclusion actions to reshape mainstream education space, time, materials, and learning environments. We think globally to act locally. We sustain the Earth on which we live, reinterpreting academic requirements for holistic student success and green economic participation. Our big picture bridges disciplines and balances arts and sciences with multiple modalities and diverse ways of knowing in classrooms, labs, and meeting rooms and across sites. We become transformative teachers who connect academics to the environment through culture for change. Collaborating on body-mind well-being to nurture stewardship, transformative teachers activate the humanization goals that motivate education.

TRANSFORMATIVE BREATHWORK AND JOURNAL

Journal Question: *How is Global Praxis a verb and Environmental Humanization a noun?*

> Mindfulness...cuts through the fundamental mechanism of ego, which is that ego has to maintain itself by providing lots of subconscious gossip and discursive thoughts.... Being aware of the whole environment and bringing that into our basic discipline allows us to become less self-centered and more in contact with the world around us, so there is less reference point to "me and "my"- ness.... We realize we have nothing to hang onto in ourselves, so we can give away each time. The basis of such compassion is nonterritoriality, non-ego, no ego *at all*. If you have that, you have compassion.[114]
>
> –Chögyam Trungpa Rinpoche

Breathwork

Wherever you are, take a mindful moment to relax. Use a timer chime if you like. Close or lid your eyes, taking several slow deep breaths, smiling slightly, noticing sensations: smells, sounds, touch, taste, and sight (if your eyes are open).

Now breathe while internally reciting the *gatha* below:

Breathing in, I calm my body.
Breathing out, I smile.
Dwelling in the present moment,
I know this is an environmental moment.[115]

Then:

Breathing in
How is Global Praxis a verb and Environmental Humanization noun?
Breathing out openness.
Repeat for as long as you like or until the timer chimes.

Journal

Imagine we're in a Diversity Circle with the transformative practitioners cited in this book. We want to support superdiverse student success in a biodiverse world. Read our answers below. Reflect on your meditation. Briefly answer the journal question above in a way that's meaningful to you.

Phil Gang

- *Global Praxis*: "We have some choices. We can persist on our current path, or we can begin to act consciously to make the Earth a fit place for humanity. Humanity created the current crisis and humanity has the potential to turn it all around. Each of us must move from knowledge to action, from thinking in a new way to being in a new way. This is the essence of the new global-ecocentric approach to living and learning in today's world."[116]
- *Environmental Humanization*: A world citizenship identity for humanity-*through*-nature as opposed to an identity of humanity-*over*-nature.[117]

Paulo Freire

In culture circles with liberation educators:

- *Global Praxis*: The oppressed detect economic-social contradictions during academic development to emancipate both the oppressed *and* oppressors through action-reflection "to *name* the world in order to transform it."[118]
- *Environmental Humanization*: Critical consciousness identity to engage academics collectively "to be more fully human."[119]

Edward Clark

Global Praxis:

- Environmental education with big-picture questions – "How much consumption can the ecological system afford?" – to support "the relationships that exist among everything that is a part of our planetary ecological system."
- "Household Earth" projects for intergenerational solutions. "Solutions which do not take into account the global context are doomed to failure. Ultimately, the goal of environmental education is to change the thinking of an entire generation of people."

Environmental Humanization:

- A world citizenship identity informed by seven "Operating Principles for Ecological Systems":
    1 "Carrying Capacity" – Conserving natural resources with homeostasis
    2 "Interdependence" – Balancing each component with the whole
    3 "Diversity "– Stability through variety
    4 "Change, Adaptation" – Short-term and long-term evolution
    5 "Competition and Cooperation" – Balance between creativity and stability
    6 "Cycles" – Rhythmic fluctuations and recycling
    7 "Energy Flow" – Dependence on external forces for survival, volatile and constant.[120]

Micaela Rubalcava

Global Praxis:

- Integrating academic engagement into world healing activities through student-centered circles.
- Engaging subjects with cultural respect and creativity for green economic participation.
- A Multicultural Mindfulness practice to apply knowledge from Culture-Conscious Listening to hands-on subject engagement for sustainability.

Environmental Humanization:

- A world citizenship identity for humanization with mindfulness, cross-cultural liberation, and ecological stewardship.
- One of three principles that distinguish Diversity Circles from mainstream education learning communities.

Notes

1 Bethell, Newacheck, Hawes and Halfon (2014); Darling-Hammond (2006); Noguera (2017, 2018); Oakes and Lipton (2007); Sleeter (2001); Sleeter and Carmona (2017); Terada (2019, February 4).
2 Goldberg and Houser (2017, July 19).
3 Cuban (2011, 2021).
4 Lewis and Diamond (2015), xix.

5 Madden-Dent and Oliver (2021, June 21).
6 Banks (all); Sleeter (all).
7 Angelo, Nilson and Winkelmes (2018); Hall, Quinn and Gollnick (2008); Oakes and Lipton (2007); Sadker, Sadker and Zittleman (2008); Wong and Wong (1998).
8 Ewing and Hannah-Jones (2018, November 29); Frankenberg, Garces and Hopkins (2016); Ingersoll (2015); Ingersoll and Smith (2003); Rothstein (all); Sleeter (all); Walter (2019, May 16).
9 Cuban (all); Darling-Hammond (all); Fried (2001).
10 Spring (all).
11 See Chapter 4 for full substructure-superstructure analysis and citations.
12 Lewis and Diamond (2015).
13 National Geographic (2019).
14 Valdés (2016), 79.
15 Valdés (2016); National Geographic (2019); Suárez-Orozco and Michikyan (2016), 15.
16 Grant and Littlejohn (2001); Rothstein (2014).
17 Freire (1985).
18 Freire (1985), 110.
19 Freire (1985), 19.
20 Gang (1991), 79.
21 Dunbar-Ortiz (2014); Emdin (2016), 218.
22 Banks (all); Emdin (2016); Howe and Lisi (2019); Gay (2000); Ladson-Billings (1995); Oakes and Lipton (2007); Urtubey (2023, June 20).
23 Kim (2022, April 6); Mcguire, Scott and Shaw (2006).
24 Giroux (1983); Spring (all).
25 See Chapter 4 for full substructure-superstructure analysis and citations.
26 Spring (2000), 18.
27 Dunbar-Ortiz (2014), 151.
28 Reece (2022), 164, 150.
29 Au, Brown and Calderón (2016); Frankenberg, Garces and Hopkins (2016); Kozol (1991); Howe and Lisi (2019); Lewis and Diamond (2015); Oakes and Lipton (2007); Nieto (all); Noguera (all); Sleeter (all); Sleeter and Carmona (2017); Sleeter and Zavala (2020); Spring (all).
30 Reece (2022), 166.
31 Ingersoll (2015); Ingersoll and Smith (2003); Sleeter (all).
32 Dweck (2007); Berry and Farris-Berg (2016); Darling-Hammond (all); Gang (1991), 78; Hall, Quinn and Gollnick (2008); Johnson, Musial, Hall and Gollnick (2017); LeFrancois (2000); Oakes and Lipton (2007); Sanders, Wright and Horn (1997, April); Sleeter and Carmona (2017).
33 Gordon (all); Olneck (1990, February), title.
34 Sleeter (all).
35 Banks (all); Olneck (1990, February); Sleeter (all).
36 Sleeter and Carmona (2017).
37 Freire (1985), 19.
38 Freire (1985), 19 and 69.
39 Reese (2022, February 9–April 12).
40 Keltner (2023), 137.
41 Hanh (all); King (2018); Middleton (2018), Reese (2022, February 9–April 12).
42 Dunbar-Ortiz (2014), 26.
43 Spring (all).
44 Sadker, Sadker and Zittleman (2008), 297.
45 Freire (1985), 59.
46 Dunbar-Ortiz (2014); Sadker, Sadker and Zittleman (2008); Reece (2022), 163; Spring (all).
47 Lewis and Diamond (2015), 77.
48 Spring (2000), 8.
49 Spring (2014), 143.
50 Lewis and Diamond (2015), title.
51 Sadker, Sadker and Zittleman (2008), 302.
52 Olneck (1990, February).
53 Temming (2021, April 14).
54 Au, Brown and Calderón (2016); Sleeter and Carmona (2017).

55 Trungpa (1993), 37, 214.
56 Lewis and Diamond (2015); Goldberg and Houser (2017, July 19).
57 Hanh (2014), title.
58 Dweck (2007).
59 Goleman (1995, 2002); Hanh and Weare (2017); Rechtschaffen (2016).
60 Dweck (2007).
61 Dunbar-Ortiz (2014), 235.
62 Urtubey (2023, June 20).
63 hooks (1994), 12.
64 hooks (1994), 12.
65 Trungpa (1993), 37.
66 Damasio (1994).
67 Whalen and Phelps (2009); Verschelden (2017).
68 Damasio (1994); Eberhardt (2019); Keltner (2023); LeDoux (1996); Verschelden (2017); Whalen and Phelps (2009).
69 Damasio (1994); Eberhardt (2019); Keltner (2023); LeDoux (1996); Verschelden (2017); Whalen and Phelps (2009).
70 LeDoux (1996).
71 Sinarski (2022, June 21).
72 Kendi (2019), 223, 23.
73 Dweck (2007).
74 Rubalcava (2001–2024).
75 United (2019, October 8).
76 Vicuña (2017, July 7), 17, 22 (author's translation).
77 Doll, Brehm and Zucker (2014).
78 Madden-Dent and Oliver (2021, June 21).
79 Gardner (1983).
80 Rubalcava (2001–2024 [2019]).
81 Verschelden (2017).
82 Brill (2018); Prakash (2013, July 16); Wilkerson (2020).
83 Daydí-Tolson (2018), and further translated by the author.
84 https://www.pcoe.k12.ca.us/apps/pages/6thGradeWatershedYear.
85 https://www.pcoe.k12.ca.us/apps/pages/6thGradeWatershedYear.
86 Bizjak, Yoon-Hendricks, Reese and Sullivan (2018, December 4).
87 Middleton (2018); https://www.bloomberg.com/news/articles/2021-08-18/california-s-dixie-fire-burns-clear-across-a-mountain-range.
88 Middleton (2018); https://www.bloomberg.com/news/articles/2021-08-18/california-s-dixie-fire-burns-clear-across-a-mountain-range.
89 Kolbert (2014).
90 Middleton (2018), 187.
91 https://datausa.io/profile/geo/quincy-ca.
92 Upton (2023, April 28).
93 Middleton (2018); https://datausa.io/profile/geo/quincy-ca; Rubalcava (2001–2024).
94 Feather (2019, April 28), 6A.
95 Crawford (2008, January 8).
96 Crawford (2008, January 8).
97 Crawford (2008, January 8).
98 Dunbar-Ortiz (2014), 183; Orange (2018); Reese (2022, February 9–April 12).
99 Clark (all); Gang (1991); US (2019, June), 3.
100 Takaki (1989), 23; Spring (all).
101 San Pedro (2017), 102.
102 Dunbar-Ortiz (2014), 14, 151.
103 San Pedro (2017), 102.
104 Rubalcava (2001–2024).
105 Vicuña (2017, July 7), 17, 22 (author's translation).
106 Whitney (2019, March 25).
107 Vicuña (2017, July 7), 22; Toledo and MacHugh (2022).

108 Emdin (2016), 23.
109 Hanh and Weare (2017).
110 hooks (1994), 14–15.
111 Bell and Delacroix (2019, Fall).
112 Bell and Delacroix (2019, Fall), quoting Ned Blackhawk.
113 Dunbar-Ortiz (2014); National Native (2012); Spring (all).
114 Trungpa (1993), 149.
115 Hanh (2008), 36.
116 Gang (1991), 87–88.
117 Gang (1991), 79.
118 Freire (1985), 19, 167.
119 Freire (1985), 41.
120 Clark (1991), 44–50.

3
BIAS, ANTIBIAS, AND CULTURE COMPETENCE

Guiding Purpose

Explain how

- Educators choose bias or antibias hourly and daily.
- Ten forms of bias pose barriers to inclusive student success, knowledge accuracy, and sustainability systems.
- Well-intentioned educators unconsciously stereotype, favor, and exclude cultures.
- Multicultural Mindfulness develops culture competence for antibias decisions.
- Transformative teachers strengthen antibias decisions by applying structural competency to academic space, time, materials, and learning environments.

Provide

- Two Multicultural Mindfulness Activities and one journal question: *Reducing Arm's-Length Bias, 4-Rs Antibias Practice*, and *How do Anglo-conformity and White Supremacy Impact My Classroom?*

Context

What's Bias?

Bias is part of human perception. Bias is judgment. It is distinguishing bad from good, as commonplace as disliking or liking something. It is part of human survival. Bias is the voice in your head, "Will this hurt or help me?" Bias consists of interpretations that categorize, sort, and separate based on feelings and assumptions. Sensed in body and mind through, bias is human discernment about things, situations, peoples, identities, and cultures. Contemporary social bias is emotional *and* structural in this way, triggered by memories and stereotypes from systemic racism, sexism, and classism; and in education, bias is a barrier to inclusive student success, teacher empowerment and diversity, and knowledge accuracy.

DOI: 10.4324/9781003364757-5
This chapter has been made available under a CC-BY-NC-ND license.

Social bias is "any attitude, belief, or feeling that results in, and helps to justify, unfair treatment of an individual because of his or her identity."[1] Reacting to impressions and expectations, social bias impacts decisions to favor or exclude unfairly. Social bias perpetuates dehumanizing cultural divisions and environmental destruction patterns. Cycling through inequity systems, social bias extends structural privileges to some and adversities to others. People who benefit from prevailing systemic norms make bias decisions to serve "personal interest to keep these rules in place."[2] It takes hard work fortified with mindfulness calm to nonviolently change the rules of injustice. Patiently, collaborations nurtured with inclusive peace practices unlock equity doors to reparative resources to grow unity.

As bell hooks explains, US systemic bias is rooted in a "white supremacist capitalist patriarchy."[3] US bias structures perpetuate Anglo-conformity, "the desirability of maintaining English institutions, the English language, and English-oriented cultural patterns as dominant and standard in American life."[4] Unintentionally, US teachers make hourly and daily decisions from Anglo-conformist bias to reproduce the dehumanization patterns within which we're ensconced. It is unpleasant for busy teachers to think about White supremacy in our classrooms, labs, and meeting rooms, but when we confront it directly, we develop the capacity to forge diversity pathways for inclusive student success and professional integrity. Only when we operate routines with structural analysis from a position of love, can we develop culture competence for knowledge accuracy to advance antibias *holism*.

As Martin Luther King, Jr. explained from a jail cell in 1963, we're wrapped into "the bondage of myths and half-truths" from cultural disinformation vis-à-vis the "dark depths of prejudice and racism."[5] We tell ourselves we're colorblind. We *want* to be colorblind, but when we look at the data, we face color-based divisions: schools are racially segregated, programs are racially tracked, the racial achievement gap persists, and holistic knowledge is politicized as anti-science and anti-diversity.[6]

Systemic racism isn't good for the planet, but it persists by feeding the short-term greed of the politicians and corporations who direct it as well as the people who benefit from its skewed profits. Many youth experience poor mental and physical health outcomes due to racism. Hate crimes are up. Gun violence hurts everyone and is a leading cause of US youth death.[7] Global warming – linked to for-profit acquisitions in a racialized economic order that devalues labor and destroys natural resources – impacts people with climate events everywhere, more adversely so in poor areas without strong infrastructures. In this context, overstandardized and understaffed teachers in the US, most of whom are White, make daily decisions that *unintentionally* divide students and omit diverse ways of knowing, thereby perpetuating bias-based suffering.[8]

Healing Bias

But there's hope! Public classrooms are *intergenerational* spaces for economic-social healing. When educators of every background collaborate to reduce bias, we prepare students to participate in democracy nourished by diversity skills. When we guide routine decisions with antibias-antiracist holism designs, we interrupt decisions from assumptions. We *can* teach that systemic bias is experienced differently by different people and that bias inclinations are part of the human condition. We *can* teach that while partialities are expressed in various ways, our healing is mutual, activated by diversity experiences that unite. As we integrate with inclusion rubrics to invite diverse students into academic project teams, we develop knowledge accuracy with multicultural analysis. We weave diverse ways of knowing into the arts and sciences to winnow out false equivalents. In classrooms, labs, and meetings rooms, we thwart assimilation and segregation patterns that divide and disinform.[9]

Our developing culture competence cogenerates knowledge about how bias operates and how to take reciprocal actions, such as voting for social justice and environmental healing. As we spot stereotypes about cultures, we regulate reactions from dislikes and likes through big-picture reflection. We ask liberation questions about mainstream academic procedures and bias requirements. We use these questions to facilitate cross-cultural story-sharing activities to flush out favoritism and exclusions *during* subject engagement. Systems analysis invites students and teachers to connect the personal to the global. As we uplift education routines with antibias-antiracist practices centered on environmental holism, we gather in diversity to uplift democracy.

What's Antibias-Antiracist Holism?

An antiracist is "one who is supporting an antiracist policy through their actions or expressing an antiracist idea."[10] To be *antibias*-antiracist for holism is to act to respect *intersectionality* from a position of love. It is examining systemic inequities to make inclusion changes with a multicultural-multiracial lens. Antibias-antiracist holism in education is participating in academic activities that (a) start by recognizing how bias streams throughout mainstream routines to fan cultural emotions and (b) develops with mindfulness breathwork and big-picture questions to guide unity experiences. Many educator decisions react to agreeable or disagreeable feelings caught into racist, classist, and sexist systems. Antibias-antiracist educators for holism "confront the issue" of unfair structures to alleviate defensiveness during reparative change.[11] We're aware of emotions from cultural assumptions palpitating through bias patterns, from extremist loathing to dulled apathy, terror to unease, intense longing to mild hope, fierce clannishness to cliquish camaraderie, and blame-and-shame. We detect and take cultural action instance by instance to replace White superiority norms in curriculum, outcomes, knowledge, communications, and interactions with inclusion practices.[12]

Some holistic antibias-antiracist practices strengthen body-mind circulation, such as conscious breathwork, healthful physical movement, wholesome nutrition and hydration, and art, music, and animal therapy.[13] Other antibias-antiracist actions for inclusion focus on mind-culture, such as multicultural content, diversifying exam rubrics, offering alternative assignments, forming multicultural-multiracial project teams with nonviolent communication protocols, assessing subject outcomes with equity benchmarks, removing names from documents, and diversifying minimum qualifications for hiring.[14] Other best practices center on culture-environment, such as assessing subject outcomes with ecological benchmarks, integrating academic requirements into climate justice activities on site and in communities (e.g., using culturally responsive scientific methods during nature experiences and regional restoration projects).[15]

Antibias-*antiracist* Environmental Liberation Education is about systemic change through inclusive sustainability actions "built around the question of race first" with the goal of a world undivided by race.[16] Antibias-antiracist educators for holism focus on economic substructure-social superstructure systems that harm people through race, class, and gender inequities as well as through Earth destruction. We name the colorblind narrative about

American world preeminence and the American Dream as disinformation. We facilitate activities to investigate how the narrative minimizes racist practices enforced violently and politically, such as stealing land from Indigenous peoples and dividing peoples by race to compel cheap and free labor.[17] Holistic liberation educators are anti-White supremacist and anti-patriarchal. We're for economic egalitarianism, and we integrate *feminist* culture consciousness into academic decisions to alleviate fear during change.[18] We attempt to reduce unconscious bias with "active/activist" peace practices for reparations.[19] We apply holistic designs to develop healthy multicultural identities, diverse student success, and accurate knowledge development for sustainability experiences during education.

Ten Forms of Bias

Bias is multidimensional. In the US, it's dominated by Anglo-conformist artifacts, practices, and beliefs. At least ten forms of bias stream through education:

1 *Institutional Bias:* Official and unofficial policies, actions, and inactions that bureaucratize assimilation, segregation, and cultural preferences and exclusions.
2 *Economic Bias:* Defensive decisions about access and participation in the means of production and consumption.
3 *Explicit Bias:* Overt clannish decisions, such as aggressive judgments (name-calling, snap accusations, and gaslighting) and violent behaviors (defacement, brutality, maiming, and killing) based on racist, classist, sexist, and other identity assumptions and stereotypes.
4 *Implicit Bias:* Unconscious decisions that marginalize or favor people unfairly to perpetrate or stand by divisions, exclusions, preferences, and other inequity patterns.
5 *Familiarity Bias:* A subset of implicit bias. In-group favoritism.
6 *Omission Bias:* A subset of implicit bias. Exclusions such as colorblind dismissals of cultural diversity, leaving out cultures, and neglecting divergent points of view.
7 *Tokenization Bias:* A subset of implicit bias related to omission bias. Dismissal of cultural integrity and the value of diversity by focusing on cultural heroes and exceptions or singling out group members to explain a whole culture.
8 *Patronization Bias:* A subset of implicit bias. When members of privileged cultures give nominal gifts to people perceived to be marginalized, reward substandard performance, or proclaim allyship without hard-won trust.
9 *Arm's-Length Bias:* A subset of implicit bias. When diverse people in segregated systems keep a distance from perceived out-groups, avoiding the effort involved in compassion-based cross-cultural interactions and authentic multicultural friendships and collaborations.
10 *Projection Bias:* A subset of implicit bias. When diverse people in segregated systems – feeling fear, shame, guilt, or resentment about perceptions of fairness and cultures – attribute their own biases and defensiveness to others, such as through transference.[20]

How Do We Reduce Bias?

Transformative teachers reduce overlapping forms of bias during routines. We counteract various facets of Anglo-conformity simultaneously. For example, Culturally Relevant Education (CRE) tackles bias with inclusion activities applicable to diverse cultures. CRE is culture-conscious academic engagement approached through concrete experiences,

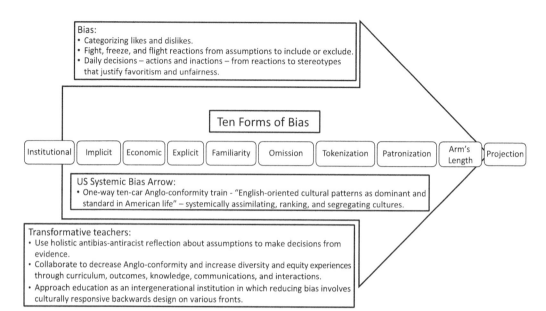

FIGURE 3.1 Ten Forms of Bias graphic. Created by the author.

dialogue, caring practices, and personal accountability.[21] Likewise, Environmental Liberation Education integrates local and global perspectives. Practitioners re-examine, *with* students and colleagues during subject development, how cultures are treated in mainstream US education and how to respect and reimagine cultures with superdiversity-biodiversity questions.

To this end, we join Diversity Circles to develop the open-minded Multicultural Mindfulness process, resisting inequity patterns and nurturing equity ecosystems with hourly and daily holism decisions. Our joyful justice practices interrupt entitlement-victimization dichotomies and the disinformation spirals that undermine academic concentration. When we're consistent with body-mind-culture-environment breathwork we design and assess academic engagement with compassion rubrics, such as outlined by the Approach-in-Dimension. The Three Transformative Tools invite diverse community supports into academics to tackle Anglo-conformity in classrooms, labs, meeting rooms, and sites. Our multiculturally creative interactions nurture inclusion experiences to change school systems with nonviolent practices that reduce multiple forms of bias simultaneously.

MULTICULTURAL MINDFULNESS ACTIVITY

Reducing Arm's-Length Bias

Outcome

- Define arm's-length bias.
- Discuss cultural stories about segregation, desegregation, and integration.
- Explain the value of diversity.

Key Concepts

- **Arm's-Length Bias:** When diverse people in segregated systems keep a distance from perceived out-groups, avoiding the effort involved in compassion-based cross-cultural interactions and multicultural friendships.
- **Bias:** Any feeling or belief that justifies divisive and unfair decisions based on assumptions, such as to favor or exclude.
- **Desegregation:** The ending of segregation policy; to be free of any provision or practice requiring isolation of the members of a particular race or ethnic group in separate units.[22]
- **Integration:** Unity designs for inclusion, holistic equity, and intergenerational sustainability.
- **Pre-prejudice:** Ignorant and defensive impressions about cultures in childhood experiences that harden into adult bias.
- **Prejudice:** A bias "prejudgment for or against" an individual, group, or thing "formed without adequate prior knowledge" or evidence. Often aggressive. Based on negative stereotypes and emotionally charged personal experiences.[23]
- **Segregation:** The separation of a race, class, or ethnic group into a restricted area, such as separate facilities or exclusion through procedural discriminations. Involves structural barriers to mixed interactions.[24]

Resources

- Written definitions of the seven terms above, journals, pencils, poster materials, board markers or sidewalk chalk (for outdoor application), an example or symbol of nature, a place to meet indoors or outdoors.

Big-Picture Question

- How do we reduce arm's-length bias and increase multicultural friendships?

Start

Diversified project teams:

- **Assign** one or more of the seven concepts above, without its written definition, to each team. (Hide the seven definitions for now.)
- Ask each team to **write** an open-ended question about the assigned concept(s), such as "Is desegregation possible or even desirable?"

Whole group circle:

- For two minutes, **discuss** each of the seven questions, with everyone sketching concept maps.
- **Reveal** the seven written definitions.
- **Discuss** the seven definitions while gallery-walking concept maps.
- **Discuss**, in a whole group circle, the posted definition of arm's-length bias.

> *Middle*
>
> Diversified project teams:
>
> - **Draw** a visual for arm's-length bias with one key word.
>
> Whole group circle:
>
> - **Compare and contrast** everyone's visuals and key words.
> - **Rewrite** one agreed-upon definition of arm's-length bias.
>
> Diversified project teams:
>
> - **Individually create posters**, featuring the agreed-upon definition with a visual of choice while discussing personal cultural stories about reducing arm's-length bias in teams.
>
> *Closing*
>
> Whole group circle:
>
> - **Discuss** ideas to resist self-segregation, how to make cross-cultural friendships, and why multicultural alliances from a position of love are part of sustainability.
> - **Discuss** how the item or symbol of nature expresses some aspect of the written definition of integration.
> - **Pair-and-share** one intention to reduce arm's-length bias this week and why its important to value diversity in friendships.

Theory and Practice

Teachers and Bias

Multiple layers of systemic bias perpetuate intergenerational economic substructure-social superstructure segregation and assimilation cycles. In the US, social bias operates structures originally founded in a *racialized* economy started by White people who seized Indigenous lands, forced the free labor of African and Indigenous peoples, and exploited the labor of poor people. These violently enforced structures rapidly propelled the US economy to global superpower status, establishing White superiority norms.[25]

Currently, US systemic bias continues when institutional participants make hourly and daily decisions, from unconscious emotions, assumptions, and defensiveness, that cumulate into racialized inequity outcomes. Unjust and unsustainable results from racist routines are part of an economic system that "requires the existence of a mass underclass of surplus labor."[26] Owing to racialized substructure-superstructure cycles, race is "a *central axis* of social relations, which cannot be subsumed under or reduced to some broader category or conception."[27] Thus, US systemic bias proceeds on preferences and aversions about identity categories, race salient among them, as the grease for social-economic stratifications.

Though no longer written into official policies, school segregation is fueled by a network of US institutions. Institutional operators make decisions about cultures that mirror systemic racism. Within schools, research shows that teachers' expectations, behaviors, and emotional connections with students significantly impact the distribution of academic resources. Teachers matter more to student success than curriculum, materials, facilities, or administration.

Study after study confirms that of all the resources schools provide, teachers are the most important for student learning, and not having a qualified teacher is particularly damaging for low income children who have fewer learning resources outside of school.[28]

However, lacking culture competence, unfamiliar with structural competence, and inexperienced in critical consciousness, many teachers unintentionally maintain academic obstacles against students of color, simultaneously easing the way for White students through implicit bias.[29]

Education Students and Bias

Most education students in the US are White and female, often with little awareness about systemic racism, while unconsciously harboring negative stereotypes about low-income children and children of color.[30] The problem is that many education students, wishing for the colorblind ideal, view social interactions and academic achievement through a lens of individualism. Some teacher credential students view multicultural education as discriminating against White people.[31] Lacking liberation education and ethnic studies coursework in teacher preparation, new teachers are hired without culture competence to address systemic bias. Many new teachers don't understand how to reduce bias with diverse students, design multicultural curriculum, or develop diversity knowledge. Many teachers don't know how to make antibias-antiracist decisions or even see the need to do so in the first place.[32]

Working Teachers

Unintentionally, working teachers unequally select and process student behaviors with culture coding. Teachers tend to forgive the negative behavior of White students. They recommend lighter consequences and use forgiving channels to negotiate penalties in comparison with what they dispense to students of color. Implicit bias determinations fuel disciplinary discrimination underneath regulations that are "typically written with neutral language." Educators dole out unjust consequences to exacerbate "racial battle fatigue" experienced by students of color. While explicit racism – as in *de jure* policies, taboo words, and blatant racial violence, such as lynching and cross-burning – has subsided, implicit bias drives bureaucratic racism. Despite "race neutral" statements, routine teacher decisions about curriculum and instruction operate outcomes that join the economic and social institutional network of systemic racism.[33]

Antibias-Antiracist Holism Teachers

Because teacher decisions are powerful, we also, collectively, have the opportunity to reverse course *with* students. We apply culture competence to make systemic change during routines for diverse student success and multicultural knowledge development. We guide change from the grassroots, diversifying academic space, time, materials, and learning environments moment by moment. Our joyful and just designs facilitate holism experiences. We rely on the Multicultural Mindfulness tool for calm during reparative work.

Multicultural Mindfulness practices release defensive clinging to the assimilation and segregation into which we have been conditioned. These clarity practices reveal hot emotions, stereotypes, favoritism, and exclusion patterns in education, on segregated and

98 Big-Picture Transformation in the Real World

relatively desegregated sites alike.[34] Environmental Liberation Education's big picture invites reflective transformation. Environmental consciousness unifies people "to renew our minds" and "to transform educational institutions – and society – so that the way we live, teach and work can reflect our joy in cultural diversity, our passion for justice, and our love for freedom."[35] We get bold with integration activities to respect differences from a position of love. Aware that diversity is central to sustainability, we synthesize antibias-antiracist actions *with* ecology practices during education. This is when critical consciousness gets holistic and "fun."[36]

Classrooms, labs, and meeting rooms become places to gather to replace systems of domination with inclusive social emotional academic learning. *Transformative* spaces grow belonging with multicultural-environmental "love" experiences while engaging subjects with diversity materials.[37] One Multicultural Mindfulness "love" activity is "Spotting Signs of Stereotypes and Bias in Education" (Figure 3.2).[38] This Multicultural Mindfulness practice outlines observational areas – the demographics of interactions, the quality of verbal and nonverbal communications, and cultures in content – to reveal patterns. We look for segregation versus desegregation, decisions from assumptions versus evidence, bias versus

FIGURE 3.2 Signs of Stereotypes and Bias in Education graphic. Created by the author.

equity experiences, grievance versus justice events, offensive versus inclusion symbols, words versus outcomes, and divisive/demeaning versus holistic/empowering identity language. Then, informed by action research during subject engagement, project teams act to reduce bias by increasing diversity and equity criteria in interactions, communications, and materials, going forward. Such critical consciousness activities are preventative, integrating academics into conflict resolution opportunities, cultural liberation modalities, peace resource use, cross-cultural respect language, and the diversity imagination that vitalizes sustainability.

Becoming an antibias-antiracist teacher for holism means acknowledging overlapping forms of bias and how everyone's defensiveness is expressed from different points of departure. We learn to recognize assumptions from positions of power and privilege as well as from disenfranchisement and marginalization experiences.

> Most of us were taught in classrooms where styles of teachings reflected the notion of a single norm of thought and experience, which we were encouraged to believe as universal. This has been just as true for nonwhite teachers as for white teachers. Most of us learn to teach emulating this model.[39]

Different standpoints impact bias variously, spinning multicultural webs. Intersectional identities and self-perceptions reference mainstream norms from simultaneous outsider and insider perspectives. Therefore, regional experiences can be at odds with statistical generalizations.[40]

For example, a five-year longitudinal study of one high school by John Diamond and Amanda Lewis describes a problematic desegregation program. "Riverview High School" has a multiracial student body with a balance of White and non-White students of relatively high economic status. The racially mixed students attend this coveted school characterized by highly qualified teachers, quality facilities, and reputable programs that support a high rate of graduation. Students, teachers, and parents from all demographics adore Riverview. However, the graduation rate masks a subsequent racial achievement gap in college attendance and completion.

When freshmen enter Riverview High School, they're still unwittingly racially tracked into programs through *academic* segregation. The study finds educators' implicit bias to be among the reasons for rankings that result in a post-graduation racial achievement gap. Well-intentioned educators unconsciously sort and separate students by race during daily academic and behavior management decisions. These reflexively racist determinations cumulate over time to divide students.

> While black and Latina/o Riverview graduates are much more likely than their peers in nearby Metro City to attend college, white Riverview graduates are far more likely than their black and Latina/o peers to attend four-year college (more than 90 percent for whites versus closer to 60 percent for black and Latina/o). While only 5 percent of white Riverview graduates end up in two-year college, 30 percent of black graduates and 40 percent of Latina/o graduates do so. Thus, while Riverview graduates overall college attendance rates are high, the institutions that they attend are stratified by race and ethnicity.[41]

Lewis and Diamond demonstrate how implicit bias racializes curriculum tracks among otherwise desegregated students, even with well-intentioned and highly qualified teachers. The results are systemic *de facto* segregation patterns. The racial achievement gap that permeates US education occurs even in a diversified school noted for excellence.[42] Therefore, antibias-antiracist teachers use holistic preventative methods, such as Multicultural Mindfulness, to advance conscientious humanization decisions.

Taproot

The stubbornness of bias illustrated in unexpected places such as *desegregated* Riverview High School is why transformative teachers address root systems diligently and with an open mind. We use body-mind-culture-environment breathwork and multimodal practices to make evidence-based decisions to connect inclusion efforts to diversity programs in other institutions. Proactive culture competence identifies divisive arrangements that propagate tricky forms of bias during economic substructure-social superstructure interactions. When teachers make antibias-antiracist decisions for inclusion, we weed culture clashes proliferating from bias on the spot while fertilizing reform. Uprooting Anglo-conformity stereotypes, favoritism, and exclusion patterns, while nourishing inclusion activities, allows integration experiences to grow. Academic transformation develops *with* public policy networks, such as when diversity programs in social services, policing, housing, and health services connect with school routines.

The more educators understand how systemic bias harms student engagement and professional efficacy, the more motivated we are to *apply* cross-institutional antibias-antiracist practices. The taproot of US systemic racism is White supremacy, protected by institutional and implicit bias casing.[43] The root maintains Anglo-conformist practices from White superiority values, propagating from an aggressive White supremacy nucleus. Awareness of one's own daily participation in institutional and implicit bias tends the ground for multicultural replanting. We dig out bias defensiveness and cultivate pluralism with culture-competence seeds. While race is the primary category in US bias, other identity categories – ethnicity, gender, sexual orientation, class, religion, geography, and ability – relate to race. Any form of bias contends with patriarchal White supremacy as the core of disinformation, such as the illusion of colorblind individualism in the American Dream that, while a worthy ideal, has yet to be reality.[44] Therefore, antibias-antiracist teachers for holism use cross-institutional measures – such as using the Three Transformative Tools for Environmental Liberation Education – to collaborate, practice, and assess decisions by gathering cultural data about academic engagement for *systemic* change.

Antibias-Antiracist Holistic Action-Reflection

Bias, in all its forms, is an action-reflection topic to deepen culture competence with structural competence.

1 *Institutional Bias* normalizes segregation, stereotypes, and cultural exclusions and preferences through formal and informal procedures. The tricky part of institutional bias is that colorblind individualism espoused in race-neutral language and policies doesn't match lived experiences and outcomes.

Bias, Antibias, and Culture Competence **101**

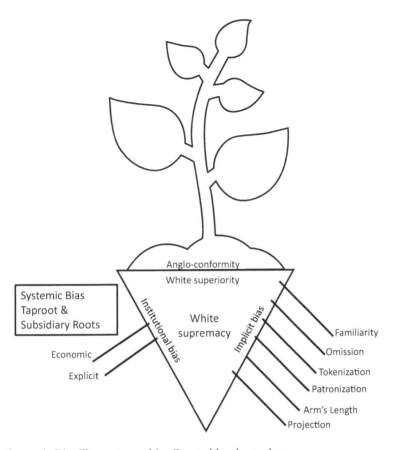

FIGURE 3.3 Systemic Bias Taproot graphic. Created by the author.

Diversity Circles help teachers resist institutional bias with action-reflection about

- Diversity-versus-colorblind individualism topics in curriculum and research.
- Racialized and gendered patterns of unequal funding, segregated sites, tracked programs, and achievement rates. Subtopics include the demographics of homework completion rates, grades and test scores, tutoring use, detentions and expulsions, and participation in Advanced Placement (AP) classes, gifted-and-talented programs, vocational education, special education, and online programs.
- The scope of diversity training, such as the amount of non-instructional time scheduled for multicultural education.
- Bullying demographics, including the investigation of "intentional and repetitive social cruelty [and] ongoing abuse that is aimed at a less powerful target" and enumerating the kinds of physical, verbal, and nonverbal cruelty manifesting in classrooms, lunch rooms, bathrooms, and playgrounds, such as violence, name-calling, derisive "laughing at others openly, eye rolling," and "embarrassing photos" that reinforce stereotypes. A subtopic is what kinds of bullying are tolerated by educators.[45]

2 *Economic Bias* consists of defensive decisions, actions, and inactions about access and participation in production and consumption. A for-profit economy stratifies human worth in

a materialistic income hierarchy. In the US, economic bias is a reaction to the threat of scarce resources in a stratified market dependent on an underclass of cheap or free labor. Desire for property and capital leads to the self-fulfilling prophecy of the "tragedy of the commons," in which two or more entities attempt to out-compete one another, each grabbing what they can, trying to dominate while depleting resources through mutual fear about perceived needs. Colorblind individualism – the hoped-for "invisible hand" in the racialized for-profit marketplace – contradicts the reality of an economy structured by cultural privilege and exclusion patterns.[46]

Diversity Circles help teachers resist economic bias with action-reflection about

- Affirmative action and reparative justice versus race-neutral policy results about student enrollment, program development, and career pathways as well as educator hiring, retention, and career pathways.
- Territorial conflicts in education, such as excluding educators and programs perceived to threaten the livelihood of others by withholding site space, time, and resources.
- Granting favors to some educators and programs with evaluations, certificates, extra resources, and access to awards.
- Ways that educators support students of immigrant and farmworker families, first-generation students, and students of color to attend and complete high-expectations academics.

3 *Explicit Bias* consists of aggressive and violent decisions and actions from defensive emotions, assumptions, and stereotypes imbued with hatred and exclusions and clinging to privileges. These are hardcore cultural prejudices conditioned by families, neighborhoods, and media. They're expressed as racial judgments, epithets, extremist labels, criminalizing language, demonizing descriptions, victimizing designations, superiority declarations, gaslighting, and defacing, destroying, and dehumanizing acts. Some people try to hide explicit bias, which is different from the unconscious process of *implicit* bias.[47]

Diversity Circles help teachers resist explicit bias with action-reflection about

- Signs of racist, classist, and sexist stereotypes in moralizing and biological depictions of groups.
- Cliques imparting typecasts and complaints verbally, visually, in writing, or through physical behaviors in ways that go beyond implicit bias microaggressions.
- Examples of physical sabotage, hate posters, and hate crimes against individuals representing identity groups.
- Ways that educators and students ignore versus call-out explicit bias messages and acts, such as racist language, book bans, and censorship of critical race theory.

4 *Implicit Bias* animates institutional bias. It consists of unconscious decisions that reinforce inequity patterns, based on preferences and aversions. These defensive likes and dislikes are different from the explicit "biases that individuals may choose to conceal for the purposes of social and/or political correctness."[48] Rather, implicit bias refers to actions or inactions from emotions, assumptions, and stereotypes associated with cultural experiences, including privileges and adversities, in contexts such as households, organizations, and neighborhoods.

Diversity Circles help teachers resist implicit bias with action-reflection about

- Assumptions and stereotypes impacting cultural representation in knowledge, curriculum, outcomes, communications, and site interactions.
- Types of fight, freeze, and flight reactions to perceived cultural threats and desires that reinforce economic substructure-social superstructure hierarchies, such as body language, phrases, tones, and decisions that divide student cultures, not for authenticity but for isolation.
- Educator favoritism of students and families who represent dominant culture groups while disfavoring marginalized groups or those represent difference from the educator's identity.
- Demographic patterns in teacher distributions of academic resources and evaluations.
- Race-neutral policies espoused by educators to treat students equally by relating to each student individually, compared with demographic results from those policies on academic ranks.
- Differences and similarities in ways White teachers versus teachers of color convey White superiority to communicate lower expectations for students of color and raised expectations for White students.[49]
- Differences and similarities in defensiveness during culture change expressed by White teachers versus teachers of color, such as fragility, hypervigilance, and pride.
- Differences and similarities in healthy multicultural identities expressed by White teachers versus teachers of color.
- White superiority-versus-double-consciousness conflicts and the development of healthy multicultural identities *between* diverse students and colleagues.[50]

5 *Familiarity Bias* is a subset of implicit bias. It is favoring members of one's in-group. It is denying that an in-group member is prejudiced by standing by the friend's bias decisions (e.g., when the friend ranks or segregates students or refuses to consider diversity content). It comes from the defensive desire to assume the best of one's own identity group.[51]

Diversity Circles help teachers resist familiarity bias with action-reflection about

- Instances of educators doing nothing during a slur or an act of exclusion or favoritism out of loyalty to the *status quo*.
- How team members protect unchecked groupthink and assimilation knowledge.
- Rules to confront stereotypes and accusations in meeting discussions, curriculum, and policies.
- How to have courageous cultural conversations among friends.
- How to talk with colleagues who maintain assimilation curriculum, racially tracked student groups, and Anglo-conformist hiring instead of engaging multicultural education, social justice enrollment practices, and diversified hiring designs.

6 *Omission Bias* is a subset of implicit bias. It is exclusionism; for instance, an educator claims to be colorblind but dismisses a student from academic engagement because of perceived differences from the educator's own cultural norms. In another example, the teacher may occasionally add cultures to subjects using a lens of sameness, such as universalized artifacts and practices, such as food, music, dance, and innovations. However, the educator skips content about authentic artifacts, practices, and beliefs developed apart from the dominant culture, such as through arts, spirituality, and true happiness experiences.

Diversity Circles help teachers resist omission bias with action-reflection about

- Cultural content and ideological frameworks for knowledge development in labs and studies.
- Cultural content in premade worksheets, looking for summaries of cultural pleasantries and intercultural similarities versus cultural values and equity practices.
- The diversity scope of seasonal holidays and celebrations observed at school.
- The representation of social justice problem-solving, cultural conflict resolution, and liberation actions *during* academic engagement.
- Welcoming ways to elicit diverse student questions and cultural perspectives and practices.

7 *Tokenization Bias* is related to omission bias. Excludes cultural integrity and diversity by placing attention on cultural heroes and exceptions or singling out members from marginalized groups to explain an entire culture. For example, it's tokenizing when a Muslim student is asked to explain a headdress or a Black student is asked to explain US racism.[52]

Diversity Circles help teachers resist tokenization bias with action-reflection about

- The range of differences and intersectional identities about cultures in knowledge and curriculum in a global context.
- The breadth and depth of cultural heroes and exceptions in knowledge and curriculum against other cultural topics.
- The representation of cultural injustice and justice themes during academic engagement.
- The demographics of people who are called on to represent cultures and explain racism.

8 *Patronization Bias* is a subset of implicit bias. It exists when members of majority cultures perpetuate cultural superiority-deficiency stereotypes by acting extra pleasantly or giving handouts to minority peoples. Another way is to declare alliance with an identity group and speak for that group without the authenticity of shared liberation experiences.

Diversity Circles help teachers resist patronization bias with action-reflection about

- Rates of passing students of color without the earning of passing grades according to completed work.
- The quality of allyship during cultural action.
- Cultural appropriations.
- Deficit-mindset-versus-growth-mindset[53] activities.
- Best practices for White educators to earn the trust of students and teachers of color during liberation collaboration, such as deep listening and doing fieldwork together.

9 *Arm's-Length Bias* is a subset of implicit bias. It is when people in segregated structures keep a distance from out-groups by self-segregating and avoiding meaningful cross-cultural friendships. As with patronization bias, one may believe oneself to be prejudice-free; however, while colorblind individualism makes segregated friendships seem circumstantial, one's own social anxiety is the barrier to deep friendships outside of one's own identity.

Diversity Circles help teachers resist arm's-length bias with action-reflection about

- Segregated-versus-desegregated social systems, such as book clubs, lunch groups, research groups, committees, teams, classrooms, and programs.
- Types of school–family communications and gatherings that segregate versus desegregate.
- Avoidance-versus-inclusion behaviors locally and globally.
- Best practices to nurture long-term cross-cultural friendships.

10 *Projection Bias* is a subset of implicit bias, occurring when diverse people in segregated systems, perceiving unfairness and feeling cultural anxiety, attribute their own assumptions, stereotypes, biases, and other distortions to others. Projection bias is hypocrisy, laying one's own defensiveness or ideology onto others. "White Fragility," a term coined by Robin DiAngelo, is a type of projection bias from repressed emotions of unacknowledged White privilege.[54] It includes accusations to others about one's own behaviors. Projection bias is the opposite of patronization bias, applying a victimization-perpetrator mindset to oneself in a way that warps reality and relationships.

Diversity Circles help teachers resist projection bias with action-reflection about

- Patterns of educators or students of all backgrounds attributing their own racism or denials of racism to others.
- White Fragility versus double-consciousness anxiety.
- Defensive transferences of cultural stress and aggression.
- Exclusions, preferences, and decisions from perceptions of power inequalities, founded or unfounded, that sew chaos into social interactions by expressing misinterpretations, misinformation, and disinformation and otherwise igniting conflicts.

History of Bias in US Education

Despite intermittent desegregation breakthroughs, education in the United States has perpetuated racialized, gendered, and class divisions since European occupation. Bias systems have been enforced from the outside with patriarchal Anglo-conformist violence and funding patterns and from the inside with segregation and assimilation procedures aligned with elitist networks of institutional rankings. From colonial times onward, educators, most of whom have been European American, have operated assimilation routines in step with the racially stratified economic substructure-social superstructure. US systemic racism was initiated through land conquest; displacing, enslaving, and killing Indigenous peoples; chattel slavery of Africans; and cheap labor extracted from other workers of color. The racial divide is between White owners, managers, and professionals over White labor on one side and free and low-wage labor of people of color on the other.[55] Figure 3.4 shows how systemic bias operates currently in education.[56]

Teachers reproduce systemic bias during hourly and daily decisions that perpetuate cultural preferences and aversions to rank students, limit curriculum, and distort knowledge construction. Teachers teach how we were taught, generalizing from personal-cultural conditioning. We decide to whom to grant high expectations and what viewpoints are permitted in classrooms, labs, and meeting rooms. Our decisions operate Anglo-conformity, conveying patriarchal and elitist White superiority. Teachers, most of whom have been European American, unconsciously wield White privilege cultural capital – artifacts, practices, and beliefs about White superiority, developed from childhood into adulthood – to reinforce US systemic bias.[57]

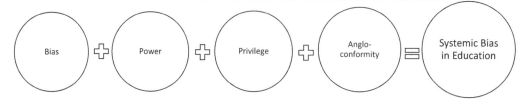

FIGURE 3.4 Bias Plus Power graphic. Created by the author.

White privilege, however, is a double-edged sword that manifests as White Fragility – defensive fight, freeze, and flight reactions to cling to power – guarding insiders and excising outsiders.[58] White privilege behaviors include the following:

- Selective listening.
- Conspiratorial, angry, and sarcastic tones.
- Denial of advantages.
- Self-justifying words and assumptions language.
- Emotional ranting about suspicions, accusations, and stereotypes.
- Opportunity hoarding.
- Self-segregation.[59]

White Fragility manifests in classroom and hallway conflicts, politicized committee meetings, and heated debates in the lounge room. Culture conflict undermines the humanization goals that motivate the profession by spreading social anxiety about scarce resources, technology in education, and ideologies in standards. Mostly European American educators, implicitly defensive about the mainstream culture to which they identify, unconsciously reinforce professional homogeneity, operate cultural tiers in curriculum, and divide groups of students. Culture clashes in education, a core institution in the social superstructure, reproduces segmented outcomes according to the systemic bias cultural divisions, thereby supplying tiered inputs for the stratified economic substructure.

Early Example of Assimilation Curriculum

Four-by-six-inch colonial hornbooks (one of the first forms of curriculum written in English in the land now called the United States), were small paddles etched with assimilation content for European American children. Colonial hornbooks illustrate how European American teachers prioritized the English language and European American cultural images with graphics, numbers, letters, and biblical quotes to teach allegiance to Eurocentric individualism and a hierarchical social-economic order believed to be God-given. The Anglo-conformist order conveyed in the hornbooks prepared some European American children for labor and others for higher education and leadership roles. Meanwhile, children of color living in the land were excluded from the curriculum altogether, expected to become free or very cheap labor, or annihilated.[60]

White colonial students physically draped the compact hornbooks around their necks with leather string toggles, much like today's ubiquitous smartphones that students and teachers carry everywhere, shown in the visual below.[61] Colonial students used hornbooks, like smartphones fisted in the hand for work and play, for academic learning and as paddles for a badminton-type games. Their Anglo-conformist content was not only linguistic but also social, emotional, and kinesthetic.[62]

Though 400 years apart, content represented by hornbooks and smartphones alike reinforces stereotypes and cultural siloes through body-mind activities patterned into economic substructure-social superstructure systems. As US curriculum developed, it continued to communicate Anglo-conformist assumptions and divisions between leaders versus labor for "agricultural age" and "mechanistic-industrial" economies. Contemporary US curriculum is delivered in cyber platforms that spread social media disinformation and dehumanize by

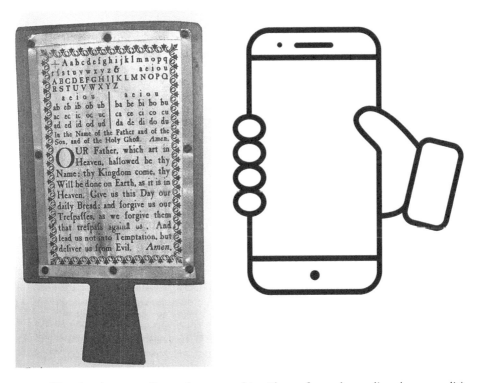

FIGURE 3.5 Hornbook versus Smartphone graphic. Photo from the earliest known edition of *The New England Primer* by Paul Leicester Ford (1899).

replacing face-to-face interactions with cyber algorithms accelerating the dissemination of Anglo-conformist assumptions and divisions. In this way, explicit curriculum reproduces tiers - globalized corporations and owners versus consumers and labor - that comprise the "technology-services" economy to perpetuate wealth inequities in the current "information-solar age."[63]

What makes bias in contemporary US education fundamentally different from the colonial epoch is climate change. The immediate future of life on Earth is in jeopardy, the stress of which sharpens cultural defensiveness. Systemic bias currently divides peoples during an epoch when unity is needed to reduce over-consumption, pollution, and fossil fuel emissions *en masse*. Education needs to increase recycle and reuse efforts in infrastructure and campus community routines to support global health. Education needs to value diversity in knowledge and curriculum for inclusive ecosystems restoration and participation in a green economy. This is why holistic antibias-antiracist educators apply a growth mindset to cultural awareness with sustainability actions. We implement procedures to engage superdiverse students in biodiversity well-being projects, facilitating academic engagement for holism experiences now.

White Supremacy, White Superiority, and Anglo-Conformity

Educators fear confronting the White supremacy, White superiority, and Anglo-conformity continuum at school. It's easier to be colorblind. However, courageous conversations and actions are unavoidable if we're to reduce bias systems that distort knowledge and undermine inclusive student achievement and diversity in our profession.

White supremacy is the conviction that White people should dominate society because they are superior to all other racialized groups. White supremacy, as executed through vigilante action, is the "frightening and highly visible reminder of the violence which has often characterized the enforcement of the racial order."[64] White supremacist spokespersons claim that "the legitimate authorities are always too weak, naïve, or corrupt to maintain the 'true' identity" of the United States. White supremacists aggressively act "to restore 'white honor' and a 'just' racial order," trying to recapture a "formerly privileged status" of yesteryear originally taken violently.[65] White supremacy is the enforcement of White superiority beliefs in Anglo-conformist policies and assimilation practices that are operated or tolerated, often unconsciously, by ordinary people in institutions, such as everyday teachers at school.[66]

Indigenous Education Example

One historical example of how Anglo-conformist bias harms is the Indigenous experience in US schools. After being forced off homelands, Indigenous families endured reservation housing and unequal access to health care and schools. While many Indigenous parents wanted to keep families together in neighborhood schools with culturally sustaining education, reservation schools were disconnected from the national economy. The majority of Indigenous families either were mandated to board children in faraway schools or found themselves sending children to boarding schools in the hopes of economic opportunity. "By 1926, nearly 83% of Indian school-age children were attending boarding schools. There were more than 350 government funded Indian Boarding schools in 30 states during the 19th and 20th centuries, enrolling over 100,000 children."[67]

However, rather than graduating Indigenous youth with humanizing knowledge and skills for the national economy, White educator bias in boarding schools dehumanized students and perpetuated substandard segregated outcomes. "By failing to provide a safe, healthy environment in which students could live and learn, and by failing to maintain an honest and timely dialogue with parents, boarding school officials alienated those American Indian families who most wanted their children to be educated."[68] For instance, White educators prevented Indigenous children from visiting with their families and communities for years at a time. White educators not only stripped Native American youth of traditional food and clothing and cut their hair, citing hygiene reasons, but also forbade speaking Indigenous languages.

Moreover, White educators didn't adequately meet basic physical and mental health needs, including basic nutrition and physical safety, of many boarded children. White educators inflicted corporal punishment as a matter of course. Rather than academic time-on-task, boarding schools were rampant with illness. "Communicable diseases flourished in the Indian boarding schools, and many students contracted serious diseases," such as measles, influenza, tuberculosis, trachoma, small pox, and meningitis.[69] Thus, as illustrated by the dehumanizing assimilation experiences of many Indigenous students, colorblind White educators perpetuate systemic bias by defaulting to inequitable Anglo-conformist policies.

Segregation and Unequal Funding

Colorblind educators who convey implicit bias are an important piece in the systemic racism puzzle. Bias is perpetuated across institutions. The more structurally competent teachers of all backgrounds become, the more empowered we are to collaborate for change. In recent decades, housing policies and patterns have produced *de facto* school segregation. Because schools are funded by family income and neighborhood taxes, income inequality has increased segregation between schools in poorer parts of cities versus affluent outer-urban and suburban regions. "The level of school segregation for black and Latino students has been steadily increasing since the 1980s.... [I]n 1997, only 5 percent of segregated White schools faced conditions of concentrated poverty, compared with 80 percent of segregated black and Latino schools."[70] Segregation and wealth gaps thus intersect.

Segregation divides classes and bifurcates cultures. White students and those of color live alienated from one another, and ethnic and linguistic groups live separated. "More than 60 years after the *Brown v. Board of Education* (1954) decision declared segregated schooling inherently unequal, Black and Latina/o students are still very likely to attend schools that are doubly segregated by race and poverty, and students attending segregated Latina/o schools are likely to experience additional segregation by language."[71] Accordingly, segregated schools signify unequal spending and disparate learning opportunities. Moreover, school segmentations interfere with cross-racial trust and multicultural communication. Segregation in schools and housing is both a symptom and a source of systemic racism.

Anglo-conformist program exclusions and academic tracking starts in early childhood education:

> Black children represent 18% of preschool enrollment but 48% of preschool children receiving more than one out-of-school suspension. In comparison White students represent 43% of preschool enrollment but 26% of preschool children receiving more than one out-of-school-suspension.[72]

This unequal access to academic engagement perpetuates through high school:

> Black students are suspended and expelled at three times the rate of White students. On average, 5% of White students are suspended compared with 16% of Black students. American Indian and Native Alaskan students are also disproportionately suspended and expelled, representing less than 1% of the student population but 2% of out-of-school suspensions and 3% of expulsions.[73]

While White students are bestowed more access to top-tier gifted-and-talented programs and advanced college-track academics, students of color are often denied such access, spending more time abiding by low academic expectations and experiencing cultural alienation from Anglo-conformist curriculum and instruction.

Segregation continues into higher education, with elite universities enrolling greater percentages of White and Asian students than other institutions of higher learning. Moreover, high-income students (most of whom are White and Asian) complete college with a BA/BS at a 60% rate, while the completion rate for low-income students (most of whom are Black, Latinx, Indigenous, and Pacific Islander) is 14%.[74]

> [W]e have ended up with systemically unequal funding in higher education. We have settled on a national framework, state by state, where public, nonprofit, and private funds for higher education are distributed in an inequitable manner, with disproportionally high levels of funding distributed to students from upper-middle- and upper-income families, while disproportionally low level are distributed to students from moderate- and low-income families.[75]

Discriminatory funding formulas throughout the education system are reinforced by assimilation curriculum and instruction delivered on site, which doles out well-funded, culturally congruent, and high-expectations education to some but perpetuating poorly funded, culturally alienating, and low-expectations education to others. For example, only 5% of segregated White schools face conditions of concentrated poverty, compared with 80% of Black and Latinx schools. Furthermore, most states spend less in high-minority school districts, with a gap averaging nationally at $1,099 for each student.[76] Spending differences worsen already racially lopsided placements in special education and gifted-and-talented programs. In this way, the cultural conditioning of Anglo-conformity steers funding unequally into segregated schools. In higher education, community colleges, which serve proportionately more students of color than other institutions, receive "the least amount of funding per fulltime equivalent student" than all other institutions. For instance, California community colleges receive $8,099 per student from the taxpayer, compared with the $32,593 per student received by elite public universities such as UC Berkeley and UCLA.[77]

> This unequal system is marked by an academic-versus-vocational divide. White and wealthy students are far more likely to be labeled as high-ability or gifted and placed in high-level classes and in programs for those assumed to be college-bound. At the same time, low-income students, African Americans, and Latinos are disproportionately identified as less able and placed in lower-level groups and classes.[78]

African American, Latinx, and Indigenous children are more likely to be identified as having a "learning disability" than European American or Asian American children and are denied access to "high-level" and "college-bound" opportunities that would lead to economic inclusion. Instead, White middle-income and wealthy students occupy those spots to "dominate society," thereby reinforcing segregation and wealth inequality.[79]

Further, racist disciplinary patterns not only drive students of color away from a sense of belonging in education but also curtail access to academic engagement. These biases reduce the opportunity for active learning between teachers and minority students. Often, White students are afforded the most academic conversations at school, while African American students are disproportionately reprimanded for talking with peers, even talking about homework.[80] Thus, well-intentioned educators unconsciously facilitate Anglo-conformist curriculum from deep-seated White superiority stereotypes to limit academic engagement in a segregated system.

White teachers of middle-class backgrounds are perplexed by what they don't perceive. For example, teachers often don't understand how cultural differences and unpredictable home experiences derail homework completion. They may not relate to domestic conditions unconducive to study, such as unreliable internet, noisy distractions, absence of partnered caregivers, overcrowded homes, before- and after-school work shifts, and lack of academic dialogue outside school. It's hard for many teachers to imagine a domicile without a desk dedicated to academic concentration. On top of that, inequitable punitive policies lower expectations, remove students from academic engagement, and ultimately hinder academic success.[81]

For instance, African American students, particularly males, are disproportionately subjected to negative disciplinary actions more than any other ethnic group, including other students of color. In contrast, White teachers apply culturally congruent "warm demander" directives and give high expectations to White students, whose home lives are culturally congruent with their own. These biases are unintentional misunderstandings about the academic engagement of Black male students living in challenging, oftentimes impoverished, conditions, in contrast to a general familiarity with the mainstreamed home lives of White students.[82]

Synthesizing Antibias Theory and Practice into US Education

Routinely, everyday teachers deal with at least ten forms of bias. Systemic bias from economic substructure-social superstructure segregation and assimilation patterns fuels the racial achievement gap and distorts knowledge. Unequal funding, racial divisions, site and program tiering, and other Anglo-conformist procedures undermine teacher capacity to humanize inclusively at school. Patterns rooted in White supremacy aggression and White superiority beliefs impact all sectors of US education.

Repairing systemic inequities involves cross-institutional changes with reparative justice policies and practices operated from a position of love. Antibias-antiracist holistic education gathers people who are otherwise invested in preserving privilege and power tiers into the unity experiences. Changing race, class, and gender inequities is hard work, involving collaborative ground-up solutions to replace divisions intergenerationally. Transformative teachers use Multicultural Mindfulness to invite peace and joy experiences into cultural awareness as we diversify curriculum and integrate diverse students into academic high expectations with world-healing activities. Transformative teachers synthesize multicultural perspectives into hands-on knowledge and curriculum indoors with nature and outdoors. We model culturally creative equity and sustainability interactions, forgiving one another for mistakes along the way and changing education one classroom, lab, meeting room, and campus at a time.

MULTICULTURAL MINDFULNESS ACTIVITY

4-Rs Antibias Practice

Outcome

- Define and discuss the 4-Rs Antibias Practice.
- Apply the *Recognize* step of the 4-Rs Antibias Practice.

Key Concepts

- **Bias**: Any feeling or belief that results in and justifies divisive and unfair decisions, such as favoritism or exclusions.
- **Culture Competence**: Cultural awareness activated with antibias-antiracist skills for cross-cultural respect and compassion from understanding cultures and biases within intersectional systems.
- **4-Rs Antibias Practice**:
   1. *Recognize* – Breathe to name bias feelings and thoughts in body and mind.
   2. *Refrain* – Breathe to pause from emotional reactions that perpetuate suffering, unfairness, or unwarranted divisions.
   3. *Restorative Action* – Breathe to respond mindfully, taking healing action with open-minded questions and cultural listening for diverse perspectives and practices.
   4. *Resolve* – Breathe to act to reduce bias and participate in reparative justice.

Resources

- Paper, pencils, board or sidewalk chalk, an example or symbol of natural food, a place to meet indoors or outdoors.

Big-Picture Question

- How do I apply culture competence now?

Start

In whole group circle:

- **Discuss** bias by holding a natural food example or symbol: Why do you like or dislike this food?
- **Discuss**: What are the cultural identities of two close friends?
- **Discuss**: What do you like and dislike about this week's academic subject? Why?
- **Discuss**: What's bias?

In diversified project teams:

- **Collaboratively write** a question about bias. For example:
  1. Why do we trust some people but not others?
  2. What cultures inform this week's academic subject? What's the evidence of cultural representation in the subject? Is the subject's cultural representation authentic, or is it biased toward the dominant culture or just about one culture, thereby lacking in cross-cultural comparison?
  3. What are the stereotypes in this week's academic subject?
- A member from each group **writes** the agreed-upon question on the board.
- All students **rotate** to checkmark a favorite question from a *different* group. The teacher erases questions with the least checks between rounds until one question remains.
- Using the question for circle discussion, everyone **takes notes** about bias.
- **Collaborate** on a definition of bias using discussion notes.

Middle

- Individually, students **make two columns** to craft a bias worksheet about a required subject:

  1. Like & Recognize (why?)
  2. Dislike & Recognize (why?)

- Students **list** likes and dislikes of facts, theories, and perspectives in the curriculum, naming a *Recognize* reason for each perception.

Closing

- In small groups, students **discuss** how to *Recognize* bias triggers by describing personal reasons for liking and disliking things in the curriculum.
- Ask small groups to **tabulate** reasons. The group with the most different *Recognize* reasons wins.
- In a whole circle, **discuss** how the *Recognize* step reveals likes and dislikes rooted in assumptions.
- **Discuss** how bias is human; it is categorizing likes and dislikes, but it's important to try to reduce social bias by asking why, what's my evidence, and increasing open-mindedness to the diversity that defines sustainability.

Discuss

1. *Recognize* – Identify emotional triggers for likes and dislikes.
2. *Refrain* – Use prevention strategies to avoid jumping to conclusions and acting on assumptions or stereotypes.
3. *Restorative Action* – Heal bias with non-defensive inquiry on the spot.
4. *Resolve* – Participate in activities for long-term antibias solutions.

Application

How Do We Make Holistic Antibias-Antiracist Decisions?

The Three Transformative Tools – Diversity Circles, Multicultural Mindfulness, and Approach-in-Dimension – start with Culture-Conscious Listening. This practice, explained in Chapter 1, unites with breathwork, prosocial body language, and open-minded reflection to calm perceptions and make better decisions. One Culture-Conscious Listening topic of concentration is intersectionality, using a "women of color" lens.[83] This focus invites a feminist interpretation into "the question of race first."[84] Women of color and other intersectional constructs reveal holistic interpretations about lived experiences – such as multicultural variations about motherhood and the subtleties of systemic racism, sexism, and classism. Holistic antibias-antiracist decisions challenge divisive economic procedures with inclusion consciousness about, as bell hooks puts it, "that moment when an individual woman or child, who may have thought she was all alone, began feminist uprising, began to name her practice, indeed began to formulate theory from lived experience."[85] By resisting "racialized hierarchies" with intersectional reflection, we encourage "multiple voices to enter the dialogue…of civic involvement."[86]

Intersectional interpretations spotlight "taken-for-granted cultural schemas and social practices that structure belonging." They help to re-imagine "civic identities" with multicultural alliances. When applied to education, intersectional consciousness confronts bias with the jolt of visionary curiosity that sparks cultural creativity to diversify academic engagement in astonishing ways. Applying a wide lens to the "formation of citizenship" energizes curriculum and knowledge transformation with "multiple identities, languages, and global sensibilities."[87] Multicultural intersections are part of intergenerational sustainability. The women-of-color construct develops culture consciousness for systemic change.

> The phrase women of color…makes clear that Black women are not the only women of color…. [The phrase] is part of their struggle to be recognized with dignity for their humanity, racial heritage, and cultural heritage as they work within the women's movement in the United States.[88]

Thus, intersectional Culture-Conscious Listening opens "third ear" understanding to overlapping diversities to connect academic engagement to the world with more accuracy.[89]

Conventional multicultural education and diversity trainings teach *about* stereotypes, using a US perspective about race, class, *or* gender categories. However, these trainings do not relate culture to *superdiversity* in *biodiversity*. Conventional diversity trainings do not connect academics to transcultural race, class, *and* gender interactions in a global context. However, prioritizing cross-cultural intersections in disciplines and subjects deepens diversity consciousness with race-class-gender awareness, which is necessary for *holistic* actions to address climate change. Whereas assimilation and segregation patterns misrepresent the "academic identity" of students of color and White students, intersectional diversity activities engage culture as "a process of regeneration, revitalization, restoration, and decolonization" to "enter the historical process as responsible Subjects."[90] We use intersectional analysis to ask questions about evidence for cultural emotions and assumptions. As we bust stereotypes, we guide "empowerment and social justice" decisions with *unity* solutions in our shared environment.[91]

How Do We Desegregate Schools?

We know working teachers say they feel less comfortable and less prepared to deal with bias and divisions than in previous decades. We also know diversity education helps. Almost twice the number of teachers who receive meaningful "diversity/multicultural education" report the ability to confront biased remarks than those who didn't receive training: 75% versus 42%.[92] Diversity education raises culture consciousness, making it harder to default to bias habits. Transformative diversity education invites educators to be part of systemic change. We learn how to de-stratify students classroom by classroom and reinterpret curriculum with multiple perspectives for academic holism.

Multicultural Mindfulness practices – such as the four holistic "nonviolent direct action" steps for change: collection of facts, negotiation, self-purification, and direct action from the Civil Rights era – bring peace to change.[93] Nonviolent solutions counter "broader social and political structures that exacerbate education inequality" by revealing colorblind racism and inserting color-conscious reparations. For example, direct action was taken to implement the goals of the 1954 *Brown v. Board of Education* decision to end legal segregation in public schools. Though temporary – occurring primarily during the 1960s and '70s in specific cases when diverse children were bused cross-district – desegregation innovations display evidence of education transformation.[94] Some desegregation efforts continued through the 1990s, when public magnet schools progressed from desegregation experiments into integrative academic arts programs – such as in districts in Florida and Chicago, which were still under court orders to desegregate.[95]

However, other studies show that desegregation does not necessarily translate into *academic* integration. Patterns from cumulative bias decisions made by well-intentioned participants working under "ostensive" race-neutral policies still end up sorting and separating students and knowledge to perpetuate the racial achievement gap.[96] Tied to the ideology of meritocracy and individualism, colorblind racism fuels inequity systems when mostly White teachers make bias decisions from the unconscious stereotypes about students of color. The key is to implement antibias-antiracist holism *experiences* by incorporating big-picture humanization activities into academic routines. Transformative teachers integrate desegregated schools by "un-standardizing" and "detracking" academic interactions with culture-conscious criteria for inclusion.[97] We reshape education space, time, materials, and learning environments with intersectional sustainability designs.

Transformative teachers use transparent big-picture diversity rubrics, like the Approach-in-Dimension, to plan and assess academic activities constructed to last "three or six months" from now, and beyond, guided by systemic equity criteria.[98] We explicitly hire diverse colleagues to disseminate Multicultural Mindfulness practices and develop culture competence through multiracial alliances to infuse "liberatory design" across departments and communities.[99] Inside classrooms, we facilitate Diversity Circles with culture and nature examples during academic engagement. We balance out rows that perpetuate deficiency-versus-superiority and punishment-versus-reward divisions with, instead, circle arrangements, getting outdoors whenever possible. We diversify textbooks, artifacts, manipulatives, and media with multicultural criteria for holistic lesson planning, worksheets, unit projects, labs, classroom libraries, and performance outcomes. We do cumulative work because hourly and daily decisions are the crux of liberation from a position of love. Our cultural actions reinterpret overstandardization and bureaucratic stagnation *with* diverse students and colleagues to shift from dehumanization divisions to inclusive humanization.

116 Big-Picture Transformation in the Real World

What's Mindfulness Praxis?

Paulo Freire explains that transformation is "the organized struggle" for "discovery." Liberation "cannot be purely intellectual but must involve action; nor can it be limited to mere activism, but must include serious reflection: only then will it be a praxis."[100] Vietnamese peace activist Thich Nhat Hanh explains *mindfulness* praxis as making "every action of our body more serene, and we become the master of our body and mind. Mindfulness nurtures the power of concentration in us."[101] Thich Nhat Hanh describes how transformative practitioners are present with suffering: "It is important that we are aware of these ugly, dangerous things in the world [such as] war, sexism, social injustice, racial discrimination, economic inequality, and hunger and starvation…so that we can begin to improve the situation." Thich Nhat Hanh emphasizes calm healing.

> If day after day, we are only in contact with our anxieties and our anger about what is ugly and corrupt, we will lose our joy and our ability to serve others.… Without mindfulness our actions are often hurried and abrupt.… When any action is placed in the light of mindfulness, the body and mind become relaxed, peaceful, and joyful.[102]

Therefore, mindfulness praxis integrates academics into holistic body-mind-culture-environment routines for peace during core routines.

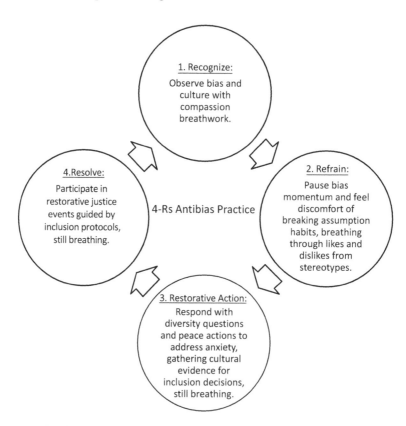

FIGURE 3.6   4-Rs Antibias Practice graphic. Created by the author.

Examples

4-Rs Antibias Practice

"Mindfulness" is popular for a reason. When practiced well, it heals suffering with three principles – interbeing, emptiness, and impermanence – for living compassion.[103] Multicultural Mindfulness uses these principles to engage culture with an expanded sense of love strengthened through body-mind breathwork, mind-culture nourishment, and culture-environment action, hourly and daily. Holism practices reduce bias defensiveness during routines. They question stereotypes about students and colleagues and help us consider cultures in curriculum. Rooted in thousands of years of Buddhist practice and science,[104] mindfulness assuages fear. The *4-Rs Antibias Practice*, adapted from the work of Thich Nhat Hanh, develops courage for open-minded change in education.[105]

First, the educator reflectively breathes to *Recognize* present moment bias, noting its fluid nature, seen and unseen, and how it divides. Second, the educator breathes to *Refrain* from reacting with bias to make unfair decisions. The educator embraces the discomfort of breaking bias habits. While abstaining from a bias action or inaction, the educator notices assumptions and feelings of preference or aversion. Third, the educator breathes for *Restorative Action*, asking antibias questions for evidence to perceive cultures respectfully and to motivate inclusion action. Such restorative inquiry brings clarity to confusion and specifies suffering, distinguishing feelings from data to invite liberation pathways. Finally, the educator breathes to *Resolve* to resist replicating unfair systems. This involves compassionately participating in multicultural reconciliation activities with reparative norms from a position of love. Commitment to equity in diversity anchors collaborations in holistic academic design, implementation, and assessment activities for sustainability.

Classroom Application

1. *Recognize* means spotting bias during classroom, lab, or meeting room interactions with reflective breathwork hourly and daily. We ask questions to notice assumptions from the dominant culture, observing privileged and marginalized access to academic engagement. We look to perceive if an individual, of any background, is unfairly asked to explain racism or a culture or if someone isn't being compassionately questioned about assimilation or segregation projections. We look to see if opportunities exist for an array of cultural voices. We acknowledge "how sloppy and how embarrassing" Anglo-conformity is by alienating students and cultural perspectives. We breathe to take responsibility for "neurotic" assimilation or segregation thoughts and behaviors, observing us-versus-them divisions that undermine civility.[106]
2. *Refrain* means applying breathwork to pause the momentum of bias in body-mind-culture circuitry, asking "do I still want to do it?"[107] We gently rework reactions from assumptions and stereotypes, such as reshuffling collaborations mid-stream to correct cultural imbalances or asking a librarian to locate multicultural resources to diversify knowledge development. Refraining is acting on the awareness "that racism, sexism, and class elitism shape the structure of classrooms, creating a lived reality of insider versus outsider that is predetermined, often in place before any class discussion begins."[108] We allow for the discomfort of anxiety during change. We use this energy to spark academic redesigns on the

spot, including flexible deadlines, multimodal alternatives, and open-ended questions. We break from vertical arrangements and facilitate cross-cultural liberation circles, indoors with nature and outdoors, during subject engagement.

3 *Restorative Action* is taking concrete steps to address harm from the bias we have recognized. It includes "joyful and just" projects with evidence-based story sharing, circle questions, and world-healing actions. We curate education to be a "humble" refuge to "respectfully learn"[109] how to detrack programs, invite academic inclusion, and organize big-picture learning community themes.

4 *Resolve* is "a further completing of that surrendering process." It is to "commit yourself as a traveler on the path" of holistic healing for the long haul.[110] We participate in bias prevention procedures. We use nonviolent communication and amends-making protocols. Hourly and daily, we collaborate on restorative design, implementation, and evaluation for sustainable equity systems, developing culture competence with structural competence during academic engagement.

FIGURE 3.7 Action to Reduce Stereotypes and Bias in Education graphic. Created by the author.

Conclusion

Holistic Antibias-Antiracist Decisions Transform

Like all humans, US educators can't escape systemic bias, which in this historical moment runs on underregulated economic substructure-social superstructure stratifications. However, we can reduce bias in our orbit. We can collaborate on antibias-antiracist decisions to transform school space, time, materials, and learning environments with cultural authenticity activities. Developing structural competence in organized Diversity Circles and culture competence with peaceful Multicultural Mindfulness practices, transformative teachers design and assess academics for belonging in diversity. We use big-picture guideposts, such as in the Approach-in-Dimension rubric, to determine a philosophy of humanity for unity planning and evaluation. We implement sustainability designs for social justice from a position of love to decrease bias in space over time. We swap cultural preferences and omissions in materials for multicultural content activated by holistic circle learning with nature, indoors and outdoors.

Transformative teachers change mainstream education with culture compassion activities. We understand that bias is a human condition. We recognize that bias is sorting and separating resources to meet perceived needs. Bias is any agreeable or disagreeable perception of a thing, sensed as feelings in the body and expressed as thoughts and actions from the mind. Bias reactions to cultural assumptions and social expectations prompt fight, freeze, and flight decisions to favor or exclude. Unfortunately, systemic inequities fuel stereotypes behind bias decisions that dehumanize people and destroy the environment.

That's why transformative teachers patiently resist ten forms of bias at school. Most educators make unconscious bias decisions day-in and day-out to further the dominant culture by restricting cultural diversity in curriculum, knowledge, and interactions. Unintentionally, we perpetuate race, gender, and class divides in academic tracks, culturally stratified achievement outcomes, and one-way communications. We sanction segmented socialization. We evaluate academic failure versus success from cultural preferences written into rubrics. We punish, pass, and reward stereotypes. We value the cultures we understand in the way we do subject design and delivery. Because most of us live and work in segregated conditions, we're conditioned to divide. However, nonviolent direct action nurtures cross-cultural relationships and advances equity breakthroughs.

Transformative teachers reform in diversity alliances to grow culture competence with structural competence while connecting subjects to world-healing events. Liberation theory recognizes that cultural trauma won't heal itself. Social action guided by reflection assuages defensiveness and territoriality by integrating diversity questions into academic development. Transformative teachers desegregate segregated sites through multicultural alliances with protocols for social trust while thwarting conflict from cultural gaslighting, hypocrisies, and false equivalents. We apply antibias-antiracist analysis to fact-check disinformation. We address implicit bias with holistic breathwork and other mindfulness practices to calm social anxiety. Transformative teachers don't ignore hurtful stereotypes when friends utter them. We rectify the absence of diversity in curriculum without falling into the trap of tokenizing or asking individuals to explain whole cultures or racism. We break the impulse to patronize or default to cultural deficiency assumptions. We unify over humanity's precarious state with global warming, researching cultural wrongdoing to guide reparations.

Education is a core institution in the systemic bias network that cycles economic and social stratifications and environmental demise. In a feedback loop, racialized wealth disparities and corporate interests undermine equity and sustainability outcomes from school. More than half the students attending K-12 schools in the US are of color, while 80% of teachers are White, and student diversity is growing.[111] The US is home to more immigrants than anywhere else in the world, almost a fifth of the global total. Currently, the US population includes 14% foreign-born, similar to the wave of immigration in the twentieth century.[112] While, historically, US education has dealt with diversity through assimilation and segregation, transformative teachers work *with* diversity, embracing it fully. We recognize bias, refrain from reacting unfairly, take restorative action for inclusion, and resolve culture conflicts with justice procedures.

Transformative teachers interact with living cultures in a superdiverse and biodiverse context. We understand that everyone must prepare for "the new economy" with green humanization skills.[113] Our students develop emotional intelligence and cultural awareness to apply subjects to vocational skills that will help repair a struggling planet. Yet most teachers are undertrained in multicultural education, environmental education, and mindfulness education. We operate individualism in ranked sites amid a violent world weaponized by the military industrial complex and accelerating climate catastrophes. However, we learn how to balance individualism with collectivism in Diversity Circles that reduce cultural barriers to liberation. We activate Multicultural Mindfulness to bridge divisions by replacing cultural assumptions with evidence during high-expectations academics. We regulate defensive emotions and bust stereotypes by reshaping subjects with culturally responsive education. We reach out to diversify our profession. We join other transformative teachers to use big-picture diversity rubrics, such as the Approach-in-Dimension. We *act* to unify academics with multicultural imagination. Guided by data we gather about equity, we *reflect* on the environment through culture to adapt to change and to advance change for holism with diverse students now.

TRANSFORMATIVE BREATHWORK AND JOURNAL

Journal Question: *How Do Anglo-Conformity and White Supremacy Impact My Classroom?*

> Mindfulness… is like swimming: you swim along in your phenomenal world. You can't just float, you have to swim; you have to use your limbs. That process of using your limbs is the basic stroke of mindfulness and awareness. It is the "flash" quality of it – you flash onto things. So you are swimming constantly.[114]
>
> –Chögyam Trungpa Rinpoche

Breathwork

Wherever you are, take a mindful moment to relax. Use a timer chime if you like. Close or lid your eyes, taking several slow deep breaths, smiling slightly, noticing sensations: smells, sounds, touch, taste, and sight (if your eyes are open).

Now breathe while internally reciting the *gatha* below:

Breathing in, I calm my body.
Breathing out, I smile.
Dwelling in the present moment,
I know this is a truth moment.[115]

Then:

Breathing in **How do Anglo-conformity and White supremacy impact my classroom?**
Breathing out openness.

Repeat for as long as you like or until the timer chimes.

Journal

Imagine we're in a Diversity Circle with the transformative practitioners cited in this book. We want to support superdiverse student success in a biodiverse world. Read our answers below. Reflect on your meditation. Briefly answer the journal question above in a way that's meaningful to you.

Milton Gordon

- *Anglo-conformity*:

    "The desirability of maintaining English institutions, the English language, and English-oriented cultural patterns as dominant and standard in American life."[116]

Ibram X. Kendi

White supremacy:

- "[White supremacists] wave Confederate flags and defend Confederate monuments, even though the Confederacy started a civil war that ended with more than five hundred thousand White American lives lost – more than every other American war combined."
- "White Supremacists love what America used to be, even though America used to be – and still is – teeming with millions of struggling White people."
- "White Supremacists blame non-White people for the struggles of White people when any objective analysis of their plight primarily implicates the rich White [politicians] they support."
- "White supremacy is nothing short of an ongoing program of genocide against the White race. In fact, it's more than that: White supremacist is code for anti-human, a nuclear ideology that poses an existential threat to human existence."[117]

George I. Sánchez

White supremacy:

- The ideology of White superiority that rationalizes segregation and discrimination, such as "IQ testing" normed to White bias in US education.

- White supremacy is "the root of the problem" and "the segregated school is a concentration camp – you may gold plate the fence posts and silver plate the bobbed [sic] wire and hang garlands of roses all the way around it, it is still a concentration camp."
- Antibias-antiracist educators are "the advance agents of the new social order" who weed out "White supremacy" as the root of US education failures, such as segregation and the racial achievement gap.[118]

Michael Omi and Howard Winant

White supremacy:

- The "new white identity" has a strong affinity "to biological notions of race and racial purity which render it fairly similar to the racism prevalent at the turn of the century."
- The "frightening and highly visible reminder of the violence which has often characterized the enforcement of the racial order."
- White supremacists claim that "the legitimate authorities are always too weak, naïve, or corrupt to maintain America's 'true' identity."
- White supremacists take actions "to restore 'white honor' and a 'just' racial order," trying to recapture a "formerly privileged status."[119]

Micaela Rubalcava

The White supremacy root of Anglo-conformity is

- Dehumanizing assimilation and segregation experiences in Eurocentric institutions perpetuating the dominant culture through over-standardization invested in systemic racism.
- White superiority rationalization for dehumanization, such as cultural profiling, land-seizing, enslavement, cheap labor procedures, mass incarceration, homelessness and substandard housing cycles, and food deserts.[120]
- Cultural censorship, such as book-banning and replacing arts and sciences with disinformation.
- Violent and fundamentalist clinging to White privilege in racialized inequity systems maintained by corporatism.
- Stereotypes to justify caste-like color-based economic-social outcomes that dehumanize all people, deplete natural resources, and destroy life on Earth.[121]

Notes

1. Derman-Sparks (1989), 3.
2. Reece (2022), 172.
3. hooks (1994), 26.
4. Gordon (1991), 249.
5. King (1964), 79–80.
6. Au, Brown and Calderón (2016); Paris and Alim (2017); Frankenberg, Garces and Hopkins (2016); Hotez (2023); Ingersoll and Smith (2003); Lewis and Diamond (2015).
7. Gramlish (2023, April 6).
8. Banks, Suárez-Orozco and Ben-Peretz (2016); Kendi (2019); Lewis and Diamond (2015).
9. Banks (all); Derman-Sparks (1989).

10 Kendi (2019), 13.
11 King (1964), 79.
12 Derman-Sparks (1989).
13 Hanh and Weare (2017).
14 Bond, Quintero, Casey and Di Carlo (2015); Banks (all); Howe and Lisi (2019); Ingersoll and Smith (2003); Sleeter (all).
15 Bigelow and Swinehart (2014).
16 Ladson-Billings and Tate (2006), 26.
17 Takaki (all); Dunbar-Ortiz (2014).
18 Butler (1989); Fiol-Matta and Chamberlain (1994); hooks (1994).
19 Derman-Sparks (1989), 3.
20 Banks (all); DiAngelo (2018); Emdin (2016); Howe v Lisi (2019); Kendi (2019); Staats (2015, Winter); Perkins (2006); Rubalcava (2001–2024).
21 Aronson and Laughter (2016); Gay (2000); Ladson-Billings (1995).
22 Merriam-Webster (n.d.).
23 Derman-Sparks (1989), 3.
24 Merriam-Webster.
25 Takaki (all).
26 hooks (1994), 29.
27 Omi and Winant (1986), 61–62.
28 Oakes and Lipton (2007), 19; Deruy (2017).
29 Lewis and Diamond (2015); Freire (1985).
30 Sleeter (all).
31 Sleeter (2001).
32 Sleeter and Zavala (2020).
33 Lewis and Diamond (2015), 50, xix.
34 Lewis and Diamond (2015), 50, xix.
35 hooks (1994), 34.
36 hooks (1994), 7.
37 Nava (2001); Reece (2022).
38 Woehr (2021).
39 hooks (1994), 35.
40 Strayhorn (2021, October 1).
41 Lewis and Diamond (2015), xvii.
42 Lewis and Diamond (2015), xvii.
43 Au, Brown and Calderón (2016), 109; Barrera (1979); DiAngelo (all); Du Bois (1909); Kendi (2019); McIntosh (1989, July/August); Omi and Winant (1986).
44 Banks (2003); Omi and Winant (1986).
45 Englander (2016), 25.
46 Hardin (1968, December 13); Smith (1776).
47 Howe and Lisi (2019).
48 Staats (2015, Winter).
49 Bland (2018, May 30).
50 Du Bois (1909), 3.
51 Du Bois (1909), 3.
52 Du Bois (1909), 3.
53 Dweck (2007).
54 DiAngelo (2018).
55 Bowles and Gintis (1976); Giroux (1983); Kozol (1991).
56 Howe and Lisi (2019).
57 Howe and Lisi (2019).
58 Bourdieu (1973); DiAngelo (all).
59 DiAngelo (2018); Lewis and Diamond (2015).
60 Johnson, Musial, Hall and Gollnick (2017); Kiefer (2010); Plimpton (1916, October); Spring (all).
61 Kiefer (2010), 68.
62 Kiefer (2010), 68.
63 Gang (1991), 79.
64 Omi and Winant (1986), 118.

65 Omi and Winant (1986), 115, 117.
66 Omi and Winant (1986), 114–118.
67 National Native (2012).
68 Child (1998), 68.
69 Child (1998), 55.
70 Oakes v Lipton (2007), 16.
71 Frankenberg, Garces, and Hopkins (2016), 1.
72 Howe and Lisi (2019), 173.
73 Howe and Lisi (2019), 173.
74 Reece (2022), 16.
75 Reece (2022), 78.
76 Oakes and Lipton (2007), 17.
77 Reece (2022), 81.
78 Oakes and Lipton (2007), 300.
79 Omi and Winant (1986), 118.
80 Bertani, Carroll, Castle, Davies, Hurley, Joos and Scanlon (2010).
81 Bertani, Carroll, Castle, Davies, Hurley, Joos and Scanlon (2010).
82 Loveless (2017, March 22).
83 Butler (1989); Fiol-Matta and Chamberlain (1994).
84 Ladson-Billings and Tate (2006), 26.
85 hooks (1994), 74–75.
86 Suárez-Orozco and Michikyan (2016), 15, 18.
87 Suárez-Orozco and Michikyan (2016), 7, 19, 63.
88 Butler (1989), 146.
89 Madison (all).
90 Freire (1985), 20.
91 Cuauhtin, Zavala, Sleeter and Au (2019), 2.
92 GLSEN (2016), 23.
93 King (1964), 79.
94 Frankenberg, Garces and Hopkins (2016), 1; Oakes and Lipton (2007); Spring (all).
95 Ewing and Hannah-Jones (2018, November 29); Obama (2018).
96 Lewis and Diamond (2015), 160.
97 Lewis and Diamond (2015), 177; Sleeter and Carmona (2017), title.
98 Angelo, Nilson and Winkelmes (2018).
99 Anaissie, Cary, Clifford, Malarkey and Wise (2022).
100 Freire (1985), 52.
101 Hanh (2006), 45.
102 Hanh (2006), 106, 46.
103 Hanh (1998); Trungpa (1993).
104 Hanh and Weare (2017).
105 Hanh (2006).
106 Trungpa (1993), 108.
107 Trungpa (1993), 111.
108 hooks (1994), 83.
109 hooks (1994), 89.
110 Trungpa (1993), 112–113.
111 Ingersoll and Smith (2003).
112 Gjelten (2015); Suárez-Orozco and Michikyan (2016), 8.
113 Johnson, Musial, Hall and Gollnick (2017); Plimpton (1916, October); Reece (2022), 40; Spring (all).
114 Trungpa (1993), 43–44.
115 Hanh (2008), 36.
116 Gordon (1991), 249.
117 Kendi (2019), 132.
118 Au, Brown and Calderón (2016), 108–109, quoting George Sanchez.
119 Omi and Winant (1986), 115–118.
120 Alexander (2010).
121 Wilkerson (2020).

4
STRUCTURAL COMPETENCE FOR TEACHERS

Guiding Purpose
Explain how

- Education is vital to economic-social systems and teachers are central to education.
- The substructure-superstructure model helps teachers visualize structural competence.
- Structural competence empowers teachers as change agents for cultural inclusion.
- Transformative teachers use structural competence to facilitate student-centered academic engagement, professional efficacy, and holistic humanization.
- Transformative teachers develop structural competence with Three Transformative Tools to advance culturally responsive holistic education for global citizenship and participation in a green economy.
- Education in Chile and Finland provides systemic reform lessons to learn from failure and success to develop Environmental Liberation Education.

Provide

- Two Multicultural Mindfulness Activities and one journal question: *Structural Competence Imagination*, *Choice Education versus Equity Education*, and *What's Culture-Conscious Listening for Equity?*

Context

What's Structural Competence?

Structural competence is a skill set to empower teachers as change agents for cultural inclusion.[1] It is critical consciousness to regulate economic and social structures in motion. Structural competence is non-defensive and innovative. It is local action to heal global systems. Transformative teachers collaborate to facilitate academic engagement to prepare students for global citizenship and the "new" green economy in a superdiverse world grappling with biodiversity destruction.[2] We are culture creators when we act with theory rather than theorize without action.

Transformative teachers use structural competence to identify evidence of inequities and ecologically damaging patterns that harm education. We use data to implement holistic classroom, lab, and meeting room activities to connect subjects, cultures, and students to world healing. We invite multiple perspectives into big-picture questions through humanization circles with nature and cultures, indoors or outdoors. We participate in culturally responsive liberation education to apply structural competence to academic activities that weave equity into success.[3]

Structural competence involves translating complex economic and social theories into solutions, which can feel perplexing in the moment. It can cause discomfort and visceral contradictions during reparations. But once moving, structural competence empowers through change. Structural competence is awareness that inequity systems are entrenched in tiered networks and territorial bureaucracies, following centuries of Anglo-conformity, impacting nearly everything that happens at school.[4] Transformative teachers develop critical consciousness to motivate change. We organize our thoughts with inclusion paradigms to integrate academics into student-centered diversity activities. We collaborate to reduce dependence on divisive routines with holistic antibias-antiracist education.

Transformative teachers assist systemic change with circle interactions among students, faculty, staff, and communities to engage arts and sciences with diverse ways of knowing. Widelens structural competence pulls together seemingly unreconcilable differences. Practitioners resist stereotypes, favoritism, and exclusions from economic-social rankings. We break victimization/perpetration dichotomies. We participate in diversity teams to reinterpret requirements with peace-giving body-mind-culture-environment questions. Our sustainability activities integrate cultural authenticity into high expectations education.

Structural competence is the bird's-eye view that connects local education space, time, materials, and learning environments to global healing. This scope expands culture competence on the ground with systemic thinking about superdiversity in biodiversity. We move from survival to thriving. Structural competence uncovers dehumanizing culture patterns beneath status quo rhetoric. It is macro knowledge about bias in education, providing micro footholds to resist "race-neutral" disinformation. For instance, when applied to Culture-Conscious Listening, structural competence reveals racism within class and gender inequities through intersectional cultural stories. Structural analysis discerns evidence about systemic suffering and cultural healing during subject development. We engage education mandates and schedules with creative problem-solving to meet requirements with sustainability designs.

The individualism in which we are embedded reinforces unconscious defensiveness and perpetuates racism despite egalitarian "best intentions."[5] When teachers apply structural competence, we question territoriality. Structural competence resists the "melting pot" and "salad bowl" symbols of hoped-for colorblindness, which distracts from the reality of assimilation and segregation. We do the restorative work of breaking bias habits that allow inequitable "opportunity hoarding" in education.[6] Structural competence empowers everyday educators to collectivize for equity ecosystems on location. We replace cultural deficiency-versus-superiority dualities with holism experiences. We make culturally responsive decisions about the academic space, time, materials, and learning environments we inhabit.

Structural competence is central to Environmental Liberation Education. With it, teachers view students, community supports, and colleagues as members of cultures in systems. We see

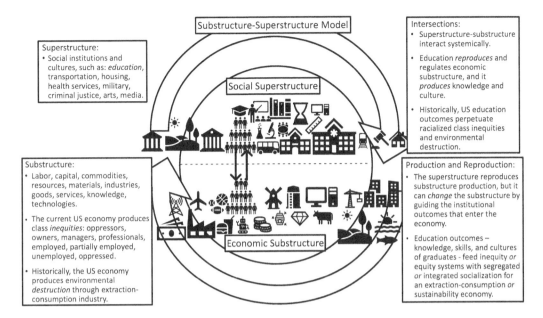

FIGURE 4.1 Social superstructure/economic substructure model graphic about the under-regulated US economy. Created by the author.

how to maneuver mainstream education procedures toward inclusion in the areas over which we have authority. We get imaginative about where to learn and how to develop knowledge with and for cultures. We diversify curriculum with local and global ways of knowing. We raise academic expectations and encourage diverse voices in the holistic learning environments we facilitate. One way to access structural competence is to visualize the substructure-superstructure model, which is the feedback loop discussed in this chapter.[7]

Substructure-Superstructure Model

The substructure-superstructure model shows an economic-social feedback loop:

- This loop is anchored by an economic base, which is the means of production, commerce, and consumption.
- The base funds and generates products and services through structural procedures for social institutions and cultural patterns on top.
- In turn, social and cultural patterns reproduce – or change – products and services through structural procedures and outcomes that feed the base.

Structural analysis, while a generalization of complex cycles, empowers educators with critical consciousness to perceive intergenerational forces and operations that divide and dehumanize. Visualizing systems globally helps practitioners make unity and inclusion decisions locally.

The substructure-superstructure model depicts how an under-regulated extraction-consumption economy produces economic-social inequities, such as those reflected in education disparities. It shows how structural immersion distracts teachers and students from big-picture context and exclude types of knowledge. The model illustrates how a poorly governed economic base *compels* teachers to make unintentional decisions that reproduce social stratifications and environmental alienation. It shows how teacher decisions about knowledge, curriculum, and students, reacting unconsciously to fear, reproduce oppression cycles, ecologically destructive industries, and wealth inequities.

The good news is that the substructure-superstructure model outlines humanity's big picture. It offers points of departure to intervene collaboratively in moving systems during lived experiences. It displays why *transformative* teachers work through intrapersonal conflict to go ahead with culturally responsive sustainability academic activities hourly and daily. Moreover, its sphere mirrors the shape that transformative teachers use for social action Diversity Circles. As we design liberation space, time, materials, and learning environments through peace *circles*, transformative teachers make authentic cross-cultural connections to grow *holistic* critical consciousness.

Multimodal circles counteract oppressor-versus-oppressed dichotomies and open doors to reshape academic experiences with diversity themes. Reconceptualizing subjects with multicultural integration, diversity is no longer a problem or an afterthought. Rather, diversity is the centerpiece of agency for substructure-superstructure solutions. This model, thus, illustrates the contour of social-emotional humanization collaborations for equity in diversity and sustainability in education for an inclusive green economy, depicted below.

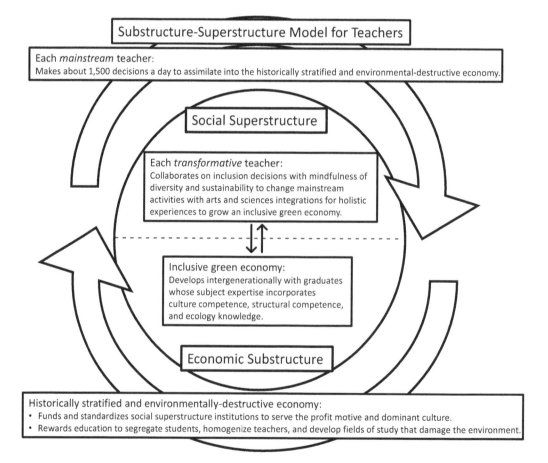

FIGURE 4.2 Superstructure/substructure model for teachers graphic about transformative teacher power. Created by the author.

The substructure-superstructure model helps educators perceive global structures in local conditions. It assists teachers to reinterpret knowledge, curriculum, and instruction with a wide view. Rather than be overwhelmed by busy timetables, we observe how institutions overlap. For example, education is an industry of knowledge production *and* a social institution that relates to other institutions, such as transportation and housing, which together shape human development to reproduce *and* impact the economic substructure. We see how under-regulation – as well as humanitarian *regulation* – of education influences experiences and outcomes. Structural competence reveals that our actions and inactions make a difference to intergenerational well-being. Our classrooms, labs, and meeting rooms impact the substructure-superstructure network. What we do shapes economic-social exchanges. Well-regulated public education is key to diversity thriving. The philosophies about humanity that guide teachers' decisions sway knowledge, students, the profession, and ultimately, the quality of goods and services toward unjust *or* just and unsustainable *or* sustainable outcomes.

The substructure-superstructure model depicts how the economy injects labor, capital, commodities, resources, materials, industries, goods, services, information, technologies, and, currently, class divisions into education. We see how the current global economy funds mainstream education procedures and merchandise to propagate inequitable product and consumption patterns. We see how the existing set-up perpetuates cultural dehumanization and environmental decline with consequences for our own classrooms as well as for generations to come. Today's global substructure-superstructure produces and reproduces tiered education, thwarting academic integration and sustainability experiences for teachers and students. Campuses, many in impoverished areas enrolling diverse students, experience some of the following characteristics:

- *Physiological insufficiencies*, such as tainted water, processed foods, dilapidated facilities, and unsustainable educator salaries.
- *Unsafe technologies and products* injurious to mental, physical, and environmental health with plastics, artificial materials, toxins, chemical substances, weapons, and disinformation media spreading stereotypes, uncivil discourse, and violence.
- *Dehumanizing engagement* due to factory-like, prepackaged, and over-standardized curriculum materials that de-professionalize and undervalue teachers and undermine student locus of control.
- *Biased requirements and assessment products coupled with low expectations* for students of color, poor students, and female students from mandated curriculum geared to vocations without humanitarian and cultural empowerment objectives.
- *Needless culture conflicts, bullying conduct, and racial profiling* during prejudicial disciplinary procedures due to divisions between oppressors, owners, managers, professionals, and the employed versus the partially employed, unemployed, and oppressed.
- *De facto segregation* of students, racialized achievement gaps, and teacher cultural homogenization.

Teachers Are the Most Important Factor to Diverse Student Success

The current systemic feedback loop propels wealth inequalities from an economic substructure defined by corporatized extraction and production of goods, services, and technologies for stratified consumption. This is how negligently supervised institutional patterns outside of school impact student success or failure, the teaching profession, and knowledge. Education is but one institution in the network. However, education *is* instrumental because of its intergenerational nature. Moreover, *within* education, teachers are the most important factor to student achievement. Teachers impact human resources that go into the economic substructure through academic and cultural decisions about students and subjects. *Transformative* teachers use professional authority to intentionally *integrate*. We use big-picture rubrics to prepare graduates with culturally relevant skills for a sustainable economy.[8] We reinterpret requirements with social-emotional circles protecting cultures and nature, indoors and outdoors, through communities of care.

How Do Global Examples Inspire US Transformative Teachers?

It's difficult to resist long-standing bureaucratic habits. The substructure-superstructure model helps educators think big as we apply structural competence and culture competence to ground-floor decisions. Our effort is assisted with global lessons. Two education reforms demonstrate how well-crafted regulations can *promote* systemic equity, while capitalist deregulations can perpetuate and *worsen* systemic inequities.

The contrasting reforms of Finland and Chile occurred during the same epoch. Finland's public education reform demonstrates a shift from economic-social stratifications to equity and quality outcomes. By comparison, education privatization in Chile shows stark substructure-superstructure inequities and poor-quality outcomes.

Finland's Healthy Substructure-Superstructure

Finland's humanitarian public education policy used structural analysis to *tame* inequitable substructure-superstructure systems. Finland reformed education in the social superstructure by un-standardizing curriculum, detracking students, reducing teaching loads, and increasing teacher academic freedom. The government fully funded teacher education and professional development to support highly qualified subject expertise, critical thinking aptitude, and collaboration skills. Finland's changes improved education outcomes, producing inclusive high-performing graduation rates and preparing students with subject expertise and social-emotional competencies. In full circle, graduates participate in the economic substructure to fund high-quality equity education for generations to come. The reform developed a competitive tuition-free teacher preparation pathway that sustains the profession, and a holistic education system that performs at the top of the world in achievement and justice measures, including with diversified subjects, such as environmental education and special education.[9]

Chile's Unhealthy Substructure-Superstructure

By contrast, Chile's privatized voucher policy mirrored for-profit substructure stratifications. Chile's *deregulation* reform had adverse results: academic achievement dropped, socioeconomic segregation between schools increased, subject development withered, school costs went up, student support declined, and teacher professionalization eroded. Education deferred to standardization and commoditization serving corporate interests. Inclusion and sustainability programs, such as special education and environmental education, were largely ignored.[10]

An analysis of Chile's deregulation confirms why proactive equity policies backed up by social superstructure implementation are necessary to moderate the rapacious modern global economy. For more than two decades, Chile conducted the longest and most comprehensive neoliberal education privatization conversion in world history. Prior to the 1980s, about 80% of Chilean students were enrolled in public schools, but by 2010 that number dropped to about 40%.[11] This cap on government spending and regulation-lifting opened up a "middle-class" exodus from Chilean public schools and an enrollment uptick in private voucher schools, which furthered segregation and inflation. Chilean students from privileged socioeconomic backgrounds made up a significant proportion of the increase in private school attendance during the decades the policy was in place. This was because students from savvy middle-class families were the first to sign up, thereby single-handedly commandeering the Ministry of Education's expenditures for private schools.[12]

Meanwhile, Chilean students from low socioeconomic backgrounds remained segmented in municipal schools because private voucher schools were often located away from their homes, making attendance difficult for those without reliable transportation. Furthermore, additional fees charged by privatized schools – for uniforms and test preparation products and services – proved to be prohibitive for low-income families. Then many Chilean students, viewed as less desirable in the eyes of private school administrators because they come to school with fewer privileges and cultural capital than wealthy students, were often denied entry to selective private voucher schools. The top institutions instead "creamed" enrollments, using bureaucratized achievement selection criteria to exclude.[13]

The exclusions of lower-socioeconomic Chilean youth from high-performing schools overlapped with other structural segmentations, such as inequitable housing regulations, health service disparities, elitist business networks, and draconian criminal justice. Conversely, privileges throughout the economic substructure-social superstructure were conferred to people in middle and wealthy classes. Advantaged Chilean youth benefited from well-informed stable households, advanced medical care, and entrée to business networks. They had better access to test preparation, dependable transportation, quiet study environments, and quality test preparation resources to matriculate through the best schools. They graduated into direct lines of employment, management, and entrepreneurial opportunities with networked family capital.[14]

Thus, Chile's education privatization doubly undermined the possibility of social integration and upward mobility through schooling because of a spate of other deregulated institutions in the social superstructure: housing, health, criminal justice, and business. The combined effect of this weakly managed for-profit system was to reproduce social stratifications produced by the free-market corporatized economic substructure. By contrast, Finland's robust public education policy furthered social integration and upward mobility supported with holistic humanitarian regulations. These global examples illustrate problems that transformative teachers solve with big-picture questions and cultural actions to humanize US education.[15]

How Do Transformative Teachers Visualize Education in Systems?

Transformative teachers visualize a circle as large as Earth bisected by a porous line. Figure 4.3, an education substructure-superstructure diagram, depicts how transformative teachers view education in the overall system and how our mind's-eye pictures change from

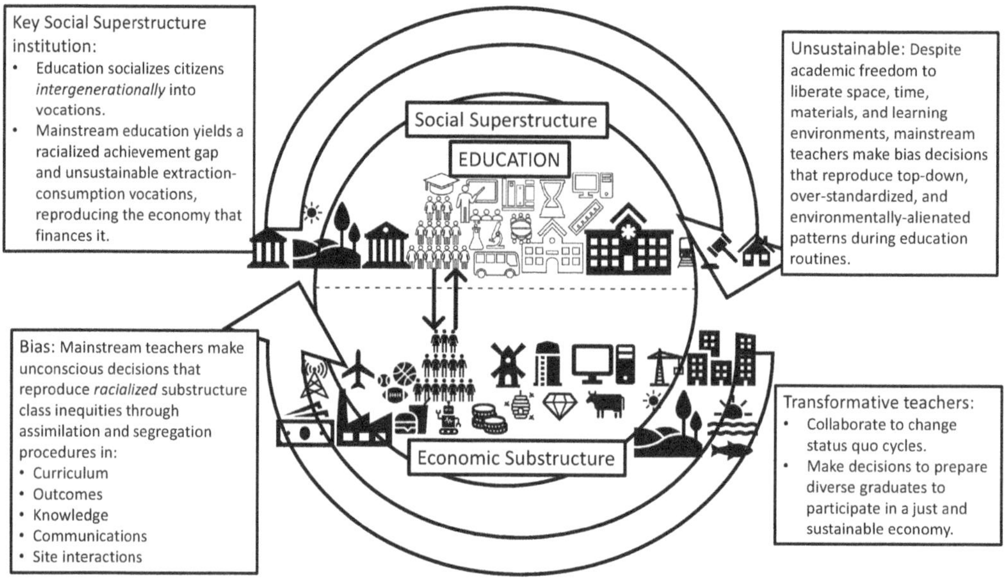

FIGURE 4.3 Superstructure/substructure education graphic about how teachers interact with the economy. Created by the author.

collective action. The circle's bottom half is the economic base of resources, income brackets, and industries, while the top half – the social superstructure – is a bustling institutional network with education, media, housing, health care, church, criminal justice, environmental protection agencies, and so on. The economic substructure in the bottom half produces content, commodities, and funding for superstructure institutions. In return, superstructure institutions operate bureaucracies to conduct and codify social exchanges and procedures for resources, goods, and services to input into the substructure. Thus, social superstructure policies and practices consume, distribute, and reproduce elements for substructure industries, which, in full circle, finance and define products and wealth categories for the superstructure.

Transformative teachers study the economic *substructure* as a foundation composed of monetizable fundamentals and resources in the means of production – raw supplies, labor (inert and living), land, materials, factories, tools, machines, and technology – along with other elements in production – capital, industries, goods, services, and markets. We pay attention to classes of people defined by involvement in the means of production, including relationships to other classes. We discuss how the substructure currently produces and markets class inequities – corporate elite, owners, managers, professionals, employed, partially employed, unemployed, and incarcerated in an oppressor–oppressed continuum.

We look for examples of how the social *superstructure* is everything not primary to production. We notice how it distributes and fulfills (or does not fulfill) human needs through cultural dynamics, reproducing hierarchies (or regulating for equity). We observe policy philosophies in superstructure bureaucracies. We investigate how superstructure institutions and culture patterns replicate, maintain, or intervene in economic substructure elements, aware that the substructure funds and defines the superstructure through production.

What Do Transformative Teachers Visualize for Sustainable Systems?

Transformative teachers understand that no one escapes the hourly and daily bias of a stratified economic-social system. But by filtering the model with a lens of superdiversity in biodiversity, we spot the illusion of colorblind individualism so we may work to manage a more just and sustainable system. We recognize how the current global economic substructure produces intergenerational cycles of racism, sexism, classism, and environmental destruction in the world's social superstructure, dividing our classrooms, labs, and meeting rooms. That's why we activate subject requirements with culture competence and sustainability knowledge to prepare graduates with prosocial skills for the substructure. We envision academic data collection to assess equity and ecology outcomes. We're clear-eyed about results, asking: Did the subject design or academic activity shift engagement away from exclusions, preferences, and unfairness cycles? Did the design or activity advance culturally responsive proficiencies and green economic skills? What's the evidence? How may we improve?

Our transformative teachers feedback loop model motivates learning communities to apply structural competence on an arch of continual improvement. One Diversity Circle activity we use is the book-club format. We team for civil discussion to grow systemic analysis about how social superstructure practices are conduits to economic substructure production. For example, we might read *The Color of Law: A Forgotten History of How Our Government Segregated America*, in which Richard Rothstein argues that historically segregationist federal government policies have enforced segregated housing patterns – and thereby a hierarchy of neighborhood schools – the legacy of which divides people by race, ethnicity, and other categories. Such systemic inequities serve the economic interests of corporate elites, owners, managers, professionals, and the employed. Resources are channeled through politics that shape superstructure policies and practices. "[E]conomic policies are conditioned by and at

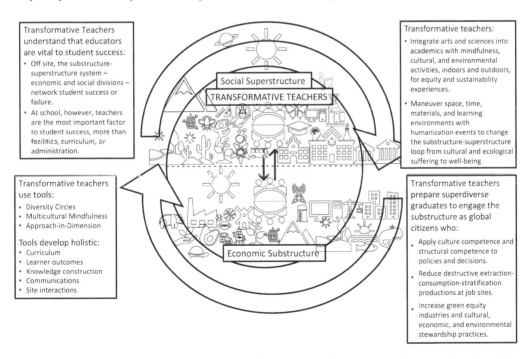

FIGURE 4.4 Substructure/superstructure graphic about transformative teacher decisions that help humanize the economy. Created by the author.

the same time modify the social and political situation where they are put into practice. Economic policies are introduced precisely in order to alter social structures."[16]

Transformative teachers research structural theory to understand how systems impact cultures at school. We compare the current dehumanization feedback loop to the holistic humanization loop we cogenerate. We develop structural competence to deepen culture competence, asking big-picture questions about superdiverse-biodiverse systems. Understanding that the economic substructure and social superstructure are inextricably linked, we see how both operate classrooms, labs, and meeting rooms. We therefore comprehend that the current system, with education prominently in it, assimilates some, segregates everyone, and perpetuates environmental devastation. That's why we face territoriality and fear about change from a position of love. We use compassion protocols to integrate nature and diverse cultures into arts and sciences activities, indoors and outdoors, reshaping academic engagement with Environmental Liberation Education.

MULTICULTURAL MINDFULNESS ACTIVITY

Structural Competence Imagination

Outcome

- Develop structural competence by comparing the "Education Substructure-Superstructure" diagram to the "Ag Program Essay."
- Draw your own substructure-superstructure diagram to imagine systemic *equity* and holism experiences in your classroom, lab, or committee.
- Brainstorm a systemic equity or holism activity to implement now.

Key Concepts

- **Structural Competence:** Critical consciousness about how systems impact education in order to change assimilation and segregation space, time, materials, and learning environments with culturally inclusive sustainability experiences.

Resources

- Journal, pencil, copies of Ag Program (below), copies of Figure 4.2 (above), an example or symbol of vegetable produce, a place to meet indoors or outdoors.

Big-Picture Question

How do I apply structural competence to my routines now?

Start

Whole group circle with Figure 4.2 (above) distributed:

- **Pass around** the vegetable produce and Figure 4.2 while **reading aloud** the Ag Program essay (below).
- **Discuss:** Who grew this vegetable? Where was it grown?

- **Discuss:** What's the most important thing you learned from the Ag Program essay about cultures and US agriculture? How is food part of culture? How is food sustainable? How do current food systems reproduce economic divisions and unsustainable practices? How does a current subject you teach or research relate to cultures in systems? How does this subject relate to sustainability?
- **Discuss** Figure 4.2. What's unclear? What makes sense? What relates to your subjects and students?

Ag Program Essay

In an education program conducted by the National Black Farmers Association (NBFA), transformative teachers and diverse students in agricultural sciences researched the history of systemic racism in agricultural industry production and discriminatory policies in the social superstructure enacted by the US Department of Agriculture (USDA). The research found that African American farmers across the nation have experienced discrimination with the USDA and state departments of agriculture. Further, research revealed that Black farm ownership dropped from 14% in 1910 to less than 2% in 2012. Substructure-superstructure cycles during those years denied Black farmers access to government loans and subsidies that were otherwise provided to White farmers.

For example, White farmers have gotten loan approvals within about 30 days, whereas loan approvals for Black farmers have taken on average about 11 months. One biased practice in the USDA was to confer Black farmers very limited times to petition for grants and loans, in some cases just one day a week, whereas White farmers were permitted to do so all week. Meanwhile, White landowners systematically denied Black farmers' private credit. Since they were hampered in getting loans in at least these two superstructure elements and were often denied emergency or disaster assistance and other aid from the USDA, many Black farmers lost their farms and homes. Through this process, a racialized industry defaulted to White-dominated big agricultural and processed foods interests, using farming practices with monocrops and pesticides that harm the environment and distract from local and natural food ecosystems.

The NBFA counteracted this structural inequity with empowerment networks. They helped farmers of color and small organic farmers form collectives, then took collaborative actions to make legislative changes to loan and credit procedures and to diversify the industry. They developed multiracial scholarships and education projects to challenge for-profit big agribusiness companies that exclude farmers of color and destroy the environment. Diverse agricultural science students now do fieldwork in environmental justice projects in multiracial alliances locally, engaging academics with outdoor education, mentorships, hands-on materials, and community-based learning environments. Ag students use diversity scholarships and NBFA-affiliated education programs to gain diversified organic farming knowledge and skills about culturally responsive cultivation and land stewardship during community empowerment sustainability activities.

Informed by systemic analysis of the agriculture industry, participants apply structural competence to transform agricultural sciences with culture-conscious sustainability activities. They analyze how bureaucrats in the social superstructure perpetuate the Anglo-conformist for-profit substructure production by segregating while harmfully exploiting the environment through industrialized big agriculture producing processed foods and fuels. By building diversity networks to develop culture competence and organic agricultural production in local food ecosystems, participants diversify agricultural experiences in the economic substructure and promote nutritious natural foods. They help reshape the industry away from extraction-consumption destruction and into healthful culturally inclusive green activities through holistic antibias-antiracist changes in education and in other superstructure institutions.[17]

Middle

Diversified project teams with copies of Figure 4.2 at each table:

- **Individually sketch**

    1 A substructure-superstructure diagram by **drawing** a circle bisected by a horizontal dotted line.
    2 **Title** it: *How I help facilitate a systemic equity feedback loop.*
    3 **Draw** a symbol for your classroom, lab, or meeting room in the center of the social *superstructure* above the dotted line. You're imagining your space and subject developing holistic humanization knowledge and global citizenship skills for cultural inclusion and green economic participation.
    4 With symbols for a culturally responsive sustainability economy, **fill in** the base. Depict a green economy *substructure* producing for a wholesome biodiverse world. Focus on careers, technologies, products, and services related to your subject.
    5 As you sketch, **think** about a liberation activity that engages a required subject, something you've rarely or never used before, such as circle seating, learning outdoors, learning with nature indoors, doing Socratic Circle inquiry, big-picture theme sequencing stations, climate justice field trips, multicultural materials, collaborating on a project with diverse community supports, or integrating cultures, mindfulness, and nature into core content activities.
    6 Consider how this activity might positively impact student success and empower you as a change agent for cultural inclusion. Consider how you act to replace status quo systemic inequities and environmental destruction routines with holism practices from a position of love.

Closing

Whole group circle:

- **Share** and **discuss** your diagram and your brainstormed activity. What kinds of inclusive green careers does your activity address? How does your activity use multimodal culturally responsive methods to deepen subject engagement? What needs to happen to implement this holism activity this week?

Theory and Practice

How Is Education Core to Systems?

Education is an institution that reproduces – or can help change – the economy. The economy finances education, counting on replications for growth. The economic substructure is maintained through education from knowledge development and by graduating students with career expertise. Mainstream education almost exclusively prioritizes the economic efficiency goal, which, in the US, is currently defined by Anglo-conformist corporate capitalism. However, *transformative* teachers redirect mainstream education to holistic humanization goals by facilitating integrative academic experiences toward a sustainability economy. In this way, we not only redefine economic efficiency away from the myth of individualism and toward public good, but we also value collectivism in the other core education goals: citizenship, self-actualization, and socialization.[18] By practicing Environmental Liberation Education, we act to reduce allegiance to an inadequately governed extraction-consumption economy that divides and destroys, and instead, we support diverse student success as we also assist an equitable green economy and multicultural-multiracial democracy through collaborations for mutual thriving.

Overcoming Substructure-Superstructure Challenges

Post-civil rights education in the US has not yet forged holistic antibias-antiracist breakthroughs, and this is largely because other institutions in the substructure-superstructure remain segregated and indifferent to sustainability. Most current institutions maintain the status quo. Culture-conscious desegregation measures, such as fair housing and equal access to quality health care, must be enacted throughout the substructure-superstructure for lasting systemic change. Alone, schools are unable to deflect the steady stream of assimilation policies that steer cross-institutional practices to divisive dehumanization patterns that harm the environment. For instance, busing, a desegregation effort enacted in parts of the country in the 1970s, resulted in positive academic achievement outcomes[19] but did not, on its own, yield system-wide economic integration. The critical consciousness to motivate desegregation efforts subsided over time, while segregation patterns continued to ghettoize and fracture space.

> Housing discrimination, racial segregation, voter suppression, and disinvestment in neighborhoods where people of color live, are a result of explicit policies which produce outcomes that reinforce our biases.... It isn't just the media that reinforces our negative racial biases (which it does), it is also the way we have historically and currently denied people of color access to opportunities in and across our communities that reinforces negative associations (crime, unemployment, crumbling infrastructure).[20]

Segregated housing, unequal access to health care, eroding infrastructure, mass incarcerations, and discriminatory enterprises have mounted to such an extent that *de facto* school segregation and the racial achievement gap persist.[21]

How, then, can we as educators change interlaced inequities and environmental destruction from US systems? The answer is to take cultural actions for humanization. We use peace processes during hourly and daily decisions about students and subjects, assessing academics with inclusion and sustainability criteria. Three Transformative Tools assist educators to break out of the fiction of individualism amid the reality of unfair systems.

We start by naming the problem. We recognize that education perpetuates systemic racism through mismanaged government funding. We observe that some students live in wealthy neighborhoods with high tax bases and attend schools with programs for higher-order cognition. We see that other students, in inadequately resourced neighborhoods, experience schools with limited academics and basic programming. We notice how colorblind stereotypes are reinforced when White youth from well-resourced schools graduate at higher rates and enter the economy as elites, owners, professionals, and managers, while many youths of color experience lower graduation rates and enter into lower-paying jobs or are underemployed, unemployed, or pipelined to prison. We see how teachers draw conclusions about such divisive outcomes, noticing that the individuals who "succeed" are often White but that the individuals who "fail" are often of color.[22]

These patterns reinforce superiority-versus-deficiency assumptions about individuals from racialized categories. That's why, during routines, many educators unconsciously justify choices that enable racialized tracking, segregated sites, and assimilation curriculum. We make culturally divisive determinations about special needs placements and individualized education plans (IEPs). We make implicit bias decisions about who gets into honors curricula and STEM (science, technology, engineering, and mathematics) tiers. We rely on assumptions about what behaviors to penalize and which perspectives we permit in curriculum. Substructure-superstructure inequities in funding and industry production enmesh into bias patterns through our own hourly and daily decisions at school. Even though we have color-blind aspirations, we maintain systemic discrimination.[23]

However, participating in holism collaborations, such as in Diversity Circles, transformative teachers reduce bias in real time. We use practices, such as those found in the Multicultural Mindfulness tool, to reshape subjects with body-mind-culture-environment activities for reconciliation. We assess academic *outcomes* with wide-lens rubrics about humanity, such as in the Approach-in-Dimension. We ask structural competence questions to reveal hypocrisies about intentions versus results. This prompts problem-solving with multicultural voices during academic development. World healing transpires as we bring cultures and nature into classrooms, labs, meeting rooms, and campus community events, thereby empowering teachers professionally and students academically as global citizens.

What Does Chile's Experience Teach US Educators About Structural Competence?

Global citizenship is learned through cultural action and by sharing international stories that illustrate how regional events relate to the world-wide substructure-superstructure. Finland's systemic reform for high-achieving and equitable public education, described throughout this book, demonstrates best practices to *transform* substructure-superstructure stratifications into inclusion and sustainability outcomes instead. By contrast, a deep dive into the *deregulation* story in Chile provides a lesson in what *not* to do.

For the politicians, business people, and others who champion privatized US education (e.g., voucher systems), Chile's recent history provides a comprehensive example of a dark cautionary tale. The January 6, 2021 violent insurrection attempt at the US Capitol provides a chilling illustration of the need to closely examine the Chilean connection to the United States. The purpose of this fanatical coup effort was to overturn the results of a democratically elected humanitarian president who had fairly won against the privatization candidate; this is similar to what happened in Chile with a bombing coup against the democratically elected humanitarian president, Salvador Allende, who died during the violent siege.

Chile's story demonstrates the fate of the current US substructure-superstructure trajectory and why transformative teachers work to change this trajectory for US education with structural competence. Chile's violent and dehumanizing privatization story mirrors the components of the US system that underpays and burns out teachers while culturally stratifying students and knowledge development with over-standardized curriculum and unequal funding procedures that serve for-profit interests. Well-meaning teachers may intend to respect student diversity when we add cultural contributions into routines, but instead we perpetuate racialized and gendered income and wealth divisions by tokenizing diverse cultures. We unwittingly ignore the systems that perpetuate substructure-superstructure inequities.[24] We may think that school choice is good for individuals in families, but instead, education deregulation drives up costs and defers to categorical ranking systems that segregate, dehumanize, and fuel an unjust environmentally damaging economy.[25]

El Teniente Mine

The copper industry in Chile illustrates the violence and dehumanization of under-regulated privatization within the substructure-superstructure loop. Chile's 200-year-old *El Teniente* Mine – currently with multinational ownership – shows the danger of permitting substructure-superstructure cycles operated by remote global interests under the policy rhetoric of individualism. This results in inequity and destruction experiences. In Chile, copper is important to social superstructure institutions, including education. One of the first metals used by humans, copper has been central to the global economy for more than 10,000 years. It is currently applied internationally in most construction, transportation, and electrical industries. Chile produces a third of the world's copper, which, as a mineral, has been in increasing demand due to its connective properties in cell phones, the internet, computers, and circuit integration. Copper comprises up to 50% of Chilean exports and 10% of its national economy.[26]

El Teniente mine is one of the largest copper mines in the world, and it shows how extraction-consumption industries in the global substructure adversely impact cultures and education in the social superstructure. The mine illustrates how corporate interests imbue the for-profit technology-services economy with dehumanization patterns. Soon after Chileans fought for liberation from Spanish colonialism in 1810, US business entrepreneurs sought to capitalize on Chile's emergence by investing in its economic substructure of raw materials in areas such as agriculture, fishing, silver, gold, and copper. *El Teniente* embodies the ambition of global enterprises with for-profit interests callous to human suffering and global warming.[27]

US Business in Chile: The Nation's First Bowling Alley and Catastrophic Fire

El Teniente Mine is part of the industrial substructure that funded and constructed the Andean Sewell Mining Town in its social superstructure with a state-of-the-art hospital, a church, social clubs, the first-in-Chile bowling alley, a movie theater, a heated swimming pool, and an education system, reaching a peak in 1968 with 15,000 inhabitants. The mine was founded in 1906 by the Braden Mining Company, and its New York executives knew the value of copper to industrial expansion, and they wanted Chile's copper to bring profit to US industry. In 1916, the mine and its village became a subsidiary in another US company, the Kennecott Copper Corporation. Its succession of US owners, engineers, and architects painted the village buildings in vivid green, yellow, red, and blue hues to brighten its visage against the stark ice and fog of its 6,500-foot altitude location.[28]

However, the mine is now infamous for its calamitous 1944 avalanche that killed 102 miners and family members, followed the next year by "*El Humo*," a deadly fire that killed another 355 miners. Up until 1970, the greater part of the copper industry in Chile was owned and operated by North American mining companies. In 1976, *El Teniente* became a loop in a tangled thread of violent events culminating when Chilean ambassador Orlando Letelier was assassinated with a car bomb in Washington, D.C. for his opposition to privatization serving international corporations off of Chile's land.[29] Rather than acquiesce to business interests headquartered in New York, democratically elected President Salvador Allende, with advisors such as Letelier, attempted to regulate the enterprise with humanitarian policies for Chilean workers. Allende nationalized copper in 1971 with the intent to remake the mining industry into a public good for the *Chilean* people.[30]

Furious US Businesses and Government Policymakers

Allende ran for president on a platform for "immediate and total nationalization" of Chilean substructure resources and superstructure institutions, including education. Within a year of his election, he signed a nationalization law in which "all of Chile's basic resources and resource industries" were "put into the hands of the State for reasons of national interest." The law also specifically called for the "immediate and total nationalization" of copper. This posed a "bold challenge to traditional standards of international law" with regard to the globally corporatized economic substructure. As Allende nationalized foreign-owned assets, he upset US business interests that had enjoyed the spoils of globalization, funneling overseas earnings back home. US corporations had been accustomed to extracting profits from developing countries with authoritarian governments, unfettered by environmental regulations or humanitarian obligations to laborers.[31]

Furious US business leaders and government policymakers resolved to reassert global corporatized campaigns against Allende's democratic humanization efforts. Allende's reforms threatened the global order of developing resource-extraction industries across the world to benefit elite corporations. For example, the US State Department established a multi-year privatization program to resist regulations in Chile. This program was led by economist Milton Friedman and other University of Chicago and Ivy League professors who trained about 100 Chilean privatization economists, known as the Chicago Boys. These US-educated bureaucrats and political operatives implemented privatization throughout Chilean institutions in the 1970s and 1980s, including re-privatizing the copper industry and privatizing education.[32]

Assassinations

The fervency of US government-backed corporations against Allende's progressive democratic policies was guided by "classical economic liberalism" ideologues such as Friedman. This ideology is not liberal in the sense of laws to support democratic inclusion; rather, it permits laissez-faire corruption, which ultimately led to the murder of Letelier, a top advisor and confident of Allende. In this way, Letelier was murdered for calling out Friedman as the US "architect" of anti-democratic privatization.

Letelier was the first high-ranking official of the Allende administration to be imprisoned after General Augusto Pinochet's 1973 military *coup d'état*, including the 17 bomb explosions at *La Moneda* – the Chilean White House – used to overthrow Allende three years into his presidency. Upon Pinochet's establishment of a military dictatorship, Letelier was immediately detained and severely tortured for a year, until, after international pressure, he was released in 1974 and exiled to Venezuela.[33]

Letelier had opposed global corporate holdings in Chile. He worked for humanization in the superstructure developing equity policies for civil and political institutions, labor unions, churches, neighborhood organizations, student groups, and schools. At one point in his diplomacy, Letelier attempted to re-negotiate the unfavorable terms of the copper mining industry under North American control. However, at an international trade meeting in Paris in 1972 with the United States, Japan, and 11 western European nations, "American negotiators wedged into the talks a consideration of the unfavorable terms of compensation Chile had offered to the nationalized copper companies" by insisting that favorable terms be negotiated into the rescheduling of Chile's debt. But Chile, represented by ambassador Letelier, refused.[34]

Within five months of the Paris accords, Allende was dead and Letelier was imprisoned, "subjected to every degrading treatment possible," torture that left the former ambassador emaciated and traumatized. After Letelier moved from his exile in Venezuela to what was presumed to be a more protected location in Washington, D.C., he continued to speak out and write about the systemic injustices perpetrated by the Pinochet government. He was a resistor who called out antidemocratic dehumanization from inadequately controlled industry and privatized education. He explained how privatization allowed US corporations to exploit Chile's economic substructure-social superstructure for their own and regulate financial interests. For this, Letelier was murdered by US operatives.[35]

In a through-line to current events in the US, and four years before the failed January 6th insurrection at the US Capitol, on January 17, 2017, Betsy DeVos was confirmed in the same building as the 11th US Secretary of Education, after answering a series of questions by Congress about her dream to privatize US education. Almost 40 years before that, six miles away from DeVos's confirmation hearing, two bodies lay sprawled near Embassy Row in Washington, D.C. On September 21, 1976, Letelier was assassinated, dead like Allende before him, by a bomb strapped to the underside of the car he was driving with two passengers. Crime scene photos included a jagged and bleeding dismembered foot in the middle of the street. One passenger had been Letelier's 25-year-old coworker, Ronni Moffitt, who died immediately, while Moffitt's husband, Michael, crawled out the back of the enflamed car to survive. The Moffitts were newlyweds whose car had broken down that morning and, graciously, Letelier offered to give them a ride to their respective workplaces. From 5,000 miles away in Santiago, Pinochet ordered the assassination of Letelier to be carried out by a team that included a US expatriate who worked for Pinochet's secret police.[36]

What's the Guise of Individualism?

Letelier was assassinated in Washington, D.C. to clear the deck for substructure-superstructure privatization in a series of events directed by US corporations and policy makers. President Allende and ambassador Letelier were resistors, attempting to reform Chile's economic-social system toward public good, such as by nationalizing copper and investing in public education. Instead, violently enforced *deregulation* to serve remote industry profits under the guise of "individualism" won the day.

The tale of copper in Chile illustrates how an *under-regulated* substructure-superstructure is anti-democratic and dehumanizing. Copper, a defining feature in the Chilean economy, was exploited through privatization in the name of free enterprise, degrading the Andean environment and regional cultures with linear-extraction production. Such mining adversely impacted the Chilean superstructure, including education, government, law, health care, and housing.

However, liberation is also part of Chile's story. The suffering that Pinochet caused prompted decades of social justice action to de-privatize the country with democratic governance. Ultimately, in 2021, the Chilean people elected student activist Gabriel Boric as Chile's president. Boric has worked to call out the masquerade of individualism, advocating for collectivism and inclusive human rights. He *re-regulated* a number of substructure-superstructure institutions, including funding free universal education, health care, and equity pensions, and he reinforced the viability of a public mining industry to pay for it.[37] Thus, Chile's privatization experience teaches US educators that applying structural competence to collective action unearths dehumanization patterns that harm schools, and such revelations motivate humanitarian public funding and policies for inclusion practices.

What Does the Invisible Hand Have to Do With Me?

Privatization theory dates to the 18th century, when Adam Smith advocated for the "invisible hand" tactic to markets and individual entrepreneurship. Smith's published work rejected government spending for public good. According to Smith, invention and efficiency are generated when economy and society interact unfettered, allowing the unconstrained initiative of individuals and industries to drive development.[38]

Smith discusses education throughout *The Wealth of Nations*, calling for minimal public services in favor of school choice by individuals. Smith asserts that when educators, as service providers, and students, as consumers, are not incentivized by competition, everyone settles for the minimum. Without competition, instruction services and student attainment outcomes are undervalued and lackluster. According to Smith, just as other service-providers and industries are motivated to modernize and improve from competition throughout the private sector, free-market competition motivates educators and students to pursue advanced education services. Smith argues that a minimally regulated or unregulated school marketplace permits education – as a superstructure institution – to reproduce and respond to consumer demand that is produced by a growth-oriented free-market economic substructure.[39]

Smith advocated for invisible hand vouchers in 1776. He called for government to step back from funding schools and to instead dole out money directly to parents to pay for the education of their own children. His idea was that individual parents want what's best for their offspring. Families are motivated consumers who demand competitive offerings rather than a government education monopoly.[40] When parents and students make choices through their own pocketbooks, Smith argued, the providers – educators and schools – are incentivized to improve and differentiate services to meet market demands. According to this theory, high quality becomes duly valued.

> The usual reward of the eminent teacher bears no proportion to that of the lawyer or physician; because the trade of the one is crowded with indigent people who have been brought up to it at the publick expence [sic]; whereas those of the other two are incumbered [sic] with very few....[41]

Smith, arguing that competition raises teacher compensation and quality, asserts that privatized education invigorates the production and reproduction of educational inputs and outputs, thereby generating value and efficiency in education.

Smith's invisible hand impacts your teaching because it valorizes negligently supervised competition and the myth of individualism. The invisible hand concept misleadingly divorces students and knowledge from the reality of racialized, gendered, and class tiering in hierarchical systems. These systems currently feed on racialized and gendered cheap labor and resources, thereby undermining fair access to economic freedom and inclusion. Without multicultural-multiracial democratic participation, or oversight of industries that prioritize profit over humanity, individualism divides. Through status quo activities in classrooms, labs, and meeting rooms, teachers unwittingly assimilate some into Anglo-conformity and exclude others, tier by abilities, culturally homogenize curriculum and knowledge, and disaffect all students from culturally responsive environmental stewardship proficiencies.

Milton Friedman, Adam Smith, and Education

Following in Smith's footsteps 200 years later, US economist Friedman applied privatization theory to policy. Friedman wrote free enterprise and rugged individualism into Chile's national policy and promoted it in the United States. At the University of Chicago, Friedman and his colleagues trained Chilean economists to define all goods and services, including education, as commodities for an open market. These economists believed in Smith's theory that government management is less efficient and effective than for-profit competition. These economists – the "Chicago Boys" – were a group of about 100 Chilean exchange students groomed by Friedman and associates. Under Pinochet, the Chicago Boys then administered privatization for many Chilean industries, including "one hundred-sixty corporations, sixteen banks, three thousand-six hundred agro-industrial plants, mines, real estate, and the education system."[42] The aim was to privatize and deregulate exchanges between the national economic substructure and social superstructure and assimilate the next generation into the theory through policy.

Friedman asserted that a voucher model for education would remove the nuisances of government protections from running schools, thereby permitting academics to be in synch with the free-market economy.

> Think of it this way: If you want to subsidize the production of a product, there are two ways you can do it. You can subsidize the producer or you can subsidize the consumer. In education, we subsidize the producer: the school. If you subsidize the student instead – the consumer – you will have competition. The student could choose the school he attends and that would force schools to improve and to meet the demands of their students.[43]

Friedman argued that vouchers avail choices to everyone, allowing low-income students to select school enrollment too. Using Smith's free-market theory, Friedman developed the school voucher strategy that he sought to instigate in Chile and the United States. Friedman was the ideological architect of Chile's decades-long privatization reform, and he personally assisted its implementation into the nation's economic substructure-social superstructure system. Therefore, according to Friedman, deregulated competition is a policy where individualism is viewed as the crux of innovation in institutions, including in education.

How Does Privatization Theory Work in US Education?

In the United States, privatization vouchers have been proposed not only for choice between public and private schools but also for schools within a public education district or state through charters and homeschooling. The choice theory is that superstructure bureaucracy hinders student achievement because "bureaucracies work against the basic requirements of effective school organizations by imposing goals, structures, and requirements." The contention is that bureaucracies don't allow educators the flexibility or the drive to meet individual students' needs. For instance, in theory, with vouchers, poor students from low-income housing would no longer be forced to attend segregated and under-resourced urban schools. "Wisconsin governor Tommy Thompson argued, 'Choice gives poor students the ability to select the best school that they possibly can. The plan allows for choice and competition, and I believe competition will make both public and private schools much stronger.'"[44]

The theory of privatized choice in the US, then, is that free-market competition incentivizes schools to improve practices and services to positively influence consumer perception. The idea is that effective schools build enrollment by marketing outcomes with a brand or status that attracts new student-consumers. Schools that are unable to successfully compete in this marketplace will, owing to their own inefficiencies, be unable to survive.

> A private company, a group of teachers, or parents can petition a local school board or state agency to establish a public school or create a special program in an existing school. Once the charter school is approved, it operates in a semi-autonomous fashion and receives public funds for its support… It is hoped that charter schools will develop and maintain unique and innovative alternatives to traditional schools.[45]

Thus, the for-profit argument is that vouchers allow individuals to choose education in a competitive superstructure, thereby bettering school programs to meet consumer demand. The belief is that schools will innovate to graduate students who, in turn, will compete in the economic substructure for the privatized feedback loop.

Political Disinformation About Privatization

President Donald Trump's Secretary of Education, DeVos, repeated Smith's and Friedman's theory.

> Educators don't need engineering from Washington. Parents don't need prescriptions from Washington. Students don't need standards from Washington.… Give parents choices through vouchers.… Let's empower the forgotten parents to decide where their children go to school. Let's show some humility and trust all parents to know their kids' needs better than we do.… Choice in education…is about freedom to learn…, freedom from Washington mandates. Freedom from centralized control. Freedom from a one-size-fits-all mentality. Freedom from "the system."[46]

DeVos dismissed the need to regulate for egalitarian humanization in education, favoring instead commoditization for individual choice. She asserted that government rules in the superstructure, or "the system," should be dismantled to allow capitalism's invisible hand to shape education through individual family decisions. Furthermore, DeVos asserted that a substructure propelled by US business interests drives innovation.

> We are the beneficiaries of start-ups, ventures, and innovation in every other area of life, but we don't have that in education because it's a closed system, a closed industry, a closed market. It's a monopoly, a dead end. And the best and brightest innovators and risk-takers steer way clear of it. As long as education remains a closed system, we will never see the education equivalents of Google, Facebook, Amazon, PayPal, Wikipedia, or Uber.[47]

In summary, politicians convey disinformation about privatization theory by portraying it as "choice" through freedom from "the system," when the deregulations they advocate permit systemic stratifications and Anglo-conformist assimilation and segregation to dominate, thereby limiting the choices that low-income and families of color have while bolstering big business "monopoly" for profit. Thus, so-called freedom for the privileged is dependent on restricting the freedom of the disadvantaged to access quality universal education.

Transformative Critique of Privatization Policy

From the perspective of liberation education theory, the main element of privatization theory to keep in mind is the concept of the *individual*. The transformative viewpoint is that when the purported *individual* interacts in privatized systems embedded in the *racialized* and *gendered* divisions of patriarchal White superiority patterns, outcomes become segmented, dehumanized, and environmentally destructive. The critique is that economic growth from the aggregate of privatized per-capita work and incomes unequally funds and biases social superstructure institutions and economic substructure industries because of lack of protection for humanity and environmental health as a whole.

Transformative structural analysis reveals that education privatization is a technocratic apparatus for undemocratic outcomes from systemic stratifications. Education privatization exploits systemic bias and feeds corporatism behind widening income inequalities in the US substructure-superstructure. There's no free-market substructure-superstructure that's fair for individual choice in the US because of ongoing inequity cycles from subsidies and tax breaks to corporations in a for-profit economy predicated on division. Racial, gender, and class divisions in the US cycle intergenerationally from a foundation of White imperialism, colonialism, land-stealing, genocide, the enslavement of people of color, and cheap labor by people of color. Transformative theory explains that school choice reinforces "banking education," wherein students are consumers, teachers are service providers, and curriculum perpetuates the standardization of individualism embedded in White superiority values.[48] In this sense, "choice" mistakes individualism for the colorblind dream, which unfortunately is, currently in the US, still a fiction. Choice seeks to wish away systemic inequities reproduced through networked institutions and, in education, through mainstream curriculum and knowledge construction standardized into tiered sites.

The transformative critique is that choice permits the stratified corporate capitalist economic substructure to determine social superstructure stratification routines. Choice perpetuates racialized assimilation-versus-exclusion outcomes through Eurocentric curriculum, overstandardized and commoditized content, and unequally funded sites. School choice by families reproduces the current extraction-consumption for-profit technology-services economy maintained by inequity structures that dehumanize and skew education quality systemically.

What Do Transformative Teachers Advocate?

Transformative teachers advocate for well-regulated universal free education paid for by a democratic government to distribute academic engagement equitably and sustainably. We call for holistic public education in all levels, as some countries around the world have managed, to support economic inclusion, social integration, multicultural-multiracial democracy, and, ultimately, climate health. The transformative critique of education privatization is that without consistent cultural inclusion practices, parents act as biased consumers. Families end up stockpiling resources – engaging in "opportunity hoarding" – to benefit their own offspring, with scant attention to social and environmental well-being. When capitalism is inadequately controlled, parent-consumers and educator-service-providers together are driven by perceived scarcities in stratified structures as they try to grab the good life where they can.[49]

Teachers have the professional capacity to reduce culturally stratified systemic patterns that serve the for-profit substructure and afflict US education. We strengthen by making unity decisions to reshape academic space, time, materials, and learning and research environments with integrative sustainability activities. Environmental Liberation Education tools assist teachers to collectivize in Diversity Circles and engage Multicultural Mindfulness peace practices that re-interpret standards and resist commoditized curriculum, designing and assessing with clear-eyed criteria for humanization, such as outlined by the Approach-in-Dimension tool. As such, we operate from a position of love, limiting screen time to make space for face-to-face socialization and hands-on culturally responsive academic activities with mindfulness and nature, indoors and outdoors.

This is reparative work, and it means resisting fear, defensiveness, and territoriality to change the status quo caught in victimization-perpetration cycles. Transformative teachers activate interdisciplinary themes with diverse community supports and social services to develop holistic education to help meet basic needs *through* culturally creative academic engagement. Illustrated by global stories, the substructure-superstructure model depicts how to see through the guise of corporatism portrayed as individualism. Structural competence equips everyday teachers to advocate for humanitarian regulations and to take big-picture humanization, mindfulness, and sustainability actions during subject routines. We act and reflect with liberation education to empower our profession with cultural inclusion activities for diverse student success and multicultural knowledge connected to world healing.

MULTICULTURAL MINDFULNESS ACTIVITY

Choice Education versus Equity Education

Outcome

- Discuss disinformation in the private-versus-public-education debate in the US.
- Apply the choice-versus-equity debate to a transformative activity in your classroom, lab, meeting room, or campus.

Key Concepts

Resources

- Journal, pencil, timer, poster paper, crayons, markers copies of Figure 4.5, an example or a symbol of a garden or an actual garden, a place to meet indoors or outdoors.

Big-Picture Question

- What is equity education?

Start

Whole group circle with Figure 4.5 distributed:

- **Read aloud and examine** Figure 4.5.
- **Answer:**

  1. What about this graphic is unclear?
  2. What makes sense?
  3. What school-community garden have you participated in? Is it on a privatized or choice site or a public education site? What are its dimensions and longevity? What are its flora and fauna? How is it an observable ecosystem? How is it integrated into academic engagement? Is it part of the campus food system? Is it part of a neighborhood farmer's market? Who maintains it? Who interacts with it? How does the garden relate to cultures and sustainability?

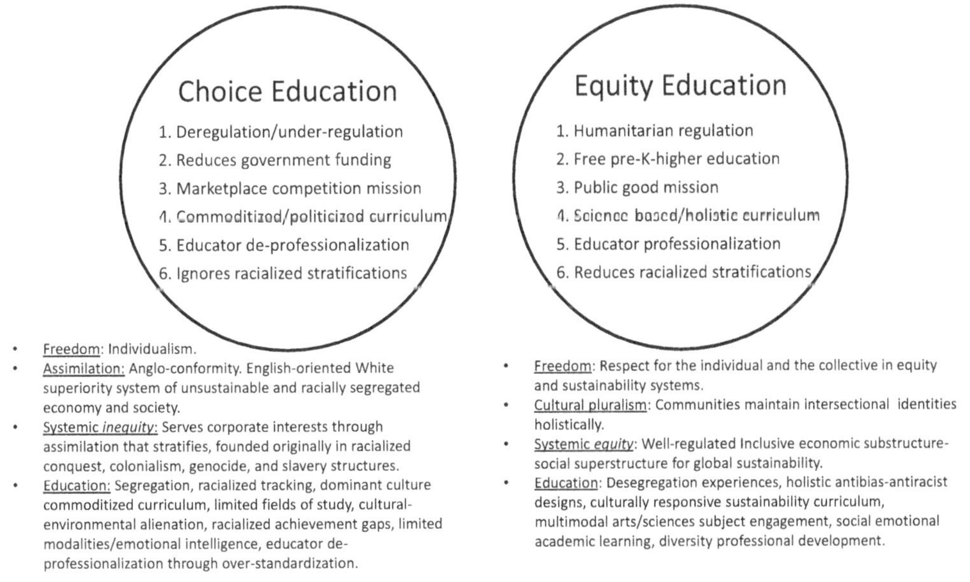

Choice Education

1. Deregulation/under-regulation
2. Reduces government funding
3. Marketplace competition mission
4. Commoditized/politicized curriculum
5. Educator de-professionalization
6. Ignores racialized stratifications

- Freedom: Individualism.
- Assimilation: Anglo-conformity. English-oriented White superiority system of unsustainable and racially segregated economy and society.
- Systemic inequity: Serves corporate interests through assimilation that stratifies, founded originally in racialized conquest, colonialism, genocide, and slavery structures.
- Education: Segregation, racialized tracking, dominant culture commoditized curriculum, limited fields of study, cultural-environmental alienation, racialized achievement gaps, limited modalities/emotional intelligence, educator de-professionalization through over-standardization.

Equity Education

1. Humanitarian regulation
2. Free pre-K-higher education
3. Public good mission
4. Science based/holistic curriculum
5. Educator professionalization
6. Reduces racialized stratifications

- Freedom: Respect for the individual and the collective in equity and sustainability systems.
- Cultural pluralism: Communities maintain intersectional identities holistically.
- Systemic equity: Well-regulated Inclusive economic substructure-social superstructure for global sustainability.
- Education: Desegregation experiences, holistic antibias-antiracist designs, culturally responsive sustainability curriculum, multimodal arts/sciences subject engagement, social emotional academic learning, diversity professional development.

FIGURE 4.5 Choice Education/Equity Education graphic. Created by the author.

> ### Middle
>
> - **Discuss** while passing around the school-community garden example or being in the garden:
>
>   4 What is privatized or choice education? How does this ideological approach operate to de-professionalize teachers, unfairly divide students, and alienate everyone from environmental holism?
>
>   5 What's public education? How does this ideological approach operate to professionalize teachers, integrate diverse students, and connect everyone to environmental holism, though imperfectly? How do we help public education be a safe and culturally responsive space? How do we empower the teaching profession? How do we diversify teachers and respect all backgrounds professionally? How do we support European American teachers to belong in diversity and develop agency in multicultural inclusion and equity efforts? How do we support teachers of color to co-lead multicultural inclusion and equity efforts? How do we integrate academic engagement to prepare diverse graduates to be global citizens who participate in a green economy?
>
> ### Closing
>
> In diversified project teams:
>
> - **Individually write** an acrostic poem on poster paper off of block lettering that spells "EQUITY EDUCATION" in a vertical line.
> - **Color in** the block lettering and write association words horizontally to correspond to each letter.
> - While coloring in the block lettering, **discuss** transformative activities that explore the above questions and relate to a subject you teach.
>
> Whole group circle:
>
> - **Discuss** the logistics of a transformative activity you will try this week.

Application

What Systems Do Transformative Teachers Change?

Transformative teachers redistribute academic resources and facilitate cultural inclusion to increase holistic diversity, mindfulness, and sustainability knowledge and experiences. Transformative teachers take action to reduce cultural tiering in disciplinary and curriculum frameworks and program tracks. We intervene in opportunity hoarding by members of the dominant culture. Opportunity hoarding at school involves backroom deals that advance members of the dominant culture, such as by accumulating advantages in a weakly managed competitive system through standards norming or the acquisition of favorable evaluations. An example is when a White parent insists on a better grade from their child's White teacher. Securing benefits in bias networks is utilitarian. It makes use of substructure-superstructure divisions in the logic of self-interest. Stratified systems incentivize advantage-leveraging by members of the dominant culture. However, leveraging is an unfair and it perpetuates inequity gaps. In a racialized system, opportunity hoarding in segregated districts result in wider achievement gaps than at desegregated ones, yet desegregated schools still produce racially tiered outcomes in college and post-secondary attendance and completion rates.[50]

For instance, at Lewis and Diamond's Riverview High School, about 50% of the students are White and 50% are of color. Riverview is a coveted, well-funded campus run by highly qualified teachers and state-of-the-art facilities and programs. However, White parents at Riverview accumulate race-based privileges to get their children into the four-year college track by championing their own children during interactions with teachers, most of whom are White. White parents sway teachers during crucial decisions about tracking, grading, and test preparation. Beyond marshalling their own children into college preparation classes, White parents simultaneously communicate cultural deficiency stereotypes about students of color during school meetings and events. Echoing desegregated "race-neutral" policy rhetoric, White parents declare a value for "diversity" at Riverview, but only with regard to optional experiences, such as extracurriculars, electives, and supplemental social events. Rather than pushing for integrative *academics*, White parents exploit racially stratified academic tracks that advantage their own children, whom they describe as hard-working or gifted rather than privileged. White parents define diversity as an *enrichment* rather a call for racial *justice* action toward a multicultural-multiracial democracy.

Parental opportunity hoarding is but one illustration of advantages-stockpiling that results in an achievement gap from Riverview. While secondary graduation rates are superior for all students compared with national statistics, White graduates from Riverview have a significantly higher four-year college enrollment and completion rate than its graduates of color. This school illustrates that choice in public education, which is enmeshed in the skewed competition of systemic racism – there's a waiting list to get into Riverview from across the district – enables White students to capture benefits while erecting barriers to upward mobility for students of color.[51] This is why transformative teachers apply equity criteria to reduce bias from hourly and daily curriculum and instruction decisions and procedures that reproduce stratified systems. Transformative teachers take action to redistribute academic resources holistically for cultural inclusion.

Opportunity Hoarding from Creaming and the Peer Effect in Privatized Education

Opportunity hoarding advantages the dominant culture through implicit bias networks in public education. In privatized education, it's more overt. Chile's story shows how privatized education divides unfairly by allowing the privileged to stockpile benefits. Chile's privatization demonstrates that rather than provide low-income students with greater educational prospects for social mobility, vouchers exacerbate social class divisions produced by the free-market economic substructure. Low-income students – staying back in remaining public schools because of transportation constraints and limited access to cultural capital for social networking to get into competitive private schools – suffer both from "creaming" and the "peer effect."[52] Creaming comes from selection criteria and marketing outreach by private schools that attract students who are academically buoyed by privileged parents and that, at the same time, deny enrollment to those without intergenerational wealth. Low-income students who don't fit the criteria of selective voucher school admissions policies are denied equal access to free choice through retail barriers erected by administrators.[53] Correspondingly, the peer effect is another superstructure process wherein the public schools that are left behind are filled with under-resourced lower-performing students. These students become peers to one another and don't gain the benefit of integration between mixed peers. Consequently, class stratifications in the economic substructure are compounded by creaming and the peer effects from education privatization in the superstructure.[54]

For example, during privatization deregulations, wealthy Chilean parents rapidly secured placement for offspring in the best schools, manipulating cultural networks to deploy vouchers for family gain. Poorer Chileans, on the other hand, without access to the cultural benefits of privileged status, operated within "a state of affairs antithetical to their own interests" by settling for underfunded regional schools rejected by wealthy families. Many dropped out before program completion after gaining access only by means of exorbitant loans that they couldn't maintain.[55] The idea of "common sense" free choice for individual upward mobility, though attractive, does not exist in under-regulated capitalist systems dependent on group divisions to reap free or cheap labor and exploit resources. Bias is simply the "common sense" of the privileged in such systems. The dream of efficiency and growth from competition motivates rewards-maneuvering through cultural hegemony. Deregulated and under-regulated schools in capitalist systems are in the business of hourly and daily structural inequities.[56]

Common sense in choice education *subsidizes* the wealthy. In Chile, upwardly mobile middle- and upper-class families – socioeconomic groups that needed vouchers the least – were the most likely to procure vouchers.[57] Middle- and upper-class families used fiscal common sense and the "cultural capital" of social status to acquire more.[58] Being educated themselves, they analyzed legislation and advised one another about tax law and financial deadlines. Wealthy families understood the value of education, and they hired tutors for test preparation. They bought success materials, uniforms, and supplies. Higher-income families used social networks to take advantage of academic and financial resources and interactions, thereby commandeering selective school logistics through choice policy to reproduce economic stratifications.[59]

Magnets and Charters Do Little to Prevent Opportunity Hoarding

Some choice policies combine privatization with targeted government regulation, such as with publicly funded magnet and charter schools. The hope is that a combination might alleviate problems like creaming and the peer effect with holistic curriculum themes and flexible schedules. Magnet schools are defined by themes for interdisciplinary creativity, and many have selection criteria. Charter schools focus on flexible schedules and curriculum catering to parental priorities. Choice in magnet and charter schools is billed as part of the larger project of supporting teacher differentiation and community preferences.[60]

However, magnet and charter schools end up perpetuating social and cultural divides due to incentives in the racialized capitalist substructure. For instance, divisions continue through the *branding* of dedicated themes that implicitly forward superiority-versus-inferiority norms. In Los Angeles, for example, gifted-and-talented magnet schools tend to produce high test scores in part because they enroll the region's best students, many of whom are accepted into the schools because of socioeconomic privileges, such as cultural capital and access to reliable transportation. Housing and class inequities and Anglo-conformity throughout the substructure-superstructure system divide magnet and charter schools from one another and from other public schools that don't share a particular magnet brand.[61]

Therefore, owing to systemic inequities, opportunity hoarding happens in public, privatized, and magnet and charter schools, all of which permit bias choices and racialized elitism, tiering, and tracking. *Transformative* teachers implement systemic changes for holistic humanization and high academic expectations with *all* students through culture-conscious public education integrations. Our efforts redistribute academic resources and interactions with inclusive antibias-antiracist designs and assessments. Our culturally responsive academic activities seek unity in diversity, deflecting opportunity hoarding on the one hand and fear of change on the other. We roll up our sleeves to overcome territoriality, clearing the path for inclusive reparations and reciprocal sustainability experiences. We embrace regional and global diversities, guiding collaborative decisions with big-picture questions to develop equity ecosystems and multiculturally creative curriculum, outcomes, knowledge, communications, and social interactions.

Examples

What Actions Advance Structural Change?

Transformative teachers change status quo structures with inclusive academic space, time, materials, and learning environments actions. We advocate for subsidized teacher training to synthesize subject expertise *with* culture competence. We join hiring and retention committees to diversify qualifications rubrics. We petition for humanitarian policies to decrease the teaching load and increase time for diversity and sustainability professional development. We get on committees to reinterpret subject standards with multicultural, mindfulness, and ecology criteria. We reduce over-standardization and ranked tracking by increasing student-centered Content Creation and integrated circle activities for curriculum engagement. We facilitate diversified project groups for hands-on community-based learning to bridge academics to the world. We use holistic assessment with social-emotional academic criteria. Our transformative actions do not come out of a vacuum; they follow the success models of culturally relevant education.[62]

Using Success Models for Structural Change – Finland

During the same time period of Chile's privatized education failures, Finland instituted a success model. Finland's free universal education reform used best practices to bring up student achievement scores equitably to the top of world rankings, simultaneously strengthening the teaching profession. Finland's fully funded education at all levels has raised academic quality, improved inclusive student engagement, increased justice outcomes, and lifted the profession by explicitly *regulating* the economic substructure to minimize for-profit corruption and hierarchies. Finland's public education has integrated social-emotional learning into academic routines to reduce standardization, tracking, and diversity exclusions. Finland's experience with holistic education with differentiated support services shows that *democratic* government support empowers educators and students with humanization experiences.[63]

Teachers in Finland instruct about 600 hours annually, whereas in the US, teachers average 1,080 annual hours. Finnish teachers use the remaining school day to make professional decisions to detrack and "un-standardize."[64] Their national curriculum guides are slim, and students don't take standardized tests for advancement until college entrance, encouraging teacher academic freedom. Finland's results: Students attain the world's top measures for academic achievement *and* equity. Teachers *love* their jobs, competing for limited spots in teacher education that is tuition-free but rigorous, requiring mentorship and master's degree research for credentialing in a process that results in a highly qualified teacher force. The respect and dignity of the profession attract interest. There's more demand to become a teacher in Finland than to become a doctor or lawyer.[65]

First-year Finnish teachers are prepared to hit the ground running in collaborations that integrate reflective teaching and subject development into social-emotional academic learning to realize *humanization* goals *with* students.[66] Finland, thus, shows how to make structural change by fully subsidizing highly qualified professional training on the front end, minimizing curriculum standards, decreasing standardized testing, detracking students, minimizing the teaching load to grant time for teachers to connect with students and collaborate, and empowering the profession with academic freedom to advance holistic education.

Structural Change through Academic Integration Connected to World

One equity ecosystem design is to integrate diverse learners into academic engagement connected to the world, such as through problem-based projects to activate subjects in multicultural ability-mixed groups.[67] Transformative teachers interrupt assimilation and segregation patterns in the Anglo-conformist racially tiered US substructure-superstructure system by *intermingling* diverse students into curriculum engagement through social justice projects.[68] Samuel Bowles and Herbert Gintis explain that the segmenting machinery of education is fueled by the capitalist substructure. In their landmark 1976 study, they found that school socialization functions through the "correspondence principle" to have more impact on the replication of the hierarchical class structure in capitalism than prescribed curriculum.

> Our econometric investigations demonstrated that little of the contribution of schooling to later economic success is explained by the cognitive skills learned in school…[but rather] parental class and other aspects of economic status are passed on to children in part by means of unequal educational opportunity.… The economic advantages of the descendants of the well-to-do go considerably beyond the superior education they receive.… Finally, our historical studies of the origins of primary school and the development of the high school suggested that the evolution of the modern school system is accounted for not by the gradual perfection of a democratic or pedagogical ideal but by a series of class and other conflicts arising through the transformation of the social organization of work and its rewards.[69]

Bowles and Gintis found that even government protections to try to equalize public education developed during the civil rights era were not enough to tame business, class, and cultural networks outside of school.

They found that civil rights regulations didn't get at the inner workings of racialized stereotypes that drive segmenting decisions hourly and daily across institutions. Equity-minded federal regulations at school, though well intended, didn't interrupt ranks compelled by capitalism because civil rights programs were not coordinated with other like-minded policies, such as desegregated housing, criminal justice reform, and multiracial labor organizing.

Unless systemically regulated with comprehensive equity policies across multiple institutions, class hierarchies inevitably reproduce through school. Thus, transformative teachers help the "transformation of the social organization of work and its rewards" by facilitating community-based diversified problem-solving groups with hands-on projects for academic engagement integrated into the world.[70] Fieldwork, internship, service, and social change projects not only facilitate multicultural socialization with cross-cultural peers and vocational mentoring but also evaluate project experiences with humanitarian criteria that minimize materialism. Culturally responsive circle education values the intrinsic rewards of collectivization for public service, sustainability, and justice outcomes.[71]

Making Structural Change with Restorative Justice

Restorative justice is a process that replaces fear, territoriality patterns, punitive academic evaluations, and tracking decisions with reconciliation circles. It is team-based holistic cross-cultural communication and evaluation to recognize how people are only as free as society's most vulnerable members. The circles gather diverse peoples to interact and solve conflicts by describing emotions, listing event facts, recognizing cultures, and regulating behaviors for civility and social justice action during academics. Restorative justice uses prosocial practices from a position of love to support inclusive cultural thriving and academic equity. The goal is to meet students' basic needs holistically *on* site, during education.[72]

Restorative justice forums connect with social services and diverse regional organizations. They're collaborations to *identify* emotions and material adversities from systemic suffering and cultural misunderstandings. Participants reflect during liberation efforts to co-generate creative ways to redistribute academic resources, integrate academic interactions into real-world healing projects, and advocate for academic inclusion. Restorative justice is an equity ecosystems design with multicultural "community circles," "mediation circles," and "restorative circles," emphasizing peer-to-peer empowerment and resolution.[73] They empower by using desegregation norms and intersectionality awareness to arbitrate oppressor–oppressed conflicts fairly and reciprocally, calming social stress and climate anxiety with the following methods:[74]

- *Feelings Observations:* Participants describe pain, joy, and the range of emotions in an experience, expressing suffering and healing, explaining contradictions in feelings and reactions, as well as emotional changes over time and space.
- *Sensory Descriptions:* Participants express local and global cultural stories, describing regional environmental events and specific characters in conflict. Participants narrate plot lines with sensory observations and explain evidence of economic and social losses and gains in micro and macro settings.
- *Perceptions and Interpretations:* Participants show mutual understanding of one another's cultural and environmental stories and themes about pain and liberation. They consider root motives, victimization and growth mindsets,[75] systemic bias, past-pain and entitlement patterns, defensiveness and territoriality habits, and adversity and privilege cycles in oppressor–oppressed and climate change events.
- *Amends-Making:* Participants offer and accept forgiveness for historical and current transgressions. They show curiosity about why and how to repair damage and change bias and environmental destruction patterns. They develop boundaries and openings for prosocial

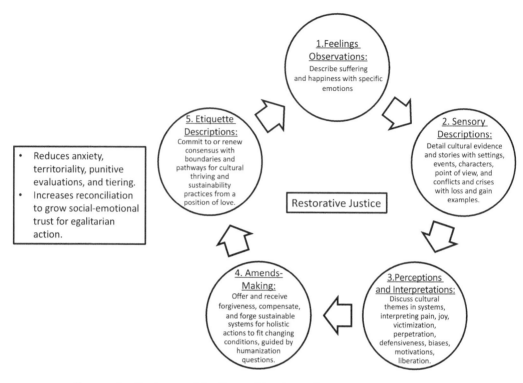

FIGURE 4.6 Restorative Justice graphic. Created by the author.

interactions in changing conditions, asking antibias-antiracist questions, such as "How may I support you in stopping this behavior? How may I support you in building goodwill and friendship?" They ask sustainability questions, such as "How can you support me in stopping this unsustainable behavior? How can you support me in taking stewardship action for inclusive goodwill, multicultural friendship, and collective action for climate healing?"[76]

- *Etiquette Descriptions:* Participants commit, or renew commitment, to consensus etiquettes. They make cross-cultural respect adjustments with boundaries to fit evolving circumstances. They apply defensiveness prevention practices and prosocial sustainability behaviors for reciprocal belonging in hourly and daily education.

Conclusion

How Does Structural Competence Empower Teachers and Students?

Structural competence is awareness that inequity systems in the United States operate in tiered networks and territorial bureaucracies following centuries of Anglo-conformist assimilation and segregation, impacting nearly everything that happens at school.[77] It is also awareness that positive change is possible.[78] When teachers collaborate with structural competence, we are empowered with big-picture awareness about local and global systems that harm students, de-professionalize, distort knowledge, dehumanize education, and destroy the environment. Structural competence is teacher agency to make changes for cultural inclusion on site.

Structural competence strengthens teacher capacity to thwart bias decisions by revealing disinformation about the fairness of individualism in inequity systems. For instance, we see that in a hierarchy, freedom for the privileged means limiting the freedom of the disadvantaged to participate in top tier institutions. Structural competence deepens culture competence to motivate inclusion action. We integrate multiple viewpoints into academic development. Environmental Liberation Education cultivates structural competence to connect student-centered subject engagement to world healing *with* cultures, mindfulness, and nature. Structural competence is the critical consciousness glue that bonds teachers and students for egalitarian participation in a new green economy.

Perspective helps. Global examples reveal connected systems. The assassination of Letelier in Washington, D.C. in 1976 illustrates the big picture. In this example, we see structural inequities that are violent, undemocratic, and entrenched in global networks. Structural analysis of this bloody car bombing reveals the carnage of under-regulated for-profit competition in a globalized free-market substructure-superstructure that entitles some, excludes others, and dehumanizes everyone. In his article, "Chile: Economic Freedom and Political Repression," published the year he was assassinated on US soil, Letelier explains how the rhetoric of freedom can mask the reality of oppression. He describes how Friedman's Chicago Boys implemented a free-market economic blueprint inside Chilean institutions. These professionals followed a 300-page instruction book, supervised by the Central Intelligence Agency and University of Chicago professors, to privatize Chilean institutions, including education, to fit the for-profit global economy serving multinational corporations, many headquartered in the US.[79] Thus, Letelier's story reveals how substructure-superstructure systems cycle inequities, following hundreds of years of European conquest and Anglo-conformist expansion. Such world systems persist regardless of policy rhetoric, perpetually biasing institutions.

In 1975, shortly after personally flying from Chicago to Santiago to advise dictator Pinochet about privatization, professor Friedman authored the proposal that the Chilean government administered through the Chilean economists he trained. Before Friedman arrived, Chile's superstructure had been progressing toward democratic socialism for public good with the peaceful democratic election of president Allende. Even with the challenges of inheriting an economic substructure formed by Spanish colonialism and US-dominated capitalism, Allende's government was able to push policies to increase economic and social inclusion for diverse Chileans. But these humanitarian regulations were wiped away in the name of "laissez-faire" freedom – policies for deregulation and under-regulation – applied by the "brutal force" of military leaders and their bureaucrats to extract remunerations for corporations through repression. The events wrecked Chile's public institutions, perpetrated violence, and led to the murder of Letelier, a Chilean diplomat, and a young US worker in Washington, D.C. who was commuting with Letelier along with her partner, who escaped the bomb blast with injuries.[80]

With systemic awareness, we see Friedman's fingerprints on US choice education campaigns. Structural competence is the skill to resist free-market economy procedures dependent on racialized stratifications to yield products and patterns that drive social superstructure bias. In education, structural competence is making the unconscious conscious, hourly and daily. Transformative teachers recognize implicit bias decisions in-the-making to pause long enough to redirect curriculum, outcomes, knowledge, communications, and interactions. Instead, we facilitate desegregation experiences, un-standardization breakthroughs, multicultural perspectives, and equity designs and assessments in high expectations academic engagement.

Culture-Conscious Listening Develops Structural Competence

Transformative teachers protect students from harmful structures by enacting sustainable equity ecosystems. We start with Culture-Conscious Listening for inclusion in substructure-superstructure analysis during holistic education. We counteract the adverse impact of racialized divisions on students and knowledge by calling out colorblind free-market disinformation. We facilitate multicultural story-telling and evidence-sharing during subject engagement to reveal stereotypes and reduce biases from assimilation and segregation cycles. According to Kathleen Osta and Hugh Vasquez:

> [W]e now live in neighborhoods that are more racially segregated than they were in the 1960s. This means that many white children grow up with very little interaction with people of color. It may also mean that the primary way white people learn about people of color are through media depictions which often serve to perpetuate harmful negative stereotypes. To complicate things further, in their own segregated communities, they may only see people of color working in lower paying service positions such as gardeners, house cleaners, dishwashers in restaurants, security guards in their schools, lunchroom supervisors, or bus drivers.[81]

We use Culture-Conscious Listening steps – Culture-Conscious Breath, Pleasant Eye Contact, Compassionate Support, Brief Summary, and Antibias Question – to welcome diverse interpretations about how mainstream social institutions reproduce economic substructure stratifications. As we sharpen structural competence by inviting cultural context, we bring superdiverse participants – privileged and marginalized – *together* in living education.

Culture-Conscious Listening establishes equity ecosystems *with* students, colleagues, and community supports through universal design. We integrate diverse learners into project groups to engage requirements with real-world problem-solving. We facilitate flexible academics and holistic interactions with restorative justice circles.[82] We engage diversity with action-reflection about dehumanization versus humanization evidence in systems, such opportunity hoarding versus multiracial alliances holism. Swapping community practices and stories and asking compassionate antibias-antiracist questions, we synthesize cross-culturally to guide academics into inclusive liberation experiences, transforming substructure-superstructure cycles piece by piece.

How Does Environmental Liberation Education Help?

Environmental Liberation Education advances holistic humanization. Transformative teachers develop structural competence to deal with global issues locally, expanding culture competence with action-reflection about superdiverse-biodiverse systems. The Three Transformative Tools assist wide-lens critical consciousness. Diversity Circles – configurations of two or more heterogenous participants for prosocial change – are the "horizontal relationship" home bases for "mutual trust."[83] In circles, we practice Multicultural Mindfulness for calm academic integrations. We reflect with Approach-in-Dimension criteria for philosophical clarity, designing and assessing humanization setbacks, stasis, and progress.

Despite glimmers of legislative hope in the 1960s, we know that systemic equity has yet to be realized in US substructure-superstructure practices. The dream for colorblind individualism has been a mirage that masks a culturally ranked and environmentally alienating system.

In a superdiverse world of scarce resources and ecological destruction, transformative teachers facilitate intergenerational experiences for biodiversity restoration through multicultural alliances. Visualizing a substructure-superstructure as large as Earth, we globalize structural competence.

In solutions teams, we deepen academics with equity ecosystems in classrooms, labs, and meeting rooms across sites and off site. We reduce fear by integrating green vocational and democratic citizenship skills into subject engagement. Transformative teachers resist the under-regulated and stratified economic production and social reproduction feedback loop. We reduce defensiveness during change by increasing holistic education from a position of love. We choose empowerment activities to balance individual and collective agency during subject development. We liberate in circles, indoors and outdoors, connecting academics to cultures, mindfulness, and nature, here and now.

TRANSFORMATIVE BREATHWORK AND JOURNAL

Journal Question: *Why do Culture-Conscious Listening?*

> You are mindful of some *thing*: you are mindful of yourself, you are mindful of your atmosphere, and you are mindful of your breath. But if you look at why you are mindful, beyond what you are mindful of, you begin to find that there is no root. Everything begins to dissolve. That is the idea of examining the nature of unborn awareness.[84]
>
> —Chögyam Trungpa Rinpoche

Breathwork

Wherever you are, take a mindful moment to relax. Use a timer chime if you like. Close or lid your eyes, taking several slow deep breaths, smiling slightly, noticing sensations: smells, sounds, touch, taste, and sight (if your eyes are open).

Now breathe while internally reciting the *gatha* below:

Breathing in, I calm my body.
Breathing out, I smile.
Dwelling in the present moment,
I know this is an equity moment.[85]

Then:

Breathing in **Why do Culture-Conscious Listening?**
Breathing out openness.
Repeat for as long as you like or until the timer chimes.

Journal

Imagine we're in a Diversity Circle with the transformative practitioners cited in this book. We want to support superdiverse student success in a biodiverse world. Read our answers below. Reflect on your meditation. Briefly answer the journal question above in a way that's meaningful to you.

Paulo Freire

Culture Circle Listening:

- "Faith" in "human liberation" and receptive "dialogue" free from "paternalistic manipulation."
- Critical consciousness that treats others not "as objects of the investigation" but as collaborators to change systems.
- "Founding itself upon love, humility, and faith, dialogue becomes a horizontal relationship of which mutual trust between the dialoguers is the logical consequence."[86]

Thich Nhat Hanh

Mindful Listening:

- "Breathing mindfully in and out" for patience in compassion "to bring joy and happiness to others and relieve others of their suffering."
- "To look and listen with the eyes of compassion. Compassionate listening brings about healing. When someone listens to us this way, we feel some relief right away."
- "One who hears the cries of the world...without judging or reacting. When we listen with our whole being, we can defuse a lot of bombs."
- Giving others "the courage to say things they have never been able to tell anyone before. Deep listening nourishes both the speaker and listener."
- Patience that "no matter what he says, even if there is a lot of wrong information and injustice in his way of seeing things, even if he condemns or blames you, continue to sit very quietly breathing in and out."[87]

Leonel Lienlaf (Mapuche poet)

Culture-Conscious Listening:

- Compassion for Earth that originates in the heart.
- "The birth of my heart has awakened.... The dream of the earth speaks through my heart."[88]

Micaela Rubalcava

Culture-Conscious Listening:

- Culture and bias reflection during restorative justice stories integrated into academic engagement from a position of love.
- A Multicultural Mindfulness practice to inform structural competence with cross-cultural observations during circle learning about subjects with nature indoors or outdoors.
- Five steps welcome diversity and increase awareness about the impact of systems on individuals and cultures: Culture-Conscious Breath, Pleasant Eye Contact, Compassionate Support, Brief Summary, and Antibias Question.

Notes

1 Lewis and Diamond (2015).
2 Reece (2022), 40.
3 Freire (1985).
4 Lewis and Diamond (2015), 173.
5 Lewis and Diamond (2015), xix, title.
6 Lewis and Diamond (2015), 119.
7 The global substructure-superstructure model explained throughout this chapter, including the diagrams created by the author, is informed by Barrera (1979); Berry and Farris-Berg (2016); Bowles and Gintis (1976); Bourdieu (1973); Deruy (2017); Hall, Quinn and Gollnick (2008); Giroux (1983); Harman (1986, Summer); Johnson, Musial, Hall and Gollnick (2017); Kozol (1991); LeFrancois (2000); Bethell, Newacheck, Hawes and Halfon (2014); Oakes and Lipton (2007); Ogbu (1982); Osta and Vasquez (2019, June 13); Pabon, Sanderson and Kharem (2011); Reece (2022); Quinlan (2016, May 6); Sanders, Wright and Horn (1997, April); Sleeter and Carmona (2017); Williams (1973, November/December).
8 Bethell, Newacheck, Hawes and Halfon (2014); Darling-Hammond (2006); Noguera (2017, 2018); Oakes and Lipton (2007); Sleeter (2001); Sleeter and Carmona (2017); Terada (2019, February 4).
9 Darling-Hammond (2010); Guarda (2015); Morgan (2014); Resnick (2013, April 9); Walker (2016, September 15).
10 Arveseth (2014); Carnoy (1998); Hsieh and Urquiola (2006); Antonio Campaña, Ximena Canelo-Pino, Claudia Heiss, Ana Muñoz, César Peña and Ivan Salinas 2017 Fulbright interviews/seminars, in Rubalcava (2001–2024).
11 Ximena Canelo-Pino 2017 Fulbright interview/seminar, in Rubalcava (2001–2024).
12 Hsieh and Urquiola (2006).
13 Carnoy (1998); Ivan Salinas 2017 Fulbright interviews/seminars, in Rubalcava (2001–2024).
14 Carnoy (1998).
15 Antonio Campaña, Ximena Canelo-Pino, César Peña and Ivan Salinas 2017 Fulbright interviews/seminars, in Rubalcava (2001–2024).
16 Rothstein (2017).
17 Boyd (1999).
18 Spring (all).
19 Frankenberg, Garces and Hopkins (2016).
20 Osta and Vasquez (2019, June 13), 3.
21 Lewis and Diamond (2015); Frankenberg, Garces and Hopkins (2016).
22 Osta and Vasquez (2019, June 13).
23 Bertani, Carroll, Castle, Davies, Hurley, Joos and Scanlon (2010); Lewis and Diamond (2015); Sleeter (2001); Sleeter and Zavala (2020).
24 Lewis and Diamond (2015).
25 Carnoy (1998); Desjardins (2017, June 21); Antonio Campaña, Ximena Canelo-Pino, César Peña and Ivan Salinas 2017 Fulbright interviews/seminars, in Rubalcava (2001–2024).
26 Desjardins (2017, June 21).
27 Dunnell (2018); Rubalcava (2001–2024).
28 Dunnell (2018); Rubalcava (2001–2024).
29 Dunnell (2018); Rubalcava (2001–2024); Letelier (1976).
30 Dunnell (2018); Rubalcava (2001–2024); Letelier (1976)..
31 Dunnell (2018); Rubalcava (2001–2024); Letelier (1976).
32 Carnoy (1998); Liu (2016, September 27).
33 Museo (2017, July & August).
34 Fleming (1973), 612–613.
35 Marcetic (2016, September 21).
36 Marcetic (2016, September 21).
37 Malinowski (2022, January 13).
38 Smith (1776).

39 Smith (1776).
40 Noguera (1998).
41 Smith (1776), 149.
42 Arveseth (2014), 4–5.
43 Friedman (2007).
44 Spring (2014), 433.
45 Spring (2014), 433–434.
46 DeVos (2018, January 16).
47 Strauss (2016, December 21).
48 Freire (1985), 59.
49 Lewis and Diamond (2015), 119–164.
50 Lewis and Diamond (2015), 119–164.
51 Lewis and Diamond (2015), 119–164.
52 Arenas (2004); Noguera (1998).
53 Parry (1996, December).
54 Arenas (2004).
55 Ivan Salinas 2017 Fulbright interviews/seminars, in Rubalcava (2001–2024).
56 Bowles and Gintis (1976); Liu (2016, September 27).
57 Arenas (2004).
58 Bourdieu (1973).
59 Antonio Campaña and Ivan Salinas 2017 Fulbright interviews/seminars, in Rubalcava (2001–2024).
60 Claybourn (2023, February 22).
61 Claybourn (2023, February 22); Resmovits, Kohli and Poindexter (2016, September 5), quoting Pedro Noguera.
62 Aronson and Laughter (2016); Gay, (2000); Ladson-Billings (1995); Nieto (2013); Reese (2022).
63 Darling-Hammond (2010); Morgan (2014); Resnick (2013, April 9); Sahlberg (2015).
64 Sleeter and Carmona (2017).
65 Darling-Hammond (2010); Morgan (2014); Resnick (2013, April 9); Sahlberg (2015).
66 Darling-Hammond (2010); Morgan (2014); Resnick (2013, April 9); Sahlberg (2015).
67 Django and Alim (2017); Freire (1985); Valenzuela (2016); Yamamura and Koth (2018).
68 Barrera (1979); Bowles and Gintis (1976); Bourdieu (1973); Frankenberg, Garces and Hopkins (2016); Giroux (1983); Harman (1986, Summer); Kozol (1991); Lewis and Diamond (2015); Rothstein (all).
69 Bowles and Gintis (1976), x–xi.
70 Bowles and Gintis (1976), x–xi.
71 Nieto (all); Rubalcava (2001–2024); Valenzuela (2016).
72 Reece (2022).
73 Oliver (2023, June 21).
74 Ellison (1998); Hanh and Weare (2017); Tutu and Tutu (2014).
75 Dweck (2007).
76 Englander (2016), 27.
77 Lewis and Diamond (2015), 173.
78 Freire (1985); Hanh and Weare (2017).
79 Arveseth (2014); Carnoy (1998); Letelier (1976); Liu (2016, September 27).
80 Arveseth (2014); Carnoy (1998); Letelier (1976); Liu (2016, September 27).
81 Osta and Vasquez (2019, June 13), 3.
82 Editors (2014, Fall); Ferlazzo (2016, February 6); Oliver (2023, June 21).
83 Freire (1985), 79–80.
84 Trungpa (1993), 32–33.
85 Hanh (2008), 36.
86 Freire (1985), 79–80.
87 Hanh (1998), 84.
88 Luis Carcamo-Huechante 2017 Fulbright lecture, in Rubalcava (2001–2024).

PART II
Three Transformative Tools

5
TOOL #1
Diversity Circles

Guiding Purpose

Explain how Diversity Circles are inclusion learning communities to

- Structure cross-cultural social-emotional trust during change for equity and sustainability in academic routines.
- Collaborate for holistic student success and teacher empowerment in a globalized world.
- Integrate cultures in phases with flexible strategies incorporating ethnic studies, diverse ways of knowing, community practices, and ecological activities into subjects.
- Organize diverse participants in Environmental Liberation Education to develop Multicultural Mindfulness peace with big-picture Approach-in-Dimension design and assessment to meet requirements.

Provide

- Two Multicultural Mindfulness Activities and one journal question: *Five Diversity Circle Projects, Diversity Circle Recipe,* and *How do Diversity Circles reconcile the oppressor-oppressed conflict?*

Context

What Are Diversity Circles?

Diversity Circles are homerooms for belonging during change. They are trust-building gatherings to meet standards through holistic education in a superdiverse and biodiverse world. Diversity Circles can start simply as book clubs for critical consciousness.[1] Diversity Circles empower teachers, students, and community supports with big-picture action-reflection during academic routines. They nurture multicultural alliances and co-generate community-healing experiences through subject themes. Diversity Circles are defined by three principles, seven adjustable types, five flexible phases, and three student-centered strategies.

DOI: 10.4324/9781003364757-8
This chapter has been made available under a CC-BY-NC-ND license.

Diversity Circles integrate culturally responsive subjects into social justice and sustainability activities to uplift high expectations education with love.

Diversity Circles aren't without conflict, given education's ideological, bureaucratic, and territorial milieu. One of Three Transformative Tools for Environmental Liberation Education, Diversity Circles are collaborations to change institutional procedures that reproduce the dominant culture. They counteract assimilation and segregation systems by integrating contradictory perspectives into culturally creative interactions. Changing disciplinary norms involves intergenerational interdisciplinary work. Diverse participants unify to make structural reparations. Creative tension is to be expected. Diversity Circles deal in the growing pains of an "hourly and daily" revolution during academic engagement.[2]

Diversity Circles mix two or more participants, as diverse as possible, "towards reconciliation" with liberation praxis to relate classrooms, labs, meeting rooms, and the campus community to the real world.[3] Diversity Circles use mindfulness *sangha* traditions, which can accommodate large groups.[4] They also draw on Paulo Freire's "liberation" education culture circles, which have a "maximum of twenty persons."[5] Diversity Circle sizes vary, but the larger they are, the harder it is to nurture social-emotional trust.

Diversity Circles co-generate culturally responsive education. Diversity Circles unite to recognize dehumanization and humanization in systems while making cultural inclusion relationships. Educators, students, and community supports collaborate to act and reflect on emotionally charged injustices and justice experiences. We communicate heartfelt cultural-environmental stories, perform and display arts, present science data, and design and facilitate subjects with wide-lens questions and hands-on projects. Our collaborations engage positive reinforcement for reparations as we reduce bias, heal cultural dissonance, and counteract environmental alienation with multicultural stewardship projects.

Diversity Circles are the structure tool for Environmental Liberation Education. They integrate body-mind-culture-environment into academics with Multicultural Mindfulness calm. For accountability, Diversity Circles design and evaluate activities with humanization guideposts, such as those outlined in the Approach-in-Dimension. Three Transformative Tools reinforce holistic academic decisions with antibias-antiracist sustainability criteria. The tools develop diversity, mindfulness, and sustainability best practices that have been modeled by transformative teachers for generations.

Diversity Circles are organic. You're probably in a version of one right now. If you're *organizing* for grassroots change toward ecological holism, you're in one. If you are collaborating on culture competence and structural competence in professional practice, you're in one. This chapter describes how to deepen and expand what you do in a way that's different from mainstream committees or learning communities. Diversity Circles are *Environmental Liberation Education* gatherings to empower students and educators on a planet with eight billion inhabitants – and growing – to take cultural action for healing during climate change.

When you are in a Diversity Circle, you're not alone dealing with the economic-social barriers to academic concentration and professional development. You're not on your own trying to motivate through humanization goals. Rather, you collectivize to resolve culture conflicts otherwise ensnared in the defensive bureaucratic grind navigating the illusion of individualism that undermines unity. You experience mindfulness *of* cultures in systems. In whatever philosophy you believe, or lived experience you perceive, your Diversity Circle nurtures cross-cultural circles to re-imagine solutions. You embrace, rather than ignore or fear, diversity in classrooms, labs, and meeting rooms and across the campus community. By connecting subjects to prosocial action, you develop "academic capital" *with* students and colleagues for global citizenship and vocational knowledge toward a green "new economy."[6]

Diversity Circles co-create multicultural-multiracial events to reduce assimilation and segregation patterns from "institutional racism/discrimination."[7] Your Diversity Circle is your joyful justice headquarters. It's where you smile during breathwork, share little meals, and exercise non-defensive protocols while exchanging cultural stories, practicing the arts, analyzing sciences data, reconciling sensitive issues with service through peace protocols. This is where you laugh, cry, and "love" for *holistic* education.[8]

You tend Diversity Circle soil with critical consciousness. Your Diversity Circle applies "mind consciousness" to cultures in the environment to liberate subjects.[9] *Seven* Diversity Circle types accommodate different sizes to connect with various campus touch-points - ranging from classroom corners to public gatherings in student centers, theaters, grounds, and off site - adjusting to school mission and conditions: Academic Faculty, Student Cohort, Student Cogen, Administrative Faculty, Community Supports, Designated Committee, and Laboratory. *Five* Diversity Circle phases develop action-reflection from simple to layered activities in antibias-antiracist progressions: Antibias Communication Norms, Required Content Inquiry, Environmental Humanization Inquiry, Student-Centered Content Creation, and Institutional and Personal Transformation. *Three* principles distinguish Diversity Circles from mainstream learning communities: Equity Ecosystems, Content Creation, and Environmental Humanization. Diversity Circles use three student-centered strategies: Sharing, Circle Questions, and Global Praxis.

In summary, Diversity Circles are big-picture learning communities, engaging requirements with holistic humanization events for inclusive student success and educator empowerment. Participants experience cultural belonging through justice and sustainability activities during subject engagement.[10] We heal economic-social systems with integrative arts and sciences to reduce, reuse, recycle, and restore from a position of love. We navigate superdiversity in biodiversity with backwards design. Our circles support academic development in an uncertain world. We join green infrastructure and campus community projects to transform education on location, facilitating multimodal stewardship activities with cultures, mindfulness, and nature, indoors and outdoors.

How Are Diversity Circles Different from Mainstream Education Collaborations?

Diversity Circles differ from mainstream education collaborations by integrating two traditions for prosocial change: the mindfulness *sangha* and the liberation circle. The mindfulness *sangha*, developed over thousands of years globally, brings people together to practice holistic consumption, compassionate speech, family responsibility, community generosity, and cultural peace.[11] The *sangha* gathers people to integrate mindfulness into all aspects of daily life: "Mindfulness is to be aware of everything you do every day. Mindfulness is a kind of light that shines upon all your thoughts, all your feelings, all your actions, and all your words."[12] The *sangha* socializes personal mindfulness practice: "You are mindful of some *thing*; you are mindful of yourself, you are mindful of your atmosphere, and you are mindful of your breath."[13] The transformative power of mindfulness collaborations is in applying awareness to action.

Similarly, the "teacher-student" "culture circles" of liberation education, field-tested by Freire in the 1960s in Brazil in 45-day cycles, brought, at the time, about 20,000 illiterate learners in poor neighborhoods to literacy through social action. Subsequently, liberation circles have been used in education across the world.[14] Like the mindfulness *sangha*, liberation circles reconcile people for holistic solutions:

> The *raison d'être* of education…lies in its drive toward reconciliation. Education must begin with the solution of the teacher-student contradiction, by reconciling the poles of the contradiction so that both are simultaneously teachers *and* students.[15]

Different from mainstream education collaborations, Diversity Circles organize teachers and students to reconcile education's present moment with peace processes that integrate diversity into action for "big, disruptive solutions" to 400-year-old problems *now*.[16] Diversity Circles gather people to practice mindfulness to reduce cultural divisions and environmental alienation during subject engagement. Diversity Circles host interactions to develop cross-cultural compassion during routines that shape knowledge and students. Diversity Circles organize for "a good kind of subversion" against systemic malaise.[17] Participants identify disinformation from "race-neutral" colorblind policies that have "good intentions and bad outcomes."[18]

Diversity Circle participants help one other recognize how our own ongoing bias decisions perpetuate the "racial achievement gap."[19] We collaborate to replace "in-group favoritism, opportunity hoarding, and racial apathy" habits from assimilation and segregation routines with culture consciousness.[20] We share stories and cultural practices to counter the narrative of hopelessness about disenfranchised teachers, subjects detached from world healing, and broken schools. We advocate to raise teacher pay, develop academic freedom to connect academics to culture creation, and nurture affirmative action to help education become a "great equalizer" institution. Diversity Circles use inclusive social-emotional designs to reduce inequity experiences in classrooms, across sites, and between campuses.[21]

Diversity Circles differ from mainstream education collaborations in purpose. Diversity Circles develop big-picture academic concentration for change. This involves quieting the

Diversity Circles are learning communities defined by:
- Three principles - Content Creation, Equity Ecosystems, Environmental Humanization.
- Seven types - Academic Faculty, Student Cohort, Student Cogen, Administrative Faculty, Community Supports, Designated Committee, Laboratory.
- Five phases - Antibias Communication Norms, Required Content Inquiry, Environmental Humanization Inquiry, Student-Centered Content Creation, Institutional and Personal Transformation.
- Three strategies - Sharing, Circle Questions, Global Praxis.

Student Cogen Diversity Circle:
- Question: How do students cogenerate academics with culturally responsive sustainability experiences?
- Student design: Multimodal science activity about evolution and biodiversity with mindfulness, cultures, and nature outdoors.

FIGURE 5.1 Diversity Circles are learning communities. Photo by the author.

mind, from the mindfulness *sangha* tradition, and applying mindfulness to academic subjects for world healing, from the liberation circle tradition. This purpose protects action. "When you have developed a basic sense of mindfulness and awareness...[you realize] that the confusion and the chaos in your mind have no origin, no cessation, and nowhere to dwell...[This] is the best protection."[22] By integrating body-mind-culture-environment *into* subjects, teachers and students intervene in substructure-superstructure dehumanization from dominant culture assimilation and segregation systems. We respond to the economically driven environmental destruction that degrades schools. We address the military–industrial complex that weaponizes global violence and fuels the culture wars, bullying, and shootings that harm education. Intersecting Diversity Circles, thus, organize a "decentralized diversity model" defined by inward-outward compassion and reconciliation for social justice action now.[23]

Where to Start?

Start with an expansive sense of culture. Teachers start by reaching out to form an Academic Faculty Diversity Circle. Initiate a conversation with a colleague this week about culture in education. Reach out to someone who self-identifies with one or more race-ethnicity-class-gender category that offers cultural difference in your partnership. Administrative educators start with the Administrative Faculty Diversity Circle. Reach out to a colleague with whom you have rapport *and* who lends cultural difference to your alliance.

Starting with someone you know lessens social anxiety about the systemic biases that you, like all of us, perpetuate hourly and daily but wish didn't exist. The spark of friendship cuts through angst about systemic racism, sexism, and classism.

Many educators strive for the colorblind ideal, but partnering with someone you trust who *also* represents cultural difference develops cross-cultural understanding grounded in reality. We explore how inequity systems ruin colorblind dreams. We allow each other grace during the discomfort of trying to reduce unconscious bias habits. We acknowledge feelings of fear, loss, anger, resentment, guilt, and shame. We partner for boldness to take holistic antibias-antiracist actions *with* students and community supports to heal education, forgiving each other for mistakes along the way.

Begin with a courageous conversation about racism or the denial of racism in education. Discuss a current global event or use ethnic studies or environmental science scholarship to address a curriculum requirement or knowledge topic. Be ready to jump into solutions. Diversity Circles are *action*-reflection meetings. Pick something in this week's academic routines on which to try a culturally responsive sustainability practice, such as one of the Multicultural Mindfulness Activity plans in this book.

After starting small, with a single partner with whom to try out non-defensive culture and sustainability ideas during familiar routines, invite other collaborators to develop *projects*. After experimenting with diversity as empowerment rather than a problem for others to solve, you notice other Diversity Circles in your midst. Transformation involves consistent collaborations with a network of students, colleagues, and community supports *during* academic engagement. From your Diversity Circle foundation, you apply Multicultural Mindfulness practices to environmental justice actions. Environmental Liberation Education unfolds as you design and assess activities with Approach-in-Dimension guideposts to adjust details with evidence guided by heartfelt and transparently discussed definitions of humanization.

MULTICULTURAL MINDFULNESS ACTIVITY

Five Diversity Circle Projects

Outcome

- Differentiate Diversity Circle types.
- Conduct a Diversity Circle meeting.
- Apply a Diversity Circle activity.

Key Concepts

- **Critical Consciousness:** Student-centered action-reflection about social-economic contradictions integrating academics into real-world healing.
- **Culture-Conscious Listening:** Five reflective breathwork steps to welcome diversity: Culture-Conscious Breath, Pleasant Eye Contact, Compassionate Support, Brief Summary, and Antibias Question.
- **Diversity Circle:** Learning community for nonviolent change, as diverse as possible, to integrate cultures and sustainability experiences mindfully into student-centered academics.
- **Socratic Circle:** Evidence-driven inquiry circle for academic development. Participants ask subject questions and explain answers with data and logical analysis for dialectical problem-solving.

Resources

- Journal, pencil, copies of Diversity Circle Cheat Sheet (below), an example or symbol of nature, a place to meet indoors or outdoors.

Big-Picture Question

- How do we activate holistic education now?

Start

Whole group circle with an example or symbol of nature in the circle's center and copies of the Diversity Circle Cheat Sheet:
Individually

- **Mark** one *type* that fits your site conditions.
- **Mark** one *phase* that gets you curious.
- **Mark** one *project* that grabs you.
- **Journal** why you like the *project* you marked and guess its *phase*.
- **Journal** about how you can adapt the project to one of your required subjects.

Middle

In partners, as diverse as possible:

- **Discuss** marked projects and diversity conditions at your site.

Closing

- **Schedule** another meeting with your partner to plan a project activity.

Diversity Circle Cheat Sheet

Types:

1 *Academic Faculty:* Two or more teachers integrate cultures, mindfulness, and sustainability into holistic academic engagement
2 *Student Cohort:* Student-enrolled group (class, program, etc.) for holistic education.
3 *Student Cogen:* Rotating Student Cohort subgroup that makes a culturally sustaining holistic classroom change.[24]
4 *Administrative Faculty:* Two or more administrators integrate cultures, mindfulness, and sustainability into institutional systems.
5 *Community Supports:* Rotating community and staff who assist and model cultures and holism at school.
6 *Designated Committee:* Specific collaborative holistic education project with an end date.
7 *Laboratory:* Campus community engages year-long big-picture themes with culturally creative interdisciplinary events featuring student-centered experiments, displays, and performances within established course schedule.

Phases:

1 *Antibias Communication Norms:* Non-defensive interactions with Culture-Conscious Listening.
2 *Required Content Inquiry:* Assess scope of cultures, mindfulness, and sustainability in a required subject or topic.
3 *Environmental Humanization Inquiry:* Pose diversity, mindfulness, and sustainability questions for global citizenship activities during required content.
4 *Student-Centered Content Creation:* Students lead curriculum development with a holistic culturally responsive sustainability activity.
5 *Institutional and Personal Transformation:* Collaborating with other Diversity Circles to analyze culture, mindfulness, and sustainability changes from integrative academic activities.

Sample Projects:

1 *Holistic Antibias-Antiracist Interview:* Each Diversity Circle participant conducts an interview with another colleague about diversity education. Ask about bias, race, and cultures, focusing on cultural fears and joys and the differences between colorblind and antibias-antiracist approaches to cultural authenticity. Apply one interview idea to an academic activity outdoors or with nature indoors. Journal and discuss experiences.

2. *Welcome Statement:* Collaboratively brainstorm a diversity statement for your site, relating cultures in subjects and student cultures to heartfelt views about sustainable humanity. Individually, rewrite this statement to tailor it to your classroom, lab, or meeting room. Make this personalized statement into a poster for display. Get feedback about emotions the poster elicits (How welcoming is the poster? What cultures does the poster unwittingly exclude?). Journal and discuss experiences.
3. *Culture-Conscious Listening:* Engage one or more of the five Culture-Conscious Listening steps – Culture-Conscious Breath, Pleasant Eye Contact, Compassionate Support, Brief Summary, and Antibias Question – during a required subject activity conducted outdoors. Journal and discuss experiences.
4. *Socratic Circle:* Integrate a whole-group inquiry circle into a required subject activity. Open the circle with breathwork about nature related to the subject (place a nature example inside the circle center). Assess for required subject mastery and culturally responsive environmental education with a pretest-posttest question. Journal and discuss experiences.[25]
5. *Outdoor Education Collaboration:* Invite others to co-create and implement an outdoor education activity that meets a shared requirement for all participants. Use a big-picture theme to guide breathwork during the activity. Assess the activity for required subject mastery and culturally responsive environmental education with a pretest-posttest question. Journal and discuss experiences.

Theory and Practice

How Do Diversity Circles Transform?

Environmental Liberation Education champions "all-inclusive" education for culturally responsive sustainability.[26] Diversity Circles organize to reduce bias from divisions during subject routines. We gather to clarify humanity in knowledge and curriculum. This section explains how Diversity Circles overlap with and differ from mainstream learning communities. It describes Diversity Circle types and phases with multicultural, mindfulness, and sustainability criteria. It depicts how to co-generate liberation education with backwards design, using three strategies for change during academic engagement.

Education Learning Communities[27]

Education learning communities have been part of positive developments in US education for decades. They have various configurations, integrating student cohorts into education through disciplinary and interdisciplinary themes. In them, students experience academic success and well-being activities, while educators experience professional development teams. Participants connect to deepen knowledge and learning outcomes.

> Learning communities represent an educational approach that involves the integration of engaged curricular and co-curricular learning and emphasizes relationship and community building among faculty or staff and a cohort of students in a rich learning environment. This educational approach may come in different forms, but typically involves/incorporates/includes at least one of the following: A curricular structure characterized by a cohort of students participating in an intentionally designed integrative study of an issue or theme through connected courses, experiences, and resources.[28]

Education learning communities gather students and teachers in space for action and reflection about topics over time.

Education learning communities engage the humanization goals that motivate students and teachers. They meet social-emotional needs through "inter-unit collaboration," "improved campus climate," "strengthened institutional culture," and "enhanced institutional reputation."

> [Educators] have been 'inventing' learning communities and modifying them as students' needs, curricular imperatives, and institutional opportunities and constraints have evolved and as newly involved individuals have brought different perspectives. Nonetheless, some patterns of learning community structures have emerged and endured as campuses found them to be effective and engaging for teachers and students. Individual learning communities rarely share the exact same structure or practices, yet they *resemble* one another in their attempts to make curricular connections and align practices across multiple courses.[29]

Education learning communities make change by using "a variety of curricular approaches that intentionally link or cluster two or more courses, often around an interdisciplinary theme or problem, and enroll a common cohort of students."[30]

US education learning communities developed from the US business sector, which is another leading institution in the economic substructure-social superstructure system.[31] Business learning communities cultivate institutional culture through professional growth and innovation. Learning communities in both business and education are premised on the human capacity to learn in two ways. First, knowledge develops through day-to-day culture connections, such as lived experiences between participants reinforced by reflection among those who share the same experiences. Second, "the creation of tension" from collaboration and culture engagement accelerates knowledge comprehension, analysis, and synthesis. The idea is that subject mastery and professional development advance during reciprocal participation in institutional change.[32]

Learning communities, thus, engage the human capacity to grow expertise and success thoughtfully through social interactions during higher-order cognition and cultural imagination events about shared topics. Education learning communities apply the business sector model – strengthening institutional culture through reflective collaboration – to school conditions.

Five Characteristics of Successful Learning Communities

Successful education learning communities have five characteristics: (1) effective student learning through cohort development, (2) learning sequences from social-emotional knowledge exchanges, (3) open-door policies for theme routines with constructive peer observations and interventions in learning, (4) reciprocal communication and knowledge-sharing, and (5) long-term teaching and learning development schemes.[33]

> [The collaboration] represents an intentional restructuring of students' time, credit, and learning experiences to build community, enhance learning, and foster connections among students, faculty, and disciplines.[34]

Structural conditions for successful collaborations include accessible meeting times and gathering spaces, physical proximity, a collective culture for academic freedom, and consistent and reliable communication. Education learning community configurations can be interdisciplinary or multi-level subject-specific; costly or cost-free; event-specific or sequential; micro or macro; experimental or prescribed; scientific or artistic; school-centered or community-centered; intergenerationally vertical in a subject or generationally horizontal; subject cohort or demographic cohort; student-led or teacher-led or co-led; gifted-and-talented or remedial; survey learning or in-depth learning.

Education learning community descriptors include "freshman seminar or interest group" or "colloquy learning community" with a "freshman year experience course" or "students from two or more regularly scheduled classes, making the additional course an integrative…colloquy"; "clustered classes" for "explicitly linking two or more separate courses" as teachers collaborate to include "an introductory skill-building class linked to a content-heavy class"; "team-taught learning communities" as "programs bring together [several classes] to create a common syllabus around integrating themes or projects"; "living learning communities" with residential cohorts that pursue "holistic curricular" experiences for students or, if students don't live together, facilitating students to interact during occasions in overlapping schedules in classrooms, hallways, cafeterias, auditoriums, and outdoors for "natural" learning community-themed activities.[35]

Education learning communities generate three core benefits: holistic education for student success and well-being; high-quality professional development for educators; and cultural collaborations for institutional development. They provide non-punitive education feedback with action-research and learning innovations for critical thinking. They intervene in the paralysis of education from over-standardization and commoditization that dehumanizes students and teachers. "[A] primary reason teachers move from high-poverty schools to wealthier ones – as well as leave the profession altogether – is lack of professional autonomy and faculty decision-making influence." Education learning communities allow participants to make reflective decisions "leading the transformation of schooling."[36] They co-generate social-emotional trust while raising education expectations.[37] Peer-observations in classrooms to coordinate themes guide knowledge development real time, making adjustments for academic efficacy. These collaborations innovate with academic engagement for "sticky campus" practices "toward reconciliation" between students and teachers and school and world.[38]

Diversity Circles as Learning Communities

Diversity Circles are an education learning community subset distinguished by sustainability themes and multicultural interactions through mindfulness and liberation circle learning. Diversity Circles gather at least two participants, as diverse as possible, to creatively and respectfully make academic change for Environmental Humanization outcomes. Diversity Circles strive for *intersectional* membership to reconcile students and teachers and integrate cultural divides through circle trust, indoors with nature or outdoors. In this way, Diversity Circles are joyful justice forums, wherein "happy teachers change the world" with ecologically minded student-centered activities.[39]

Three Principles Differentiate Diversity Circles

Three mindfulness principles – interbeing, impermanence, and emptiness – distinguish Environmental Liberation Education from mainstream approaches to diversity and sustainability in education. These "three dharma seals" of mindfulness assist "the transformation of suffering" through "peace, joy, and liberation" experiences.[40] These principles center Diversity Circles on healing activities for inclusive student success and multicultural knowledge development in an ecological world. Martin Luther King, Jr., friend of Thich Nhat Hanh, described how antibias-antiracist freedom involves leadership by the oppressed: "We know through painful experience that freedom is never voluntarily given by the oppressor; it must be demanded by the oppressed."[41] Diversity Circles, thus, support co-leadership by people of color, people with lived experiences in poverty, and people whose identities have been marginalized historically. Applied to Diversity Circles through liberation theory, the three mindfulness principles become Equity Ecosystems, Content Creation, and Environmental Humanization.

Principle #1: Interbeing/Equity Ecosystems

Reflecting interconnections in nature, Equity Ecosystems are sustainability designs for holistic cross-cultural action. They grow trust during social justice with ecological motifs. Equity Ecosystems adjust to conditions: cross-district and cross-institution,[42] cross-class campus-wide,[43] whole-classroom,[44] multicultural-multilingual cohorts,[45] and subset circles of two to 20 people.[46] Informed by action research and cultural and sustainability surveys, transformative teachers facilitate Equity Ecosystems to meet basic needs: physiological, safety, love, self-acceptance, curiosity, and aesthetics.[47] This principle is about realizing inclusion face to face as much as possible, co-led by historically marginalized peoples with ideological transparency. It is circle learning activated during multimodal openers, core content projects, and social-emotional closures throughout academic routines.[48]

Principle #2: Impermanence/Content Creation

Content Creation is cultural expression, performance, and displays to refresh knowledge for humanization. This is cultural action for prosocial change during academic routines. Students and teachers co-generate findings, works, materials, and presentations integrating mainstream disciplinary approaches with interdisciplinary analysis and diverse ways of knowing in the

Diversity Circles:
- Integrate cultures into holistic academic development with liberation experiences.
- Paulo Freire facilitates a critical consciousness culture circle.

Diversity Circles:
- Change collaborations for critical consciousness education, integrating mindfulness, cultures, and nature into subject engagement, indoors and outdoors.

Three strategies:
1. *Sharing* – Engage subject through culture and nature stories, readings, data, and artifacts with mindfulness inquiry.
2. *Circle Questions* – Pose change questions and integrate Sharing information into labs and field experiences.
3. *Global Praxis* – Refresh lab and field experience design with Sharing and Circle Questions information to revitalize environmental liberation and cogenerate new stories, readings, data, and artifacts for feedback loop.

Equity Ecosystems

Diversity Circles:
- Integrate diverse students into inclusive academic engagement with real world problem-solving.
- Culture circle at the UCLA Paulo Freire Institute.

Paulo Freire Institute, UCLA April 22, 2014. Photo by Fang-Tzu Hsu

FIGURE 5.2 Equity Ecosystems in action. Photo by the author.

FIGURE 5.3 Content Creation in action. Photo by the author.

real-world. Content Creation is reducing pre-packaged assimilation content and increasing holistic knowledge with ethnic studies, women's studies, other identity studies, environmental studies, and field investigations.[49] Developed through action-research about cultural suffering and thriving during subject engagement, this principle expands arts and sciences with diversity and ecology themes through evidence and hands-on imagination.[50]

Principle #3: **Emptiness/Environmental Humanization**

Environmental Humanization is local and global citizenship for sustainability to unify the humanization goals that motivate education. It is an inclusion identity that shifts students and teachers from individualistic extraction-consumption behaviors to collective praxis.[51] It is a holistic state of being that expands social justice with open-minded awareness of superdiversity in biodiversity. It is the spacious process of regulating consumption patterns with conservation and restorative designs. During academic engagement, this is the principle of generosity to shift consciousness from "humanity-over-nature" to "humanity-through-nature" with[52]

- Culturally responsive nature or outdoor activities integrated into subjects.
- Community–school sustainability gardens with cultural arts and life-cycle activities, such as dedications, fertilizing, planting, weeding, harvesting, and nourishment.
- Regional flora and fauna interdisciplinary projects.
- Green career programs.

FIGURE 5.4   Equity Ecosystems. Photo by the author.

- Reduce, reuse, recycle, and renew activities during academic routines for sun, earth, air, and water interbeing experiences.
- East, south, west, and north stewardship journeys with nature, indoors and outdoors, to meet subject requirements.[53]

How Do Diversity Circles Develop Culture Consciousness?

Compassionate interactions develop culture consciousness. As diverse collaborators act and reflect for liberation, we discern how race-neutral policies and wishful colorblind individualism mask systemic divides. Culture consciousness advances by listening to diverse perspectives while researching equity and applying cultural practices and evidence to academic activities. We find that in US education:

- Student racial and cultural diversity is increasing.
- The racial achievement gap persists between European American and some Asian Pacific American students versus students of color.
- School segregation, and racialized tracking within desegregated schools, continues.
- Mainstream curriculum assimilates toward the dominant culture.
- About 80% of teachers are European American.
- The numbers of African American and Indigenous teachers are decreasing.
- A decline in teacher education enrollment for a highly qualified teacher pool.
- Scant multicultural education or ethnic studies in teacher education.
- High teacher turnover and more so in underfunded schools.
- Negligible holistic antibias-antiracist teacher professional development.

Our findings prompt cultural inclusion activities. For example:

- Academic integration projects to counteract segregation and racialized tracking.
- Big-picture backwards design with multicultural perspectives and sustainability criteria for knowledge and curriculum development.

- Multimodal subject activities with cultures, mindfulness, and nature, indoors and outdoors.
- Guided diversity field experiences linking education to world.
- Mentorship for employed teachers of color to lead culturally responsive sustainability education.
- Advocacy for higher teacher pay, reduced class sizes, and holistic professional development anchored in ethnic studies.[54]

How Do Diversity Circles Develop Liberation Content?

Culture consciousness is a starting point for liberation content. Diversity Circles empower teachers and students with praxis about economic-social contradictions to *transform* knowledge with ethnic studies, cultural ways of knowing, and real-world problem-solving.[55] Liberation content starts from "curiosity" about inclusion during the "hourly and daily practices and processes that are the substance of what we think of as 'school.'"[56] Liberation from assimilation and segregation procedures that distort cultures with a fixation on individualism – rather than recognizing individuals as members of cultures in systems – generates holistic knowledge. Transformative teachers debunk the portrayal of racism, sexism, and classism as individual pathologies. We replace the colorblind yearning that poses racism as someone else's problem with, instead, collective critical consciousness.[57]

Many teachers think of racism as a malady which they don't personally suffer from and which doesn't exist inside their classrooms or committees.[58] We wish racism didn't harm our students and colleagues, and when we're made aware that racism's structural, we don't know what to do about it. We intervene in victim/perpetration behaviors as best we can, but we don't know how to deal with the White supremacy root of anxiety, aggression, and chaos.[59] Systemic racism divides, undermining the unity needed to combat global warming.

Liberation content features cultures and seeks to understand communities in systems. It uses "community-based pedagogies" to investigate economic, social, and political oppression structures, and freedom from such structures.[60] Liberation content transforms knowledge with "lived experiences" to offset systemic racism with "intersectionality and multiplicity" evidence.[61] It shifts racialized assumptions by "opening space for knowledge from marginalized communities" to empower *diverse* students by engaging subjects with "structural analysis."[62] Dr. King explained:

> Nonviolent direct action seeks to create such a crisis and foster such a tension that a community which has consistently refused to negotiate is forced to confront the issue. It seeks to so dramatize the issue that it can no longer be ignored… [T]here is a type of constructive, nonviolent tension that is necessary for growth…. The purpose of our direct-action program is to create a situation so crisis-packed that it will inevitably open the door to negotiation.[63]

Diversity Circles, thus, develop liberation content as personal commitment to cultural negotiation. When applied to *Environmental* Liberation Education, Diversity Circles integrate environmental science with cultural arts to engage the creative tension *everyone* shares during "crisis-packed" climate change.[64] Subjects are reframed with planetary data, not to produce "a separate subject matter, but rather" to provide "a reconceptualization of subject matter that takes into account state standards and assessment for which students will be held accountable."[65] Diversity Circles develop multicultural liberation content on "a cosmic scale" for intergenerational thriving.[66]

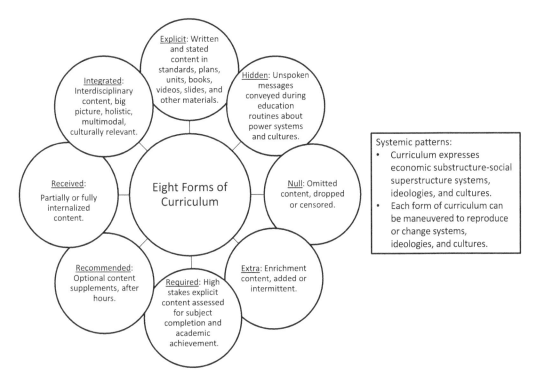

FIGURE 5.5 Eight forms of curriculum graphic. Created by the author.

Eight Forms of Curriculum[67]

The more educators understand curriculum, the more transformative our collaborations become. We do not have to be confined to top-down busy-making explicit curriculum. There are at least eight forms of curriculum, and when we apply academic freedom to them, we empower the profession and students[68]:

1 *Explicit:* Official guidelines and content, written, produced, and stated, such as national and state content standards, program requirements, course learning outcomes, lesson plans, textbooks, resources, classroom and lab materials, media packages, project kits, cultural and arts items, visuals, manipulatives, and things in subjects and routines. Explicit curriculum is what is directly propounded: mainstream or transformative; standardized or unstandardized; misinformed or from scientific peer-reviewed scholarship. The bureaucracy of explicit curriculum can absorb teachers in make-work, tight schedules, and closed-minded perceptions of standards that restrict the exercise of academic freedom.
2 *Hidden:* Hourly and daily embedded messages conveyed through routines. For example, in US mainstream education, this is instructions about individualism, power divisions, ranked identities, and assimilation and segregation norms. Hidden curriculum is transmitted through language (e.g., using dominant culture language or multiple languages) and non-verbal cues; modalities (cyber versus face-to-face); disciplinary and procedural patterns that exclude *or* include students and cultures from subjects; academic tracking and segmentation *or* programmatic integration experiences; and unconscious evaluations of students

and cultures that inform design decisions for space, time, materials, and learning environments in classrooms, labs, and meeting rooms.
3. *Null:* Omitted content. Censorship such as the banning of critical race theory. Information intentionally kept out of or unconsciously removed from curriculum when its applicability is culturally relevant to the subject.
4. *Extra:* Optional activities. Intermittent enrichment content interspersed in core content without being part of required curriculum, such as noncompulsory handouts, worksheets, clubs, committees, service projects, sports, visual art, theater, band, or robotics.
5. *Required:* Evaluated explicit curriculum mandated for subject completion, performance, and graduation, used to define achievement. It's standardized core content assessed with assignments and exams through approved rubrics. Required curriculum provides evaluation criteria. For example, US mainstream required curriculum relies on an assimilation economic efficiency rubric, wherein knowledge is deemed to be valuable as "a market product to be consumed by individuals for their own private use (such as to get a job)."[69]
6. *Recommended:* Explicit academic content available but provided intermittently, if at all. It's typically negotiated for after-hours use in the form of specialized readings, research projects, and tutors.
7. *Received:* Content the student internalizes. The content is *received* when it's *understood* and applied. If explicit curriculum isn't comprehended or used, it becomes null curriculum; for example, a graduate from high school with low civics scores may not have *internalized* the rights and duties of citizens in a democracy from school.
8. *Integrated:* Holistic academics with interdisciplinary themes for humanization, often developed in learning communities. When applied to multicultural project teams with social justice themes, integrated curriculum engages intersectional liberation experiences. Its backwards design starts with "big ideas" for "connections between persons, between the individual and the community, between humanity and nature, between the material and the spiritual." It supports a "reverence for life" with a "holistic worldview."[70] Integrated curriculum is "not linear." It focuses on "students and their questions rather than on teacher-identified central ideas." The "teacher acts as facilitator" to develop subjects for "deep intellectual engagement and principled activism in a diverse society."[71]

What Shapes Curriculum?

Eight forms of curriculum are impacted by disciplinary norms and sanctioned languages, cultures, modalities, and topics. In US mainstream education, curriculum prioritizes the interests and divisions of the for-profit global economy. It delivers largely vocational curriculum marketed to individuals "rather than as a public resource that develops a citizenry who can act on behalf of the good of both their own communities and others with whom they share space and resources."[72] Mainstream curriculum mandates are dominated by privatized consumption and materialism values. Because curriculum, in its various forms, reproduces economic substructure productions, transformative teachers do not passively comply with curriculum mandates. Instead, we ask critical consciousness questions to shape curriculum toward equity and sustainability solutions.

What's Explicit and Required Mainstream Curriculum?

Explicit and required mainstream forms of curriculum are standardized to pin student learning outcomes to tiers defined by Anglo-conformity, and they are often commoditized. These

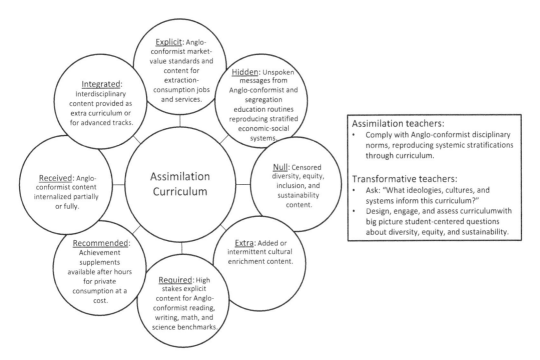

FIGURE 5.6 Assimilation curriculum graphic about the current US system. Created by the author.

forms are manufactured for "a market product to be consumed" by individuals.[73] Mainstream subjects serve the economic efficiency goal of US education.

> Setting standards for quality has become conflated with standardization. Standardization refers to making things exactly the same. Content standards, which specify what students should know (Lewis 2000), have become the basis for standardizing what students should learn and what testing should cover.... Standardization is a consequence of standards setting when attempts to improve student learning become bureaucratized and curriculum is defined in detail in terms of what is measurable and is established at state or national levels.[74]

Focused on "what is measurable and is established" in institutions, standardization curriculum in mainstream education is rooted in systemic inequities.

Status quo educators obediently deliver explicit and required mainstream curriculum to serve commerce in the stratified economy. Some of the resulting schisms are obvious – segregated sites and racialized tracking between schools and programs – but others are harder to spot. Cultural divides *within* classrooms, labs, and decision-making rooms occur as teachers unwittingly distribute mainstream curriculum inequitably according to systemic bias. Explicit and required forms of curriculum are *not* necessarily materially or culturally available to everyone equally. Moreover, commoditized curriculum trivializes the teaching profession, weakening academic freedom by absorbing educators into the dominant culture of consumption. Mainstream curriculum stifles critical thinking with the expediency of predetermined standards and prepackaged units. Banking education makes it convenient to avoid humanization problem-solving and cross-cultural imagination through multiple perspectives during subject engagement.

What's Explicit and Required Multicultural Curriculum?

Like explicit and required mainstream forms of curriculum standardized into US education, *multicultural* curriculum reacts to disciplinary norms and sanctioned languages, cultures, modalities, and topics in economic-social systems. Categorized into two sets, explicit and required multicultural curriculum either delivers market-based supplemental products about diversity framed by individualism or empowers teachers to integrate diversity framed by a dialectic about the individual and collectivism. Depicted in the transformative planning and assessment tool, Approach-in-Dimension explained in Chapter 7, these are the two sets:

1 The *Contributions* and *Additive* approaches, which are extracurricular diversity topics and materials appended to mainstream standardization. This set of explicit multicultural curriculum delivers diversity content packages that comport with the existing substructure-superstructure model of Anglo-conformity. This set omits critical consciousness and intersectionality topics from ethnic studies about indigeneity, culture conflict-reconciliation, interdisciplinary counternarratives, and structural analysis.[75] It neglects implementing academic engagement for participation in an equitable and sustainable economy.[76]
2 *Transformative*, *Social Action*, and *Environmental Liberation Education* approaches, which are education strategies for systemic change. This set of explicit multicultural curriculum empowers teachers to reshape assimilation and segregation knowledge with diverse ways of knowing and liberation circles for collective action. This set develops critical consciousness and intersectionality topics from ethnic studies and other identity studies.[77] It facilitates academic engagement designed for a just and sustainable economy.[78] For example, Christine Sleeter and Judith Carmona describe a systemic change strategy to un-standardize required curriculum by infusing a culturally relevant "Concept, Big Idea" into the creative process for "Transformative Intellectual Knowledge."[79]

How Do We Make Culturally Relevant Change?

While inroads have been made to change mainstream curriculum away from Anglo-conformist standardization and commoditization, most multicultural curriculum has been delivered through *Contributions* and *Additive* approaches. Diversity has been tokenized into one-off explicit, hidden, and required forms with little impact on systemic inequities and assimilation curriculum.[80] This book offers Three Transformative Tools that start with Diversity Circles to organize for big-picture action-reflection. Intersecting Diversity Circles on a single campus make change by tackling various education dimensions simultaneously. As one classroom transforms its curriculum, outcomes, knowledge, communications, or social interactions with antibias-antiracist sustainability activities, neighboring classrooms get inspired to change. As we network classrooms, we shift departments, schools, and districts. One district intersects with others, and culturally relevant change ripples.

Seven Types of Diversity Circles

Diversity Circle configurations are unlimited. However, at least seven types provide variations to meet different site conditions. As a transformative educator, you might participate in any or all of the seven Diversity Circle types, personalizing collaborations to changing circumstances.

All Diversity Circle types feature cultures and nature, indoors or outdoors, integrating mindfulness and liberation activities into subjects for inclusive academic equity and sustainability experiences:

1. *Academic Faculty:* Two or more academic faculty, as diverse as possible, in professional development for *culturally sustaining holistic change*. This is home base for social-emotional trust among teachers. It develops multicultural alliances for humanization knowledge and student-centered action-reflection during big picture academic development.
2. *Student Cohort:* A variable-sized student group based on academic enrollment with one or more educator-facilitator striving for *culturally sustaining holistic education*. This humanization home base can be a whole class (e.g., everyone in Political Science 101), all classes in a major or program (e.g., a STEM [science, technology, engineering, and mathematics] field), a larger group (e.g., a graduating class), or a campus affinity club, team, or student organization (e.g., *Men of Color*).
3. *Student Cogen:* A Student Cohort subgroup of two or more members to design and implement a *culturally sustaining holistic classroom change*. Drawing on Freire's co-generative culture circles, Christopher Emdin uses the term "cogen" as follows: "Cogens are simple conversations between the teacher and their students with a goal of co-creating/generating plans of action for improving the classroom."[81] The teacher ensures that, by term's end, every student in the cohort has been in a Student Cogen once, collaborating apart from class meeting times with snacks, background music, and mindfulness practices. This humanization homeroom builds social-emotional trust among peers and models education for academic development.
4. *Administrative Faculty:* Two or more administrators, counselors, and/or other staff, as diverse as possible, in professional development for *systems change*. This humanization home base grows social-emotional trust among non-teaching employees who engage culturally sustaining holistic education. It develops multicultural allies to fund and manage big picture academics and student success.
5. *Community Supports:* Rotating variable-sized groups of local volunteers and aides, as diverse as possible, assist and model multicultural holistic education. Organized by the educator, community supports nurture *intersectional belonging* and intergenerational humanization during academic development.
6. *Designated Committee:* Two or more education participants across categories, as diverse as possible, on a project time line for *culturally sustaining holistic change*. This humanization home base advances a *specific* activity for big picture academic development.
7. *Laboratory:* A variable-sized campus-wide interdisciplinary learning community, as diverse as possible, for *culture creation*. Organized from the existing academic schedule, this humanization home base experiments with holistic education during a year-long big-picture theme with interactive student-centered events. Participants act and reflect on a holistic question.

Five Diversity Circle Phases

Just as Diversity Circle types are ideals that adjust to conditions, the five Diversity Circle phases are also flexible. In collaborative evolution, not every Diversity Circle type engages each phase, but all start with some variation of the first:

1. *Antibias Communication Norms:* Respectful civil interactions. Non-defensive reciprocity protocols for discussions and activities, such as Noun/Pronoun Use, Turn-Taking, Creative Tension, Culture-Conscious Listening, and Academic Accuracy (detailed below).
2. *Required Content Inquiry:* Identifying limitations and biases in school and curriculum mandates. This is evaluating how a subject treats big picture topics and cultures. It's assessing if the subject is defined with diversity, equity, inclusion, and sustainability criteria, and engages a transparent philosophy of humanization.
3. *Environmental Humanization Inquiry:* Experimenting with global citizenship activities for subject engagement. Based on Required Content Inquiry findings, this is designing and inserting an academic activity to integrate cultures, mindfulness, or nature, indoors or outdoors, into world-healing experiences.
4. *Student-Centered Content Creation:* Students engage big-picture change. Students co-generate and disseminate materials to replace assimilation and segregation curriculum with multicultural and sustainability imagination. This is action-research to deepen required subjects with diverse ways of knowing and interdisciplinary themes. Using backwards design toward a capstone assignment, educators support students with suggested steps:

- Examine core content with a big-picture question.
- Design an activity for a holistic capstone assignment shared with others.
- Implement the activity.
- Reflect on subject mastery and change from the activity.

5. *Institutional and Personal Transformation:* Networking with other Diversity Circles for integrated policy change. This is sharing data about diversity, inclusion, equity, or sustainability changes from activities to coordinate efforts. This is terminating or refreshing stagnant circles and starting new ones, diversifying further and connecting for solidarity to synchronize cross-institutional change. This phase uses Approach-in-Dimension or another big-picture rubric to gauge academic transformation.

Global Nonviolent Liberation Traditions in Diversity Circles

When we collaborate for liberation education, we participate in a version of the seven Diversity Circle types, engaging some or all of the five phases. Our grassroots struggle for prosocial change engages what Dr. King describes as the "constructive, nonviolent tension necessary for growth."[82] As Sleeter and Carmona explain:

> Knowledge itself is embedded in social power relations. Curriculum, and who gets to define it, is political because knowledge in a multicultural democracy cannot be divorced from larger social struggles. It is a medium through which a society defines itself and forms the consciousness of next generations. In [William F.] Pinar's...words, "The school curriculum communicates what we choose to remember about our past, what we believe about the present, what we hope for the future...." It has long mattered because, "at stake was nothing less than the nation's definition of itself."[83]

Diversity Circles use global nonviolent traditions for "multicultural democracy," drawing from liberation theologians and justice organizers, such as Dr. King, Mohandas K. Gandhi, and Freire.[84] Advancing Indian Independence, Gandhi practiced civil disobedience with "four sustaining pillars" for nonviolence: "Sarvodaya" (inclusive justice), "Swaraj" (self-rule), "Swadeshi" (local intelligence), and "Satyagraha" (active resistance).[85] Gandhi's work illustrates the "action" and "faith" cycle developed by liberation theology priests with oppressed peoples in Latin America in the mid-1900s.[86]

Like Gandhi, liberation theologians *listen* to the oppressed, facilitating self-determination in "the concrete conditions" of neighborhoods for community action. Then, with revitalized faith co-generated by the camaraderie of action, a growth cycle unfolds between material liberation *events* and the formation of humanization *systems*. Emancipation faith reinforces the "praxis of solidarity in the interests of liberation," and evidentiary reflection on newfound justice experiences informs further liberation actions.[87]

Freire developed liberation theology into liberation education with culture circles, wherein illiterate students gain literacy *through* social action. Freire facilitated critical consciousness wherein students co-generate themes and codes, connecting subjects to justice events. Learners analyze actions while collecting community knowledge to transform dehumanization patterns into humanization experiences for inclusive systemic change.[88]

Dr. King developed nonviolent direct action for civil rights with four steps: (1) "collection of the facts in determining whether injustices are alive," (2) "negotiation," (3) "self-purification," and (4) "direct action."[89] Likewise, other structural change methods, such as critical race theory activities, social justice education, Youth Participatory Action Research, and critical pedagogy, are informed with global liberation tenets.[90] Thus, Diversity Circles organize with nonviolent liberation methods to structure economic-social change through collaborative praxis.

Three Diversity Circle Strategies

Diversity Circles expand nonviolent liberation methods with mindfulness and sustainability education, integrating academics into body-mind-culture-environment activities, indoors and outdoors. These best practices are encompassed in three strategies that adapt to Diversity Circle types or phases: *Sharing*, *Circle Questions*, and *Global Praxis*. The three strategies un-standardize curriculum and reinterpret subjects with backwards design from a position of love.[91] They engage fundamental mindfulness principles – interbeing, impermanence, and emptiness – to activate the Multicultural Mindfulness peace process that distinguishes Diversity Circles from mainstream committees and learning communities. The strategies start with compassionate Culture-Conscious Listening during Sharing and Circle Questions and culminate with Global Praxis to meet requirements with critical consciousness experiences. Evaluated with philosophical transparency, such as by selecting among the ideologies in the Approach-in-Dimension matrix, the three strategies shape education with diversity, equity, inclusion, or sustainability priorities for *holistic* educator empowerment, student success, and knowledge development.

Sharing

Rather than following explicit curriculum objectives uncritically, participants engage objectives with culture and nature stories, readings, artifacts, and data with big picture themes about the subject. Participants connect topics to sustainability elements, such as sun, earth, sky, and water, investigating economic and social systems that destroy or steward. Participants research and explain emotionally charged regional and global issues for labs and field experiences about topics. Participants use breathwork and social-emotional openers, core content engagement, and closures during indoor and outdoor culture circle activities. Sharing develops the subject with multi-modal materials, evidence, and arts and sciences integrated into hands-on projects.[92]

Circle Questions

Participants ask subject-related questions about cultural and environmental suffering and healing: What makes communities work, or fall apart? How does this topic inform what it means to be human? What does this topic say about how to "live responsibly in the global community?"[93] Circle Questions nurture curiosity during social-emotional academic learning.[94] The questions motivate academic engagement with generative themes and data collection and coding.[95] Related to a topic, participants ask these questions:

- What are our cultural assets and expressions?
- What are our communities especially good at?
- What will our environment be like 10 years from now? Seven generations from now?
- What current cultural practices help or hurt sustainability?
- What are barriers to culturally responsive sustainability? What do we know about reducing those barriers?
- What basic needs are we meeting ecologically? What needs are yet to be met?
- How might we change our approach to this subject to connect to world healing?[96]

Global Praxis

Participants apply Sharing and Circle Questions to world healing activities. We integrate diverse ways of knowing and cultural and environmental evidence from lab projects, field experience, and community observations and participation into academic development. We answer questions to engage real-world humanization, continually refreshing problem-solving activities with big picture themes in a feedback loop.

In summary, Sharing, Circle Questions, and Global Praxis encapsulate best practices in holistic education. They reduce stereotypes, academic tiering, resource inequities, and environmental alienation in education. The strategies un-standardize with student-centered experiences, reshaping subjects for "cultural change."[97] When multicultural collaborators practice mindfulness during academic routines, oppressed and oppressor dichotomies deflate. When participants pose questions to resist "structural inequalities, institutional practices, and racial ideologies," we integrate multiple perspectives and arts into scientific evidence through liberation themes. We work *with* students and colleagues from "historically underserved communities," and we develop culture competence with structural competence to grow ecological knowledge for an inclusive new green economy.[98]

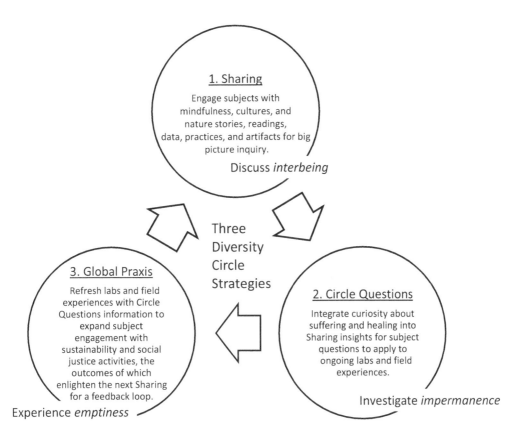

FIGURE 5.7 Three Diversity Circle strategies graphic. Created by the author.

MULTICULTURAL MINDFULNESS ACTIVITY

Diversity Circle Recipe

Outcome

- Conduct a Laboratory Diversity Circle meeting.
- Outline a one-year Laboratory Diversity Circle time line.

Key Concepts

- **Laboratory Diversity Circle**: Experimental learning community with interdisciplinary participants to reimagine academics with multiple perspectives during a year-long campus-wide theme and creative student-centered action-reflection events.
- **Nonviolent Direct Action**: Collection of facts, negotiation, self-purification, and direct action.

Resources

- Journal, healthy potluck meal sign-up sheet filled-in by participants, an example or symbol of nature, a place to meet indoors or outdoors.

Big-Picture Question

- How do we activate big-picture holistic education now?

Start

- **Reach out** and schedule a one-hour potluck meeting with one or more colleagues, as diverse as possible, to try a Laboratory Diversity Circle.

Middle

Whole group circle meeting:

- **Popcorn read** and **discuss** *Recipe for a One-Year Laboratory Diversity Circle* (below) while sharing a potluck meal and observing nature.
- **Outline** your own Laboratory Diversity Circle time line.

Closing

- **Share** stories and arts or science data related to your requirements, campus cultures, and the world.
- **Discuss** big-picture questions from the stories or data and select a theme that connects subjects to the world.

RECIPE FOR A ONE-YEAR LABORATORY DIVERSITY CIRCLE

(Used to develop Truckee Meadows Community College's [TMCC's] annual FREE events described further below)

1 COLLECTION OF FACTS — 1st MEETING — EARLY FALL:

A group of two or more interdisciplinary teachers and students, as diverse as possible, convenes over a potluck to explore a big-picture theme. Most participants have similar schedules. Participants use civility norms, such as Noun/Pronoun Use, Turn-Taking, Creative Tension, Culture-Conscious Listening, and Academic Accuracy. Along with food to share, people bring active curriculum and disciplinary materials and resources.

- **Warm-up:** Pass around resources while eating and sharing stories and scientific data about campus cultures and the world. Pose transformational questions. Explain curriculum goals for the year. Describe required subjects, relating content to suffering and healing. Discuss student and teacher cultures, observing diversity, culture clashes, and intersections about race, ethnicity, class, gender, ability, and other categories.
- **Required Content Inquiry:** In the meeting's second half, discuss the theme that was determined the previous spring. Or if this is the first time doing the Laboratory, identify a common topic in required subjects, naming cultures and bias in curriculum and knowledge. Pose academic questions related to the environment. Explore interdisciplinary methods. Propose action-research and readings or projects about emerging themes. Near the end of the meeting, everyone writes a possible the theme for everyone to see. Everyone stars a favorite version (not one's own). The most starred theme guides activities going forward.

2 NEGOTIATION — 2ND & 3RD MEETINGS — MID-FALL & WINTER:

- **Scheduling:** At the second meeting, a date and place for a spring teach-in are determined by surveying class schedules. While some participants' schedules might not overlap, selecting one date with one or two assembly times totaling three hours ensures a ready-made crowd of enrolled students from various classrooms with an estimated assembly size. Participants who can't attend the assembly can market and develop projects with other classes.
- **Open Enrollment:** Cultivating diversity is important. If the initial Laboratory group does not represent race, class, gender, and ethnic diversity, then diversification is actively pursued. Welcoming newcomers into the circle happens all year long. There is no end date to invite participants.
- **Ongoing Required Content Inquiry:** In these two meetings and during spontaneous hallway chats, participants investigate the Laboratory theme in core content. Participants try theme activities during routines, collecting and discussing emerging cultural data, reflecting on how academic space, time, materials, and learning environments address the theme.

3 SELF-PURIFICATION — 4TH & 5TH MEETINGS — EARLY SPRING:

Design and practice theme activities for global citizenship experiences during the spring assembly. Assess how theme activities deepen core content and explore how the big-picture theme impacts curriculum and knowledge. Develop required subjects with student-led action-research. Allow imagination to guide activities into culture, mindfulness, and nature experiences, indoors and outdoors.

- **Critical Consciousness Connections:** Connect theme resources and discoveries to spring assembly activities. Share stories and data and pose questions about in-progress projects, discussing how the spring assembly might engage critical thinking to connect subjects to the local and global context through hands-on arts and sciences activities, performances, and displays with flexible seating, walking, and moving through problem-solving materials and sequences.

- **Shared Learning Experiences:** Teachers may conduct short cross-discipline lessons in each other's classes (10–30 minutes), exploring theme data for the spring assembly.
- **Assembly Logistics:** Participants finalize spring assembly logistics, discussing how students co-generate the theme, such as with subject demonstrations or interdisciplinary projects. Finalize assembly presentations, activities, and displays.

4 **DIRECT ACTION – THE ASSEMBLY – MID-SPRING:**

- **Student-Centered Content Creation:** This is the big-picture student-centered event!
  1 **The Spring Assembly:** Students, teachers, and community supports gather in a flexible a public space, indoors and outdoors, to pose big-picture questions, debate answers, co-create content, and disseminate arts and sciences knowledge, synthesizing multiple perspectives about the theme.
  2 **Creative Assessment Display:** An interdisciplinary assessment display about the assembly is gathered and exhibited shortly afterwards to sustain community involvement in theme reflection.

5 **DIRECT ACTION/ASSESSMENT – 6th MEETING – LATE SPRING:**

- **Wrap-up Meeting:** Reflect on the most important things learned, identifying areas for improvement from data. Evaluate for required content outcomes and theme expressions, discussing academic changes from the year's experiments.
- **Call-to-Action for Next Year's 1st Meeting:** Calendar a 1st Meeting for the next fall. Give a call-to-action to gather fresh cultural stories, scientific data, and resources about human suffering and healing and hold a meeting to determine a new theme to relate academic subjects to the region and world for next year's projects.

Application

How Do Diversity Circles Help Resolve the Teacher-Culture Paradox?

The paradox is that teachers are the most important factor to student success within education[99]; however, US teacher demographics and lack of multicultural education are barriers to *diverse* student success.[100] Educators don't like this, but we're stuck with it until we take cultural action. We resolve the paradox by training and mentoring highly qualified culture-conscious teachers, of all backgrounds, to integrate disciplinary standards and subjects into liberation education assessed for equity and sustainability.

One reason the teacher-culture paradox exists is that US teachers have high turnover while the incoming pool is shrinking. Nearly half of newly hired teachers leave the profession in the first five years of employment.[101] Enrollment in teacher education has dropped, narrowing the professional pipeline.[102] In a self-defeating cycle in states such as California, where enrollment in teacher preparation declined by 75% during the 2000s[103] – an uptick in *alternate* credentials corresponds with the simultaneous increase of diverse school-age children. This means that ill-prepared teachers are with students in the most need of highly qualified teachers.

Moreover, the numbers of teachers of color – particularly African Americans and Native Americans – are declining within the contracting and unstable teacher pool.[104] Nationally, about 20% of PreK-12 educators are professionals of color while 50% are students of color.[105] Employed teachers of color are often placed in segregated, underfunded schools that nonetheless require mainstream curriculum. This is a culture conflict that spreads job dissatisfaction. The profession is straightjacketed by the trend of hiring alternatively credentialed teachers with substitute provisions in a culturally incongruent system hamstrung by mainstream standardization. However, Diversity Circles offer grassroots organization for professional development to grow teacher diversity with multicultural, mindfulness, and environmental education.[106]

Diversity Circles Reduce Barriers to Academic Belonging

Diversity Circles remove barriers to belonging through imaginative culture-conscious activities. We enact inclusive social-emotional academics *unified* by systems analysis for Earth stewardship. This is what Juliana Urtubey does. Urtubey, a Spanish-English bilingual special education teacher and 2021 National Teacher of the Year, had been discouraged by demoralized teachers at her school. Campus culture was caught in bureaucratic loops and hardship at a Title I school marked by poverty and segregation in Las Vegas, Nevada. But when a transformative colleague encouraged her to apply for a collaborative project grant for a school garden, Urtubey, without much gardening experience, organized teams to make it happen. Urtubey's holistic approach combined arts and sciences to bring together special needs *and* mainstream students, culturally diverse families, and educators across the curriculum to cultivate vegetables and flowers with murals, and sculptures to heal "racial apathy" with botanical-cultural habitats. Their STEAM (science, technology, engineering, arts, and mathematics) projects focused on reducing cultural deficit thinking and increasing cultural "nutrition" and "nourishment" activities.[107]

Urtubey's gardens and murals illustrate how culturally relevant environmental education changes educational systems. As teachers stepped outdoors, taking lounge conversations into the gardens, the project evolved organically into neighborhood farmer's markets and cooking camps for healthy meals at summer school. Collaborators engaged curriculum requirements through sensory and cultural explorations of sun, earth, sky, and water, shifting from victimization thinking to a growth mindset.[108] Environmental justice experiences during school–community gardening reduced classroom–home divides as educators worked side by side with local families, developing subjects during naturally occurring field interactions and garden art projects, such as community painting and sculptures.[109]

Urtubey explains that gardens are just one of the many projects that effect change with five pillars for inclusion: (1) reframing reality *with* diverse students, (2) intergenerational learning, (3) assets mindset from social justice work, (4) holistic learning to meet academic needs, and (5) joyous and just design.[110] Thus, multicultural collaborations on big-picture projects integrate majority and minority identities to remove cultural barriers to success by engaging diversity *during* academics.[111]

Mentorship Projects

Another illustration of Diversity Circle efficacy is diversity mentoring. Naturally occurring diversity mentorship activities develop multicultural, highly qualified teachers. Mentorship is a best practice for teacher education and retention. When new teachers enter jobs with immersion experiences inside diverse classrooms guided by master teachers who model multicultural education, they are empowered with culturally responsive "clinical expertise" skills.

They accelerate higher-order teacher competency development, such as critical thinking about cultures during curriculum interactions.[112] Being mentored in diversity education *with* diverse students helps future teachers become transformative.

> Teachers teach from what they know. If policymakers want to change teaching, they must pay attention to teacher knowledge and make investments in those things that allow teachers to grapple with transformations of ideas and behavior.[113]

Teachers of all backgrounds and career stages benefit from mentoring with action-research. When mentoring is strengthened with culture competence development, teachers gain success skills and networks from guided interactions, such as illustrated by the San Francisco Teacher Residency (SFTR) program.

> SFTR is a consortium that includes the San Francisco Unified School District, the United Educators of San Francisco, and two area college…teacher education programs. SFTR pairs graduate students ("residents") from both universities with mentors…who are classroom teachers in San Francisco. And it provides residents and [mentors] with coaches who observe lessons and support each pair in working together. After completing the program, SFTR graduates are guaranteed teaching positions in San Francisco public schools. Just as important, the program continues to provide each new teacher with coaching during [the] first two years on the job.[114]

Reflective mentorship about multicultural education fosters collaboration for universal design.[115] Thus, cross-cultural mentoring not only *models* teacher diversification but also provides hands-on professional development about how to remove cultural barriers sustainably.

What Makes a Good Diversity Circle?

Minority-Serving Institutions

Minority-Serving Institutions (MSIs) are an education sector innovating with diversity collaborations for mentorship through multicultural imagination. They host "grow your own" teacher education to scaffold "career ladders for educational aides and paraprofessionals seeking to become teachers" and to "train highly qualified" teachers with field experience.[116] Moreover, the open-door access of *community college* MSIs widens demographic entry into a variety of professions, including teacher education, providing a learning environment for diversified curriculum.

MSIs enroll a critical mass of diverse students and hire more professors of color and student services professionals proportional to predominantly White institutions (PWIs). With a diversity mission, the best MSIs experiment with inclusion methods, advancing ethnic, women's, and other identity studies in curriculum during equity programming.[117] MSIs, mostly public, include Asian American and Native American Pacific Islander–serving institutions (AANAPISIs), Alaska Native and Native Hawaiian (ANNH), Native American–serving non-tribal institutions (NASNTI), Hispanic-Serving institutions (HSIs), historically Black colleges and universities (HBCUs), and Tribal colleges and universities (TCUs). As of 2023, there were over 800 MSIs in the US.[118]

In contrast to PWIs, especially "highly selective universities" that insert diversity words into campus mission statements but otherwise use "discriminatory practices," MSIs are funded for equity and inclusion.[119] For example, the Hispanic Association of Colleges and Universities states that the HSI mission is "to promote Hispanic student access to and success in higher education; encourage the diversity of faculty and staff at institutions in higher learning; and provide a network of support for faculty and staff committed to Hispanic higher education."[120] With race awareness and minority perspectives explicitly valued, the best MSIs facilitate integrative activities and culturally responsive curriculum. Thus, MSIs, through the demographics and programming that define them, promote naturally occurring Diversity Circles.

MSIs are productive in diversifying teacher education, awarding half of all education degrees to minority students.[121] They're instrumental in strengthening the K-12 teacher pool with highly qualified diversity competencies. For example, HBCUs train 2% of the nation's teachers overall, but they provide content and skills to 16% of African American teachers.[122]

Data suggest that over a third of Black, Asian Americans, and American Indian/Alaskan Natives receive their education degrees from MSIs. Over half of Hispanics receive their education degrees from MSIs. Notably, HSIs alone account for 44% of all education degrees conferred to Hispanics.[123]

MSIs innovate to meet the "needs of new" enrollments in teacher education with inclusion strategies that change "the course of study in traditional certification programs."[124] For instance, the best MSI teacher education programs develop social justice and community service diversity activities.[125] MSIs provide their relatively more diverse preservice teacher candidates with field experience in schools *with* children of color and ethnic studies assignments for portfolio development.

The antiracist-antibias mission and funding of MSIs confront systemic bias – "collective bias backed by legal authority and institutional control" – by interrupting PWI dominance in teacher education.[126] MSI teacher education engages multiracial-multicultural students in proactive programs with hands-on holistic curriculum. For example:

- Multiculturally imaginative subject engagement.
- Diverse peer and teacher mentorship activities for guided inclusion.
- Concurrent courses to pair ethnic studies with education curriculum.
- Socratic Circles about environmental education.
- Culturally relevant STEAM projects.
- Community-designed units.
- Sister-school relationships.
- Culturally relevant sustainability field trips.[127]

MSI's thereby disrupt Anglo-conformity in institutions and teacher education to counteract assimilation standardized into the US education system over hundreds of years.

In summary, MSIs illustrate Diversity Circles. They show how naturally occurring diversity collaborations support students across racial and ethnic categories through culturally responsive education. MSIs illustrate what Freire calls "*cultural* action" for *change*, which is deliberate action to intervene in and transform social structures that are *preserved* by the status quo.[128] Specifically, MSI teacher education innovate on cultural action in four ways to challenge systemic racism:

- *Inclusive enrollment:* Open admissions and support teams invite historically underserved students to matriculate proportionately more teachers of color than from PWIs.
- *Diverse educators:* By employing more highly qualified faculty of color than at PWIs, MSI education programs set the context for diversity alliances.
- *Explicit multicultural curriculum:* MSI educators collaborate on diversity grants to which they're uniquely eligible to advance diversity curriculum.
- *School-world culture connections:* Graduates of MSI teacher education enter careers with the benefit of guided *diversity* field experiences to activate subjects with best practices through hands-on teaching projects and reflective multicultural education mentorship.[129]

Teachers of color in Diversity Circles

When teachers of color with culturally responsive education expertise participate in demographically mixed Diversity Circles, we help address the racial achievement gap with cultural actions that

- Reduce cultural homogeneity and increase cross-cultural balance in curriculum, outcomes, knowledge, communications, and interactions.
- Model desegregation.
- Raise academic expectations for diverse students.
- Counteract stereotypes and bias with multicultural education during core routines.
- Diversify educator teams in school-community projects, such as "detracking" programs and sustainability gardens, to model how to work together "to succeed in an increasingly diverse society" for a sustainability economy.[130]

Teachers of color are essential to prosocial antibias-antiracist change. Though no one is free of systemic bias, teachers of color have been found to promulgate less bias than White teachers, thereby modeling culturally responsive skills.[131] Upon hire, teachers of color are obligated to respond professionally to bias assessments in an Anglo-conformist system, a burden that is also the seed for antibias-antiracist consciousness. Further, teachers of color hold students of color to higher expectations in academic achievement, as well as civility, while maintaining high and fair expectations for White students.[132]

White teachers, conversely, susceptible to Anglo-conformity, have been found to inadvertently reevaluate criteria according to the perceived racial identity of individual students. This may be because White teachers may have internalized racialized *privileges* from a filial identity that comports with *assimilation* stereotypes. For example, White teachers unconsciously favor culturally congruent names. In a study of 55,000 students, it was found that "observationally equivalent siblings with similar test scores but different types of names are treated differently by teachers."[133] For instance, in a behavior known as "aversive racism," if a Black student uses more descriptive writing, and a White student uses more cited writing, and both descriptive and cited criteria exist in the rubric, the White teacher, expecting less because of unconscious stereotypes, may give the Black student a worse grade. Then, in another case in the next year, the White student might use more descriptive writing and the Black student uses more cites, but this time the White teacher, expecting *more* because of other unconscious stereotypes, still gives the White student the better grade.[134]

With fewer biases invested in racism, teachers of color have been found to motivate academic success among students of color by facilitating culturally congruent empowerment. For instance, community empowerment is cultivated between Latinx teachers and students, which is particularly important for Latina students who experience low levels of self-confidence at school. "Latino/a faculty contribute a positive campus climate for Latina students and…more supportive climates are related to better retention and graduation rates for these students."[135] Latinx teachers are important in their "capacity to build positive relationships with students, to understand and value local community funds of knowledge, and use these to organize rigorous learning activities, and engage in ongoing inquiry to assess participation and learning."[136] Having lived experiences with oppression, teachers of color are less likely to dismiss cultural difference as a cultural or intellectual deficit.[137]

Further, teachers of color recognize that as students of color learn to *use* community services, basic physiological and psychological needs can be met.[138] Teachers of color often access social workers to make health connections for students with doctors, clinics, nutrition programs, clothing, diapers and other family supplies, as well as immigration specialists. "'Teachers of color do more than teach content. They dispel myths of racial inferiority and incompetence and serve as surrogate parents, guides, and mentors for their students.'"[139] Teachers of color recognize that developing cultural-emotional intelligence through empathy and love grows multilingual skills and cross-cultural socialization to improve academic engagement.[140]

Teachers of color advance the value of diversity education applicable to students and teachers of every background.

> In a study of 80 teacher educators recognized for their success in preparing teachers in both multicultural and global education, [it was] found that personal experiences with people different from themselves, experiences with discrimination, and an outsider status were among the reasons the teacher educators gave for their commitment to multicultural and global education.[141]

For example, bilingual Latinx teachers use linguistic skills to support Latinx student success. We explain to Spanish-speaking families how to support youth to enroll and succeed in higher education. Consequently, Latinx students from immigrant families who maintain Spanish at high levels as "balanced bilinguals" are more likely to go to college than those who lose their primary language.[142] In another example, a one-year same-race pairing of students and teachers significantly increased math and reading test scores of both Black and White students, more so for Black students. All outcomes, from graduation to gifted-and-talented program placement, improve with diverse student–teacher pairings.[143]

In summary, teachers of color with culture competence training are important to diversity collaborations. Highly qualified teachers of color shape curriculum and knowledge with diverse ways of knowing, inclusive high expectations, desegregation modeling, and holistic antibias-antiracist practices. Teachers of color cultivate cultural compassion by approaching adverse lived experiences in the Anglo-conformist system as touch points to develop academic engagement for *all*. Conversely, often unconsciously, White teachers without antibias-antiracist training perpetuate White bias due, in part, to identifying with economic and social privileges in the Anglo-conformist system. Moreover, structural stratifications outside school propel middle-income and wealthy student success regardless of the boost from teacher-culture congruence. However, impoverished students of color at the bottom of the achievement gap gain profoundly from high expectations by teachers of color, who simultaneously confer the value of diversity-modeling to all students. Thus, teachers of color with subject proficiency deepened by culture competence are essential to diversity collaborations for equity education, empowering the profession with diversity and opening pathways to prepare students inclusively for a sustainability economy.

How to Start a Diversity Circle from Scratch

Try an Ethnic Studies Book Club

Most US teachers are European Americans who enter the profession with scant ethnic studies coursework, little experience with multicultural academic integration, and limited involvement in multiracial collaborations. Instead, many educators are territorial, unintentionally operating individual classrooms or programs guardedly with procedures caught into assimilation and segregation systems. Given US education's tiering, mainstream Anglo-conformist curriculum, diversity censorship campaigns, and implicit bias procedures, many teachers are unaware or confused about how to innovate or what to do with cultures at school.

Some teachers understand that systemic racism harms schools, but still take the path of least resistance to avoid the controversy of culture, race, and identity topics, especially in post-pandemic years with teachers under attack and schools caught into media-fanned culture wars. Some states have issued classroom-level book removal policies, and a quarter of all teachers say they have cut diversity content to avoid potential punitive consequences. Others have quit, with already-distressing departure rates increasing since the pandemic. For instance, one social studies middle school teacher, who was told by the superintendent to cut content that stated "slavery was wrong," quit teaching instead.[144]

Grassroots collaborations empower teachers of all backgrounds to develop philosophical clarity about how cultures and education are intertwined. To do this, one simply reaches out to a colleague to form an ethnic studies book club tasked with applying scientific scholarship about justice to routines. If, owing to educator demographics in your area, you form a Diversity Circle without racial diversity, allow what you do in your book club to guide foresight strategies to reach out for racial diversification going forward.

For now, there are no wrong answers in this book club. This is a journey, and ethnic studies is a treasure trove of critical consciousness and cultural knowledge about systemic racism to prompt justice action.[145] Because most educators have dutifully learned, through mainstream institutions, to interpret race through the lens of individualism rather than through systemic analysis, many of us are perplexed about how structural inequities operate in our institutions. Many teachers perceive racism as an almost-solved problem, now existing only among extremist individuals, not within *us*, even while we maintain cultural silos at school.[146] We may not understand that systemic racism drives our own routine decisions, unconsciously leading to self-segregation and dehumanization experiences.

Believing ourselves not to be racist and yearning for the colorblind ideal, we perceive White colleagues and students as individuals with free choices and unlimited opportunities for upward mobility. We perceive colleagues and students of color as individuals hampered by cultural deficits that interfere with the American Dream. We don't want to see ourselves as perpetuators of the racial achievement gap or the cultural homogeneity that characterizes our profession, so we try not to see race at all. In one study:

> Even the teachers who recognized White privilege defined it in individual terms rather than in terms of collective use of power. Most of the teachers (and administrators) found culture a more comfortable concept to work with than race, although they tended to see culture as something people of color (but not White people) have. Many of them framed culture within the narrative of immigrant groups becoming culturally assimilated, a narrative that fit their own European immigrant family story.[147]

Consequently, an ethnic studies-based Diversity Circle develops global antiracist knowledge. We use structurally informed criteria to conduct a Required Content Inquiry about mainstream curriculum. For instance, an ethnic studies examination of 47 elementary textbooks published between 1980 and 1988 across disciplines shows biased words and prejudiced illustrations.

> [T]he texts consistently gave the most attention to Whites, showing them in the widest variety of roles and giving them dominance over storylines and accomplishments. African Americans were represented more than earlier, but still in a limited range of roles and with only a sketchy account historically, mainly in relationship to slavery. Asian Americans and Latinxs' appeared only sporadically, receiving virtually no attention in history. American Indians, conversely, were depicted almost solely, but sporadically, in history texts.[148]

While some recent textbooks portray fairer representations, especially with more inserts about African Americans, significant omissions and stereotyping remain. Many textbooks ignore race and racism and default to a superficial treatment of *culture* in a manner that demeans the living communities of people of color who carry forward with cultural practices despite systemic inequities. The "White perspective" dominates, and "the overall framing of the curriculum is still White, and with respect to issues of race and racism, lack criticality."[149] An ethnic studies book club format for Diversity Circles develops interdisciplinary resources and inclusion themes about distortions in curriculum, outcomes, knowledge, communications, and interactions and opens the site to cultural arts and scientific evidence from diverse ways of knowing.

Ethnic Studies Inspires Change

Ethnic studies energizes through student-centered cultural content and practices. Ethnic studies came to fruition in the US as a *student* movement in the 1950s and '60s after thousands of years of development. "Since before the arrival of Europeans, Indigenous communities had their own complex bodies of knowledge."[150] This body of knowledge – known as Traditional Ecological Knowledge (TEK) – demonstrates the environmental stewardship that has been dismissed by the "industrial civilization" ideology of mainstream education. "Industrial civilization justified exploitation and destruction of whole societies and expansion without regard for the sovereignty of peoples; it promoted individualism, competition, and selfness as righteous character traits."[151] Likewise, African American, Latinx, and Asian Americans have for generations been compiling, testing, and transmitting knowledge and practices for cultural sovereignty about local and global topics apart from Eurocentric conquest ideologies.

Today, there are more than 700 ethnic studies programs nationally, advancing diverse perspectives, equity academics, liberation theory, and community histories through interdisciplinary scholarship that provide book club–worthy works.[152] Your Diversity Circle can engage these resources to discuss ethnic studies interdisciplinary themes and cross-cultural understanding to deepen requirements. You can discuss local and global interpretations of diverse experiences in structural racism, investigating works about critical race theory, feminism, egalitarian economics, and multicultural-multiracial democracies. You can relate subjects to systems of domination – perpetration by oppressors, victimization of the oppressed, and dehumanization of both – as well as to cultural empowerment for holistic humanization. A few examples of accessible book club readings include Teaching Strategies for Ethnic Studies by Banks. Rethinking Ethnic Studies by Cuauhtin, Zavala, Sleeter, Au, Becoming a Multicultural Educator by Howe and Lisi, and Multicultural Education by Noel.[153]

How Is Ethnic Studies Inclusive?

Ethnic studies encompasses bilingual, multilingual, and multiracial cross-cultural analyses of systemic oppression as well as overlapping and contradictory *liberation* experiences, inside and outside of institutions. Your ethnic studies book club could start with a classic text such as *A Different Mirror: A History of Multicultural America*, in which Ronald Takaki describes racialized diversity dehumanization from structural inequities and exclusions as well as resistance and community self-determination experiences.[154] He documents demographic diversity that defines both the capacity of *and* limitations to US democracy. Takaki explains that one way to transform oppression is through interdisciplinary liberation education that balances traditional scholarship with cross-cultural knowledge from poetry, songs, journals, work logs, letters, and stories expressed in multiple languages and modalities. Using primary sources, Takaki explores "liminality" perception to develop intersectional critical consciousness. Liminality – operating multiple perspectives simultaneously – is an advanced culture competence skill. Liminality aptitude helps teachers become agents for cultural inclusion by co-investigating, co-analyzing, and sharing cultural knowledge across contexts. Liminality skills develop subjects holistically to grow an intersectional "reorientation of our consciousness."[155]

Why Student-Centered *Ethnic Studies?*

Student-centered ethnic studies develops intergenerational consciousness. For example, in a middle school program for a Peer Assistance and Leadership program, multiracial students co-lead restorative justice "to make a difference in their lives, schools, and communities" in an "advocacy homeroom." This is a Diversity Circle variation that teams to reduce social alienation among its members at the "big" school they attend. In the homeroom, multiracial students swap cultural stories and data using a "community circles" format to learn about campus cultures. Then the homeroom group practices reconciliation skills through "mediation circles" with case scenarios. Finally, outside the homeroom, students bring newfound skills to the campus community using "restorative circles" to referee conflicts and host cultural expressions on site. Therefore, rather than top-down punitive measures for behavior, peers ask each other to identify emotions and perceptions about why the conflict occurred and what the resulting harm was; then they formulate steps for peace practices going forward.[156]

Another way to support peer-to-peer consciousness-raising is to facilitate a student-centered ethnic studies book club in a Student Cohort or Cogen Diversity Circle. After phase 1, Antibias Communication Norms, to feel safe sharing cultural stories and prepare for consciousness change, the Diversity Circle enters the Required Content Inquiry phase with an ethnic studies antibias textbook analysis, using categories such as "invisibility or omission," "stereotyping," "imbalance and selectivity," "unreality," "fragmentation and isolation," "linguistic bias," and "cosmetic bias."[157] Then, from findings, the Diversity Circle engages the Environmental Humanization Inquiry phase to fill bias gaps in the textbook with ethnic studies resources and cultural assets information. This phase is about applying cultural content to academic requirements integrated into activities with nature indoors or outdoors. Finally, during Student-Centered Content Creation, students integrate ethnic studies into the subject during capstone projects.

In this Student-Centered Content Creation phase, students learn that ethnic studies originated from cultural movements. Students recognize how previous youth generations pushed ethnic studies to change US education. Students make cultural connections during critical consciousness, applying ethnic studies holistically to curriculum and knowledge. They ask questions about distortions from individualism about "what America *should* be" that misrepresent racism as a relic of the past.[158] When diverse students are given permission to lead critiques of mainstream education in their own classrooms, they identify assimilation and segregation education *fallacies* such as the following:

- Knowledge universally worth knowing mostly originated in Europe (or among European-Americans).
- Individuals rather than communities, social institutions, and organized groups should be the focus of education.
- Mobility is assumed, and problems will sort themselves out, particularly problems about inclusion in democracy.
- Racism and colonization are tragic vestiges of the distant past.
- White people are the "real" Americans who built this country, deserving the right to governance.[159]

This is when Diversity Circles co-create joyful justice academics *through* ethnic studies, reinterpreting curriculum with knowledge about the following:

- *Indigeneity and roots:* The "sovereignty and autonomy of the Indigenous peoples/first nations of the land where" schools reside.
- *Coloniality, dehumanization, and genocide:* The "totalizing practice of dehumanization, domination, oppression, and the theft that involves the subjugation of one people to another."
- *Hegemony and Normalization:* The "explicit and intersectional power relationships based on colonization [that have been rendered] implicit, institutionalized, and 'normal.'"

- *Decoloniality, regeneration, and transformational resistance:* Scholarship and cultural expressions integrating social action, community practices, cultural wisdom, and diverse world views into holistic education.[160]

In summary, the ethnic studies book club format for Diversity Circles helps participants overcome confusion about what to do with cultures at school. The format surmounts the lack of diversity education, segregated conditions, and assimilation curriculum in mainstream US education. Participants ask questions to reveal bias in curriculum, making interdisciplinary connections with big-picture questions to develop cultural diversity resources and practices. When educators facilitate student-centered Diversity Circles, sites shift from dehumanization to empowerment for humanization, integrating cultural arts into scientific evidence. Diversity Circles overcome barriers to inclusion with critical consciousness about *outward* aspects of cultures in substructure-superstructure systems. They also develop authenticity and social change *within* communities by engaging with cultures apart from outsider appraisal. Thus, ethnic studies is a resource for Diversity Circles to advance Environmental Liberation Education solutions.[161]

Examples

Example #1: An Academic Faculty (and Student Cohort) Diversity Circle

An Academic Faculty Diversity Circle between TMCC's Chicana education professor (the author) and a Jewish European American administrator at Marvin Picollo School in Reno, Nevada, illustrates cross-cultural collaboration for change. Started in 2013, this ongoing circle transformed curriculum at both sites with integrative academics between college students at an HSI and students with severe special needs, ages 3 to 22 at a public school. I wanted my teacher preparation students to have career guidance to become professionals with diversity skills. The administrator wanted his older students, whose ages overlap with college students, to experience social-emotional learning with peers without severe special needs. He also wanted to open career doors by hiring TMCC students as aides after course completion. The innovation resulted in college class meetings *at* Marvin Picollo, which is a relatively desegregated public school because of regional busing for special needs learners, mixing culturally diverse as well as wealthy and low-income families.[162]

Our Diversity Circle conducted a Required Content Inquiry to identify culturally alienating curriculum at both sites. We noted limited modalities and cognitive range in academic engagement at both spaces. The Marvin Picollo administrator observed how older students with severe special needs didn't have opportunities to make cultural connections during academics with peers without severe special needs. He also found that the district lacked a special education career pathway from teacher preparation programs, even though the district had many unfilled special education jobs. I observed that regional special education courses were light on field experience, especially to develop diversity competencies because most district schools are segregated. Therefore, we researched best practices for field experiences with mentorship to develop highly qualified teachers while supporting the academic engagement of students with special needs.

Zone of Proximal Development

We theorized that by integrating TMCC students with Marvin Picollo students, everyone could experience what Lev Vygotsky coined the "zone of proximal development," which accelerates learning with interactive guidance.[163] We designed an Environmental Humanization Inquiry project to socialize students intergenerationally between both sites, facilitating multicultural connections and multimodal cognition to engage state requirements with sustainability activities, such as outdoor education (horse therapy and greenhouse gardening) and holistic education (music therapy, aquatic therapy, and adaptive physical education). The project aimed to facilitate social-emotional academics with advanced peers (TMCC students) modeling learning behaviors with less advanced peers (Marvin Picollo students with severe special needs). In turn, the TMCC students would experience a zone of proximal development with site mentors while problem-solving in Marvin Picollo classrooms. Both sets of students would have the opportunity to develop multicultural relationships and hands-on culture competence, engaging academics through multiple modalities and cognitive range guided by diverse educators.

Grassroots Collaboration

This early immersion project illustrates grassroots change. The Marvin Picollo administrator carved out site space for college students to hold circle reflections and to interview diverse educators and support staff. He organized mentor teachers and gathered site curriculum. I obtained clearance to hold class on the other side of the city. I replaced lectures with hands-on assignments and reduced prefabricated textbook readings with site-based special education curriculum and a case study manual. I swapped indoor lectures with outdoor-indoor *student-centered* learning. The transformative result was that TMCC's diverse education students – in contrast to those who take the same course elsewhere – gain about 30 hours *more* field experience in a richly diverse school, guided by a wide range of experienced educators.

Student Cohort Off-Shoot

An unexpected project outcome was the emergence of naturally occurring Student Cohort Diversity Circles. Student cohorts form each semester to meet "students' need for affiliation" with emotional "family like" bonds.

> A cohort is defined as a group of about 10-25 students who begin in a program of study together, proceed together through a series of developmental experiences in the context of that program of study, and end the program at approximately the same time.[164]

Each semester, the TMCC students form hallway packs, collaborating on assignments and interspersing hands-on student-to-student interactions (often punctuated with dramatic events given the severity of the special needs on the Marvin Picollo site) with impromptu and scheduled dialogue circles. The diverse college students lean on one another, sharing cultural stories about classroom data collection and analysis about learning setbacks and breakthroughs. They interview rotating professionals on site and discuss sensory journals about visual, sound, touch, taste, and olfactory observations. They pose questions to one another, applying analyses of shared experiences to the case studies they write. The case studies analyze academic strategies that result in the progress, stasis, or setbacks of a Marvin Picollo student or group of students over time within a multicultural framework. The college students, 40% of whom are Latinx in TMCC's education program, compare their own lived cultures with those at Marvin Picollo. They discuss culture shifts when their mentors adapt strategies to communicate between students, families, and school. Moreover, they experiment with inclusive antibias-antiracist practices and describe how theory develops from hands-on experiences.

Career Pathway

Another project outcome is that the college students interact on site with an extraordinarily wide array of special education professionals, including classroom teachers, music therapists, horse and aquatic therapists, occupational and physical therapists, adaptive physical education specialists and librarians, adaptive culinary arts educators, nutritional specialists, bilingual educators, social workers, speech pathologists, registered nurses, vocational educators, early childhood educators, special education administrators, and school psychologists. During the semester, some students rule out special education careers, while others seek employment, inspired by experiences in the field. Others discover special education pathways besides classroom teaching.

For example, one TMCC student, mentored by a middle school teacher, invented a numeracy board game. The board game set high expectations for nonverbal students and engaged alternative modalities for math. She conducted her interactive lesson observed by the district superintendent. The experience led her toward a career in occupational therapy. Another student set up a horse therapy visitation with peers from elsewhere in the district to expand same-age interactions. This led to exploration about becoming an adaptive physical education specialist.

After obtaining teaching credentials, some cohort participants become teachers at Marvin Picollo. At any given time, several teachers and staff employed there have taken the course, now mentoring the next generation. For instance, a former TMCC student became employed as a full-time culinary arts teacher, and she resurrected the school garden to develop a farm-to-fork curriculum. Another former student became the lead teacher with teenagers with behavioral problems, and he mentors TMCC students to dispel fears about working with the behaviors.[165]

In this Diversity Circle project, older students with severe special needs benefit from *integrating* with mainstream peers, and younger students benefit from one-on-one interactions with college students, advancing academic learning from proximal development. College students benefit from mentorship and seamless access to entry-level teaching jobs while gaining holistic education about subjects and methodologies on a richly diverse site. All participants have the opportunity to develop culture competence through hands-on social-emotional interactions during big-picture circle academics with communities and nature, indoors and outdoors.

Example #2: An Administrative Faculty Diversity Circle

Starting in 2018, an Administrative Faculty Diversity Circle at TMCC conducted a Required Content Inquiry about diversity in course syllabi across the curriculum. Syllabi function as a first encounter between students, teacher, and curriculum. Syllabi can either welcome student cultures or alienate. This investigation identified, collected, and analyzed data from TMCC syllabi across four divisions: Business and Social Sciences, Liberal Arts, Sciences, and Technical Sciences. It analyzed four diversity factors, establishing a baseline for transformation. Review of the 32 syllabi focused on diversity and equity messaging (or lack thereof) in language, statements, required readings, and assignment rubrics.[166]

Shifting Away from Uniform Colorblind Messaging in Curriculum

The inquiry showed this sample of TMCC syllabi display a uniform colorblind Anglo-conformist message to students and academic subjects. The syllabi didn't offer holistic antibias-antiracist content. Seventy-five percent combined "Mainstream," "Contributions," and "Additive" approaches to diversity through use of language, statements, required readings, and assignment rubrics, evaluated by Approach-in-Dimension criteria (see Chapter 7). The syllabi topics omitted race and structural competence. Three fourths of the syllabi used Anglo-conformist individualism to discuss course subjects and classroom norms, ignoring systemic racism as an element of education. The syllabi deferred to an assimilationist framework for student failure or success.

Twenty-five percent of the syllabi were marginal-proficient with diversity and equity ideas, expressing an Additive-Transformative approach. These syllabi inserted statements to acknowledge culture, and they listed race, ethnicity, class, and gender categories. However, they equated cultures using colorblind logic by omitting language about structural racism. These syllabi used some inclusion language, itemizing student-centered activities, civility expectations, and student success resources. One syllabus used she/her, he/him, they/them pronouns.

However, none of the syllabi mentioned the HSI status of the campus, and none asserted diversified required materials or assignment rubrics. They didn't back up words about diversity or resource lists with Transformative or Social Action curriculum *requirements* for assessment. None meets exemplary Transformative-Social Action criteria for structural competence in language, statements, required content, or graded assignments.

Experimental Curriculum Transformation Workshops

The next step was to design diversity statement workshops to assist curriculum transformation with the goal to support diverse student success. The workshops' objectives challenge faculty to use academic freedom to develop a philosophy of humanity for their classrooms. Participants reflect, write, and insert syllabus statements to invite students of varying identities into academic standards.

The workshops engage faculty in sequenced activities to reshape course learning outcomes by reflecting on how disciplinary training and subject expertise relate to a philosophy of education that engages diversity. A participant reads explanations and examples of six approaches to diversity education from the Approach-in-Dimension rubric and identifies an approach that best matches personal beliefs about humanity related to course standards. Then the participant finds an inspiring quote to link diversity to course subjects and writes a welcome statement.

A Science Teacher in STEM Transformation

Wow! That was an awesome journey. The creativity, the passion, the frankness, the joy in those statements speaks to me. I would imagine it speaks to our students as well. After reading these, I had to go read my syllabus – how depressing. I believe there is a generic Title IX statement, provided to me by a colleague when I was first writing a syllabus. I suppose that this does not constitute much of a diversity statement. Considering the important roles that diversity, equity, and inclusion play in the sciences, it's a bit of a shame I do not have one.

As a science teacher, I try to highlight issues of diversity, equity, and inclusion in the sciences – and there are many. There are major issues in the STEM workforce – especially when various occupations and pay are considered. In higher education, there is a problematic achievement gap between under-represented minorities and their White counterparts in STEM subjects. Further, it is my opinion that STEM students do not get much in the way of the humanities in their education or job training. Therefore, I do try to highlight issues of equity in the classroom. For my students, this is a life-or-death lesson. Many will go into health care. In our current health-care system, the Black population of the US has a death rate 3.7 times higher than that of Whites from Covid-19. This is an issue of systemic racism in our health-care system. I want our students to be prepared for this reality so that they can be part of changing it when they enter the workforce.

What struck me in general about the reading was the fact that it did not sound like the generic Title IX statement from my syllabus. I landed on "Social Action." Landing on "one" is clearly a very linear way of thinking, but I was led down this line of thinking reading the categories. I suppose what drew me in the most was the focus on a student-centered approach to writing the statement.

Bilingual Student Cogen Diversity Circle:

Question
- How do Monarch butterfly migrations to Mexico relate to people migrations from Mexico?

Activity
- Read Spanish-English book, Señorita Mariposa by Gundersheimer and Rivero, about Monarch butterflies and regional cultures with liberation themes - life cycle, migration, and ecology. Discuss leaving home, collaborate on a butterfly poster, move like a butterfly, and write poetry about protecting pollinators in food ecosystems that nourish diverse cultures.

Environmental Humanization

FIGURE 5.8 Bilingual Student Cogen Diversity Circle. Photo by the author and Fe (fee) Danger.

Reading the examples, however, I found the Transformative writings much more suited to my pedagogy. I most appreciate the emphasis on questions. I approach science as a process and less as a series of facts, so inquiry is a dominant theme in my courses. Further, I appreciate the extremely welcoming tone of the statement and its emphasis on understanding and acceptance. I think that writing something for my syllabus with a mix of both the Transformative and Social Action approaches would work well for both myself and my students.[167]

A Paralegal/Law Teacher

Workshop participants learn how writing welcome statements helps them reconceptualize course content to invite diverse students and cultural perspectives into core subjects. Changed statements encourage students to develop culture competence and structural competence during academic engagement. Students are encouraged to participate in course-related careers for world healing. For example, a civil evidence instructor wrote a statement for her syllabus that acknowledges the impact of colorblind bias and cultural deficit thinking on investigation techniques:

> I want students from all diverse backgrounds and perspectives to be well served by this course, that students' learning needs be addressed both in and out of class, and for the diversity that students bring to this class to be viewed as a resource, strength, and benefit. When we acknowledge differences between us it builds a bridge to an open and honest relationship between us as students and teacher, and between all of you as classmates. It is my intention to present materials and activities that are respectful of diversity, including but not limited to: race, color, national origin, language, sex, disability, age, sexual orientation, gender identity, religion, creed, ancestry, belief, veteran status.... In this course we explore investigative techniques that can be affected by our pre-existing biases. We will learn how to arrive at accurate and objective conclusions by acknowledging implicit biases and the negative impact they can have in our investigations.[168]

In drafting the statement, the instructor researched how implicit bias influences fact-gathering and interpretations of evidence and law. She considered information from the 2020 California Racial Justice Act (RJA),[169] with strategies to reduce discrimination in criminal justice by authorizing legal professionals to use systemic analysis for decisions about evidence. The RJA documents that people of color are disproportionately accused and incarcerated, for longer sentences, relative to White people. This instructor learned that colorblind investigators, police, lawyers, judges, and jurors strive to assume nothing and treat everyone as individuals. However, because of cultural conditioning in the institutions that perpetuate systemic racism, they harbor unconscious racial bias. Unless professionals within the criminal justice system use antibias-antiracist measures, the reflex persists and professionals identify criminal suspects based on racial stereotypes despite colorblind intentions. Inaccurate conclusions are then drawn by denying the influence of these stereotypes.

To train *holistic* antibias-antiracist investigators, this instructor now has a framework to design assignments for students to look for signs of systemic bias: Students read cases to explore how structural racism directs what professionals say and do and why. Students gather data about implicit bias and racialized systemic trends. Students integrate bias data during the fact-finding process of particular cases, matching antibias-antiracist analysis to the body of uncovered evidence. Thus, after composing a new syllabus statement, this instructor reflected: "Thank you for your guidance during this course. I have learned a great deal, perhaps the most important being the need for reflection and change."[170]

A Visual Arts Instructor

Developing critical consciousness by composing welcome statements, everyday teachers explore how to be *transformative* teachers. A visual arts instructor shifts from a stock diversity statement to a heartfelt statement that guides discussion topic rules and projects to social justice communication. Here is an excerpt:

> Through group discussion after each project, we aim to learn, understand, enlighten and empower. We listen to diverse perspectives, and forgive miscommunications.
> Printmaking is a levelling medium. It involves the production of multiples of a single artwork, which can contain text, and image. Printmakers are usually community spirited, devoted to social justice, equal rights and equity. Printmaking is the original physical mode of communication to the masses, responding to events and ideas, and questioning our ways of being on this planet.
> I teach to transform with you. The world benefits when you graduate to be an antibias-antiracist citizen with subject expertise, culture competency, and sustainability skills. I have high expectation for your success, critical thinking, and creativity.
> We are diverse together.[171]

An English Teacher's "Revolutionized" Syllabi

In back-and-forth dialogue between workshop instructor and participants, teachers consider other aspects of curriculum, such as the language used throughout their syllabi, required reading selections, and assignment rubrics.

> This is one of the most challenging and meaningful Professional Development sessions I have participated in. I have realized that a Diversity Statement – without intentionality and finding a way to integrate it into the core of the course itself – is simply paying lip service to diversity. To make reviewing easier – all of the diversity statement and additional materials that I have added to the syllabus are in green font so you can see some of my rationale for how and where I have included them.[172]

This English teacher declares: "The final transformation! I feel that the first impression my students will have and their familiarity with my intentions has been revolutionized!"[173]

Example #3: A Laboratory Diversity Circle

In operation continuously since 2003, this Laboratory Diversity Circle – Faculty for Radical Empowerment and Enlightenment (FREE) at TMCC, introduced in Chapter 1 and explained in the Diversity Circle Recipe above – gathers students, educators, and community across campus to act-reflect imaginatively on interdisciplinary themes. FREE adapts Freire's culture circles for praxis *by* the oppressed for liberation from dehumanizing systems for *both* the oppressed and oppressors. Freire explained how critical consciousness develops humanization through "codification" stages during academic development: (1) identification of themes and problems and (2) action-investigation for real-world solutions. The two stages elicit community stories and data about injustices to create problem-posing questions and themes for "cultural change," thereby facilitating students to be "responsible Subjects" in liberation education.[174]

As such, FREE involves students, with facilitating teachers, in identifying "hinged themes" to extrapolate subjects with the research, writing, and diagraming of a "thematic fan." Students develop literacy and analytical skills by applying academic subjects to lived experiences. "Once the thematic demarcation is completed, each specialist presents to the interdisciplinary team a project for the 'breakdown' of [the] theme." Students categorize contradictions to "develop codifications to be used in thematic investigation." The codifications document dehumanization and reveal cultural data points for humanizing actions. Thus, students and teachers become "critical co-investigators," co-generating an intergenerational academic-world-healing event.[175]

FREE adapts Freire's model to integrate mindfulness *and* environment into *experimental* interactions. The program gathers participants from an overall student body of 57% European American, 27% Latinx, 6% Asian American, 4% mixed race, 2% African American, and 1% American Indian. FREE activates a yearly average of about 10 to 20 faculty, staff, and community supports, and 100 to 400 students in outdoor and indoor activities. Some FREE themes have been *vision, censorship, binary opposition, freedom of expression, "color-blinders," paradigm shifts, evolution versus creation, organic, mythology, diversity, water, "(hum)animals," fear, nature versus nurture, food, problem solving, magic & logic, a brave new world, belonging, sustainability*, and *seventh generation*.[176]

> FREE teachers are 'cultural creators' supporting one another in Victor Turner's concept of the *'communitas'* that generates 'social dramas' and ritual metaphors such that faculty and students learn how to take educational risks together in order to empower thinking and transform understanding.[177]

Sustainability Theme Project

One FREE project was embedded into a collaboration with environmental activists on the *2022-23 Year of Sustainability* theme, with 280 documented sustainability activities that culminated in an event with about 450 participants on Earth Day, involving biology, visual arts, education, anthropology, English, and geology, and community groups. Some of the activities that happened during the year were exhibited throughout the year in the Student Center on six recycled mosaic mega-fire-manzanita display trees made by visual arts, education, and counseling faculty and students in an upcycling activity. These activities led to structural transformation; for instance, the mosaics are used in academic events, and a land acknowledgement plaque was installed permanently in a campus pollinator garden with a Great Basin Tribes ceremony to honor living Numu (Northern Paiute), Wašiw (Washoe), Newe (Western Shoshone), and Nuwu (Southern Paiute) peoples.[178]

Another activity – "*Seedfolks* Planting" – was a small beautification garden made by diverse English Language Learners (ELLs). Students read *Seedfolks*, a book about a neighborhood garden. To apply reading comprehension, the students painted wooden plant tags and planted 29 plants at the entrance of a campus building, followed by storytelling about their project to Earth Day participants. Thus, students from around the world developed the campus-wide sustainability theme to deepen subject engagement with outdoor education and story sharing.[179]

206 Three Transformative Tools

Transformative teacher:
- Heather Haddox facilitates subject requirements with reading, discussion, and writing about *Seedfolks* by Paul Fleischman, using critical consciousness circle methods to sow twenty-nine plants to beautify campus community.

Laboratory Diversity Circle:
Question
- How do students develop academically and experience belonging in diversity and sustainability outdoors?

Activity
- Students from Cambodia, Columbia, Ecuador, El Salvador, Guatemala, Haiti, Japan, Mexico, Peru, Thailand, and Ukraine do planting project during a sustainability literacy theme.

FIGURE 5.9   Transformative teachers. Photo granted by permission from Rain Donahue.

Water Theme – Hornbook Ping Pong and Student-Made Mural Project

In 2017, the FREE Laboratory Circle activated a water theme. Because TMCC is in a high desert region confronting water scarcity, the theme is culturally and environmentally relevant. In one culminating event, students as "co-investigators" played Hornbook Ping Pong, linking US education history to cultural stories, questions, and healing actions about water science and use.[180] Students integrated required subjects into interdisciplinary curriculum about water. They coded water topics and proposed intersectional solutions for water protection.

About 200 students played Hornbook Ping Pong on round tables, preparing for the game by reading, writing, illustrating, and talking about water after studying it for months during existing coursework. As shown in Figure 5.10, students played this question-and-answer game with the recycled cardboard ping pong paddles they designed with cultural information from student presentations and the water mural they made.[181] Then, playing the game, they activated cultural knowledge kinesthetically, just as European-ancestry colonial students in the Americas had done when globalization was developing with their own hornbook paddles generations before. Game rules were that, upon missed shots, players had to shout out water facts written and drawn onto the paddles. After playing, students attached their paddles to the nearby mural to develop culturally responsive artwork for the rest of the campus to view. Students, therefore, collaboratively and imaginatively integrated curriculum about anthropology, printmaking, psychology, education, mathematics, English, and sociology, connecting academics to the world.[182]

Playing with hornbook paddles symbolizes "transformational resistance" to mainstream education textbooks that have a US children's literature history dating back some 600 years. In other words, curriculum delivered to children by Catholic and European colonist educators in the land now called the United States is framed by conquest. Facilitators at this event explained that the hornbooks – rectangle paddles of 4 to 6 inches – were handcrafted by

FIGURE 5.10 Hornbook Ping Pong. Photo by the author (FREE 2017).

FIGURE 5.11 Interdisciplinary Laboratory Diversity Circle. Photo by Candace Garlock (FREE 2017).

educators who engraved cultural literacy curriculum onto animal horns or stamped wooden paddles protected by a sheer layer of horn leaf. During US colonial schooling, educators conveyed Anglo-conformist content in visuals and phrases onto both paddle sides. During the FREE event, students made their own paddles but used ethnic studies content to resist the conquest paradigm, relating culturally responsive water sustainability questions and stories to cultural actions.[183]

Therefore, FREE illustrates a Diversity Circle for campus-wide academic experiments to meet the humanization goals that motivate students and teachers with big-picture cultural themes. By deepening curriculum with ethnic studies, participants address the teacher-culture paradox with inclusive and holistic multicultural education for change.

The greatest promise of multicultural education is that it will serve as a vehicle for general curriculum reform and transformation. If ethnic content is merely added to the traditional curriculum, which has many problems [Citation], then efforts to modify the curriculum with ethnic content are likely to lead to a dead end. The total school curriculum should be transformed.[184]

Conclusion

Why Try a Diversity Circle Now?

While teachers are not the cause of US education problems, *transformative* teachers are vital to solutions. We know education serves the economy, but we also understand that our hourly and daily decisions can be redirected to education outcomes that change the economy toward public good. Rather than unconsciously reproducing an economy that stratifies and destroys, transformative teachers advance equity and sustainability experiences with students to reshape subject engagement and learning outcomes from a position of love. Our proactive multicultural collaborations facilitate holism activities during core routines. We organize for cultural belonging in diversity from which to resist

FIGURE 5.12 Laboratory Diversity Circle water mural. Photo by the author.

FIGURE 5.13 Three Diversity Circle strategies. Shutterstock photo.

Three Diversity Circle Strategies:
1. *Sharing:* Circle-read *Earth Day Every Day* by Lisa Bullard and Xiao Xin on a field trip to a watershed park.
2. *Circle Question:* How do we support water and cultures every day?
3. *Global Praxis:*
   - Students collect leaves, rocks, and branches.
   - Students arrange nature in circle designs.
   - Students sketch nature outlines to make coloring booklets, Water & Earth, to fill in coming weeks.
   - When booklets are complete, students discuss questions and ideas for watershed stewardship inspired by art.

systemic inequities at school. Counteracting Anglo-conformist procedures – such as racialized tracking, biased determinations about student behavior, curriculum development that marginalizes cultures, and site segregation – is hard work and cannot be done alone. Diversity Circles are trust-building alliances to integrate multicultural, mindfulness, and environmental education into nonviolent liberation action and reflection during academic development.

Diversity Circles thwart disinformation from colorblind "race-neutral" policies that ignore systemic racism in our midst. From our culturally responsive home bases, we co-create hands-on alternatives to "banking education."[185] We support diverse student success and well-being by *reducing* mainstream over-standardized curriculum as we *increase* backwards design. Posing big-picture questions, Diversity Circles practice Multicultural Mindfulness peace to integrate humanization and structural competence into academic activities. We guide and evaluate outcomes with transparent philosophies of education, such as those outlined by the Approach-in-Dimension. We strengthen the profession by advocating to train, recruit, and mentor diverse highly qualified educators. We call for reduced teaching loads, increased pay, and more time for professional collaboration to reconceptualize education with diversity. We help hire and retain educators with subject expertise *and* culture competence for holistic education.

Diversity Circles build on an important innovation in US education – unbolting desks from the industrial rows in school houses in the 1800s.[186] Going with this simple yet radical historical change, transformative teachers continue to unlock the dehumanizing structures that divide through circle activities with cultures, mindfulness, and nature, indoors and outdoors. Our circles counteract exclusion and destruction socialization with unity experiences. We expect creative tension in teams involved in making change. We assuage inevitable defensive reactions during uncertainty by celebrating social-emotional well-being moments as we solve problems together. We prevent and resolve territorial conflict by reconceptualizing mainstream academics with local and global perspectives from ethnic studies and diverse cultural ways of knowing. We decrease top-down prepackaged materials and busy-making curriculum with Culture-Conscious Listening in classrooms, labs, committee rooms, and offices connected to campus-wide inquiry projects about world healing.

Happily, Diversity Circles need few props and minimal funding. These grassroots roundtables are accessible to illiterate, preliterate, and highly educated participants of all ages in any topic with any cultures or languages. We form cross-cultural alliances to imagine antibias-antiracist themes that connect personal experiences to real-world solutions. *Embracing* diversity and sustainability with compassion practices, transformative teachers activate "natural awe," reflecting on sun, land, sky, and water to integrate subjects and cultures into environmental consciousness. Try a Diversity Circle now to participate in holistic humanization during academic engagement that flowers like "a lotus that grows from the mud."[187]

TRANSFORMATIVE BREATHWORK AND JOURNAL

Journal question: *How do Diversity Circles reconcile the oppressor–oppressed conflict?*

> Mindfulness…is composed of psychological phenomena that exist as seeds in our store consciousness. We have the chance to become aware of them when they manifest as mental formations in our mind consciousness. As soon as a mental formation rises, we should breathe in and out and identify it. As we continue to observe it, we can see its connection with the whole of our mind…. 'I breathe in and out and identify the mental formation that is present at this moment in me.' To identify a mental formation with the help of conscious breathing means to recognize, embrace, and become one with that mental formation. It does not mean to drown in that mental formation, because the subject that is recognizing, embracing, and becoming one with the mental formation is the energy of mindfulness. When our mindfulness is one with the mental formation, the mental formation quite naturally changes for the better.[188]
>
> —Thich Nhat Hanh

Breathwork

Wherever you are, take a mindful moment to relax. Use a timer chime if you like. Close or lid your eyes, taking several slow deep breaths, smiling slightly, noticing sensations: smells, sounds, touch, taste, and sight (if your eyes are open).

Now breathe while internally reciting the *gatha* below:

Breathing in, I calm my body.
Breathing out, I smile.
Dwelling in the present moment,
I know this is a reconciliation moment.[189]

Then:

Breathing in *How do Diversity Circles reconcile the oppressor–oppressed conflict?*
Breathing out openness.
Repeat for as long as you like or until the timer chimes.

Journal

Imagine we're in a Diversity Circle with the transformative practitioners cited in this book. We want to support superdiverse student success in a biodiverse world. Read our answers below. Reflect on your meditation. Briefly answer the journal question above in a way that's meaningful to you.

Paulo Freire

Culture circles:

- Nurture culturally relevant social trust to liberate from the oppressed–oppressor duality.
- Support the oppressed to co-generate academic themes by reflecting on economic-social contradictions in communities.
- Listen deeply, ask clarity questions, and facilitate the oppressed to apply "critical consciousness" to real-world liberation experiences for everyone.[190]
- Educate resourcefully by using a best practices model – originally tested in the 1960s with 20,000 culture circles of mostly Afro-Brazilian farmworkers and urban poor – to bring illiterate participants to literacy through social action in 45-day cycles.[191]

Thich Nhat Hanh

Mindfulness circles:

- Apply thousands of years of evidence about communities of care for holistic well-being.
- Practice mindfulness together hourly and daily, such as "mindful walking, mindful speaking, [and] mindful eating.... People in our *sangha* standing near us, practicing with us, support us so that we are not pulled away from the present moment."[192]
- Use breathwork and sensory reflection for nonviolent collectivization now. "Breathing in, I see that I am part of a *sangha*, and I am being protected by my *sangha*. Breathing out, I feel joy."[193]
- "The rich also suffer … They may be rich materially, but many are poor spiritually, and they suffer a lot. I have known rich and famous people who have ended up committing suicide… Nonviolence means we act with love and compassion."[194]
- Work through relationship conflicts by activating three peace principles: interbeing, impermanence, and emptiness.[195]

Micaela Rubalcava

Diversity Circles are

- Learning communities of two or more participants, as diverse as possible, to make holistic change by connecting academics to real-world liberation experiences.
- Homerooms for social-emotional trust through cross-cultural understanding to reduce assimilation and segregation procedures and increase integrative space, time, materials, and learning environments.
- Grassroots action-reflection alliances that work through cultural conflict with peace practices to grow structural competence during academic engagement.

- Inclusion collaborations for diverse student success, knowledge development, and sustainability experiences with cultures, mindfulness, and nature indoors and outdoors.
- The *structure* tool for Environmental Liberation Education, with three principles, seven types, five phases, and three core strategies.

Notes

1 Freire (1985), 19.
2 Lewis and Diamond (2015), xix.
3 Freire (1985), 59.
4 Hanh (all); Trungpa (1993).
5 Freire (1985), 22 and 110.
6 Reece (2022), 61, 40.
7 Reece (2022), 14.
8 Nava (2001), title; Reece (2022), 165.
9 Hanh (2002a), 70.
10 Yamamura and Koth (2018).
11 Hanh (all); Trungpa (1993).
12 Hanh (1999), 18.
13 Trungpa (1993), 32.
14 Aubrey and Riley (2016); Elias (1975); Freire (1985), 59, 113.
15 Freire (1985), 59.
16 Reece (2022), 21, 3.
17 Reece (2022), 1.
18 Lewis and Diamond (2015), xix.
19 Lewis and Diamond (2015), xiii.
20 Lewis and Diamond (2015), 178.
21 Reece (2022), 15.
22 Trungpa (1993), 99–101.
23 Yevonne Allen: February 26, 2021 email to the author, in Rubalcava (2001–2024).
24 Emdin (2016).
25 Paideia (2018); Ross (2003).
26 Fiol-Matta and Chamberlain (1994), 141.
27 Scholarship describing education learning communities, including "Equity Ecosystems": Bell (1991); Berry and Farris-Berg (2016); Doig and Groves (2011); Freire (1985); Geri and MacGregor (1999, January); Gutierrez (1973); Hanh (all); King (1964); Putman and Rock (2018); Roberts and Pruitt (2009); Vescio, Ross and Adams (2008, January); Smith, MacGregor, Matthews and Gabelnick (2004); Vescio, Ross and Adams (2008, January); Yamamura and Koth (2018).
28 www.lcassociation.org.
29 Smith, MacGregor, Matthews and Gabelnick (2004), 69–70.
30 Smith, MacGregor, Matthews and Gabelnick (2004), 20.
31 Vescio, Ross and Adams (2008, January).
32 King (1964), 79.
33 Vescio, Ross and Adams (2008, January).
34 Smith, MacGregor, Matthews and Gabelnick (2004), 67.
35 Smith, MacGregor, Matthews and Gabelnick, 71–91; Rubalcava (2001–2024).
36 Berry and Farris-Berg (2016), 13.
37 Vescio, Ross and Adams (2008, January).
38 Reece (2022), 73; Freire (1985), 59.
39 Hanh and Weare (2017), title.
40 Hanh (1998), 3.
41 King (1964), 80.

42 Frankenberg, Garces and Hopkins (2016).
43 Freire (1985).
44 Doll, Brehm and Zucker (2014).
45 Sleeter and Carmona (2017); Sleeter and Zavala (2020).
46 Paulo Freire's circles have a "maximum of twenty persons." Freire (1985), 110.
47 Maslow (1943).
48 Doll, Brehm and Zucker (2014); Emdin (2016).
49 Butler (1989); Fiol-Matta and Chamberlain (1994); Freire (1985); Sleeter and Carmona (2017); Sleeter v Zavala (2020); Urtubey (2023, June 20).
50 Fiol-Matta and Chamberlain (1994); Sleeter and Carmona (2017); Sleeter and Zavala (2020); Valenzuela (2016).
51 Fried (2001); Rubalcava (2005).
52 Gang (1991), 79.
53 Ardoin and Bowers (2020); Bigelow and Swinehart (2014); Clark (all); King (2018); Vergou and Willison (2016); Middleton (2018); Rubalcava (2001–2024).
54 Frankenberg, Garces and Hopkins (2016); Ingersoll (2015); Noguera (2017, 2018); Rubalcava (2001–2024); Sleeter (all); Sleeter and Carmona (2017); Sleeter and Zavala (2020).
55 Sleeter and Zavala (2020).
56 Sleeter and Zavala (2020), 8; Lewis and Diamond (2015), xix.
57 Sleeter (all).
58 Sleeter (all).
59 Emdin (2016); Englander (2016); Kendi (2019); Kleinrock (2021); Lewis and Diamond (2015); Omi and Winant (1986); Osta and Vasquez (2019, June 13); Sleeter (1994); Temming (2021, April 14); Verschelden (2017).
60 Sleeter and Zavala (2020), 8.
61 Sleeter and Zavala (2020), 8.
62 Sleeter and Carmona (2017), 87; Sleeter and Zavala (2020), 8.
63 King (1964), 79–80.
64 King (1964), 79–80.
65 Sleeter (2011), 20.
66 Vicuña (2017, July 7), 22.
67 Drake and Burns (2004), 7, 17; Ebert and Culyer (2008); Rubalcava (2001–2024).
68 Drake and Burns (2004), 7, 17; Ebert and Culyer (2008); Rubalcava (2001–2024).
69 Sleeter and Carmona (2017), 167.
70 Sleeter and Carmona (2017), 167, 47; Miller (1991), 2–3.
71 Sleeter and Carmona (2017), 157.
72 Sleeter and Carmona (2017), 167.
73 Sleeter and Carmona (2017).
74 Sleeter and Carmona (2017), 3.
75 Banks (2003); Sleeter and Zavala (2020); Cuauhtin, Zavala, Sleeter and Au (2019).
76 Bigelow and Swinehart (2014).
77 Banks (2003); Sleeter and Zavala (2020); Cuauhtin, Zavala, Sleeter and Au (2019).
78 Bigelow v Swinehart (2014).
79 Sleeter and Carmona (2017), 24
80 Fiol-Matta and Chamberlain (1994); Hu-DeHart (1993); Sleeter and Carmona (2017); Sleeter and Zavala (2020); Sleeter (all).
81 Emdin (2016), 65.
82 King (1964), 79.
83 Sleeter and Carmona (2017), 3.
84 Sleeter and Carmona (2017), 3.
85 Prakash (2013, July 16).
86 Boff and Boff (1987), 2.
87 Gutierrez (1973), 40, 38.
88 Diaz (2018); Freire (1985).
89 Kunhardt (2018); King (1964), 79.
90 Nieto (2016).
91 Sleeter and Carmona (2017).

92 Rubalcava (2001–2024).
93 Clark (2001), 84–89.
94 Madden-Dent and Oliver (2021).
95 Freire (1985).
96 Sleeter and Carmona (2017).
97 Freire (1985), 113.
98 Reece (2022), 25.
99 Bethell, Newacheck, Hawes and Halfon (2014); Darling-Hammond (2006); Noguera (2017, 2018); Oakes and Lipton (2007); Sleeter (2001); Sleeter and Carmona (2017); Terada (2019, February 4).
100 Sleeter (all).
101 Gray and Taie (2015).
102 Quinlan (2016, May 6).
103 Ellison and Freedberg (2015, May 21).
104 Quinlan (2016, May 6).
105 Deruy (2017); Ingersoll (2015).
106 Ellison and Freedberg (2015, May 21).
107 Urtubey (2023, June 20).
108 Dweck (2007).
109 Dweck (2007).
110 Dweck (2007).
111 Blake (2018, March); Felice (1977).
112 Dubin (2017, Fall); Mascio (2016, Summer).
113 Campbell (2000), quoting Linda Darling-Hammond, 349.
114 Dubin (2017, Fall).
115 Gay (2000); Ladson-Billings (1995).
116 Bond, Quintero, Casey and Di Carlo (2015), 3.
117 California (2017, October 11); Espinoza, Turk and Taylor (2017); Flores (2017); Gasman, Samayoa and Ginsberg (2016); Petchauer and Mawhinney (2017); Rubalcava (2001–2024).
118 NASA (2023–2024).
119 Reece (2022), 150.
120 Flores (2017).
121 Petchauer and Mawhinney (2017).
122 Roberts and Pruitt (2009).
123 Gasman, Samayoa and Ginsberg (2016), 7.
124 Gasman, Samayoa and Ginsberg (2016), 5.
125 California (2017, October 11).
126 Dastagir (2018, May 28), quoting Robin DiAngelo.
127 Rubalcava (2001–2024).
128 Freire (1985), 131.
129 Gasman, Samayoa and Ginsberg (2016); California (2017, October 11).
130 Lewis and Diamond (2015), 177; Bond, Quintero, Casey and Di Carlo (2015), 1.
131 Lewis and Diamond (2015), 177; Bond, Quintero, Casey and Di Carlo (2015), 1.
132 Gay (2000); Nieto (2013).
133 Bond, Quintero, Casey and Di Carlo (2015), 6.
134 Kayes (2006).
135 Gandara (2015), 14; Vigil (1988).
136 Mercado (2016), 26.
137 Gay (2000); Ladson-Billings (1995).
138 Vigil (1988).
139 Nieto (2016), 214.
140 Nava (2001).
141 Nieto (2016), 212.
142 Gandara (2015), 11.
143 Bond, Quintero, Casey and Di Carlo (2015), 6.
144 Natanson (2023, March 6).

145 Banks (2003); Cuauhtin, Zavala, Sleeter and Au (2019); Hu-DeHart (1993); Muñoz (1989); Sleeter and Zavala (2020); Takaki (all).
146 Sleeter (all).
147 Sleeter and Zavala (2020), 26.
148 Sleeter and Zavala (2020), 27.
149 Sleeter and Zavala (2020), 35.
150 Au, Brown and Calderón (2016), 19; Hu-DeHart (1993).
151 Dunbar-Ortiz (2014), 168.
152 Hu-DeHart (1993).
153 Au, Brown and Calderón (2016).
154 Takaki (1993).
155 Kendi (2019), 23; Rubalcava (1995).
156 Editors (2014, Fall); Oliver (2023, June 21); https://palusa.org; Ferlazzo (2016, February 6).
157 Howe and Lisi (2019), 191–192.
158 Reece (2022), 8.
159 Sleeter and Zavala (2020), 36–37.
160 Sleeter and Zavala (2020), 70–71.
161 Au, Brown and Calderón (2016).
162 Bouweraerts (2015, March 12).
163 Ormrod (2000), 45.
164 Maher (2005), 195–196.
165 Matt Barak 2016 Marvin Picollo interview, in Rubalcava (2001–2024); Bouweraerts (2015, March 12).
166 Rubalcava (2001–2024).
167 Rubalcava (2020).
168 Salisbury (2021).
169 Assembly (2020, September 30).
170 Salisbury (2021).
171 Melhop (2023).
172 Maynard (2021).
173 Maynard (2021).
174 Freire (1985), 20.
175 Maynard (2021), 20, 105–115.
176 Elena Bubnova: February 14, 2018 email to the author, in Rubalcava (2001–2024); Truckee (2018).
177 Truckee (2018).
178 Libby (2023, May 9); Cecilia Vigil: 2022–23 emails to the author, in Rubalcava (2001–2024).
179 Heather Haddox: March 29, 2023 email to the author, in Rubalcava (2001–2024).
180 Freire (1985), 97.
181 Sleeter and Zavala (2020), 70–71; Kiefer (2010); Young, Bryan, Jacobs and Tunnell (2020).
182 Rubalcava (2001–2024).
183 Young, Bryan, Jacobs and Tunnell (2020); Rubalcava (2001–2024).
184 Banks (2003), 13.
185 Freire (1985), 59.
186 Cuban (1993).
187 Hanh and Weare (2017), 132; Keltner (2023), 14.
188 Hanh (2008), 70–71.
189 Hanh (2008), 36.
190 Freire (1985), 69, 19.
191 Elias (1975); Aubrey and Riley (2016).
192 Hanh (2002b).
193 Hanh (2002b).
194 Hanh (1995) 79–81.
195 Hanh (2002b).

6
TOOL #2

Multicultural Mindfulness

Guiding Purpose

Explain how Multicultural Mindfulness is an inclusive peace process to

- Apply holistic curriculum and knowledge to big-picture humanization.
- Nurture cultural inclusion and diversity belonging for academic concentration during change.
- Integrate body-mind-culture-environment activities into subjects for student and teacher reconciliation.
- Use backwards design to engage subjects with culturally responsive systemic questions.
- Prompt reflective liberation and sustainability action to link subjects to human superdiversity in Earth biodiversity.
- Develop inward calm to address fear of change and outward compassion to resolve creative tension non-defensively.
- Collaborate on joyful justice academic projects to integrate academics into global citizenship and a sustainability economy.

Provide

- Two Multicultural Mindfulness Activities and one journal question: *Shaping Space for Interbeing*, *Drive-All-Blames-Into-One*, and *What's Multicultural Mindfulness?*

Context

What's Multicultural Mindfulness?

Multicultural Mindfulness facilitates cultural action-reflection with peace. Multicultural Mindfulness is process practices for cultural inclusion and equity experiences during academics. Its integrations support *holistic* student success, teacher empowerment, and curriculum and knowledge during change. It is one of Three Transformative Tools for Environmental

DOI: 10.4324/9781003364757-9
This chapter has been made available under a CC-BY-NC-ND license.

Liberation Education to reform mainstream education with antibias-antiracist activities for sustainable systems. The Diversity Circles tool *organizes* cross-cultural collaborations for change. The Approach-in-Dimension tool *guides* philosophical for the design and evaluation of change. The Multicultural Mindfulness tool *facilitates* hourly and daily non-defensive decisions and calm conflict resolution during change. Multicultural Mindfulness is present moment awareness of living cultures and compassion for creative tension during humanization.

Multicultural Mindfulness supports educators and students in "joyful and just" academic activities.[1] The practices invite teachable moments to integrate subjects into culturally responsive Earth stewardship experiences. The practices counteract assimilation and segregation patterns and destruction systems with cross-cultural creativity circles to reduce, reuse, recycle, and restore in real time. The practices ease anxiety while connecting subjects to local and global reparations. Multicultural Mindfulness integrates body, mind, culture, and environment into academic engagement for multicultural democracy and a sustainability economy.

Multicultural Mindfulness engages body-mind breathwork to motivate five culturally responsive and environmentally sustainable practices: wholesome nourishment, caring communications, compassionate relationships, community service, and nonviolent "reverence for life" on Earth.[2] Consistent breathwork fertilizes "everyday awe" to "animate action," connecting the present moment to the world.[3] Holistic action-reflection eschews false equivalents and challenges extremism while opening "the middle way" for synthesis.[4] At school this means balancing research and development of pinpointed disciplinary topics, subject details, and precise technological advances, with transformative middle way interdisciplinary engagement.[5] In this sense, academic freedom – the "unfettered pursuit of truth"[6] – connects to generosity from a position of love. Multicultural Mindfulness empowers educators and students to address suffering by nurturing social-emotional trust during academic learning. Multicultural Mindfulness, thus, personalizes the humanization goals that motivate students and teachers.[7]

Multicultural Mindfulness engages participants in the "natural awe" of Earth during otherwise bureaucratized schedules that have become "the substance of what we think of as 'school."[8] Its practices intervene in unconscious bias patterns from mainstream procedures and grow true happiness through reciprocity on the ground.[9] These action-reflection practices replace territoriality with integrative classrooms, labs, and meeting rooms. They calm social anxiety from the dehumanization of over-standardization, racialized tracking, and departmental silos. These peace practices elicit cultural authenticity and work through culture clashes while we solve systemic contradictions. "When we are mindful, we can see our roots of affliction clearly and transform them."[10]

Multicultural Mindfulness activities reveal false dichotomies with critical consciousness about ecosystems.

> Mindfulness is the energy that can embrace and transform all mental formations. Mindfulness helps us leave behind 'upside-down perceptions,' and wakes us up to what is happening.… This training tells us not just to refrain from taking what is not ours or exploiting others. It also exhorts us to live in a way that brings about justice and wellbeing to society.[11]

When we're mindful *of* education, we detrack and un-standardize to socialize for unity during knowledge development accountable to human superdiversity in Earth's biodiversity.

Multicultural Mindfulness shines a light on disinformation that confuses people who are victimized by or who profit materially from skewed systems. It reveals assumptions and stereotypes that alienate students "from historically underserved communities" and inspires culturally responsive academic engagement.[12] It gently exposes favoritism of those with intergenerational wealth or racial privileges that insulate against the spiritual value of diversity in education. Multicultural Mindfulness nurtures belonging at school. It invites an array of perspectives into subjects to assist transformative teachers to translate requirements into holistic projects for global citizenship and green vocations.

Three Multicultural Mindfulness Principles

Transformative teachers guide antibias-antiracist education toward unity with environmental consciousness through three mindfulness principles: interbeing, impermanence, and emptiness. These big-picture principles relieve suffering from stratified systems with holistic awareness. The three principles support cultural inclusion and academic accuracy with middle way liberation. Applying one engages all three.[13]

Interbeing

Interbeing refers to holistic relationships in ecological systems. It is interconnectedness in changing cosmos.[14] As Thich Nhat Hanh explains in *Happy Teachers Change the World*:

> 'Interbeing' means that you cannot be by yourself alone – you have to inter-be with everything else. Suppose we look at a rose deeply with mindfulness and concentration. In a short time, we discover that a rose is made of only non-rose elements. What do we see in a rose? We see a cloud, because we know that if there is no cloud there will be no rain…and no rose can grow. The sunshine…is also a non-rose element that is there in the rose. If we remove the cloud and the sunshine from the rose, there is no rose left….A rose has to inter-be with the whole cosmos.[15]

Interbeing is non-defensive. Mindfulness *of* interbeing reveals clouds and sunshine in the rose *and* ourselves. Interbeing bridges structural competence logic with lived experience emotion. It frees classrooms from the straightjacket of individualism and top-down "banking education" through relational circles.[16] As transformative teachers and students resist oppressive structures that divide and destroy during mainstream education, we develop interbeing activities about the "mud" that nourishes the "lotus."[17] We appreciate individuals as members of cultures in a shared environment. Interbeing imbues *Multicultural* Mindfulness with ecological perception to help educators take action to detrack programs and integrate peoples and subjects "here and now."[18]

Impermanence

Impermanence is flexibility in change every moment everywhere – past, present, and future. As educators recognize that all things change "here and now" in a constant state of flux, we see that even system-wide change is possible. As Thich Nhat Hanh puts it:

> Mindfulness…is the capacity of being present in the here and now. Focus your attention on what is going on. If mindfulness is there, concentration will be there, too. If you continue to be mindful of something, then you will concentrate on it; it will become the object of our concentration."[19]

Multicultural Mindfulness centers academic concentration on diversity change. Impermanence releases psychological entrapment in culture-based suffering. It frees us from Anglo-conformist data collection and analysis. Mindfulness *of* economic-social pain releases self-justifying assumptions and cynical hypocrisies ensnared in systems that distort truth. We breathe to recognize streaming stereotypes to discern tiers in an economy dependent on systemic bias. We breathe to counteract entrenchment in extremes. Rather, impermanence engages mindfulness practitioners in present moment equity actions to discern fact from fiction in unfolding subjects. It collects holistic evidence from perceptions about good versus bad for integrative decisions to un-standardize subjects and collectivize to refresh reconciliation during change, here and now.

Emptiness

Emptiness is spacious relief from the impulse to fix meaning and cling to ego. Mindfulness *of* emptiness assuages fear of change and territoriality with *open-mindedness*. We concentrate on non-defensive growth to encourage cultural inclusion behaviors.

> When your mindfulness and concentration are good, you will be able to receive insights; you will begin to understand in depth what is really happening in the here and now. So, the process is mindfulness, concentration, and insight. The insight helps you to understand, and it liberates you from your wrong perceptions. It makes you stop suffering.[20]

Multicultural Mindfulness of emptiness poses big-picture intersectional questions during topic development. It frees people in cultures to evolve and unify with imaginative healing themes. It strengthens prosocial feelings with universal connections in suffering and happiness. It is looking deeply for unconditional love as we adapt actions to unbounded liberation.

Why Apply Multicultural Mindfulness Hourly and Daily?

Like breathing, culture consciousness is a living practice. It's engaged moment by moment to respond to divisions from poorly regulated or corrupt economies and societies, which, in the US context, is reinforced with the desire for individual freedom defined by materialism. Culturally responsive academic concentration in US schools involves hourly and daily decisions about changing diversity. These decisions cannot be made in isolation. Multicultural Mindfulness is collaborative. That's why Multicultural Mindfulness works in concert with two other tools. Diversity Circles *structure* cross-cultural alliances for change. The Approach-in-Dimension is wide-lens *planning* and *assessment* during change. Multicultural Mindfulness *resolves* inward-outward conflicts inherent to change. Transformative teachers apply Multicultural Mindfulness for "tremendous generosity" during economic-social dehumanization experiences. We engage Multicultural Mindfulness moment by moment for peace while making holistic space, time, materials, and learning environment adjustments to connect education routines to living cultures now.[21]

Why Change Mainstream Education Space, Time, Materials, and Learning Environments?

Culture-conscious decisions interrupt extraction-consumption habits by maneuvering education elements – space, time, materials, and learning environments – to support sustainability. By redesigning these elements holistically, educators in history have reformed education by doing the following:[22]

- Unbolting desks from fixed rows, which opened student-centered collaborations.
- Desegregating schools with busing programs to integrate diverse students, which narrowed the racial achievement gap and increased cross-cultural socialization in places where busing occurred.
- Supporting student-led ethnic studies to expand curriculum and knowledge beyond assimilation and segregation paradigms with cultural pluralism, equity, and diverse ways of knowing frameworks.
- Mainstreaming students with special needs through team-supported Individualized Education Programs (IEPs), which increased academic engagement of students with special needs and supported inclusion interactions among all students.
- Opening access to global resources through cyber modalities, with differentiated curriculum and instruction through flexible online programs and the reach of remote education. (It bears noting that cyber technology, while presenting as empowering, appears also to have several dehumanizing consequences, such as accelerating socio-economic inequities and replacing face-to-face interactions and cultural development with screen representations that blur cultural authenticity. For more, please see footnote.[23])

Space[24]

Multicultural Mindfulness *space* is holistic place-based sustainability experiences. For example:

- Outdoor education.
- Face-to-face culture consciousness circles.
- Interdisciplinary and intergenerational site-based education learning communities.
- Faculty mentorship "teas" and circles.[25]
- Student-to-student support circles.
- Global-multicultural classroom and school library resource centers.
- Interdisciplinary and intergenerational field trips and exchange events.
- Peace corners.
- Teacher-student one-on-one conferences.
- Community-support-student one-on-one conferences.

Time[26]

Multicultural Mindfulness *time* is scheduling holistic sustainability experiences, such as during:

- Openers and closures.
- Core content activities.
- Hourly, daily, and quarterly transition routines.
- One-time and adaptable intermittent events.
- Balanced semester, whole-year units, or multi-year schedules.

Materials[27]

Multicultural Mindfulness *materials* is finding and using holistic sustainability content, selecting topics and alternative modalities that

- Observe or immerse in nature.
- Empower historically alienated cultures.
- Investigate intergenerational interdisciplinary themes.
- Develop student-centered research, scholarship, works, and performances.
- Advance sensory-based multimodal social-emotional academic learning, including with animal, music, and water therapy.
- Diversify subjects.
- Reduce consumption, reuse and recycle.
- Restore ecosystems.
- Relate subjects to community practices and interactions about liberation, mindfulness, and environmental themes.
- Foster green careers.

Learning Environments[28]

Multicultural Mindfulness *learning environments* is designing academic integrations with holistic sustainability designs. For example:

- Equity ecosystems for peer-to-peer behavior management and emotional regulation during restorative justice experiences.
- Socialization activities and whole-campus events with equity and mindfulness criteria.
- Across-the-curriculum projects that connect academic engagement to the real world.
- Promoting campus systems that reduce, recycle, and restore.
- Classroom, lab, and meeting room well-being themes to integrate body, mind, culture, and environment into routines, such as conscious breathing, mindful walking, and reflective journaling outdoors.
- Collaborations to invite Indigenous stewardship knowledge and practices to lead education reform.
- Experiments to develop green citizenship and healthy multicultural identities through local and global collaborations.

How does Multicultural Mindfulness engage systems?

Multicultural Mindfulness engages systems with cross-cultural academic concentration outside of the self to relieve "anxiety, rumination, depression, and self-criticism" that "can overtake us."[29] Multicultural Mindfulness helps to recognize how dehumanization-versus-humanization systems impact this personal moment. We use the practices to counteract the "interfering neurotic" who "tries to run the show."[30] Multicultural Mindfulness of systems adjusts *what* knowledge is engaged and *why*. Transformative teachers facilitate culturally responsive social-emotional academic learning *with* students and colleagues to uplift subjects with environmental consciousness.[31] This holistic approach shifts participants away from intermittent or add-on approaches. Instead, we change mainstream bureaucratic systems in motion. We integrate big-picture questions into academics to shape subjects personally and multimodally.

Multicultural Mindfulness develops culture competence in real time. We swap Anglo-conformity for equity ecosystems. We use structural analysis to moderate judgment with curiosity about multicultural perspectives and clashing emotions. We recognize the need for cultural belonging in sustainability with local projects. That's why we address inequities *before*, and *concurrent* with, this learning moment. Multicultural Mindfulness brings peace to arts and sciences integrations, assuaging the creative tension of forging inclusion. It reduces structural barriers to justice while growing community compassion with environmental consciousness.

Multicultural Mindfulness Systems Illustration

Inspired by breathwork methods in Thich Nhat Hanh's *No Mud, No Lotus*, the chalk mural in Figure 6.1 illustrates a Multicultural Mindfulness activity to recognize systems and inspire

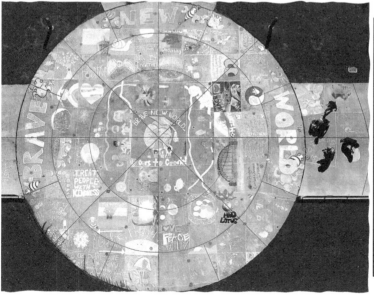

FIGURE 6.1 Brave New World mural. Photo created by Tim Ill & Kate Kirkpatrick (FREE 2020).

cross-cultural and environmental holism. Seventy students, staff, and educators created a 50-by-50-foot chalk mural called *Brave New World*. This outdoor mural involved diverse participants in the existing academic schedule to reflect on real-world suffering and healing in October 2020 during the Covid-19 pandemic. Conducted on campus grounds and adhering to public health protocols, the project integrated math, psychology, veterinary science, biology, anthropology, sociology, and other fields of study. Diverse subjects came together through mindfulness principles – interbeing, impermanence, and emptiness – for critical consciousness about economic-social systems.[32]

How Can Multicultural Mindfulness Strengthen Public Education?

Multicultural Mindfulness weaves superdiversity-biodiversity into body-mind-culture-environment integration. Transformative teachers and superdiverse students act and reflect together to guide academics to public good outcomes. A social democratic institution, public education is meant to be the "great equalizer," a place for social integration and opportunity.[33] Public education classrooms should be cross-cultural spaces for true happiness, not by denying material threats or retreating to structural habits but by entering the world through integrated subjects.[34] Multicultural Mindfulness practices invite superdiverse youth, educators, and communities into big-picture problem-solving. "During times of crisis and national disasters we turn to our public schools for safety and refuge."[35]

Brave New World mural squares (5'x5') depict intergenerational belonging:

- Preschoolers, college math students and professors, and an education professor draw a "Mud Lotus" interacting with a "Parabolic Bridge" on campus center plaza.
- Rangoli rice powder designs throughout the mural symbolize cultural beliefs about human suffering and healing.

FIGURE 6.2 Brave New World mural squares. Photo created by the author (FREE 2020).

Multicultural Mindfulness calms anger, releases tension, and restores communication.[36] Poverty, marginalization, and displacement are all factors that inhibit well-being. Students from "disfavored communities" graduate from college at much lower rates than students from privileged groups.[37] For instance, wealthy and upper-middle income White and some Asian students have an overall college completion rate of about 70%, whereas poor and lower-middle income students of color and students from other cultural identities have an overall completion rate of about 30%.[38] While overall statistics have cultural variations requiring specific solutions, mindfulness of intersectionality and differences helps develop middle-way universal design.[39]

Thich Nhat Hanh explains that prison inmates in violent conditions can experience sustainable freedom with mindfulness *of* incarceration.

> No matter where you find yourself, if you have freedom, you are happy. I have many friends who spent time in forced labor camps and because they know how to practice, they did not suffer as greatly. In fact, they grew.... By freedom I mean freedom from afflictions, from anger, and from despair. If you have anger in you, you have to transform anger in order to get your freedom back. If there is despair in you, you need to recognize that energy and not let it overwhelm you. You have to practice in such a way that you transform the energy of despair and obtain the freedom you deserve – the freedom from despair. You can practice freedom every moment of your daily life. Every step you take can help you reclaim your freedom. Every breath you take can help you develop and cultivate your freedom.[40]

Multicultural Mindfulness transforms public education classrooms, labs, and meeting rooms into indoor-outdoor spaces to develop "the talent of knowing how to be happy" wherein "happiness is a habit that each of us needs to learn."[41] As everyday teachers replace cultural victimization with growth mindsets, true happiness experiences reduce the systemic suffering that disrupts academic concentration.[42] Transformative teachers strengthen the profession, support public education, and assist diverse student success with prosocial projects for a livable world.

MULTICULTURAL MINDFULNESS ACTIVITY

Shaping Space for Interbeing

Outcome

- Apply the Multicultural Mindfulness principle of *interbeing* to shape indoor or outdoor classroom space.

Key Concepts

- **Interbeing:** The interconnectedness of everything in the universe, including superdiverse people in biodiverse ecosystems.

Resources

- Catalogues or examples of natural, low-cost, and culturally relevant furniture and resources for indoor and outdoor education, a place to meet indoors or outdoors.

Big-Picture Question

- How do I feature environmental interbeing in my learning environment?[43]

Start

Whole group circle (while passing around catalogues and viewing examples):

- **Individually journal** one assignment or activity planned for next week and title it with a one-sentence description.
- **Individually write** a big-picture sustainability question about "interbeing" to guide a space redesign for your activity or assignment.
- **Read aloud** Redesign Example (below).
- Discuss:

    1 What's confusing?
    2 What's clear?
    3 What's one doable idea?

Middle

- **Individually sketch** an interbeing redesign for your planned activity or assignment.
- **Everyone shares sketches** and **brainstorms** change logistics for each redesign.
- After everyone shares and brainstorms, **individually journal** a to-do list.

Closing

- **Individually calendar** a redesign.
- **Individually journal** reflection criteria to assess the redesign for required subject learning and inclusion and sustainability outcomes.

Interbeing Redesign Example

Current Assignment Title and Description

- "Weekly Chapter Summary"
- Students submit weekly one-page descriptions about textbook chapters.
- Weekly, teacher orally reviews chapter topics described in the summaries while students take notes.

Big-Picture Question

- How do I activate unconditional love?

> ### Sustainability Redesign
>
> - New Assignment Title: "Weekly Chapter Summary Circle."
> - Students submit a 2/3-page description of the chapter *with* a 1/3-page brainstorm about "systems" in chapter topics.
> - Weekly, students lead circle discussion (outdoors when possible or with seasonal nature inside circle center) about systems brainstorms, taking notes during discussion.
>
> ### Changes
>
> - Students replace some "comprehension" academic writing about textbook chapters with "analysis" and "synthesis" writing about systems in chapter topics.
> - Students reshape classroom space with interbeing by replacing top-down teacher talk about chapters with student-generated content discussed in a circle about systems in chapter topics, outdoors when possible, or reflective of seasonal nature in circle center.
>
> ### To-Do List
>
> - Change the assignment rubric to assign points to circle participation and systems analysis writing.
> - Communicate schedule for student-led circle discussion and seasonal nature example drop off.
> - Design feedback "Yes/No" cards such as the following:
>
>   1 Did you feel included in the circle discussion? Why? Why not?
>   2 Did you identify systems in chapter topics? Why? Why not?
>   3 What did you notice about nature systems that relate to chapter topics? How did nature deepen or distract your academic concentration?

Theory and Practice

What Are Intergenerational Pre-Prejudice and Prejudice Cycles?

Dr. Martin Luther King, Jr. describes intergenerational pre-prejudice and prejudice cycles.

> When you suddenly find your tongue twisted and your speech stammering as you seek to explain to your six-year-old daughter why she cannot go to the public amusement park that has just been advertised on television, and see tears welling up in her little eyes when she is told that *Funtown* is closed to colored children, and see the depressing clouds of inferiority begin to form in her little mental sky, and see her begin to distort her little personality by unconsciously developing a bitterness toward white people; when you have to concoct an answer for a five-year-old son asking in agonizing pathos, "Daddy, why do white people treat colored people so mean?"[44]

Cultural feelings and ideas cycle intergenerationally through body and mind. In people who have experienced oppression, the cycles translate into "tongue twisted" and "speech stammering" body reactions to adversities in inequity systems. They include physical-emotional signals emitted through eyes, such as "tears welling" and "agonizing pathos" in vocal cords. In prejudice systems where class-race-gender-entwined cultures negotiate violent injustices, people experience institutional bias daily in ways that "begin to distort" the "mental sky" of perception that, in time, imprints implicit bias.[45]

Caste systems worldwide perpetuate intergenerational prejudice through inferiority-versus-superiority stereotypes centered on race as a "central axis" cultural category. Unfortunately, race persists as a primary classification in modern "social relations" in the United States.[46] Moment by moment, people reiterate its saliency. "A racist idea is any idea that suggests one racial group is inferior or superior to another racial group in any way."[47] Ideas of racialized inadequacy versus supremacy accumulate inwardly but are expressed through confusion, anxiety, and anger outwardly. Thich Nhat Hanh explains:

> Often our mind is not there with our body. Sometimes we go through our daily activities without mind consciousness being involved at all. We can do many things by means of store consciousness alone, and mind consciousness can be thinking of a thousand other things.... When someone touches the seed of anger by saying something or doing something that upsets us, that seed of anger will come up and manifest in mind consciousness as the mental formation...of anger.[48]

Thus, untreated fear and anger in "store consciousness" distorts daily experience with cultural defensiveness to fuel individual divisive decisions that perpetuate racist systems.

How Does Multicultural Mindfulness Reduce Pre-Prejudice and Prejudice?

Multicultural Mindfulness reshapes education with compassionate antibias-antiracist exercises to identify "pre-prejudice" *feelings* before they harden into divisive habits.[49] It provides exercises for treat prejudice *ideas* conditioned by economic-social systems. The practices reveal, as Dr. King put it, the "depressing clouds of inferiority" and "superiority" that develop inside youth over time to solidify into adult bias.[50] Social divisions are "culturally conditioned" by assimilation and segregation systems and propaganda about dominance-versus-weakness.[51] *Racialized* categories in US class-divided power systems have been cycling for centuries, fomenting superiority complexes and cultural inferiority stereotypes. These systems alienate people from one another and lead to cultural category rankings involving gender, ethnicity, age, and ability tiers that intersect with economic divides.

Pre-prejudice impressions about economic-social hardships *or* advantages from inequity systems start at home. People translate personal family experiences about economic status into neighborhood stories developed through institutional networks, such as media, government, church, school, and criminal justice.[52] Early childhood experiences with race occur within macro systems that pattern community beliefs about how "one racial group is inferior or superior to another racial group."[53] However, Multicultural Mindfulness cultivates open-mindedness. It detects cultural assets, valuing people of all backgrounds. It counters disinformation serving inequity systems. It grooms body-mind receptivity to cross-cultural relationships. It develops healthy multicultural identities to strengthen diversity alliances working for economic egalitarianism solutions.

Multicultural Mindfulness practices with young children connect people in contexts to systems. The practices are like Venn diagrams, visualizing similarities among contrasts to grow pre-tolerance. They reflect on multicultural interactions *with* compassion to assuage anger, panic, and entitlement feelings while building holism memories. They clarify the meaning of cross-cultural respect. Just as the pliability of the developing brain is amenable to language learning, Multicultural Mindfulness strengthens holistic antibias-antiracist awareness by tapping into the elasticity of youth consciousness. The practices cultivate interest in diversity, priming "collective effervescence," which happens during cultural inclusion events to develop the "life force that merges people into a collective self...an oceanic 'we'."[54]

Multicultural Mindfulness interrupts pre-prejudice and prejudice cycles by intervening in dehumanization conditioning with non-defensive action-reflection. Its practices shift misperceptions with openness to forgiveness. They locate sources of confusion and stress, spotting pre-prejudice feelings and prejudice anxieties from fear-based assumptions during intergenerational interactions. The practices calm emotions about perceptions. Valuing diversity during the reciprocation of sustainability, the practices help people identify with diversity unity. They integrate body, mind, and culture into the environment to dissipate assumptions and stereotypes before they habituate into bias. They interrupt pre-prejudice developments in youth with holism awareness. Likewise, Multicultural Mindfulness practices intervene in the bias habits of adults, interrupting prejudice with awareness of belonging in diversity.[55]

How Does Multicultural Mindfulness Integrate Body-Mind-Culture-Environment?

Multicultural Mindfulness is awareness of diversity intersections. It examines how race, class, and gender diversities have been constructed hierarchically and alienated from the environment through substructure-superstructure stratifications. Transformative teachers work to

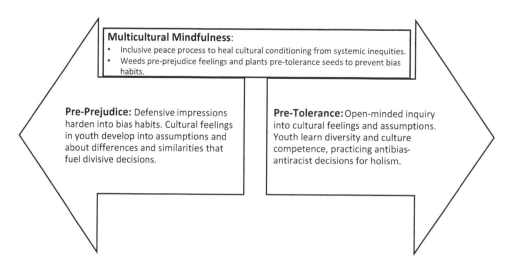

FIGURE 6.3 Multicultural Mindfulness graphic. Created by the author.

change unequal education outcomes. Mindfulness *of* race, gender, and class tiers in programs investigates how big emotions attach to rankings. We notice resentment from disenfranchisement, the desperation of entitlement, and fear about reparations. We reflect to counteract unconscious reactions to inequity systems with curiosity about stereotypes, blame cycles, and ideological reactions. The process motivates generosity actions to soften misunderstandings and renew relationships during change. We take classrooms, labs, and meeting rooms outdoors when we can, do calming breathwork, share nourishing meals, and offer words of affirmation and actions of forgiveness.

Mindfulness questions assumptions and examines dehumanizing mental formations. *Multicultural* mindfulness reviews the brain's store consciousness to cultivate the cultural seeds of interbeing, impermanence, and emptiness. The practices gather cultural evidence to look deeply into the humanizing mental formations that motivate inclusion actions. Transformative teachers facilitate holistic practices during subject engagement with diversity rubrics for collaborations that encourage multiple languages and modalities. Diversity teaming on hands-on projects interrupts US dominant culture bias, which involves the pretense of colorblind individualism that distorts the reality of cultural divisions. Participants learn how hierarchical systems warp knowledge, and we use culture-conscious interpretations to welcome multiple perspectives into subjects. We circle to experience cultural practices and listen to cultural and nature stories in classrooms, labs, and meeting rooms. We compare mainstream knowledge with ethnic studies scholarship to expand learning outcomes with big-picture questions.

Multicultural Mindfulness prompts social-emotional inclusion activities to foster "[a]n environment in which children feel free to ask questions and make comments about disability, gender, and race." We nurture intersectionality during face-to-face circle discussions and projects designed to "reflect children and adults who are of color, who are differently abled, and who are engaged in non-stereotypic gender activities." We nurture prosocial collective action by eliminating "stereotypic and inaccurate materials from daily use."[56] Our integration experiences reroute dehumanization patterns with the body-mind-culture-environment holism academics *we* design and implement. Multicultural Mindfulness prompts changes to education space, time, materials, and learning environments to break segregation and assimilation habits with "love and compassion" world-healing projects.

> A person is comprised of…form, feelings, perceptions, mental formations, and consciousness. Anger belongs to the aggregate of mental formations, and the unpleasant feeling that goes along with the anger belongs to the aggregate of feelings…. Our anger is a field of energy. Thanks to our mindful observation and insight into its roots, we can change this energy into the energy of love and compassion – a constructive and healing energy.[57]

Healing agitation, disgust, obsession, and hopelessness at school from superiority-versus-inferiority systems, Multicultural Mindfulness integrates cultural inclusion and diversity belonging into academic engagement connected to the world one activity at a time.

MULTICULTURAL MINDFULNESS ACTIVITY

Drive-All-Blames-Into-One[58]

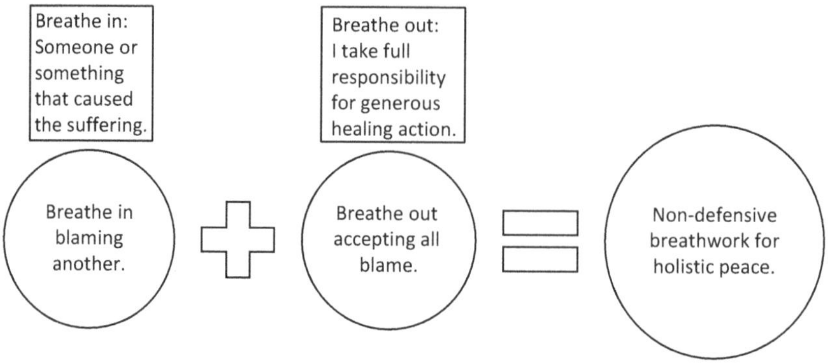

FIGURE 6.4 Non-Defensive Breathwork graphic. Created by the author.

Outcome

- Conduct advanced *Tonglen* breathwork for game-changing conflict resolution.
- Personalize Multicultural Mindfulness by writing a *gatha* about cultural defensiveness.

(Please note: This practice does not apply to criminal or violent interactions. Rather, use it for day-to-day conflict resolution.)

Key Concepts

- **Gatha:** Uplifting verses, songs, or "small practice poems," recited self-reflectively or aloud with others during mindfulness breathwork, daily activities, or meditative study.[59]
- **Tonglen:** A counterintuitive non-defensive mindfulness practice to breathe in bad and breathe out good to reduce territoriality and increase generosity.[60]
- **Drive-All-Blames-into-One:** Advanced *Tonglen* practice to take responsibility during a conflict or unfortunate situation. You declare that the issue is "not somebody else's fault." You reverse judgment unconditionally and take compassionate action: "Even though someone else has made a terrible boo-boo and blamed it on you, you should take the blame on yourself. In terms of power, it is a much simpler and direct way of controlling the situation." You forgive others, regulate your own emotions, and engage solutions.[61]

Resources

- Journal, pencil, a timer, copies of Figure 6.4 (above), an example or symbol of nature, a place to meet indoors or outdoors.

Big-Picture Question

- How do I access unconditional love?

Start

Whole group circle with Figure 6.4 distributed; example or symbol of nature is visible:

- **Read** the non-defensive breathwork Figure 6.4. What part of this have you done before, and how did it work for you? If you haven't tried anything like it, why not?
- **Select** a person, process, culture, or organization that you blame for a wrongdoing, predicament, conflict, or crisis.
- **Breath consciously.** Close or lightly lid eyes. Breathe in through the nose deep into the belly and breathe out relaxed, slightly smiling mouth for a couple of minutes. Breathe in wanting someone else to apologize or behave in a particular way, and breathe out handling the issue non-defensively, releasing condemnation.

    1   During in-breaths, inhale blame against someone, a culture, or something other than you or your culture as the problem's cause.

    - **Breathe in**, fear and exasperation: "Don't you see you should not make me suffer like this?"[62]
    - **Breath in**, accusing someone or something else for the predicament.
    - **Breathe in**, acceptance of the unfairness of taking on *all* blame. Remind yourself that blame, shame, and desire are part of perpetration-victimization cycles.

    2   During out-breaths, take onto *yourself* all the blame you attributed to another or an outside force.

    - **Breathe out**, release from blame.
    - **Breathe out**, the freedom of unconditional love during problem-solving.
    - **Breathe out**, the strength of forgiveness *and* taking "calm transformative action" to reduce your own bias obstructing reciprocal healing.

Middle

1 **Individually Journal** your observations about replacing blame with generosity.
2 **Read aloud** antibias *gathas*[63]:

    Breathe in depressing clouds of inferiority; breathe out interbeing.
    Breathe in arrogant clouds of superiority; breathe out interbeing.
    Breathe in tears welling; breathe out impermanence.
    Breath in desire; breathe out impermanence.
    Breathe in tongue-twisted anger; breathe out emptiness.
    Breathe in bitterness toward another; breathe out emptiness.

3 Inspired by nature in circle's center, **individually write** your own personal antibias *gatha* about a current predicament.

Closing

Whole group circle:

1 **Stand, sit, or lie** down indoors or outdoors to breath consciously. Each participant uses the personally written *gatha* and gazes at nature in the circle center for a few minutes.

Application

How Does Multicultural Mindfulness Heal?

Multicultural Mindfulness empowers teachers to support inclusive student success with unifying *sustainability* pathways for academic engagement. This isn't extracurricular. It heals systemic bias with personal calm for cultural inclusion during subject interactions, such as holistic openers, core activities, *and* closures. It guides decisions about space, time, materials, and learning environments with interbeing, impermanence, and emptiness principles to cultivate diversity belonging. Its process practices replace suspicion with "tremendous generosity," shepherding "basic goodness" reciprocation.[64] Multicultural Mindfulness involves big-picture antibias/antiracist questions. For example: How can this requirement be reimagined for multiracial democratic citizenship and green economic participation?

Multicultural Mindfulness practices shift territorial disputes from bureaucratized banking education into compassion education with cultural and environmental consciousness, indoors and outdoors. Our joyful justice circle activities develop healing pathways. For example:

1 Principles for loving-kindness.
2 Reconciliation.
3 Peace precepts for ecological systems.
4 Sharing, Circle Questions, and Global Praxis.

Healing Pathway #1: Principles for Loving-Kindness

One Multicultural Mindfulness healing pathway features the three mindfulness principles discussed throughout this book: interbeing, impermanence, and emptiness.[65] These distinguish Environmental Liberation Education from other education philosophies by integrating liberation, mindfulness, and environmental education. The principles engage subjects with open-minded action-reflection for ecological well-being from a position of love.

Interbeing is the interconnectedness of everything (e.g., superdiverse people in biodiverse ecosystems within the cosmos).[66] Multicultural Mindfulness breathwork on interbeing develops inward-outward compassion for unity through diversity. *Impermanence* is change. Multicultural Mindfulness breathwork on impermanence develops a capacity for cultural adaptability. *Emptiness* is spacious release from the impulse to fix meaning and cling to desire. Multicultural Mindfulness breathwork on emptiness develops "everyday awe" in nature and in other universal "wonders," including the "moral beauty" of expressing "love without expectation, without demand, without possession."[67] As a healing pathway, the three principles develop loving-kindness skills through culturally creative subject activities, such as through participating in visual and performing arts projects about culture change, problem-solving two-sided judgments with multiple perspectives through language arts writing assignments, applying diversity topics to math problem sets, and comparing polarized stereotypes – you versus me and black versus white – by integrating ethnic studies, other identity studies, and diverse ways of knowing about community topics into social science projects.

Loving-Kindness Skills

The three mindfulness principles grow loving-kindness skills to diminish defensiveness from dehumanizing policies that deceive with the rhetoric of individualism that masks inequity systems. The culture of competitive individualism in education undermines diversity collaborations for social justice solutions.[68] However, pressing existential threats – global warming – coalesce purpose. We rally to *cooperate*, reducing preoccupation with "competitive advantage" and for-profit ranks. According to Dacher Keltner in *Awe: The New Science of Everyday Wonder and How it Can Transform Your Life*, the more we act to resist the status quo structures of harm, the more we develop intergenerational skills for thriving.

> We perceive natural phenomena like tide pools, pollinating bees, or ecosystems gathering around a "mother tree" as a result of intricate interacting *systems* of causal forces. We see human affairs as the result of complex webs of cause-and-effect relations in history that transcend an individual's intentions.[69]

Mindfulness practices dedicated to "*taming* the mind," shift the ego from a "state of being tamed" to a state that relates with others by "*training* the mind" with "loving-kindness" through generosity progressions: (1) fulfilling basic needs – physiological, safety, belonging, self-acceptance, and curiosity – through public service; (2) courage – "the gift of fearlessness" to resist systemic oppression with nonviolent liberation activities; and (3) "knowledge" – curiosity and words of praise about diversity assets to fertilize justice "discipline."[70] Thus, everyday educators uplift professional identities trapped into punitive cycles, over-standardized bureaucracy, and "self-obsessed digital technologies" to instead develop peace skills in transformative teams, acting and reflecting on restorative breakthroughs for collective change.[71]

As educators join Diversity Circles to engage loving-kindness with core mindfulness principles, we minimize social anxiety from "ego battles" at school.[72] We "volunteer more time" to facilitate multicultural equity activities.[73] We support students "from historically underserved communities" with success strategies that humanize all students.[74] Non-defensive academic activities include such Multicultural Mindfulness practices as conflict resolution protocols for peer circles, engaged mentoring, and co-creating social emotional academic learning units.[75] Teaming for humanizing systems, we "experience a sense of gentleness toward ourselves, and a sense of friendliness to others."[76] This friendliness opens up non-defensive communication proficiencies to work through reparative justice.

Rather than running away, shutting down, or lashing out, we embed breathwork into routines to grow "complete openness" to love in education's "home ground" of standards and procedures.[77] Beyond breathwork, we can develop loving-kindness consumption by supporting wholesome meals, organic produce from community gardens, and green cutlery and plates in school food systems. In this way, we reduce anxiety from processed foods and increase the time we

> share a meal in mindfulness ... we chew with real awareness, not chewing anything else, such as our thoughts, our fears, or even our aspirations.... When we eat together in this way, the food and the community of co-practitioners are the object of our mindfulness. It is through the food and one another that the ultimate becomes present... to live deeply.[78]

Verified by thousands of years of practice across world cultures and supported by science, mindfulness practices develop prosocial skills not as bureaucratic chores to grit through but as flow activities for joyful and just healing during education.[79]

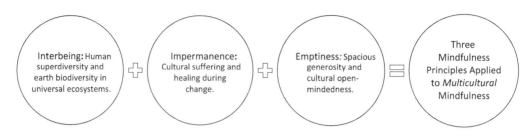

FIGURE 6.5 Three Mindfulness Principles graphic. Created by the author.

Healing Pathway #2: Reconciliation

The Multicultural Mindfulness process permeates nonviolent direct action, described in four steps by Dr. King: "collection of the facts in determining whether injustices are alive, negotiation, self-purification, direct action."[80] Peace begins by recognizing the need for ongoing data collection and analysis for accuracy during change. Nonviolence involves negotiation about shared existence. When negotiation stalls, healing skills develop through self-purification exercises to overcome fear during reconciliation. Mindfulness practices help to recognize "there is no ground to get, that we are ultimately free, nonaggressive, open. We realize we are actually nonexistent ourselves.... Then we can give. We have lots to gain and nothing to lose."[81] Nonviolence develops receptivity to truth from open-minded listening and reconciliation during restorative action.[82]

Multicultural Mindfulness reconciliation is modeled by diverse peace activists who illustrate how to reduce systemic racism and increase cultural inclusion with calm to resolve conflict. An example of stalwart commitment is shown by six-year-old African-American Ruby Bridges, when in 1960, she attended first grade at previously all-White William Frantz Elementary. Ruby and her family and allies faced angry mobs of White parents. They participated in the nonviolent civil disobedience steps of justice change.[83] According to Dacher Keltner:

> [Restorative Justice] dates back to Gandhi and MLK, in our deeper history to Indigenous practices from around the world and further back in our evolutionary history to mammalian peacemaking tendencies. It is grounded in the conviction of moral beauty, that all people, including those who have murdered and those who've lost loved ones and are overheated with thoughts of revenge, can find kindness and overcome. A central practice of restorative justice is the talking circle, in which individuals sit in a circle and take turns sharing where they are at that day while other simply listen.[84]

Self-purification for reconciliation develops during talking circles with deep listening in "the new science" of transformative brain patterns wherein "emotions animate action."[85] Prosocial brain patterns are galvanized during "peak experiences" in circles with story-telling, kinesthetic and musical chanting and singing, choral clapping and drumming, dancing, theatrical role-playing, constructing visuals and artwork, demonstrative reading and writing, non-defensive civility circles, and group meditation and spiritual invocation.[86] Exchanging cultural stories about "everyday reverence" motivates activism for "inspired and optimistic" commitment to holistic change. Multimodal circle activities stir people to do "likeminded actions," changing self-serving behaviors into prosocial practices, such as giving money and resources and volunteering in the community. Self-purification thus develops during collective generosity experiences to motivate peace actions "integrated in their community."[87]

Method Training

An illustration of collaborative reconciliation is the liberation work of Vietnamese Zen Master Thich Nhat Hanh and Dr. King in Chicago in 1966. Dr. King nominated Hanh for the Nobel Peace Prize in 1967 for his mindfulness "peace mission."[88] Hanh explains social action mindfulness as method training. He describes how nonviolent world healing without bias starts with acceptance. "Mindfulness accepts everything without judging or reacting.... Mindfulness is remembering to come back to the present moment."[89] Both human rights leaders of color taught the art and science of self-purification for nonviolent action-reflection. Multicultural Mindfulness uplifts cross-cultural social justice movements with the planetary unity for environmental justice. Environmental Liberation Education is accepting the present moment as an opportunity for holistic antibias-antiracist reconciliation with the educational objective of Earth stewardship now.

Multicultural Mindfulness is method training to elicit cultural truth, cross-cultural amends, and unity reconciliation. Participants engage restorative justice to grow culture competence while granting and receiving forgiveness during negotiation (see Figure 4.6). The diversity accords we nurture during education heal social relations one meeting at a time. We use nonviolent communication circle protocols to engage a subject or resolve conflict, such as the following five protocols:

- *Feelings Observations:* Describe emotions.
- *Sensory Descriptions:* Offer understanding through cultural and environmental practices, evidence, and story-sharing.

- Thich Nhat Hanh, a Vietnamese Zen Master, poet, feminist, and human rights activist collaborated with Martin Luther King, Jr. in Chicago.
- Dr. King nominated Hanh for the Nobel Peace Prize in 1967 for his global mindfulness "peace mission."
- They used self-purification training for nonviolent justice actions from a position of love.

FIGURE 6.6 Martin Luther King, Jr. and Thich Nhat Hanh together at a news conference. Photo by permission from Newscom.

- *Perceptions and Interpretations:* Clarify suffering and healing experiences in systems that impact everyone.
- *Amends-Making:* Make reparations by apologizing and offering and receiving forgiveness for behavior.
- *Etiquette Descriptions:* Commit to or renew relationships with holistic interactions guided by specific mindfulness boundaries and pathways for reciprocal thriving practices and egalitarian resource distribution.

Reconciliation cannot be done through disjointed online modalities or hurried timeline meetings that perpetuate the status quo. Rather, non-defensive reparations involve patient process to acknowledge how marginalized-versus-privileged experiences impact cultural interpretations of projects and purposes. Reconciliation involves restorative activities to overcome shared adversities from world systems in local contexts. Applied to education, reconciliation involves cultural authenticity experiences during academic routines to integrate individuals in cultures into shared sustainability.[90]

Healing Pathway #3: Peace Precepts for Ecological Systems

After winning the Nobel Peace Prize in 1964, Dr. King nominated Thich Nhat Hanh for the same prize. Hanh brought together isolated monasteries into sites of nonviolent resistance during the Vietnam War.[91] After witnessing monk brothers setting themselves on fire to protest an unjust war that killed children, razed communities, and ravished ecosystems, Thich Nhat Hanh, in 1966, established peace precepts for feminist "Engaged Buddhism." The precepts prompt "looking deeply" into social, political, economic, and environmental injustices to activate humanization without aggression.

> We practice mindfulness in order to realize liberation, peace, and joy in our everyday lives.... Mindfulness means awareness and it also means looking deeply.... Mindfulness is transformation.[92]

Thich Nhat Hanh worked to replace cultural-political suffering with liberation experiences through mindfulness.

Thich Nhat Hanh traveled out of Vietnam on a peace mission, meeting with Pope Paul VI and US Secretary of Defense Robert S. McNamara to appeal for an end to the US bombing of Vietnam. During the mission, Hanh was barred from returning to Vietnam and subsequently was denied access to his homeland after the war.[93] In his global work, Thich Nhat Hanh taught that mindfulness is an inward-outward process for calm to process world pain through daily transformative action. He explains the connection between mindfulness and social action.

> Mindfulness must be engaged. Once there is seeing, there must be acting.... We must be aware of the real problems of the world. Then, with mindfulness, we will know what to do and what not to do to be of help.[94]

Thich Nhat Hanh's works describe a multitude of best mindfulness practices defined by interbeing, impermanence, and emptiness, such as the 14 peace precepts. The first of Hanh's 14 precepts emphasizes broad-minded patience so activists don't cling to single-minded ideologies caught into fundamentalism. The peace precepts explain how to transform cultural alienation by participating in ecosystems for climate justice. The peace precepts underscore the following:

- Healing involves *all* sentient beings and environmental elements, such as the oppressed and vulnerable (children, the elderly and infirm, impoverished peoples, endangered animals, imperiled plants, and natural resources) and also the oppressors, who suffer spiritually.
- Transformation is continual *action*, consequences, and reflection to overcome dualistic thinking with holistic compassion.
- Cultural inclusion involves spacious *imagination* about the unknowable universe.[95]

In summary, the peace precepts call for action from a position of love because "nonviolence does not mean non-action. Nonviolence means we act with love and compassion."[96]

Revolutionary nonviolent action for *public* good is generated with self-purification techniques also modeled by Brazilian Paulo Freire's liberation education. Freire's culture circles use peace precepts and have empowered thousands of disenfranchised people of color with literacy through critical consciousness for community healing, developed from liberation theology.[97] Liberation theology is a movement facilitated by Catholic bishops across Latin America in the 1950s and 1960s. Its practices display how self-purification links to community activism for structural change.

Liberation theology categorizes self-purification as two cyclical phases: (1) "liberating action…[in which] the poor can break out of their situation of oppression only by working out a strategy better able to change social conditions" and (2) building "faith" through deep reflection on "liberating practice."[98] These phases are the basis of Freire's work on holistic "praxis," explained in *Pedagogy of the Oppressed*. Reflective engagement strengthens as marginalized peoples self-determine knowledge with analytical skills. The oppressed develop academically while cogenerating "lived faith that finds expression" through civic commitment.[99] Thus, nonviolent action-reflection methods for social justice span world cultures and inform Multicultural Mindfulness, modeling global peace precepts for self-purification during systemic change.

Together, Thich Nhat Hanh's teachings about engaged mindfulness, US nonviolent civil disobedience steps – fact-gathering, negotiation, self-purification, and direct action – and Latin American liberation methods, demonstrate how to apply "the energy of concentration" to resolve conflict.[100] Multicultural Mindfulness draws on these traditions to counteract fight, freeze, and flight reactions during the academic routines that divide. Multicultural Mindfulness reduces either-or dualities that warp knowledge by unifying through diversity consciousness for a better world. "Actively aware in all of our activities and to be truly present with what we are doing…. The first function of mindfulness is to recognize and not to fight."[101] Multicultural Mindfulness reshapes dehumanization at school with circle configurations to develop knowledge and curriculum with nonviolent calm during creative tension. Thus, peace precepts in Multicultural Mindfulness connect academics to individuals in a shared environment locally and globally, cultivating cultural inclusion for diversity belonging.

Seven Operating Principles of Ecological Systems[102]

Environmental Liberation Education integrates mindfulness world peace precepts into environmental education. Edward Clark explains seven operating principles of ecological systems that, when applied to multicultural and mindfulness education, form a human equity and climate sustainability paradigm. These principles bring interbeing, impermanence, and emptiness down to Earth. They illustrate that diversity is crucial to healthy natural systems:

1 *Carrying Capacity:* Conserving natural resources with homeostasis.
2 *Interdependence:* Balancing each component with the whole.
3 *Diversity:* Stability through variety.
4 *Change, Adaption:* Short-term and long-term evolution.
5 *Competition and Cooperation:* Balance between stability and creativity.
6 *Cycles:* Rhythmic fluctuations and recycling.
7 *Energy Flow:* Dependence on external energy forces for survival, volatile and constant.

These ecological principles prompt transformative teachers into "remembering to come back to the present moment" of the natural universe during education. The principles pose diversity as a strength in the changing environment in which academics transpire. Applying liberation peace precepts to ecological systems reveals the inadequacy of colorblind Contributions and Additive approaches to multicultural education. Rather, Transformative, Social Action, and Environmental Liberation Education approaches synthesize cultures and the environment into subjects connected to diversity through our human and biological world.

In summary, Multicultural Mindfulness is about the big-picture antibias-antiracist process. Its three principles – interbeing, impermanence, and emptiness – bridge peace precepts to ecological systems. Multicultural Mindfulness practices do not fixate on the "frightening...dimensions of environmental crisis" but rather engage "lively and playful" sensory circles for climate justice.[103] The activities link human superdiversity to ecological biodiversity during subject engagement.[104] They involve restorative justice for environmental "liberation, peace, and joy in our everyday lives."[105] Transformative teachers facilitate Multicultural Mindfulness through academic engagement designed with stewardship activities so students experience resilience during the climate crises that impact school.[106] Thich Nhat Hanh emphasizes the bond between nonviolent liberation and holistic happiness:

> Liberation and happiness are linked to each other; if there is liberation, there is happiness, and greater liberation brings greater happiness. If there is liberation, peace and joy exist in the present moment. We don't need to wait ten or fifteen years to realize them. They are available as soon as we begin the practice. However modest these elements may be, they form the basis for greater liberation, peace, and joy in the future.[107]

Thich Nhat Hanh describes body-mind liberation, available to everyone, even the incarcerated, war-torn, and despairing. Liberating joy is "available as soon as we begin the practice"; in other words, diversity belonging in humanizing ecological healing is here and now.[108]

> **Laboratory Diversity Circle:**
> Question
> - How do we belong in diversity?
>
> Activity
> - Teacher displays Earth art at public exhibit, made with basic classroom supplies and recycled materials about interbeing, impermanence, and emptiness principles.
> - Students compare and contrast all displays in the exhibit with questions about visual arts elements and principles.
> - Students circle for critical consciousness about visual arts, to make identity collages about belonging in diversity.
> - Students adapt identity collages to thesis statements to engage academic writing language arts standards.

FIGURE 6.7 Laboratory Diversity Circle belongingness. Four-foot recycled materials artwork display and photo created by the author.

Healing Pathway #4: Sharing, Circle Questions, Global Praxis

Three Diversity Circle strategies described throughout this book – Sharing, Circle Questions, and Global Praxis – form a Multicultural Mindfulness healing loop to change mainstream space, time, materials, and learning environments in classrooms, labs, and meeting rooms with cultural inclusion.

Sharing: Participants form a circle to take turns to listen, talk, and apply a subject to cultural and environmental themes through data and emotional-impact expressions and stories. The circles generate passion while gathering and analyzing science and arts evidence and practices. The goal is to reconceptualize disciplinary norms with multiple modalities and diverse ways of knowing. Participants develop academically by exchanging multicultural perspectives and languages. Participants use Culture-Conscious Listening with antibias breathwork and supportive body language, offering thoughtful summaries of content. Participants practice emotional regulation by naming unpleasant, neutral, and pleasant feelings about the subject with reflections about events in systems. Participants use compassion dialogue to reveal assimilation and segregation experiences, seeking non-defensive solutions to contradictions with intersectional understanding.

Circle Questions: Participants deepen inquiry with progressive big-picture questions from data, scholarship, works, expressions, and stories. Participants gather, code, and generate themes to inspire liberation actions in ongoing labs and field experiences. Circle Questions are informed by cultural and academic information from Sharing. Sample questions include the following:

- What's in the universe?
- How does the universe sustain itself with diversity?
- How do cultures relate to the universe?
- What do people do with cultural pain?
- How do cultures participate in economic equity?
- How do cultures engage in environmental healing?
- How do cultural experiences affect sustainability skills?
- How do we counteract disinformation that harms cultures?
- What cultures model sustainability?
- How do individuals develop culture competence with structural competence in global context?
- How does the systemic past impact our region now?
- How does the systemic now impact our region's future?
- What regional institutions need to change?
- How do we steward the environment with joy in a shared cultural context?[109]

Global Praxis: Participants continually refresh labs, field experiences, and real-world projects about the subject with information from Sharing and Circle Questions. Participants take culturally responsive liberation actions to reduce, recycle, reuse, and restore for community healing. Participants engage in critical consciousness social action to resist systemic oppression with environmental awareness, such as with holistic sun, land, sky, and water activities. Participants make multicultural connections with antibias-antiracist practices during ecology projects.

Global Praxis Iceberg

The Global Praxis Iceberg is a visual to imagine social action with environmental awareness. First, the iceberg tip is perceiving diversity in local context. We observe facts to ascertain "whether injustices are alive."[110] Second, at the waterline, we engage diversity negotiation. We apply culturally responsive academic practices to space, time, materials, and learning environments in our orbit. Third, we submerge for systems research, gathering data and analyzing how fundamental human needs are met or unmet by the economy. We discern cultural beliefs and conditioned biases in this economic subterrain. In full circle, we collaborate to deal with the substructure productions that shape the social superstructure we see at the tip, both parts of which, in this historical moment, are defined by inequities and unsustainability patterns. We use cultural evidence and stories to refresh restorative actions at the waterline.

The Global Praxis Iceberg reveals our complicity in unjust systems. We connect local habits to global patterns seen and unseen. We resolve to reject the "punitive evaluation model" that imprisons US education. We engage "an affirming professional development model," teaming for social justice with student-centered best practices.[111] We construct knowledge and evaluate outcomes with a transparent education philosophy, such as with one of those outlined by the Approach-in-Dimension. We engage subjects holistically through Multicultural Mindfulness practices to integrate body-mind-culture-environment. "Witnessing other's acts of courage, kindness, strength, and overcoming activates…the cortical regions [of the brain] where our emotions translate to ethical action…The soul of our bodies is awakened."[112]

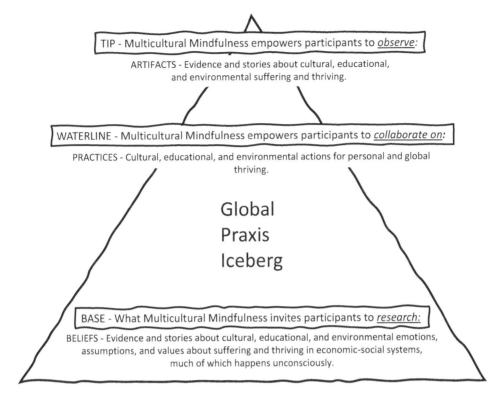

FIGURE 6.8 Global Praxis Iceberg graphic. Created by the author.

Deep dive action research, coupled with breathwork and other mindfulness practices, stimulates the "oxytocin" and "the vagus nerve" to prime compassionate energy for global healing in a local context.[113] We discern cultural *beliefs* that enable dehumanizing and unsustainable economic productions. While we're there, we seek cultural evidence about liberation beliefs. We synthesize beliefs into *reciprocal* restorative actions. Rather than inadvertently reproduce an economy of inequity systems, we reduce cultural defensiveness and grow multicultural reconciliation at the waterline. With Global Praxis, we change outcomes for a new green economy from the equity ecosystems we co-create.

Thus, teachers and students use Sharing, Circle Questions, and Global Praxis strategies during academic engagement in a unifying feedback loop. We participate in hands-on circle activities and holistic inquiry projects for diversity belonging in a sustainable world.

Examples

The following examples illustrate the Multicultural Mindfulness process. They show how teachers empower by unstandardizing subjects and de-tracking students with holism practices to reduce bias with compassionate big-picture reconciliation experiences now.

Example #1 – Multicultural Mindfulness Classroom

"Shaping the space" of a "mindful classroom" is an immediate and low-cost way to implement holistic education. "Mindfulness is a way of being. It is an open-minded and open-hearted view we can take" into routines, such as while "chatting with friends," "walking to class," transitioning between activities, doing activities, studying in the library, standing in lines, and eating and relaxing in student centers and on school grounds. When educators design mindful classrooms, we establish peace spaces. *Multicultural* Mindfulness classroom designs integrate diversity and sustainability into "five realms of mindful literacy": physical, mental, emotional, social, and global. While it's easiest to design classrooms when a teacher is assigned a room, roving educators who share spaces apply movable designs with portable mindfulness materials and circle configurations.[114]

The design starts with "circles" for "relaxation and group cohesiveness." Multicultural belonging in environmental stewardship is facilitated by arranging objects for interbeing, impermanence, and emptiness reflection and interactions. It starts with cultural relevance, involving diverse students in design decisions. Students involve home and community members in developing cultural materials and peace resources for the classroom. Everyone brings in culturally respectful artifacts, practices, and beliefs from home cultures. Participants provide simple soothing objects, such as breathwork chimes, water jars, and seasonal nature items. Overhead fluorescent lights are reduced by increasing lamps and natural light from windows. Students select culturally responsive nature materials and "soft ambient" music.[115]

As budgets allow, transformative teachers insert flexible seating, such as benches, pillows, yoga balls, bean bag chairs, seat pillows, and circle rugs with culture and nature motifs. Chair legs are modified to ease moving existing furniture into circle variations. Students care for plants, maintain insect and reptile terrariums, and refresh classrooms with nature materials to reflect country/community-of-origin stories. The classroom library or resource area features multicultural, environmental, and mindfulness materials. Resources are easy to use with an egalitarian schedule corresponding to reflection about required subjects. Resources balance local and global information, such as with sun, land, sky, and water topics. Body-mind, cultural-social, and economic-environmental well-being resource posters and displays spotlight holism themes to deepen academic concentration.[116]

Transformative teachers schedule outdoor and community activities as often as possible. Outdoor seating on campus is designed with blankets, benches, and stations so students are comfortable engaging academics in nature by studying, exploring, and touching Earth respectfully. Sequential field trips are planned for regional activities to integrate arts and sciences standards into C-STEAM (culture, science, technology, engineering, arts and math) projects about trees, plants, gardens, and seasonal ecosystems.[117] Thus, Multicultural Mindfulness classroom designs support inward reflection and outward action for sustainability belonging *during* academic development.

Example #2 – Multicultural Mindfulness Chill Center to Reduce Bias

Unlike whole classroom designs or resource areas accommodating several students at once, the Multicultural Mindfulness chill space is a privacy corner for individuals to restore calm and process social anxiety and bias. It's a contemplative place to consider personal-cultural assumptions, stereotypes, and difficult emotions about race, class, and gender differences at home and school. It's a place for conscious breathing and journaling to take "brain breaks" during challenging projects, exam schedules, and reflect on social conflicts, such as bullying for friendship loss. It's to reflect on body-mind clarity during culture-conscious social emotional development and identity formation.

The design involves partitioning a spot and either removing all objects or carefully displaying a few "beautiful art" objects, "natural things," and items representing student home cultures. It can include visual instruction posters about cultures and Earth as well as charts about emotions, conscious breathing, relaxation methods, and healthful postures. It can have a basket of stress-relieving toys for self-regulation. Students can do art or journal about suffering from culture conflict or about joy from culture healing, registering sad and happy body-mind feelings. They can reflect on ideas from stories and events.[118]

Thus, a Multicultural Mindfulness chill center helps to remove social stress that disrupts academic concentration. It grows personal capacity for culture conflict resolution and antibias efforts. Students notice body-mind signs of culture stress from head to toe and choose relaxation postures and behaviors. Students draw or write about gratitude, generosity, and peace experiences inspired by student-curated music with earphones. They reflect on unifying environmental questions. They compose *gathas* (contemplation poems) to guide classroom breathwork. The space isn't only for behavior episodes, it is also for consistent equitable use so everyone experiences the value of regulating everyday fight, freeze, and flight reactions. Everyone learns how to marshal fear responses during problem-solving dilemmas. Everyone has the chance to practice breathwork to activate the vagus nerve, calm the amygdalae, and encourage the prefrontal cortex to consider cultural truth and meaning.

Example #3 – Multicultural Mindfulness in Diversity Circles

Chapter 5 explains Diversity Circles as learning communities for multicultural reconciliation and environmental consciousness, linking subjects to local experiences in the world. With seven types, five phases, and three strategies, they're cross-cultural alliances for big-picture change. Examples below about a few subject areas illustrate how Multicultural Mindfulness reshapes academic engagement through Diversity Circles.

Mathematics Illustration

Multicultural Mindfulness *of* math prompts the formation of social-emotional relationships to lessen math anxiety with culturally diverse peers and community supports, thereby helping learners experience math as a language.[119] Students engage culturally relevant mindful mathematics by immersing in the math language, internalizing math principles, problems, and rules through face-to-face circle interactions.[120] Social-emotional support deepens by integrating cross-cultural references into math materials, such as with the Inca Counting System, Egyptian math, Mayan math, and math about unity topics such as geometric shapes and statistics about plants, animals, and the planet.[121]

Multicultural Mindfulness inspires basic math skills such as numeracy, decimals, fractions, and exponents into problem sets and math discussions about examples of regional themes. Math circles work together with soothing culturally inspired background music, cultural poetry to interpret statistics, and geometric artwork, such as tessellations and other visual numerical patterns in global architecture, mosaics, and tapestry. Students engage math through kinesthetic intelligence by exercising fine motor skills like finger painting, collaging, and knitting about numbers with cultural themes. They activate naturalistic intelligence when math circles go outside to chalk math problems on sidewalks, tabulate environmental data from word problems, investigate Indigenous stewardship practices involving timelines and sequencing, and compare local data to scientific climate data, enumerating changes.[122]

Science Illustration

The Earth Day Bark Beetle Clay Project was implemented through Multicultural Mindfulness backwards design. This interdisciplinary collaboration between visual arts, education, and counseling departments was a subset in a year-long Laboratory Diversity Circle about "The Year of Sustainability." This theme supported diverse departments in about 280 sustainability activities during the year across science, social sciences, humanities, and math divisions. The project developed with the three strategies described throughout this book: Sharing, Circle Questions, and Global Praxis.

Sharing

Participants met in a ceramics lab hosted by transformative teacher, Candace Garlock, to share cultural stories about sustainability elements, such as leaves, ferns, sunflower husks, sand dollars, and other nature items collected by participants. One item, lodgepole pine branches, gathered at a nearby Northern California mega-fire site, inspired the project. Participants examined how the bark beetle (Scolytinae) marked the branches, discussing texture and designs made by burrowing larvae feeding on living tissues below the bark.

Participants researched how

- Bark beetles are part of healthy decomposition in undisturbed forest ecosystems.
- Beetles help recycle and decompose dead and dying trees for healthy forest renewal.
- Too many larvae kill trees prematurely, creating fire tinder.
- Beetle infestations – predicted to increase with human-caused global warming – destroy vulnerable forests and human communities with mega fires.
- Beetle stewardship for healthy forests involves cultural practices, such as prescribed burns, as well as innovations integrating chemistry, engineering, math, environmental education, and other fields of study.

Circle Questions

- "What's my universe?"
- "What's the full scope of my environment?"
- "How do I interact with the physical environment?"
- "How does the universe work?"
- "How do my cultural experiences affect the decisions I make as a global citizen?"
- "How has our past shaped our present, and how will our present shape our future?"

Global Praxis

Inspired by Circle Questions, diverse participants designed and implemented the Earth Day Bark Beetle Clay Project for local sustainability experiences. They

1 Gathered fallen beetle-burrow branches, hypothesizing that gathering may help reduce flammable excess tinder.
2 Rolled recycled clay with the bark beetle–carved branches to stamp natural "landscapes."
3 Cut rolled clay into medallion shapes, stamped the words "breathe," "earth," and "sustainability" onto the medallions, and fired and glazed them.
4 Practiced Multicultural Mindfulness breathwork inspired by the medallions.
5 Distributed medallions to the campus community and displayed them on Mindful Manzanita Mosaic trees in the Student Center. Circle participants made six trees with broken pottery outside the lab and dead manzanita collected in the same Northern California megafire region as the beetle branches.
6 Reflected on further animal projects, such as the C-STEAM (culture, science, technology, engineering, arts, and math) Turtle Tables implemented the following year. This project featured living tortoises, the Haudenosaunee turtle island symbol for Earth, hexagonal turtle-scute math problems, and investigations into hexagonal geological formations.

Conclusion

"Our Precious Planet"

When students are unequally served, teachers depreciated, and public education segregated, participatory democracy for a sustainable world is unattainable. Nourishing culturally responsive ecosystems at school for a healthy planet is a monumental undertaking. Yet, transformative teachers facilitate present moment *joyful* justice. We shift dualistic thinking and centuries-old systems with a collective growth mindset for personal, cultural, and institutional holism

Laboratory Diversity Circle: Earth Day Bark Beetle C-STEAM Project

Activity
- Diverse students cogenerate curriculum with mindfulness, cultures, and nature indoors.
- Students use backwards design with bark beetle branches from regional megafire site to engage campus community in climate justice experiences.

FIGURE 6.9 Laboratory Diversity Circle Earth Day Bark Beetle STEAM project. Photos created by Candace Garlock and the author.

experiences, here and now. Multicultural Mindfulness develops community respect through inward-outward peace practices during subject engagement. It integrates body, mind, culture, and environment into humanizing academics for global citizenship and green economic participation. Multicultural Mindfulness is hands-on intergenerational education for well-being in classrooms, labs, and meeting rooms. As Thich Nhat Hanh explains in his "letter to a young teacher":

> Our mission as teachers is not just to transmit knowledge, but to form human beings, to construct a worthy, beautiful human race, in order to take care of our precious planet.... With mindfulness, concentration, and insight you can generate a feeling of joy and happiness whenever you want. With the energy of mindfulness, you can also handle a painful feeling or emotion. If you do not have the energy of mindfulness you will be afraid of being overwhelmed by the pain and suffering inside.[123]

As transformative teachers resist extraction-consumption systems, we confront status quo divisions that distort perceptions. We use mindfulness to handle painful feelings and suffering from cynics and disparagers. We take responsibility to collaborate for healing. We engage *public* education with mindfulness of diversity during imaginative academic engagement. We act and reflect on the "worthy, beautiful human race," addressing politicized manifestations of structural inequities on-the-spot.[124] We patiently shift mainstream homogenization with culture-conscious diversity experiences. Environmental Liberation Education integrates teachers, students, and subjects into social-emotional Earth stewardship now.

Peace Process

Calming yet energizing Multicultural Mindfulness inspires transformative teachers to remove bias barriers to holistic student success. This is prosocial decision-making. Our healing journey deepens culture competence with structural competence in cross-cultural circles. Mindfulness *of* cultures in the environment is as antibias as it is ecological. We engage cultures and nature, indoors and outdoors, co-creating belonging in sustainable systems.

One basic Multicultural Mindfulness practice discussed throughout this book, 4-Rs, involves first *recognizing* inequities in the space, time, materials, and learning environments we inhabit. Then we pause to *refrain* from habituating bias in the moment. By interrupting the habit, we open to *restorative action* to reconcile now, such as by using holistic backwards design. We button up the 4-Rs with *resolve* to participate in long-term restorative justice through integrative sustainably projects.

Transformative teachers, thereby, resist economic-social tiering, materialism, and the territoriality of the racialized systems with peace practices. We make "sticky campuses" for multicultural-multiracial socialization.[125] We transform cultural pain and suffering, misrepresented by individualism, by nurturing individuals through collectivism. An advanced Multicultural Mindfulness practice, *Drive-All-Blames-into-One* empowers participants to calm big emotions from perpetrator-victimization dichotomies. We assuage fear and power struggles on the spot, replacing anxiety with curiosity about diverse perspectives and intergenerational reciprocation. We take responsibility to regulate our own feelings, reframing unfair problems with generosity. We don't see the issue as "somebody else's fault."[126] Rather, we respond with compassion to grow unity.[127]

Multicultural Mindfulness Is a Labor of Love

We organize in Diversity Circles to practice Multicultural Mindfulness by sharing cultural and environmental practices, stories, and data. We pose diversity questions about social action to develop subjects through justice problem solving. We use the Approach-in-Dimension for clear-eyed holistic design and evaluation. Multicultural Mindfulness is a labor of love about the "dangers and risks which [will] confront" the next generation.[128] The process works through cultural misunderstandings during alliances to develop healthy multicultural identities together.

Transformative teachers arrange space, time, materials, and learning environments for Multicultural Mindfulness experiences in classrooms, labs, committee rooms, and offices. We use multicultural-environmental compassion themes to curate furniture, lighting, sounds, and resources, doing as many activities as possible outdoors. We know that economic and social chaos is structural, but restoration is personal, cultural, and environmental.[129] That's why we apply loving-kindness practices to creative tension. Transformative teachers understand that clinging to colorblind individualism in color-coded systems perpetuates structural oppression. We know that environmental alienation is reproduced in many education routines. Then emotions flair during campus politics fanned by global crises. That's why Multicultural Mindfulness is friendly, calming, and patient, conducted, whenever possible, during face-to-face academic integrations.

Multicultural Mindfulness is the heartbeat of Environmental Liberation Education. It is hands-on peace practices for culturally responsive science and arts connected to communities and nature. Transformative teachers reduce deficiency-versus-superiority divisions from systems by increasing holistic academic concentration. We engage subjects through an ecological lens, observing regional diversity in environmental context. We make inclusion changes and take deep-dive soul searches for cross-cultural reconciliation at school. We are curious about dehumanization and humanization outcomes, practices, and beliefs. We take direct action for multicultural, environmental, and mindfulness education guided by three humanizing principles: interbeing, impermanence, and emptiness. We practice body, mind, culture, and environment unity during routines to experience intergenerational liberation through academic engagement here and now.

TRANSFORMATIVE BREATHWORK AND JOURNAL

Journal Question: *What's Multicultural Mindfulness?*

> As you continue to practice mindfulness and awareness, the seeming confusion and chaos in your mind begins to seem absurd. You begin to realize that your thoughts have no real birthplace, no origin, they just pop up.., unborn. And your thoughts don't go anywhere, they are unceasing.... [N]o activities are really happening in your mind.[130]
>
> —Chögyam Trungpa Rinpoche

Breathwork

Wherever you are, take a mindful moment to relax. Use a timer chime if you like. Close or lid your eyes, taking several slow deep breaths, smiling slightly, noticing sensations: smells, sounds, touch, taste, and sight (if your eyes are open).

Now breathe while internally reciting the *gatha* below:

> Breathing in, I calm my body.
> Breathing out, I smile.
> Dwelling in the present moment,
> I know this is a mindfulness moment. [131]

Then:

> Breathing in **What's Multicultural Mindfulness?**
> Breathing out openness.

Repeat for as long as you like or until the timer chimes.

Journal

Imagine we're in a Diversity Circle with the transformative practitioners cited in this book. We want to support superdiverse student success in a biodiverse world. Read our answers below. Reflect on your meditation. Briefly answer the journal question above in a way that's meaningful to you.

Thich Nhat Hanh

Mindfulness:

- Engaging "our active awareness in all of our activities and to be truly present with whatever we are doing."
- Awareness that "the first function of mindfulness is to recognize and not to fight."[132]
- "The energy of concentration" to heal anger, confusion, and fear.
- Perceiving *interbeing*, *emptiness*, and *impermanence*.
- Peace action here and now.

Chögyam Trungpa

Mindfulness:

- Steadily refreshing one's view with relaxed generosity and open-hearted curiosity.
- Present moment gratitude to "experience a sense of gentleness toward ourselves, and a sense of friendliness to others."
- Where compassion meets generous action: "love without expectation, without demand, without possession."[133]
- Accountability in one's own feelings while shifting unwholesome thoughts with calm action-reflection.
- Problem-solving pain from aggression, arrogance, envy, clinging, and delusion with nonviolent consciousness for healing with joy.

Micaela Rubalcava

Multicultural Mindfulness:

- Present moment body-mind-culture-environment awareness during high expectations education.
- Deciphering cultures in systems to reveal streaming assumptions and stereotypes.
- Culture consciousness to perceive fight, freeze, and flight biases during routines.
- Calm action-reflection about interbeing, impermanence, and emptiness for holistic antibias-antiracist subject engagement from a position of love.[134]
- Restorative justice to invite cultural ways of knowing into academic engagement.
- The peace *process* tool for Environmental Liberation Education.

Notes

1. Dweck (2007); Urtubey (2023, June 20).
2. Hanh (1999) 94-96.
3. Keltner (2023), 23, 30.
4. Hanh (1998) 7–8.
5. Hanh (1998) 7–8.
6. Reece (2022), 98.
7. Rubalcava (2005).
8. Reece (2022), 13; Lewis and Diamond (2015), xix.
9. Hanh (all); Hanh and Weare (2017).
10. Hanh (2006), 115.
11. Hanh (1998), 81, 95.
12. Reece (2022), 25.
13. Hanh (all); Trungpa (1993).
14. Bigelow and Swinehart (2014); Gang (1991); Vicuña (2017, July 7).
15. Hanh and Weare (2017), xxiii.
16. Freire (1985), 59.
17. Hanh (2014).
18. Hanh (2002a), 59.
19. Hanh (2002a), 59.
20. Hanh (2002a), 59.
21. Trungpa (1993), 12.
22. Cuban (1993); Frankenberg, Garces and Hopkins (2016); Mcguire, Scott and Shaw (2006); Smith and Tyler (2006); Spring (all).
23. Shaer (2018, March); Haraway (1991). In addition to distorting human interactions, screens limit sensory social-emotional learning experiences, thereby fomenting anxiety and other mental health problems from lack of occasions to regulate emotions holistically in real time, such as with human touch, vision, sound, smell, and taste. The absence of place-based, hands-on academic engagement undermines relational academic concentration for collective critical consciousness to change material conditions toward holistic humanization. All that said, screens remove some ability and geographic barriers to communication, and they appear to open affinity-based identities to relate humans to unity with animals and the world.
24. Derman-Sparks (1989); Iberlin and Ruyle (2017); Rechtschaffen (2016); Rome and Martin (2010, July 1).
25. Reece (2022), 23.
26. Madden-Dent and Oliver (2021).
27. Banks (all); Bigelow and Swinehart (2014); Clark (all); Gang (1991); Urtubey (2023, June 20); Valenzuela (2016).

28 Doll, Brehm and Zucker (2014); Mountain (2023, August 11); Middleton (2018); Rechtschaffen (2016); Reece (2022).
29 Keltner (2023), 33.
30 Keltner (2023), 33., quoting Aldous Huxley, 32–33.
31 Bigelow and Swinehart (2014); Block (2016); Clark (all); Gang (1991); Summers and Smith (2014).
32 Hanh (2014).
33 Noguera (1998); Reece (2022), 15.
34 Hanh (all); Hanh and Weare (2017).
35 Noguera (1998).
36 Hanh and Weare (2017).
37 Reece (2022), 59.
38 Reece (2022), 59.
39 Hanh (1998), 7.
40 Hanh (2002a), 6–7.
41 Hanh and Weare (2017), xxvi–xxvii.
42 Dweck (2007).
43 Rechtschaffen (2016), 63.
44 King (1964), 81.
45 King (1964), 81.
46 Omi and Winant (1986), 61.
47 Kendi (2019), 20.
48 Hanh (2010), 9–10.
49 Derman-Sparks (1989), 3.
50 King (1964), 81.
51 Madison (all).
52 Alexander; (2010); Barrera; (1979); Bowles and Gintis; (1976); Bourdieu; (1973); Kozol; (1991); Freire; (1985); Giroux; (1983); Harman (1986, Summer).
53 Kendi, (2019), 20.
54 Howe and Lisi; (2019); Keltner, (2023), 13.
55 Derman-Sparks (1989).
56 Derman-Sparks (1989), 6, 7, 11.
57 Hanh (2006), 74–75, 78.
58 Trungpa (1993), 76–88.
59 Hanh (2008), 5.
60 Trungpa (1993).
61 Trungpa (1993)., 77–88.
62 Trungpa (1993)., 78–79.
63 Adapted from King (1964), 81.
64 Trungpa (1993), 37, 241, 12.
65 Hanh (all); Trungpa (1993).
66 Banks, Suárez-Orozco, Ben-Peretz (2016); Bigelow and Swinehart (2014); Gang (1991); Vicuña (2017, July 7).
67 Keltner (2023), 11, 23, 37; Trungpa (1993), 24.
68 Reece (2022).
69 Keltner (2023), 40.
70 Trungpa (1993), 2, 10, 11, 12.
71 Keltner (2023), 33.
72 Trungpa (1993), 7.
73 Keltner (2023), 41.
74 Reece (2022), 25.
75 Reece (2022), 56–57.
76 Trungpa (1993), 1.
77 Nava (2001); Reece (2022); Trungpa (1993), 11, 12, 37, 214.
78 Hanh (1995), 32–33.
79 Hanh (all); Hanh and Weare (2017); Rechtschaffen (2016).

80 King (1964), 79.
81 Trungpa (1993), 14.
82 Editors (2014, Fall); Oliver (2023, June 21); https://palusa.org; Ferlazzo (2016, February 6).
83 Coles andandand Ford (2010).
84 Keltner (2023), 87–88.
85 Keltner (2023), 30.
86 Ellison (1998); Hanh and Weare (2017); Keltner (2023), 7; Kunhardt (2018); Tutu and Tutu (2014).
87 Keltner (2023), 83–86.
88 Niebuhr (1999, October 16).
89 Hanh (1998), 64, 67.
90 Ellison (1998); Hanh and Weare (2017); Tutu and Tutu (2014).
91 Niebuhr (1999, October 16).
92 Hanh (2006), 9.
93 Niebuhr (1999, October 16).
94 ReShel (2018).
95 Hanh (all).
96 Hanh (1995), 81.
97 Diaz (2018); Elias (1975); Freire (1985); Nyirenda (1996).
98 Boff and Boff (1987), 2–4.
99 Gutierrez (1973), 38.
100 Hanh (2010), 15.
101 Hanh (2010), 9, 14.
102 Clark (1991), 44–47.
103 Bigelow and Swinehart (2014), xii.
104 Bigelow and Swinehart (2014), xii; Clark (1991); Gang (1991); Urtubey (2023, June 20).
105 Hanh (2006), 9.
106 Bigelow and Swinehart (2014).
107 Hanh (2006), 9.
108 Hanh (2006), 9.
109 Clark (all); Gang (1991); Sleeter and Carmona (2017).
110 King (1964), 79.
111 Reece (2022), 98.
112 Keltner, (2023), 82–83.
113 Keltner, (2023), 83.
114 Rechtschaffen (2016), 5–7, 63.
115 Rechtschaffen (2016), 63.
116 Rubalcava (2001–2024).
117 Bigelow and Swinehart (2014); Urtubey (2023, June 20).
118 Rechtschaffen (2016), 63.
119 Ehlers (2023).
120 Rechtschaffen (2016).
121 Bazin and Tamez (2002).
122 Rubalcava (2001–2024).
123 Hanh and Weare (2017), xvii–xviii.
124 Hanh and Weare (2017), xvii–xviii.
125 Reece (2022), 73.
126 Trungpa (1993), 77.
127 Keltner (2023).
128 Noguera (1998).
129 Takaki (all).
130 Trungpa (1993), 99–101.
131 Hanh (2008), 36.
132 Hanh (2010), 9, 14.
133 Trungpa (1993), 1, 24.
134 Hanh (all).

7
TOOL #3

Approach-in-Dimension

Guiding Purpose

Explain how the Approach-in-Dimension is a philosophy of education rubric to

- Determine a transparent approach to humanization through academic design and evaluation, adaptable to professional passion, subject requirements, and site cultures.
- Analyze six ideological *approaches* to five education *dimensions* for holistic planning and assessment.
- Change assimilation and segregation education with activities for holistic and integrated student success, educator empowerment, and accurate knowledge for a sustainable world.
- Collect cultural data and achievement results about progress, stasis, or setbacks from academic engagement changes.
- Compare philosophical intentions to data and results to guide decisions about space, time, materials, and learning environments.

Provide

- Two Multicultural Mindfulness Activities and one journal question: *Healthy Multicultural Identity Quest, Superdiverse Biodiverse Me Turtle,* and *What's the Approach-in-Dimension?*

Context

What's the Approach-in-Dimension?

The Approach-in-Dimension is an academic engagement guide to compare humanization goals to cultural outcomes. It helps educators make holism decisions about education space, time, materials, and learning environments. It is a design and assessment tool to stay on the humanization path with a clear philosophy of education. This rubric pinpoints how to adapt subject priorities, professional passion, and site cultures to equity and sustainability criteria.

It assists educators to change assimilation and segregation education with holism and integration activities for student success, educator empowerment, and accurate knowledge in a superdiverse and biodiverse world. The Approach-in-Dimension describes six *approaches* – Mainstream, Contributions, Additive, Transformative, Social Action, and Environmental Liberation Education – to five education *dimensions* – curriculum, outcomes, knowledge, communications, and interactions.

The Approach-in-Dimension is based on the multicultural education scholarship of James A. Banks, who wrote about two models: four *approaches* and five *dimensions*.[1] The Approach-in-Dimension reconceives Banks's models by synthesizing them and inserting "Mainstream" as the first approach and "Environmental Liberation Education" as the last, resulting in *six* approaches to five dimensions. The Approach-in-Dimension supports academic transparency. It helps teachers determine a philosophy of humanity in education to channel the cumulative effect of the roughly 1,500 decisions we make every day.[2] With collaborative reflection, everyday educators become transformative teachers who *change* practices when we find outcomes don't match intentions.

The Approach-in-Dimension is distinct from top-down assessments required in our overstandardized and segmented system that serves the prevailing economic substructure and social superstructure. Rather, this tool is a way to handle requirements in context with academic freedom for cultural creativity and diversity inclusion. The tool empowers educators with inward-outward awareness to reconceptualize requirements and reshape mainstream space, time, materials, and learning environments. The Approach-in-Dimension spotlights teachers' vital role in intergenerational knowledge development within broad systems. This matrix empowers teachers to support diverse student success by mindfully curating subject details in classrooms, labs, meeting rooms, and programs. The teacher uses this tool to plan and evaluate for inclusive subject engagement in real-time local and global conditions. It eases the challenging process of weaving multiple perspectives into banking education's punitive procedures that alienate and exclude. It supports the project of culturally responsive social-emotional academic learning for a sustainable world.[3]

What sets this tool apart is its integrative function. There exists a number of best practices and rubrics for *multicultural* education as well as an array of *environmental* education parameters.[4] Further, *mindfulness* education criteria are well-defined with interbeing, impermanence, and emptiness fundamentals.[5] The Approach-in-Dimension *combines* these three areas, offering teachers cohesive action-reflection guideposts for *holistic* education.

With this map, transformative teachers identify when we perpetuate the status quo that divides and destroys and when our hourly and daily decisions facilitate unity and sustainability experiences. We ascertain if our own developing culture competence and structural competence support egalitarianism and planet health during academic engagement. As transformative teachers, we want to prepare diverse students for inclusive participation in an environmentally sound infrastructure and economy. By synthesizing multicultural, environmental, and mindfulness education, the Approach-in-Dimension steers our projects. This planning and evaluation tool points to the ideology advocated in this book: Environmental Liberation Education. In this way, the Approach-in-Dimension assists educators to reduce implicit bias practices that stratify, dehumanize, and destroy the environment by increasing social justice activities, culturally responsive humanization events, and ecological well-being *during* academic routines.

The Three Transformative Tools explained in this book combine to help educators do big-picture work. The tools do the heavy lifting to move being caught into dis-empowerment and segregation cycles to advancing the prosocial education that motivates us. Transformative teachers use variations of these tools to organize, apply, and measure inclusion and sustainability activities in context:

1. *Diversity Circles* provide a learning community *structure* with two or more participants, as diverse as possible. These environmental justice homerooms grow social-emotional trust during culture change. We collaborate on nonviolent liberation methods, experiment with holism diversity projects, and facilitate local-global sustainability activities during academic engagement.
2. *Multicultural Mindfulness* is our peace *process* for inward-outward change. We use reconciliation practices to integrate body-mind-culture-environment into classrooms, labs, meeting rooms, and site routines. We act and reflect to distinguish what we *do* from mainstream education; for instance, we change academics through consistent

   - Critical consciousness circles with hands-on culture and nature activities, indoors and outdoors to respect sun, earth, sky, and water.
   - Antibias-antiracist project teams.
   - Student-led sustainability teach-ins.
   - Holism experiences, such as restorative breathwork and journaling, arts and sciences integrations, animal, plant, and water therapy, and multimodal and multilingual interactions.
   - Well-being physical education, natural foods cultivation and consumption, and other healthful routines.
   - Nonviolent communication for diversity belonging and cultural empowerment with intergenerational generosity and restorative justice activities (see Figure 4.6).

3. *Approach-in-Dimension* is a *planning* and *evaluation* rubric to interpret academic requirements and guide outcomes from the transformative activities we implement, distilling intentions from results with six approaches to humanity in five education dimensions.

A Hands-On Tool

The Approach-in-Dimension is hands-on, assisting educators to identify bias versus antibias, dehumanization versus humanization, and unsustainability versus sustainability outcomes. It plans for diversity and inclusion experiences, such as organizing circle formations, culturally responsive positive reinforcement exercises, students choice and question formats in multiple modalities and languages, and peace breathwork during core content. It assesses for equity, social-emotional academic learning, and environmental well-being. For example, a teacher who chooses the Environmental Liberation Education approach may use the Approach-in-Dimension to figure out student-led subject activities with intergenerational interactions around green themes, and then evaluate how the activities reduced plastics or replaced ecologically unsound school supplies, such as throw away lab projects. A teacher who chooses the Transformative approach may use the Approach-in-Dimension to prepare for and gauge the academic efficacy of culturally creative materials from community cultures to meet requirements or integrating culturally responsive music, dance, or recycled art collaborations into core content.

Six *approaches* – Mainstream, Contributions, Additive, Transformative, Social Action, and Environmental Liberation Education – demarcate activities in five *dimensions* – curriculum, outcomes, knowledge, communications, and interactions.[6] First, the educator ascertains the scope of diversity, mindfulness, and sustainability in six philosophies of education. Second, after choosing a philosophy that resonates with professional passion and cultural authenticity balanced with regional and site demographics, the educator endeavors to decrease unmindful bias and unsustainability decisions during routines. Taking one or more of the five dimensions at a time, the educator collaborates to research how dimension routines reproduce Anglo-conformity, environmental destruction, or dehumanization systems. Then the collaboration experiments with change designs. Third, the collaboration assesses design implementation for outcomes, looking for the scope of change or lack thereof.

The Approach-in-Dimension is hands-on this way because it empowers educators to maneuver academic space, time, materials, and learning environments with goals to "detrack" students or "un-standardize" academics.[7] We use the matrix for holistic backwards design and assessment of the humanization philosophy we determine.[8]

Summary of Approaches and Dimensions

Six Approaches

1 *Mainstream:* Dominant culture assimilation and segregation academics. Little or no diversity, mindfulness, or sustainability.
2 *Contributions:* Appends positive diversity, mindfulness, and/or sustainability lists and extra-curriculars to the Mainstream approach. Celebrates palatable cultures, well-being, and environmental elements. Tokenizes with one-time worksheets and projects, and tip-of-the-iceberg cultural categories and examples.
3 *Additive:* Augments Contributions lists with some cultural, mindfulness, and sustainability comprehension but without holistic *action*. Focuses on civility and cultural studies without developing structural competence for solutions to systemic inequities. Views racism and other structural problems associated with diversity, public health, and environment as individualistic, to be dealt with case by case mostly outside classroom or department routines, and entertains diversity in discrete events or as a theoretical, anomalous, or overwhelming topic.
4 *Transformative:* Integrates diversity, mindfulness, or sustainability into academics *on site*. Breaks from above three approaches with actions to reduce assimilation and segregation by reshaping academics structurally. Reduces allegiance to banking education and increases diversity, mindfulness, or sustainability practices for inclusive academic concentration. Infuses diverse, social-emotional, or ecological ways of knowing into subject engagement with ethnic studies, women's studies, and other identity studies theories and evidence. Advocates for intersectional culture competence, structural competence, and inclusive antibias-antiracist academics.
5 *Social Action:* Expands the *on-site* Transformative approach with *off-site* solutions and restorative activities. Activates unifying antibias-antiracist culture circles co-generated by the oppressed for community empowerment experiences. Integrates academic engagement into critical consciousness about community suffering and thriving. Develops culture competence and structural competence to reshape subject engagement by reducing assimilation

256 Three Transformative Tools

Approach-in-Dimension	1. Mainstream No/little diversity, mindfulness, *or* sustainability. Systemic assimilation, segregation, environmental destruction in:	2. Contributions Mainstream *plus* diversity, mindfulness, *or* sustainability positives lists in:	3. Additive Contributions *plus* civility norms with diversity, mindfulness, *or* sustainability comprehension in:	4. Transformative Intersectional diversity, mindfulness, *or* sustainability integration In:	5. Social Action Intersectional diversity, mindfulness, *or* sustainability empowerment with community healing experiences from:	6. Environmental Liberation Education Intersectional diversity, mindfulness, *and* sustainability empowerment with holistic healing experiences in:
1. Curriculum	Required subjects, mostly on site.	Required subjects with some extra cultural content, mostly on site.	Required subjects with some extra cultural content, mostly on site.	Culturally revised required subjects, mostly on site.	Student-cogenerated required subjects, on/off site with cultures or nature.	Student-cogenerated required subjects, on/off site, indoors/outdoors, with cultures and nature.
2. Outcomes	student knowledge and skills upon subject completion about dominant culture.	Student knowledge and skills upon subject completion about dominant culture.	Student knowledge and skills upon subject completion about dominant culture.	Student knowledge and skills with culture and structural competence upon subject completion.	Student knowledge and skills with real-world culture and structural competence upon subject completion.	Student knowledge and skills with real-world culture and structural competence upon subject completion.
3. Knowledge	Disciplinary development, data collection, and dissemination.	Disciplinary development, data collection, and dissemination.	Disciplinary development, data collection, and dissemination.	Interdisciplinary development, data collection, and dissemination.	Interdisciplinary development, data collection, and dissemination for solutions.	Interdisciplinary development, data collection, and dissemination for solutions.
4. Communications	Cultural status quo messages and exchanges.	Largely cultural status quo messages and exchanges.	Largely cultural status quo messages and exchanges.	Multicultural inclusion messages and exchanges.	Cultural liberation messages and exchanges.	Multicultural environmental liberation messages and exchanges.
5. Interactions	Assimilation, stratification, and environmental alienation socialization events, mostly on site.	Assimilation, stratification, and environmental spectator socialization events, mostly on site.	Assimilation, stratification, and cultural and environmental socialization events, mostly on site.	Holistic culturally relevant equity and environmental socialization events, largely on site.	Holistic culturally relevant liberation or climate justice socialization circle projects, on/off site.	Holistic culturally relevant environmental liberation socialization circle projects, on/off site, indoors/outdoors.

FIGURE 7.1 Approach-in-Dimension graphic. Created by the author.

and segregation space, time, materials, and learning environments, and increasing hands-on action-reflection for humanization and liberation experiences connected to the world.
6 *Environmental Liberation Education:* Takes *planet* justice action *on site and off*, featuring diverse cultures and nature, indoors or outdoors. Merges Social Action circle activities with mindfulness and environmental consciousness. Superdiverse students co-generate academics with critical consciousness about community suffering and thriving toward biodiversity sustainability. Develops culture competence and structural competence by reducing assimilation and segregation education space, time, materials, and learning environments and increasing multiple perspectives and authentic practices during hands-on action-reflection for humanity-through-nature activities during holistic subject engagement connected to the world.

Five Dimensions

Each dimension operates patterns of assimilation/segregation *or* equity/integration; alienation *or* mindfulness; unsustainability *or* sustainability:

1 *Curriculum:* Discipline and subject design, access, and use. Eight forms.
2 *Outcomes:* The scope and application of acquired knowledge and skills upon subject completion or lack thereof.
3 *Knowledge:* Concept, design, collection, observation, experimentation, analysis, creation, and dissemination of data, evidence, or a subject in pursuit of truth through arts, sciences, and/or diverse modalities, practices, and skills and cultural ways of knowing.
4 *Communications:* Information and cultural perspective exchanges and messages in education dimensions, implicit and explicit, among educators, students, and communities.
5 *Interactions:* Socialization involving economic, cultural, emotional, and environmental systems, relationships, and projects associated with academic communities, and between education and the world.

Macroscopic Rubric

Educators are powerful. We regulate much of what happens in classrooms, labs, meeting rooms, departments, and sites. We have authority over vital aspects of school space, time, materials, and learning environments. The Approach-in-Dimension is macroscopic in this way. It helps to see mislabeled courses, workshops, and meetings that impart dehumanization activities and experiences through the pretext of standardization and scheduling. The Approach-in-Dimension offers acumen to counteract disinformation and the devaluation of arts and sciences. We perceive causes of economic-social chaos and disenfranchisement from hate and ignorance. Unintentionally or calculatedly, status quo territorial divides perpetuate systemic inequities, dehumanization, and environmental harm through the Mainstream approach. Mainstream routines perpetuate dominant culture curriculum, the racialized achievement gap, biased research, monocultural or conflict communications, and site segregation. Status quo procedures underrate teachers with inadequate pay, over-standardization, and unsafe schools. The existing state of affairs serves overprocessed foods and plastics to students and delivers environmental education as extra curriculum. The Approach-in-Dimension helps everyday educators marshal academic freedom to pursue truth and take cultural action in education dimensions guided by big-picture diversity, mindfulness, and ecological criteria.

Microscopic Rubric

The Approach-in-Dimension is also microscopic. It pinpoints specific instances of diversity, mindfulness, and sustainability in passing learning moments. The tool spots cultural inclusion or exclusion in weekly quizzes and unit exams. It ascertains student locus of control during projects, such as who makes choices about topics and materials and what cultural ways of knowing occupy project analysis and evaluation. The Approach-in-Dimension assesses the cultural relevance of academic behaviors, such as modalities, perspectives, and languages in reading comprehension activities and research assignments. It discerns bias in educational objectives and school–home communications about required content, comportment, and grading curves. It identifies diversity or homogeneity during classroom interactions, pinpointing equitable or inequitable participation in units and study groups.

The Approach-in-Dimension enumerates details about how students in programs meet or do not meet basic human needs sustainably. Educators attend to healthy food, clean water, consistent exercise, physical safety, cultural belonging, self-acceptance growth, and higher-order aesthetics and curiosity tasks, such as diversity field trips and community service projects. This inventory focuses not only on student access, but also on student *agency*, thereby transforming education design and evaluation from cultural victimization to empowerment criteria.[9]

Metacognition

While checklists are useful, the Approach-in-Dimension is another kind of rubric. For example, thoughtful antibias-antiracist checklists – like the "Equitable Classroom Practices Observation Checklist" and the "Teaching Tolerance: Observing Equity" worksheets – assist diversity reflection.[10] However, in contrast to strategic checklists, which are valuable for data observation and collection, the Approach-in-Dimension prompts metacognition about cultures and sustainability.

It offers a bird's-eye view for critical thinking about humanization adjustments to academic activities. It is for flow reflection about cultural perspectives in humanity relative to professional passion, subject priorities, and student demographics during academic decisions. Rather than checking off components, the Approach-in-Dimension provides humanity *themes* for hands-on cultural interactions during the ongoing choreography of education space, time, materials, and learning environments.

The Approach-in-Dimension hones philosophical clarity to motivate design and assessment actions to remove barriers to academic inclusion. The six approaches delineate cultural choices about systems in a globalized world. The educator commits to a growth mindset[11] for diversity and sustainability, tailoring operations to subject expertise, disciplinary standards, academic requirements, and site cultures. The five dimensions are the areas where *transformative* teacher collaborations practice Multicultural Mindfulness peace processes to work through fear of change and creative tension during integrative decisions. In Diversity Circles, we use the Approach-in-Dimension for big picture criteria during subject specifics. In concert, the Three Transformative Tools assist teachers to resist cultural defensiveness and bias habits, and instead take clear-eyed action to reduce assimilation and segregation systems. The tools facilitate inclusive and un-standardizing academic activities for holistic *change* through the humanization and ecological stewardship that students and teachers co-create.

MULTICULTURAL MINDFULNESS ACTIVITY

Healthy Multicultural Identity Quest

Outcome

- Develop a healthy multicultural identity with others.

Key Concepts

- **Healthy multicultural identity**: Inward-outward mindfulness of cultures within systems to develop multicultural belonging for healing actions in a superdiverse-biodiverse world.

Resources

- Journal, pencil, copies of Figure 7.2 (below),[12] a place to sit indoors or outdoors.
- A nature example brought in by each participant to symbolize cultural identity.

Big-Picture Question

- How do I belong in diversity?

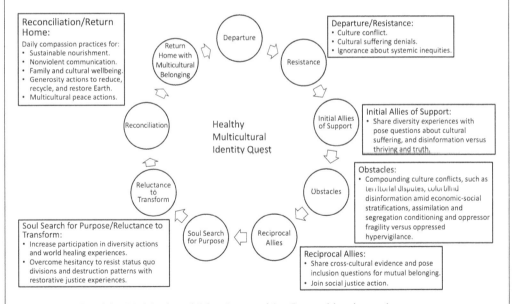

FIGURE 7.2 Healthy Multicultural Identity graphic. Created by the author.

Start

Whole group circle:

- **Passing around** the nature examples, each participant **describes** identifying with or feeling alienated from the example by sharing an emotional experience or cultural question.
- **Hand out** and **discuss** Figure 7.2. What's confusing? What inspires? With whom do you share cross-cultural connections?
- **Individually reflect** for a minute, imagining one's own healthy multicultural identity quest.
- **Journal** about what to expect on your quest. What is your cultural identity suffering versus your cultural identity joy?

Middle

Diversified project teams:

- **Collectively write** or **draw** one of the following:
  - **Obstacle Stories** about challenges to a healthy multicultural identity.
  - **Reciprocal Multicultural Allies Stories** about diversity friends.
  - **Homecoming Stories** about: (1) the cultural symbols, practices, and beliefs of your healthy multicultural identity and (2) how you are a global citizen for sustainability.

Closing

Whole group circle:

- Teams **share** stories.
- Go around the circle to **explain** individually where one is at now in a healthy multicultural identity quest.

Theory and Practice

How Does the Approach-in-Dimension Address Systemic Bias?

The Approach-in-Dimension prompts reflection to identify barriers to big-picture transformation. Despite how professionally energizing it is to participate in holistic education, it's hard to change what we do. We feel tethered to requirements, afraid to rock the boat. We often feel anxious and defensive at school. We perceive resource scarcities, disinformation, and extremism. We observe weapons and patterns of violence. We are overwhelmed about climate change. We are concerned about safety. But we still have a hard time stepping away from the mainstream biases and patterns in which we are immersed. Because systemic inequities are baked into standards, we gravitate to Contributions and Additive approaches, which append diversity, mindfulness, or sustainability elements to the Mainstream such as using prefabricated cultural worksheets and activities as extra curriculum.

We might feel comfortable with single culture topics but exhausted by the prospect of integrating ethnic studies or women's studies into requirements. We don't know how to participate in multiracial liberation teach-ins or critical consciousness circles. We're too busy to get creative with culture action or sustainability initiatives. Teaching from a position of love makes us feel vulnerable. Many of us identify with colorblind values we learned in our own schooling, and which have been reinforced in disciplinary training and professional development. Moreover, we are evaluated with individualism and banking education criteria, and we don't want to be penalized for change.

Educators make decisions with either/or thinking, conditioned in the career by academic "punitive" evaluations and life-long cultural routines in the divisive systems of the racialized extraction-consumption economy.[13] Further, many educators do not have structural competence or systemic transformation skills.[14]

> [O]ne of the main reasons for gaps that persist is that [educators] collectively have low equity skills…. If we hope to close the equity gap, we all need to become better at what we do through a lens of equity-mindedness.[15]

Everyday educators simply don't know what to do about the economic and social contradictions that dehumanize students and distort knowledge.

Many teachers in the US, 80% of whom are European American, have been accustomed to White privilege since birth.[16] One benefit from identifying with Anglo-conformity is control. Contributions and Additive approaches maintain a sense of control with boilerplate diversity statements and textbook cultural celebration days. However, advanced approaches to diversity can feel unnerving. Transformative education can feel like "losing control in a classroom where there is no one way to approach a subject – only multiple ways and multiple references."[17] Thus, transformative teaching involves a leap of faith.

It takes courage to reach out to collaborate against systems and the stratified economy that finances social institutions. Stepping into the transformative arena isn't for the faint of heart.[18] For White educators to voluntarily relinquish White privilege embedded in mainstream education means facing "White Fragility" (Chapter 3). When antibias-antiracist actions for change disrupt hourly and daily expectations, fear lashes out. We suffer from defensive reactions in hot-headed culture conflicts. As explained by Robin DiAngelo:

> White people in North America live in a social environment that protects and insulates them from race-based stress. This insulated environment of racial protection builds white expectations for racial comfort while at the same time lowering the ability to tolerate racial stress, leading to what I refer to as White Fragility. White Fragility is the state in which even a minimum amount of racial stress becomes intolerable, triggering a range of defensive moves. These moves include the outward display of emotions such as anger, fear, and guilt, and behaviors such as argumentation, silence, and leaving the stress inducing situation. These behaviors, in turn, function to reinstate white racial equilibrium.[19]

White Fragility is what Martin Luther King, Jr. referred to as "gravely" detrimental to civil rights. Writing in 1963 from a "filthy roach-infested" jail cell in Birmingham, where he was incarcerated for nonviolent civil disobedience, Dr. King described

> the regrettable conclusion that the Negro's great stumbling block in the stride toward freedom is not the White Citizen's Council-er or the Ku Klux Klanner but the white moderate…who constantly says, 'I agree with you in the goal you seek, but I can't agree with your methods of 'direct action.'[20]

As such, White moderates may deny personal complicity in systemic racism, but White moderate *teachers* delay "direct action" at school with anxiety behaviors, such as shouting, whining, crying, leaving the room, or refusal to participate.

Some of these "defensive moves" are passive-aggressive – hiding in classrooms or offices to avoid integration experiences or deflecting change to curriculum or knowledge development by not participating whole-heartedly in diversity or cultural inclusion projects to which one has signed onto. Other moves are aggressive – throwing fits, yelling, name-calling, accusing, projecting, stomping out, slamming doors, writing inflammatory messages, filing complaints, and getting litigious about bias and culture events.[21] Some moves are deceptive, such as teachers who outwardly disagree with censorship or stifling nonviolent student protests. These teachers may object to encroachment on academic freedom, but quietly they omit diversity resources, critical race theory, diverse cultural ways of knowing, and intergenerational integrations in the learning environments they manage. They choose not to explicitly support nonviolent student protests and justice teach-ins. Then, agonized by hypocrisy, such teachers might emote anger, fear, sadness, or guilt while still carrying forward with Anglo-conformist curriculum and knowledge decisions.[22]

Because educators wield power over students, unconscious bias decisions unfairly direct who speaks, the language, tone, and content of communications and the heterogeneity or homogeneity of interactions. Teacher bias impacts curriculum engagement and research projects, such as the availability of cultural voices and points of view in materials and data points. Bias is involved in determining who participates in higher order tasks. Teacher bias limits the diversity of identities of classroom volunteers and service supports who guide site interactions. Teacher bias skews behavior management and conflict resolution procedures that impact academic outcomes. For example, a colorblind teacher might be unaware of authorizing White students to dominate academic discussions, while consenting to Latina students' back-of-the-room silence. Part of such silence is cultural dissonance with the Mainstream approach because of its history of exclusions. The resulting monocultural subject engagement limits the range of participation in academics, and homogeneous classroom and lab activities reinforce social divisions on campus at large.[23]

When teachers experience White Fragility, the agitation can be disconcerting to students of color who wish to please the teacher. Some students stay out of the way, repressing the frustration they feel. Conversely, other students of color display anger, for which they get punished.[24] To reinforce this dynamic in lounges and committee meetings, teachers may explain emotional discomfort from cultural dissonance against students of color and ethnic studies and women's studies scholarship by asserting how they don't like political correctness and don't feel safe discussing systemic racism or sexism.[25]

Teachers may be aware of White supremacy, critical race theory, and social justice action as topics but believe them to be inappropriate for classrooms, labs, or campus events. Bryan Reece describes a professor with this perspective who said: "The subject matter is the subject matter…[there's no] connection between these students' lives and…pedagogy…[There's] no reason to make changes in the classroom" to respond to diverse cultures.[26] Such educators might concede the existence of systemic inequities but believe these problems to be outside the scholarly norms of academic space, time, and materials. For example, attempting to apply race-neutral standards to *individuals*, educators exhibiting White Fragility may view student underperformance to be about personal choices rather than an outcome of systemic patterns. They thereby blame the victim for design biases and cultural deficiency stereotypes from cultural conditioning in the assimilation and segregation procedures that define mainstream education.

Reducing Systemic Bias by Removing Barriers

Reacting with annoyance, shame, or distress, many experiencing anger, numbness, or fear about culture change are nonetheless well-meaning. Many educators aspired to teach since childhood, seeking employment in schools that are similar to those they attended.[27] Teachers have fond memories of neighborhood schools with warm recollections that inspire best practices to replicate those good feelings in their own classrooms.[28] Good feelings are a starting point to nurture alliances through the shared goal for humanity. With a lens of intersectionality, teachers join Diversity Circles to swap stories and data about best practices from different cultural standpoints, posing *cross-cultural* questions for inclusion experiences on site. In this way, transformative teachers model integration during the Diversity Circle gathering itself while engaging fond memories to energize real-time humanization activities with students.

Collaborating on prosocial definitions of humanity engages teachers to work through cultural discords in over-bureaucratized conditions that may not comport with fond childhood recollections. Deep-dive reflection increases teachers' cultural engagement with local diversity. US teachers work in increasingly diverse and segregated sites dealing with physical and mental health issues, safety uncertainties, environmental calamities, and social disconnect from students. Teachers need to feel cultural belonging *with* students.[29] Educators reduce cultural and bureaucratic barriers by facing the "sincere ignorance" about racism, sexism, and classism that warps perception and alienates people from one another.[30] To thrive professionally, teachers actively heal culture clashes through circles of care, using culture consciousness in the solutions that interpret and guide change.

Diversity Circles practice Multicultural Mindfulness and evaluate design results with the Approach-in-Dimension to awaken teachers from colorblind delusions. Many educators are – "proud not to see any differences between their students...[trying] to treat them absolutely in the same manner"- but transformative teachers value cultural authenticity and differences[31]: "Successful groups move in unison and integrate different talents into a smoothly functioning, synchronized whole."[32] As transformative teachers collaborate on diversity activities, and develop social emotional academic learning experiences for cultural inclusion, we empower with holism.

Closer Examination of the Approaches

Translating theory into practice means understanding the rubric's approaches and dimensions. Four of the six approaches were originally conceived by Banks for use in multicultural education. They are "Contributions," "Additive," "Transformative," and "Social Action."[33]

Contributions

Banks describes Contributions as an intended departure from Anglo-conformist education into cultural awareness. The Contributions approach includes knowledge *about* cultures in subjects and disciplines. It features exceptional individuals, events, and innovations from non-dominant groups, presenting a positive and colorblind list. Unintentionally, educators who use it reinforce Anglo-conformist individualism by tokenizing and romanticizing heroes, holidays, festivals, foods, and fun within topics selected to emphasize human sameness rather than differences.[34]

As extra curriculum, Contributions lists are side stories to academic requirements. The lists don't prompt analysis or synthesis of diverse cultural perspectives in the subject. They ignore systemic oppression and segregation and emphasize cultures palatable to Eurocentric sensibilities. For instance, US Contributions curriculum may note Indigenous cultures and individuals, but it uses the Anglo-conformist framework to start US history with the *arrival* of White *colonists*, who *developed wild lands* and *civilized savages* through *westward expansion* as *pioneers*, rather than as using culturally accurate terms such as invaders, nature destroyers, cultural annihilators, violent murderers, and enslavers. The Contributions version of historical dating dismisses how diverse Indigenous communities stewarded the land sustainably for thousands of years previous to European conquest. Further, it ignores how Indigenous nations currently live as sovereign communities with vibrant languages and practices, including humanizing governments despite ongoing systemic violence.[35] Diverse cultural ways of knowing are vital to evidence-based ecological conservation and restoration practices to solve climate change, but they go largely dismissed in the Contributions approach.[36] Rather, this approach tacitly poses cultural diversity as a problem, best solved through assimilation.

The Approach-in-Dimension tool presented here reworks Banks's Contributions approach with mindfulness and environmental education criteria. So defined, Contributions are found to neglect social-emotional academic learning, inequity structures, diverse ways of knowing, cultural liberation and humanization models, and restorative and climate justice projects during academic engagement.[37]

Additive

Banks's Additive approach is Contributions plus studies into single cultures and attention to negative issues associated with diversity. Positive multicultural attributes are listed, and diversity is posed as a source of problems that individuals – rather than systems – perpetuate through stereotyping, bias, discrimination, and culture wars. The approach sets out civility norms and entreats descriptions of cultures for cross-cultural tolerance. Otherwise, diversity is viewed as political with extracurricular topics about broad systems that have little station in the set curriculum or subject.[38]

The Approach-in-Dimension tool expands Banks's formulation with a mindfulness and environmental education, showing how body-mind-environmental holism topics are ignored when cross-cultural and structural analyses are omitted from academic engagement. Such topics include pollution, plastics, food waste, megafires, rising oceans, habitat loss, extinctions, and much more. This expansion of the Additive approach reveals that educators who employ it see little point in tackling systems during subject engagement. They may strive to respect various cultures, but they decline collective action to change the institutional routines that propagate systemic oppression, segregation, dehumanization, and Earth destruction.[39]

Additive educators might declare themselves to be allies of marginalized communities and student inclusion, participate in mental health and cultural awareness months, and attend Earth Day events, but they speak *about* the issues of others with whom they claim to be allies. In the curriculum they implement, Additive adherents might investigate single cultures or exceptional individuals in topics, but they do not critically relate these topics to global systems or sociological solutions. They overlook how ways of knowing in communities and regions relate to equity and sustainability. Instead, Additive educators unconsciously defer to

Anglo-conformity. They frame diversity, mindfulness, or the environment as addendums to the subject and academic achievement as individualistic.[40]

Transformative

Banks's Transformative approach explains how educators take the bold leap toward integrative change.[41] It engages intersectional systems and "antiracist, anticlassist, and antisexist" criteria across the curriculum.[42] It incorporates multiple ways of knowing from race, ethnicity, class, gender, and other identity experiences into subject engagement. Educators and students define and engage knowledge development with an inclusion lens while critically analyzing mainstream education. Synthesizing multiple perspectives during academic engagement, educators actively resist social-economic dehumanization experiences on site.[43]

The Approach-in-Dimension deepens Banks's Transformative category with mindfulness and environmental education. The Transformative approach becomes about "balancing, integrating, transforming" learning environments with body-mind-culture integration and ecology activities through requirements.[44] It engages interdisciplinary knowledge holistically to understand cultures with awareness of intersections in oppression and resistance to systemic inequities. It deepens culture competence in subject topics with mindfulness or sustainability thriving practices on site.[45]

Social Action

Banks's Social Action approach is Transformative plus applying cultural empowerment academic activities to the real world. Social Action engages subjects through liberation education culture circles.[46] It is Paulo Freire's pedagogy of student-centered action-reflection for community empowerment through academic development. Participants redirect academics to systemic contradictions with collaborative justice projects on site and off.[47]

Expanded by the Approach-in-Dimension, Social Action is reformulated to incorporate mindfulness or climate justice projects. This approach integrates holistic race-class-gender intersectionality experiences, well-being, or environmental sustainability criteria into regional and global justice events. Participants who experience race, class, or gender privilege become unassuming "allies" of the oppressed. Educators listen, value, and engage *with* students intergenerationally to act and reflect on oppression, mental and physical health systems, or environmental injustices. Students co-lead academic engagement integrated into community humanization experiences.[48]

Two Additional Approaches

The Approach-in-Dimension tool adds two more approaches to develop Banks's four, like bookends: *Mainstream* and *Environmental Liberation Education*.[49]

Mainstream

The Mainstream approach comes *before* Banks's Contributions approach. It's added as reference for the unconscious bias decisions educators make in-synch with prevailing systems.

Mainstream education trivializes culture, mindfulness, and environment during academic routines. It devalues diversity, social-emotional learning, and environmental conservation during requirements. This is Anglo-conformist banking education. The mainstream approach racially segregates, tracks students into achievement gaps, enforces Eurocentric disciplinary biases, and dissociates education from cultures and nature. It serves the stratified extraction-consumption economy that funds US education and produces environmental destruction. This approach, therefore, reinforces structural bias and climate demise by deferring to individualism and industry profiteering. It spreads race-neutral disinformation through standardization that omits diverse ways of knowing and ranks students and knowledge racially. Perhaps fortunately, however, according to liberation theory, cultural suffering from the Mainstream approach is the catalyst that spurs collective action for systemic change.[50]

Environmental Liberation Education

The sixth approach – Environmental Liberation Education – comes *after* Banks's Social Action.[51] This is holistic Social Action with liberation multicultural education, mindfulness education, *and* environmental education. Antithetical to the Mainstream approach and going further than classic liberation education, this approach joins cultural empowerment with mindfulness of ecology. This is education for intergenerational nonviolent planetary justice.[52]

Environmental Liberation Education relates academics to superdiversity in biodiversity. It uses subjects to motivate teachers and students to problem-solve about resource scarcities, health maladies, and climate crises. It removes standardized individualism blinders, inspiring community projects to integrate structural equity into culturally relevant conservation and restoration activities. The Environmental Liberation Education approach integrates the "perspectives of women of color" and the "roles" of diverse oppressed peoples into planetary healing now.[53]

Environmental Liberation Education does not stop at diversifying "pre-existing course topics." It does not just begin "to alter the structure" of curriculum with antibias-antiracist culture, mindfulness, *or* sustainability topics.[54] It's not intermittent environmental education. Environmental Liberation Education involves collaborative big-picture student-centered reconceptualization of the disciplinary norms, and national, state, and district standards that define mainstream curriculum and knowledge. It meets requirements with holistic reinterpretations of standards using diversity criteria for "joyful and just" interdisciplinary practices and projects outdoors and with nature indoors.[55] Its diversity collaborators co-create change through integrated liberation circles, on site and off. During subject activities, its educators listen to, value, and interact *with* diverse communities for body-mind-culture-environmental holism experiences now.

Closer Examination of the Dimensions

Banks lists five dimensions of *multicultural* education:

1 "Content integration."
2 "An equity pedagogy."
3 "The knowledge construction process."
4 "Prejudice reduction."
5 "An empowering school culture and social structure."[56]

The Approach-in-Dimension tool rephrases Banks's five dimensions and applies them to education broadly. The hourly and daily routines that typically occupy educators fly by in a blur. Professional efficacy develops when we consistently pause to understand cultures and multicultural synergy. When we reflect on how each of the five education dimensions influences assimilation/segregation *or* equity/integration; alienation *or* mindfulness; unsustainability *or* sustainability, we are motivated to make decisions for change.[57]

Five dimensions rephrased:

1 *Curriculum* is disciplinary and subject design, access, and use. Curriculum is ideological and cultural. Eight forms of curriculum are explicit, hidden, null, extra, required, recommended, received, and integrated (Figure 5.5). Some curriculum examples are *written*, such as content standards, guidelines, lesson plans, textbooks, scholarship, readings, library resources, assignments, quizzes, and exams. Other examples are content materials, practices, and artifacts, such as arts, visuals, media excerpts, manipulatives, and lab and project items.
2 *Outcomes* is the scope of student acquired knowledge, comprehension, application, analysis, synthesis, and evaluation upon subject completion or lack thereof.
3 *Knowledge* is the conception, design, collection, observation, experimentation, analysis, creation, and dissemination of data, evidence, and the subject by educators, students, and communities in pursuit of truth. It is arts and sciences disciplines and research, and can include diverse modalities, practices, skills, and ways of knowing, such as cultural arts and story sharing.
4 *Communications* is information, cultural exchanges, and messages about education dimensions, implicit and explicit, among educators, students, and communities. Information is transmitted in limited or multiple languages, monocultural or multicultural expressions, and limited or multiple modalities. Spoken, written, visual, and body language surveys and routines perpetuate or reduce ten forms of bias (Figure 3.1).
5 *Interactions*: Socialization involving economic, cultural, emotional, and environmental systems and relationships during routines, programs, and projects. Interactions disempower or empower cultures and permit violence or encourage nonviolence. Interactions facilitate unequal or equal access to and use of resources individually or collaboratively, indoors or outdoors, on site or off. Interactions connect education participants to a sustainability infrastructure, society, and economy or alienate from the real world.

In summary, within education dimensions, teachers translate theory into practice by applying an approach – a philosophy of humanity in education – to hourly and daily decisions. We can choose to reproduce the mainstream philosophy of assimilation, segregation, and environmental alienation. Or we can choose to reduce divisions and dehumanization by collaborating for change with subject activities connected to multicultural and environmental respect and engagement. There's a profusion of rubrics asserting education best practices for student success and knowledge accuracy. The Approach-in-Dimension is one. It is a big picture map. It guides busy teachers to work *with* human superdiversity and ecological biodiversity during real-time academics. This rubric engages global reflection locally. With it, educators diagnose and apply academic freedom to maneuver space, time, materials, and learning environments to reduce bias. We empower ourselves professionally to facilitate *holistic* and *integrated* student success with subject proficiency uplifted by global citizenship skills for a sustainable world.

268 Three Transformative Tools

MULTICULTURAL MINDFULNESS ACTIVITY

Superdiverse Biodiverse Me Turtle

Note: this activity takes about an hour, which can be split into two 30-minute segments or simply skip to the closing segment for one 30-minute session.

Outcome

- Develop culture competence with structural competence to address climate change.

Key Concepts

- **Biodiversity:** "The variety of living species on Earth, including plants, animals, bacteria, and fungi" currently "at risk" due to "human activities."[58]
- **People of Color:** Diverse peoples without European ancestry (or with mixed ancestry) who are excluded from or dehumanized by racialized systems dominated by White peoples.
- **White People:** Diverse peoples with mostly European ancestry who benefit from racialized systems dominated by White peoples.
- **Superdiversity:** Human contact and recontact during local-global interactions through the "movement of goods and capital," "mass migration," and other phenomena for cross-cultural intersections within systems, all of which is currently experiencing the uncertainties and scarcities of climate change.[59]

Resources

- Journal, pencil, timer, copies of Figure 7.3, copies of the two essays below, a living turtle or turtle symbol inside the discussion circle center, and a place to meet indoors or outdoors.

Big-Picture Question

- How does my cultural identity relate to Earth?

Start

Whole group circle around the turtle example; distribute Figure 7.3.

- **Glance** at Figure 7.3.
- **Read aloud** Key Concepts above.
  - What's confusing?
  - What's clear?

- **Popcorn read aloud** *Turtle Island* below.
- After reading, **discuss:**
  - How does reflecting on diverse Indigenous perspectives nourish your healthy multicultural identity quest?
  - What's a topic in your core content that relates to Turtle Island?
  - How does nurturing your own cultural identity as part of Turtle Island help you understand your belonging in diversity and Earth stewardship?

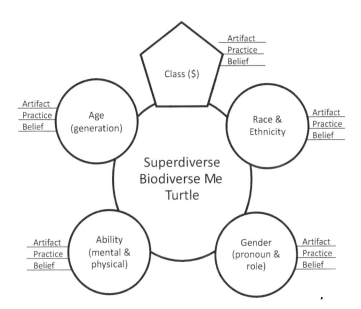

FIGURE 7.3 Superdiverse Biodiverse Me Turtle graphic. Created by the author.

Turtle Island

Turtle Island, from the Anishinabee peoples, represents the land known as North America, and it symbolizes Earth. Turtle Island thrives with clean water. Turtle Island motivated Nokomis Josephine Mandamin (no-kuh-miss, "grandmother" in Ojibwe) to organize walks across North America to raise awareness and make policy changes for water protection.[60]

Another story about Turtle Island, told by Robin Wall Kimmerer, Potowatomi Nation, is that one day Sky Woman fell from eternity with a bundle of seeds and roots to blue Earth spinning in the vast galaxy. Geese caught Sky Woman, and a turtle offered its shell as a place for Sky Woman to land. Diverse animals swam to ocean's bottom to try to gather red mud to fortify the turtle's back for Sky Mother, but to no avail. At last, Muskrat, a brave but weak swimmer with clever claws, dove, dug, and passed away from exertion while pushing a precious dab of red mud onto the turtle's shell. Sky Mother offered gratitude songs to Muskrat and the red mud. She planted seeds and roots, cultivating blue Earth to become Turtle Island, a vast land with diverse plants, animals, and peoples co-existing in life cycles.[61]

Middle

Whole group Circle:

- **Popcorn read** *Cultural Standpoints* below.
- After reading, **discuss**: What emotions do you feel? Do the cultural standpoints resonate with you? Why/Why not?

Cultural Standpoints

If you're White:

You want to extract yourself from White supremacy and exist in an authentic cultural identity. You also want to extract yourself from White supremacy and learn more about your authentic cultural identity. You also feel defensive or guilty about your identity because the colorblind American dream has you deny your unearned advantages from systemic racism. Because you experience fight, freeze, or flight reactions about White supremacy and being part of the historically dominant culture, you view diversity as a problem to solve. You're daunted by the prospect of repairing the inequity systems into which you were born. While you claim to be an ally, you tend to speak *for* others rather than listen. You struggle with developing a healthy *multicultural* identity and nourishing professional practice with culture consciousness and structural competence. Fearing plurality and losing structural benefits from reparations, you avoid participating in multiracial alliances to dismantle systemic racism and take organized action for a sustainable world. Or you go in the other direction, passionate about social justice and sustainability, but you struggle with your own biases and you face resistance or distrust about your participation in liberation projects.[62] However, you want to apply a growth mindset, so you are ready to manage social anxiety and instead learn how to effectively integrate cultures into sustainability.

If you're of color:

You want to extract yourself from White supremacy and exist in an authentic cultural identity. You also want to extract yourself from White supremacy and learn more about your authentic cultural identity. You also are *weary* of the burden of the racialized category imposed on you. You're *wary* of the White people with whom you work. You experience defensively pessimistic fight, freeze, or flight reactions about White supremacy, systemic inequities, and the daily prejudice and violence you negotiate. Self-segregation feels like a buffer against systemic racism, and you feel good about cultural empowerment; or you take an assimilation path of least resistance, but resentment builds from demoting your culture.[63] You struggle with developing a healthy *multicultural* identity and nourishing professional practice with culture consciousness and structural competence out of exhaustion. You resist joining multiracial alliances to dismantle unjust systems and take organized action for a sustainable world. Or conversely, you might go in the other direction, passionate about culture empowerment, but you struggle with your own biases and face resistance or distrust about your participation in liberation projects.[64] However, you want to apply a growth mindset, so you are ready to manage social anxiety and instead learn how to effectively integrate cultures into sustainability.

Closing

Diversified project teams:

- **Draw** a *Superdiverse Biodiverse Me Turtle* visual, copying loosely from Figure 7.3. Copy shapes and lines, not words.
- **Write** inside the turtle body: "Superdiverse Biodiverse (insert your first name)."
- **Fill the rest in:**

  1 **List** your own culture identifiers inside each shape category (e.g., for "class," you might write "wealthy," "professional," "student," "middle class," "working class," "poor," "unemployed," or some combination).

2. **List** one artifact, practice, and belief on the lines outside each shape category; for example, I might write for "professional" (class): "reliable Subaru commute car" (artifact), "check emails daily" (practice), "community college teaching is a service career that helps the world" (belief).
3. **Draw** jagged culture-clash lines between list categories and items that conflict; for example, I might note the clash between "reliable Subaru commute car" (artifact) as a "professional" (class) versus "green values" (belief) as a "mother of three in the next generation" (gender).
4. **Write** "P" next to cultures of privilege and "M" next to cultures of marginalization; for example: P for "light brown skinned mixed-race" (race & ethnicity) and M for "baby boomer" (age) as an elder who has aged out of the new job market.

- **Individually journal** answers to one or more questions below:

Reflecting on your class, race, ethnicity, gender, ability, and age cultures:

1. Why is the diagram a turtle? Why is "class" culture the turtle's head?
2. How do each of your cultures relate to assimilation and segregation?
3. What is a bias you have from each cultural viewpoint? How do you express bias?
4. What are the consumption-versus-stewardship patterns of each of your cultures? How do these patterns impact Earth?
5. Which culture do you want to get to know better to develop your healthy multicultural identity so that you can actively collaborate for a sustainable world?

Whole group circle:

- **Discuss** journal answers, showing your turtle selves, and brainstorm ideas from this activity to apply to your subject or students.

Application

Diversity Statements

One way to use the Approach-in-Dimension to lessen fear about change is to write a heartfelt diversity statement personalized to your subjects. By committing to one of the six approaches (or devising your own), you delineate how to make cultural shifts in curriculum, outcomes, knowledge, communications, and interactions. For example, in one *Curriculum Transformation Diversity Statements* workshop, a White psychology instructor expresses unconscious allegiance to the mainstream. She discloses stress about making education change:

> I wasn't sure what to expect prior to watching the video and exploring the canvas course and this intimidated me and felt overwhelming to think about.... After watching the video, I have an especially clear understanding of the expectations and benefits of including a diversity statement. The video also helped me feel supported, encouraged and engaged. I was surprised that the introduction video in and of itself would create such a dynamic change in my ease and excitement.... It is pretty clear to me upon reflection and after reviewing my syllabus language that I currently employ a mainstream [approach].... After looking at the video and the reading assignment, I could have sworn my syllabus had at least hints of [diversity]. It totally doesn't, not even a little.[65]

After watching an Approach-in-Dimension video, this teacher was given permission to feel "ease and excitement." While she realized how her syllabus language had been unintentionally mainstream, with a sense of relief she was "encouraged and engaged" to apply academic freedom to her subject (Psychology). The diversity statement she ultimately wrote for her "Lifespan Human Development" course anchors changes to make in other education dimensions going forward:

> Welcome! We are in it together! Throughout the lifespan, both genetic and socio-cultural factors (such as race, ethnicity, poverty, policy, law, family environment) are aspects of human growth and development. This course is designed to help you gain critical skills using empirical science and theory as a lens to consider cross-cultural issues relative to human development. My hope is for you to become more actively engaged as community members and leaders with respect for humanity and our planet, so we help create a healthier, more sustainable future. We will use critical thinking, real-life issues and settings, and assumptions you might have, to explore how socio-cultural and cross-cultural settings impact developmental milestones along an individual's life-course and the lifespan. An understanding of diversity issues is crucial to all careers that intersect with human beings and is a first step toward social action.[66]

The Approach-in-Dimension offers touchpoints for everyday educators to redefine education with cross-cultural compassion to apply to routines. It navigates social anxieties that belie academic concentration, heels dug into mainstream bureaucracy with unprocessed emotions about culture conflicts in education. The tool shows how to adjust space, time, materials, and learning environments with the transparent humanization criteria we assert in the statements we write. Seeing the harm of dehumanizing systems in our own classrooms, labs, and meeting rooms motivates change. Matching a statement to one of the six philosophies in the Approach-in-Dimension helps educators gauge how deeply held cultural beliefs impact professional decisions.

From there, educators can choose action-research *with* students to integrate diverse ways of knowing and culturally responsive materials into curriculum and knowledge development. We can decide to welcome multiple languages into subject discussions and school–home communications. In segregated sites, we can experiment with race-class-gender *integrated* academic project circles. Reaching out to sister schools and community groups, we find creative ways to diversify academic socialization. We join hiring and retention committees to diversify staff. The Approach-in-Dimension equips educators of all demographics with culture, equity, and sustainability yardsticks to reform mainstream assimilation, inequity, and unsustainability procedures with liberation experiences.

As we apply transformative theory to practice, any welcome statement we write is a departure, to a lesser or greater extent, from Anglo-conformity. A Contributions statement celebrates diversity but does not take a stand against systemic racism, thereby preserving biases patterned by the stratified global extraction-consumption economy that destroys the environment. An Additive statement augments the Contributions list with civility norms and cultural awareness; however, without calling for collective action against systemic racism with structural changes for climate justice, it too preserves segregating bias and environmentally alienating outcomes. For profound change, statements conveying Transformative, Social Action, or Environmental Liberation Education approaches each assert holistic

Approach-in-Dimension ⇩	1. Mainstream No/little diversity, mindfulness, or sustainability.	2. Contributions Mainstream *plus* diversity, mindfulness, or sustainability positives lists in:	3. Additive Contributions *plus* civility norms with diversity, mindfulness, or sustainability comprehension in:	4. Transformative Intersectional diversity, mindfulness, or sustainability integration In:	5. Social Action Intersectional diversity, mindfulness, or sustainability empowerment with community healing experiences from:	6. Environmental Liberation Education Intersectional diversity, mindfulness, *and* sustainability empowerment with holistic healing experiences in:
Curriculum	• Required stock or no welcome statement. • Defaults to Anglo-conformity and unsustainability required curriculum procedures, mostly on site.	• Required stock or personalized welcome statement. • Survey of exceptional heroes, identities, innovations, or festivities as extra-curricular, mostly on site.	• Required stock or personalized welcome statement. • Survey plus respect as extra-curriculum, mostly on site.	• Personalized welcome statement. • Combines race-class gender ways of knowing into inclusion activities during revised required curriculum, mostly on site.	• Personalized welcome statement. • Justice liberation projects during required curriculum, on site and off.	• Personalized welcome statement. • Sustainability justice liberation projects indoors and outdoors, during required curriculum, on site and off.

[Diversity Welcome Statement]

FIGURE 7.4 Diversity Welcome Statement graphic. Created by the author.

antibias-antiracist humanization and sustainability subject methods. These statements express an inclusion vision of humanity that portrays diversity not as a problem but as a source of solutions to academic engagement.

Examples

How Does Your Philosophy of Education Impact Your Hourly and Daily Decisions?

The following examples illustrate how the Approach-in-Dimension guides hourly and daily decisions. They show that collaborating to diversify one dimension can diversify other dimensions as well. Participants transform present moment academics, reducing mainstream routines by increasing equity and sustainability experiences. These examples occur at Truckee Meadows Community College (TMCC), designated a Hispanic-Serving Institution (HSI), a form of a Minority-Serving Institution (MSI). MSIs are sites with a mission to serve ethnic minority students, often integrated with majority students during academics. MSIs aim to hire diversity-minded educators to collaborate on culturally relevant curriculum for diverse student success.[67] The examples below describe experiments in using the Approach-in-Dimension to lower barriers to equity and sustainability during education by increasing intersectional designs. The examples are an assignment rubric, a classroom inclusion poster project, and a collaborative mural.

Example #1 – Learning Outcome Rubric Redesign

This example is part of a Designated Committee Diversity Circle project. It shows changes to a required assignment rubric about Children's Literature made by an educator striving for Environmental Liberation Education.[68] The rubric redesign engages diverse students in mandatory course outcomes – to list and explain materials in a high-quality active-use classroom library – while developing culture competence, structural competence, and sustainability

274 Three Transformative Tools

Learning Outcome Rubric Redesign for Children's Literature Signature Assignment

Learning Outcome	Exceeds Expectations	Meets Expectations	Approaches Expectations	Does Not Meet Expectations
Explain children's literature classroom library categories: *Fiction* - prose, poetry, fantasy, modern fantasy, folklore, science fiction, realism, historical fiction, contemporary realistic fiction. *Nonfiction* – biography, informational, cultural ways of knowing.	The student identified and explained 12 categories. The student profiled 1 book in each category, including books about 6 cultures and 6 about ecology, authored by authentic cultural representatives and/or scientists. The student engaged and analyzed culturally relevant social action for environmental justice inspired by 1 or more nature books *outdoors*.	The student identified and explained 12 categories. The student profiled 1 book in each category, including books about 3 cultures and 3 about ecology, authored by authentic cultural representatives and/or scientists. The student engaged and analyzed culturally relevant social action for environmental justice inspired by 1 book *about* a nature.	The student identified and explained 12 categories. The student profiled 1 book in each category, including books about 3 cultures and 3 about ecology, authored by authentic cultural representatives and/or scientists. The student theorized about a culturally relevant environmental social action inspired by 1 book, but did not participate.	The student was unable to accurately identify and explain 12 categories. The student provided less than 12 book profiles with less than 3 books about cultures and 3 about ecology. Authors were not vetted. Explanation of culturally relevant social action about the environment is lacking.
Mainstream	Environmental Liberation Education	Environmental Liberation Education	Transformative	Fail

FIGURE 7.5 Learning Outcomes Rubric graphic. Created by the author.

skills. The reformulated rubric expects students to identify and describe a balance of library resources with a mix of literature categories and multiple cultures in two collection themes: diversity *and* ecology. The "exceeds" and "meets" expectations categories use Environmental Liberation Education, Social Action, and Transformative criteria. The "approaches expectations" is Additive. The "does not meet expectations" is Contributions. Using the Environmental Liberation Education approach to frame big picture questions about the subject, the educator rewrites a signature assignment rubric. The educator breaks from Anglo-conformity to use an antibias-antiracist *sustainability* philosophy of education for subject engagement that supports inclusive student success.[69]

Example #2 – Classroom Inclusion Welcome Statement and Poster

Welcome statements, introduced above, reside in the *curriculum* dimension, but they can be applied to other dimensions. One way to apply a welcome statement to the Communications dimension is to turn it into a classroom poster illustrated by students. The Contributions welcome statement lists cultural categories and examples to feature commonalities and minimize differences during academic engagement:

> This course is committed to providing equal opportunity, and access to learning, free of discrimination, to students from all walks of life. When you sit down to program a computer, it does not care about your sex, age, race, color, religion, physical or mental disability, creed, national origin, veteran status, sexual orientation, genetic information, gender identity, gender expression, or political affiliation. While I feel inclined to tell you socially

constructed cultures and identities don't matter to humans, I have to tell you that diversity does matter. I will do my best to use diverse examples and culturally relevant approaches to the exercises, quizzes, discussions, and lectures we engage. One thing I can guarantee is this: each person in this course is part of a community and just as welcome as the next. We are all responsible for treating each other with integrity as mature members of our community. Let's have a good time in this course and grow in our ability to make computer applications together![70]

A welcome poster based on the Contributions approach includes classroom norms. For example[71]:

- Be courteous and polite.
- Take care of our classroom.
- Be in class on time and have academic materials ready.
- Listen to teacher directions, lectures, and diversity examples.
- Pay attention to one another during discussions.
- Complete assignments so you're prepared.

Students might illustrate the poster with a familiar cultural hero who represents a regional demographic, such as Chavez, Dr. King, Yuji Ichioka, or Sitting Bull (Tatanka-Iyotanka, Lakota Sioux).

Additive Classroom

An Additive welcome statement is Contributions plus attention to resolving issues associated with diversity. It includes information about the importance of *everyone* feeling equally safe with one another's differences by recognizing that it takes effort to show mutual respect for *cross*-cultural understanding through civility norms:

> You are welcome here! TMCC values every race, ethnicity, nationality, family structure, LGBTQ/A+ status, ability, language, political affiliation, socioeconomic status and background, DACA/DAPA [Deferred Action for Childhood Arrivals/Deferred Action for Parental Accountability] status, belief and religion, body type, age, and more! Let's treat each other with kindness and respect so that we can all feel safe to learn, think, and grow![72]

The welcome poster provides culture respect norms[73]:

- Respect others' cultures, be polite, and treat each other with kindness.
- Take care of our classroom and cultural values.
- Be in class on time and have academic materials ready.
- Listen to teacher directions, lectures, and diversity examples.
- Pay attention to different cultural perspectives during discussions.
- Complete assignments so you're prepared to participate.

Students might illustrate with a school mascot to show school unity or a picture of children with different skin tones holding hands.

Transformative Classroom

A Transformative statement makes bold change. It invokes interdisciplinary scholarship to acknowledge oppression, resist systemic inequities, and advance culture competence with feminist standpoints, mindfulness, and/or sustainability within required subjects:

> This course strives to cultivate diversity, equity, and inclusion in all matters: theoretically, academically, and personally. Towards those efforts I will try to highlight the historical and present biases in the literature, underscoring its white supremacy and white privilege. I encourage diverse perspectives in the classroom, particularly marginalized standpoints that challenge the dominant culture and 'common sense' understandings. Please ask questions. Discuss with me any concerns you may have regarding your ability to participate in this class and whether they require accommodations for learning or health challenges. I hold extended office hours and generally am flexible in making myself available to all students, and particularly those on non-traditional paths.[74]

Poster norms transparently acknowledge systemic racism, sexism, and classism[75]:

- Respect cultures and be polite because systemic inequities cause social anxiety.
- Take care of our classroom diversity by reaching out to make cross-cultural connections.
- Be in class on time, have academic materials ready, and participate in cultural practices, stories, and diverse ways of knowing during subject engagement.
- Recognize featured culture(s) during directions, lectures, and diversity examples.
- Apply antibias-antiracist compassion to treat classroom materials respectfully and complete assignments, encouraging and listening to diverse perspectives during discussions and collaborative projects.

The poster graphic that students make might show several women of color, such as Dolores Huerta, a Chicana environmentalist and farmworker rights activist who secured voting rights and policing reform and was the 2012 winner of the US Presidential Medal of Freedom; Joy Haro of the Muscogee Creek Nation, first Indigenous woman to hold the position of U.S. Poet Laureate; Kalpana Chawla, Indian American Astronaut and Engineer, the first woman of Indian descent to go to space; or Barbara Jordan, African American Texas Congresswoman instrumental in the Richard Nixon impeachment hearings.

Social Action Classroom

A Social Action welcome statement is Transformative deepened by real-world justice *action*:

> No matter where you're from, your dreams are valid.
>
> *–Lupita Nyong'o*

Introduction to Women's Studies is meant to highlight the current gender, race, culture, and class issues in our society today and to consider what social action can be taken. In this class, all are valued; no matter the gender, race, culture, class, ability, and other diversities, all voices will be heard. By doing this we create an understanding that we are all in this together and that everyone has the power to defeat socially constructed stereotypes. If you are curious about accommodations based on a disability, please contact or visit the Disability Resource Center.[76]

Poster norms emphasize nonviolent community action[77]:

- Respect cultures, be polite, call out bias and racism because systemic inequities dehumanize, and take nonviolent social justice actions.
- Take care of our classroom and relate our diversities to local and global healing.
- Be in class on time, have academic materials ready, and respond to cultural practices, stories, evidence, and diverse ways of knowing to develop liberation experiences during subject engagement.
- Recognize featured culture(s) during instructions, explanations, and diversity examples.
- Apply antibias-antiracist compassion to treat classroom materials respectfully and complete assignments, encouraging and listening to diverse perspectives during circle discussions and projects connected to the world.

The student graphic here might show Dolores Huerta and César Chavez side by side, working with multiracial alliances during nonviolent social justice actions to reduce pesticides, develop organic farming, and establish habitable conditions and living wage insurance for farmworkers.

Environmental Liberation Education classroom

The Environmental Liberation Education statement is Social Action plus attention to human superdiversity in biodiversity to connect academic engagement to resource conservation, ecosystems restoration, and climate justice:

> We speak, we listen, we wonder, we move. Our knowledge is good. We've understood what it is for. We hear and we've seen what is great and small, under the sky and on the earth.
> *(Popol Vuh, circa 600 BCE)*

Welcome!
I teach to transform *with* you. The world benefits when you graduate as an antibias-antiracist global citizen for holism with subject expertise and critical thinking skills. Together we develop culture competence with stewardship practices. I have high expectations for your academic success and cross-cultural creativity. We grow during diversity collaborations, taking subjects outdoors and learning with nature indoors in academic circles. We connect mindfulness to regional communities and Earth. We resist systemic bias and over-standardized curriculum. We reduce, reuse, recycle, and restore with equity ecosystems. We ask joyful justice questions, listen for inclusion, and readily forgive miscommunications. We integrate body-mind-culture-environment, developing critical consciousness to connect subjects to sustainability.[78]

Poster norms feature environmental justice action[79]:

- Respect local and global cultures, be polite, call out injustices compassionately while recognizing that systemic inequities dehumanize and alienate everyone from Earth.
- Take care of our indoor-outdoor classroom, relating diversity to cultures and environment.
- Be in class on time, have academic materials ready, and participate in culture practices and story and evidence sharing with diverse ways of knowing in liberation circles during subject engagement.
- Participate in cultural and environmental sustainability mindfulness experiences with instructions, explanations, and diversity examples.
- Apply holistic antibias-antiracist materials to stewardship experiences.
- Complete assignments so you're prepared for academic projects with superdiversity in biodiversity questions to take justice action from a position of love.

The student graphic might show an illustration from the 2021 Caldecott-winning book *We are Water Protectors* by Carole Lindstrom (Ojibwe Turtle Mountain Band) and illustrated by Michaela Goade (Tlingit and Haida Indian Tribes of Alaska) that concludes with an "Earth Steward and Water Protector Pledge."[80]

Example #3 – Collaboration Mural

Described briefly in Chapter 6, this mural project started with a syllabus welcome statement written for the Environmental Liberation Education approach. This curriculum statement turned into a collaborative mural design during the Covid-19 pandemic for healing in communications and interactions education dimensions.

Participants from education, psychology, mathematics, counseling, veterinary science, and visual and performing arts, practicing physical distance, co-generated a chalk mural entitled "Brave New World," in the shape of Earth, with more than 70 diverse students, faculty, staff, and children in October 2020. Upon completion, two physically distanced dances were performed by diverse students around the 50-foot-diameter circular mural. Two student lead muralists – one a White female Visual Arts major and the other a deaf Latina in an English as a Second Language program in Adult Basic Education – collaborated to design the mural, while others filled in individual 5-by-5-foot grids. In all, the mural involved intergenerational, multiracial, varied class, and gender-balanced peoples.[81]

Brave New World

The Brave New World mural was organized through Faculty for Radical Enlightenment and Empowerment (FREE), a Laboratory Diversity Circle that uses the established academic schedule to facilitate imaginative sensory events with diverse students across the curriculum. For example, all classes that meet at 9:30 a.m. on Tuesdays walk out of respective classrooms for a few minutes or more to engage in activities about a shared theme. FREE un-standardizes and detracks bureaucracy by integrating otherwise divided curriculum with academic inclusion experiences.[82]

During the Covid-19 pandemic, the FREE Laboratory adjusted to public health mandates. The outdoor Brave New World mural enlisted diverse students to come to campus one by one to break the detachment of online course attendance. Students came to the mural site during a scheduled one-hour time slot over a week. The dance students performed together outdoors after the mural was completed during their scheduled class meeting. FREE announced the mural as follows:

> We welcome students and faculty to participate in our Fall 2020 physically distanced event: "A Brave New World," a collaborative chalk mural on the Dandini Plaza.... Students and faculty/staff will – in their own designated grid square – relay one-at-a-time to chalk-illustrate an interpretation of our Brave New World, and how it relates to their Fall 2020 coursework.
>
> The project will divide the Plaza into grid squares. Participating students and staff will fill one grid for one hour according to a physically distanced schedule during October 12–17. Join us for this FREE event that involves TMCC's diverse students, faculty, and staff in a collaborative project, that will be accompanied by dance interpretation as performed by TMCC dance students. Join us and help to bring a sense of belongingness and humanization despite the global crisis.[83]

Among the challenges to translating a welcome statement from the curriculum dimension to the communications and interactions dimensions was figuring out how to facilitate *diverse* participation. This was solved by reaching out to Adult Basic Education, the campus childcare center, and the Diversity and International Student Center Office. Further, the Rangoli artwork initiated by a math professor was replicated throughout the mural to show respect for the rice powder sidewalk artwork practice in East India that processes cultural transitions through visuals about faith during suffering.[84]

Diverse participants posed antibias questions about the world during a global pandemic and then answered those questions with social-emotional outdoor artwork linked to academics. Preschoolers from the Childcare Center posed questions about the mural and illustrated

FIGURE 7.6 Hand mural art by Jenny Krupka and a teacher credential student. Photos created by the Jenny Krupka and the author.

their perspectives about the pandemic. Counseling staff illustrated mental health, grappling with questions about systemic racism in health care. Veterinary Technical students depicted the value of pets in mental health during the pandemic. One illustration from staff in Information Technology displayed a yearning hand pointing to Earth from celestial skies. Math students drew a parabolic bridge about the symmetry of hope mirroring despair. Education students participated in the mural as an extension of an assignment to write, illustrate, and hand-bind children's books, transferring book illustrations to the chalk grids. The Brave New World mural is an example of how writing a welcome statement for change in the curriculum dimension guided by the Environmental Liberation Education approach can lead to corresponding academic changes in other education dimensions.

Conclusion

"The Way Out Is In"

Education transformation involves outward action from inward reflection. Liberation educators take economic and social justice action from personal and cultural reflection. As Ibram X. Kendi puts it in *How to Be an Antiracist*, systemic change entails a "reorientation of our consciousness."[85] We collaborate to apply critical consciousness to diversity to develop humanization and equity for unity systems. In this era of mass migration and global warming, we use the wide lens of superdiversity in biodiversity to reimagine space, time, materials, and learning environments holistically. Our big picture redefines cultural freedom and happiness. In *Happy Teachers Change the World*, Thich Nhat Hanh and Katherine Weare explain:

> Within the school, first you have your class and you transform your class. Your class becomes a happier place. Your class can become like a family. Finally, with our families, our colleagues, our students, and the whole school behind us, we are stronger. Together we can take the next step and help still more people. The transformation begins to affect even the families of our students and our colleagues, and the ripples spread far and wide. But we always remember, the principle is this: the way out is in.[86]

The Approach-in-Dimension is pragmatic. It provides design and evaluation guideposts to spread liberation ripples far and wide. Everyday educators help reorient consciousness by planning and assessing multicultural, mindfulness, and sustainability activities hourly and daily. The Approach-in-Dimension outlines criteria from six philosophical approaches for educators to make decisions in five education dimensions. When transformative teachers choose Environmental Liberation Education, we engage creative tension from change. This means resolving ongoing conflicts with peace precepts as we team to restructure requirements. We adapt to an unfolding arch of improvement in local and global contexts. By integrating subjects *with* diverse students through multicultural circle activities and intergenerational hands-on nature projects, indoors and outdoors, on site and off, we steward the forest through the trees.

Humanization Goals Motivate Education

Teachers are hardworking, and on top of that, we negotiate political and technological distractions within an over-standardized and punitive bureaucracy.[87] Most of us don't notice how our "best intentions" don't result in inclusive or sustainable outcomes.[88] We're unaware that our own classrooms, labs, and meeting rooms perpetuate the racial achievement gap, lower-order cognition, teacher disenfranchisement, and ecologically unsound routines. Unintentionally, our moment by moment decisions obstruct what little multicultural and sustainability education we manage to introduce. Intergenerational cycles produce economic-social divides and the environmental alienation that dehumanizes us all. The distance between our education system and an equitable and sustainable economy precludes the humanization goals that motivate academic engagement.

Yet teachers Yet teachers teachers are *people* people.[89] The Approach-in-Dimension helps to steer teacher decisions toward culturally responsive humanization activities for a livable world. When teachers discover that Mainstream, Contributions, and Additive approaches aren't inclusive or sustainable, we turn to Transformative, Social Action, and Environmental Liberation Education. We ask thematic questions and use compassionate prompt-and-response sequences to redefine subjects *with* living cultures. We change curriculum, outcomes, knowledge, communications, and interactions toward cultural freedom that learns from history, one activity at a time.

The primary determinant of academic achievement is socio-economic status. Our current socio-economic system is stratified. Macro structures and forces are hard to change. However, highly qualified teachers *are* the most important *school* factor to student success.[90] The micro context of the routines that good teachers operate positively influences student behaviors and knowledge development, opening doors to subject proficiency, critical thinking, and humanization. Good teachers who apply culture competence and structural competence are *transformative* teachers who act locally and think globally. Transformative teachers apply personal passion and professional authority to reduce cultural barriers in education. The underlying function of the Approach-in-Dimension is to support academic freedom with big-picture mindfulness. This wide lens helps good teachers translate theory to action for intergenerational inclusion, cultural expression, and diversity belonging in equity and ecology activities.

What's Deep Diversity?

In "The White Man's Burden, Revisited," Gerald Porter describes humanization practices for "educational freedom." Freedom comes from "deep diversity that challenges modern objectivism by recognizing that knowledge is merely a description or a representation of experience."

> Deep diversity assumes that the subject is commingled with the object, that what we can know is our experience of an essentially mysterious reality. Experience should not be confused with the reality it represents but is merely the portion of reality we allow ourselves to consciously acknowledge. Reality is full of an indeterminate number of possibilities that we reduce to what our culture has taught us to believe is possible.[91]

The Environmental Liberation Education approach strives for deep diversity, and the Approach-in-Dimension is a deep diversity rubric. A culturally expansive paradigm, deep diversity is for people on a planet in need of healing. This paradigm assists people navigating superdiversity and biodiversity intersections with "transnational population flows" during "globalization and mass migration" in an epoch of climate change.[92]

Environmental Liberation Education engages participants to consider how immigrant groups layer onto existing "segmented assimilation" patterns. Immigrant groups have been pitted against "native minorities" in worldwide racial systems that segregate and oppress, the recognition of which provides an opportunity to unite and liberate.[93]

> Deep diversity goes beyond tolerance or even concepts of mutual coexistence or interdependency. Deep diversity implies that differences between people and their ideas are indicative of a level of organization that is more fundamental than the comparatively superficial structures imposed by conventional thinking about racial/ethnic, cultural, or ideological differences.[94]

Opening Possibilities

The Approach-in-Dimension breaks us out of conventional thinking. It helps educators apply Multicultural Mindfulness, developed through social-emotional Diversity Circle bonds, to collectivize freedom by reimagining "what our culture has taught us to believe is possible." We shift from "tolerance [of] coexistence" to reconceptualization. We liberate from overstandardization through multicultural creativity from deep diversity.[95] Transformative educators recognize how assimilation obstructs diverse cultural ways of knowing. We correct dehumanization in US education, described poignantly by Luther Standing Bear, Sicangu and Oglala Lakota, who was a student in the Carlisle Indian Industrial School:

> [He] recounts numerous occasions on which the Carlisle Indian Industrial School students were displayed as docile and educable Indians. The Carlisle band played at the opening of the Brooklyn Bridge in 1883 and then toured several churches. Students were carted around East Coast cities. Standing Bear himself was placed on display in Wanamaker's Philadelphia department store, locked in a glass cell in the center of the store and set to sorting and pricing jewelry.[96]

Luther Standing Bear was in the first graduating class of the Carlisle Indian Industrial School, a boarding institution modeled after Fort Marion prison by Captain Richard Henry Pratt. Pratt administered the internment of captive Cheyenne and other Plains Indians in the late-1800s. Luther Standing Bear broke through the inhumanity he experienced in the US education system to become a transformative professional, taking restorative actions for living Lakota sovereignty. He worked to change unsustainable US assimilation/segregation policies into practices for an active "community of interbeing."[97]

How Do We Move from One Approach to the Next?

Like Luther Standing Bear, Environmental Liberation Education teachers integrate healthy multicultural identities into justice action from a position of love. Using clear-eyed Approach-in-Dimension markers, we move from one approach to the next with Multicultural Mindfulness to ease fear of change. Diversity Circles organize us to address culture conflicts with non-defensive protocols for holism designs and equity assessments. We nurture a philosophy of humanity that welcomes themes, problems, and disciplinary concepts from several points of view. One social sciences educator describes social justice community-building routines: "I maintain a sense of authority…not by hiding behind the illusive cloud of objectivity that is sometimes advocated particularly in political science courses. I reveal my work in the community as it substantiates what I teach."[98] A language arts educator weaves in alternative funds of knowledge:

Short of securing a foundation in literary criticism that includes the traditionally marginal literatures, we challenge our fundamental assumptions about the nature of creative expression. Transforming the curriculum to reflect the lives and works of women of color implies the primary objective of securing greater understanding and appreciation, but it also implies the critical step of exploring cultural traditions. Orality, the literary tradition of Native Americans and African Americans, is a window through which to view tradition.[99]

We phase out Anglo-conformist education by developing subjects with diverse perspectives. We balance mainstream curriculum and knowledge with historically marginalized standpoints, such as the construct of women of color, and by identifying individuals and groups who resist dominant cultural practices and systems. We facilitate academic engagement by defining how people live, survive, and thrive when they are not part of the dominant culture. Welcoming diverse ways of knowing accelerates change from disciplinary homogeneity and exclusions to interdisciplinary holism. Approach-in-Dimension criteria offer footholds in classrooms, labs, and meeting rooms to connect subjects to "powerful 'action' antidotes" for healing.[100] Teachers and students move from ego suffering to active engagement through empathy and joy during liberation action.

> Research on evolutionary psychology is suggesting that the human race [is] fundamentally prone to some slants of mind such as a "negativity bias" that cause us to tend toward rumination, pessimism, worry, anger, over-planning, and hypervigilance. These tendencies may have once kept us safe as a prey species surviving in dangerous environments, and allowed the gloomiest and most aggressive among us to pass on our genes, but they no longer serve us well in helping us to get along together or meet the modern challenges of a pressurized and hyper-connected age. If we are to live a happy and compassionate life, we need to take positive action.[101]

What are we Liberating from?

The Three Transformative Tools facilitate two healing steps: action and reflection. In communities of practice, educators link academics to regional and global cultures. We liberate from "socially constructed stereotypes" so "all voices will be heard." We "consider what social action can be taken" and flex "the power to defeat" systemic bias. We liberate from colorblind individualism set in systemic racism, inviting students to "create an understanding that we are all in this together." A social sciences educator explains liberation as social justice on the spot:

> I bring guest speakers into my class that I actually know very well because of our shared efforts to address social justice issues, and I create a space for students to reveal their vision of themselves as change agents in society.[102]

Teachers liberate to *engage* diversity through mixed race, class, and gender interactions. A liberation educator explains:

> To be eligible for the Search for Education, Elevation, and Knowledge (SEEK) Program, a student must have a high school average of 79 percent or below, must come from a low-income family, and must have attended school in an 'educationally disadvantaged' neighborhood.... My students are, for the most part, in their late teens and early twenties.

Approximately 80 percent are women. There is presently an Asian majority made up of young people from Hong Kong, The People's Republic of China, South Korea, Vietnam, and Cambodia; approximately one fourth are Haitian; and about 20 percent are Latina.[103]

This educator facilitates diversity-responsive "materials and methodology" that are "carefully selected to match the ability levels and interests of students." She describes academic freedom to insert the "medium of content that has intrinsic value to my students' lives." She gathers evidence from cultural surveys and adapts curriculum and routines to reflect demographic shifts over time, supporting students to replace the victimization mindset with culturally relevant growth mindsets.[104] She observes that her typical student

> (1) rarely uses English as a medium of communication outside of the classroom; (2) is employed, working an average of twenty hours per week; (3) travels long distances to come to school. When we add to this picture the fact that many of our students struggle with problems of ill health and domestic difficulties, it is understandable that they tend to be prone to stress, depression, and fatigue.[105]

Therefore, this educator's "primary goal" is to co-generate empowerment by developing healthy multicultural identities *and* practical English language skills.[106] Thus, we liberate from dehumanization in systemic oppression by finding balance. We use holistic humanization activities to meet individual needs within the existing system as we engage cultural action to change the system.[107]

Transformative teachers ask deep diversity questions. Working through anxiety about uncertainty in a globalized world, we activate joyful justice academic projects toward multicultural unity. We plan and evaluate diversity and sustainability activities in five education dimensions. We make adjustments to projects by resisting territoriality to redistribute resources inclusively. We reinterpret subjects non-defensively with restorative justice and arts and sciences integrations. We develop curriculum and knowledge by comparing philosophical intentions to cultural data collection and analysis. We use the Approach-in-Dimension, or other educational philosophy rubrics, to guide hourly and daily decisions for holism. We tailor our philosophy of education to professional passion and diversity reflection, aware of how site cultures are represented in, or excluded from, subjects, disciplines, fields of study, and school-career pathways. *We* design and assess *with* students and colleagues in real time, using the diversity, mindfulness, and environmental criteria *we* value. We continually check academic outcomes for equity and inclusion, refreshing the humanization activities that motivate education with subject engagement connected to Earth.

TRANSFORMATIVE BREATHWORK AND JOURNAL

Journal Question: *What's the Approach-in-Dimension?*

> [Mindfulness is] ongoing awareness.... If things become heavy and solid, you flash mindfulness and awareness into them. Your attitude is that the phenomenal world is not evil, that "they" are not going to attack you or destroy you or kill you. Everything is workable and soothing.[108]
>
> —Chögyam Trungpa Rinpoche

Breathwork

Wherever you are, take a mindful moment to relax. Use a timer chime if you like. Close or lid your eyes, taking several slow deep breaths, smiling slightly, noticing sensations: smells, sounds, touch, taste, and sight (if your eyes are open).

Now breathe while internally reciting the *gatha* below:

Breathing in, I calm my body.
Breathing out, I smile.
Dwelling in the present moment,
I know this is a reflection moment.[109]

Then:

Breathing in **What's the Approach-in-Dimension?**
Breathing out openness.
Repeat for as long as you like or until the timer chimes.

Journal

Imagine we're in a Diversity Circle with the transformative practitioners cited in this book. We want to support superdiverse student success in a biodiverse world. Read our answers below. Reflect on your meditation. Briefly answer the journal question above in a way that's meaningful to you.

James A. Banks

Approaches and dimensions:

- Four *approaches* to multicultural education ("contributions," "additive," "transformative," and "social action").[110]
- Five *dimensions* to multicultural education ("content integration," "the knowledge construction process," "prejudice reduction," "an equity pedagogy," and "an empowering school culture and social structure").[111]

Thich Nhat Hanh

Two approaches to education:

1. "Without [mindfulness] teachers can make students suffer and students can make teachers suffer, and the gap widens between the two generations with . . . a sort of loneliness."
2. "Administrators may be attracted to mindfulness because they think it will improve academic performance and prevent teachers burning out. But the practice of mindfulness can be much more. The practice of right mindfulness can help both teachers and students suffer less; they will be able to improve communication and create a learning environment that is more compassionate and understanding. Students can learn very important things, such as how to handle strong emotions, how to take care of anger, how to relax and release tension, how to restore communication and reconcile with others."[112]

Micaela Rubalcava
Approach-in-Dimension:

- Big-picture planning and assessment rubric to clarify a philosophy of humanity and change assimilation and segregation education, adaptable to professional passion, subject requirements, and site cultures.
- Six *approaches*: Mainstream, Contributions, Additive, Transformative, Social Action, and Environmental Liberation Education.
- Five *dimensions*: curriculum, outcomes, knowledge, communications, and interactions.
- The *design* and *evaluation* tool for integrated and holistic Environmental Liberation Education with diversity, equity, inclusion, and sustainability criteria.

Notes

1. Banks (1988, 1993).
2. Goldberg and Houser (2017, July 19).
3. Freire (1985); Reece (2022).
4. Banks (all); Clark (all); Bigelow and Swinehart (2014); Gang (1991).
5. Hanh (all); Rechtschaffen (2016); Trungpa (1993).
6. Adapted from Banks (1988, 1993).
7. Lewis and Diamond (2015), 177; Sleeter and Carmona (2017).
8. Banks (1988, 1993).
9. Maslow (1943).
10. Louisiana (2010), 1; Teaching (2015); Doll, Brehm and Zucker (2014).
11. Dweck (2007).
12. Hanh and Weare (2017), 316–318; Young, Bryan, Jacobs and Tunnell (2020), 153.
13. Reece (2022), 98.
14. Lewis and Diamond (2015).
15. Reece (2022), 107.
16. Ingersoll (2015); Deruy (2017).
17. hooks (1994), 36.
18. Brown (2018).
19. DiAngelo (2018), 54.
20. King (1964), 84, 89, 84.
21. DiAngelo (all).
22. DiAngelo (all).
23. Petchauer and Mawhinney (2017); Rubalcava (2001–2024).
24. Lynch (1983); Sleeter (2001).
25. Sleeter and Zavala (2020).
26. Reece (2022), 96.
27. Darling-Hammond (2006).
28. Rubalcava (2001–2024).
29. Ingersoll (2015); Deruy (2017).
30. Madison (all).
31. Ogay and Edelmann (2016), 393.
32. Keltner (2023), 111.
33. Banks (1988).
34. Banks (1988).
35. Dunbar-Ortiz (2014); Reese (2022, February 9–April 12).
36. Reese (2022, February 9–April 12).
37. Rubalcava (2001–2024).
38. Banks (1988).
39. Rubalcava (2001–2024).

40 Rubalcava (2001–2024).
41 Banks (1988).
42 Fiol-Matta (1994a), 7.
43 Giroux (1983).
44 Fiol-Matta (1994b), 143.
45 Rubalcava (2001–2024).
46 Banks (1988).
47 Freire (1985).
48 Rubalcava (2001–2024).
49 Rubalcava (2001–2024).
50 Rubalcava (2001–2024).
51 Rubalcava (2001–2024).
52 Clark (all); Bigelow and Swinehart (2014); Gang (1991).
53 Fiol-Matta and Chamberlain (1994), xi.
54 Ries (1994), 38.
55 Urtubey (2023, June 20).
56 Banks (1993), 5–7.
57 Bloom (1974); Clark (all); Gardner (1983).
58 National Geographic (2019).
59 Valdés (2016), 79.
60 Robertson (2021).
61 Kimmerer (2013).
62 DiAngelo (all); McIntosh (1989, July/August).
63 Du Bois (1909); Kendi (2019); Paris and Alim (2017).
64 hooks (1994).
65 Reynolds, P. (2021a).
66 Reynolds, P. (2021a).
67 Blake (2018, March); Espinoza, Turk and Taylor (2017); Kim (2022, April 6); Li and Carroll (2007); Petchauer and Mawhinney (2017); Gasman, Samayoa and Ginsberg (2016); Savage (2017, September 6); Rubalcava (2001–2024).
68 Young, Bryan, Jacobs and Tunnell (2020), 93.
69 Rubalcava (2001–2024).
70 Reynolds, T. (2021b).
71 Wong and Wong (1998), 145–146.
72 Rubalcava (2001–2024 [2018]).
73 Wong and Wong (1998), 145–146.
74 Mascarenhas (2020).
75 Wong and Wong (1998), 145–146.
76 Rubalcava (2020).
77 Wong and Wong (1998), 145–146.
78 Rubalcava (2001–2024).
79 Wong and Wong (1998), 145–146.
80 Lindstrom (2020).
81 Rubalcava (2001–2024 [2020]); Truckee (2018).
82 Rubalcava (2001–2024 [2020]); Truckee (2018).
83 Eckland (2020, October 19).
84 Rubalcava (2001–2024 [2020]); Truckee (2018).
85 Kendi (2019), 23.
86 Hanh and Weare (2017), 287.
87 Reece (2022).
88 Lewis and Diamond (2015), title.
89 Rubalcava (2005).
90 Bethell, Newacheck, Hawes and Halfon (2014); Darling-Hammond (2006); Noguera (2017, 2018); Oakes and Lipton (2007); Sleeter (2001); Sleeter and Carmona (2017); Terada (2019, February 4).
91 Porter (1995), 177.
92 Valdés (2016), 79.
93 Suárez-Orozco and Michikyan (2016), 15.

94 Porter (1995), 178–179.
95 Porter (1995), 178–179.
96 Dunbar-Ortiz (2014), 157.
97 Hanh and Weare (2017), xxiv.
98 Angelo, Nilson and Winkelmes (2018).
99 Clair (1994), 251–252.
100 King (1964), 89.
101 Hanh and Weare (2017), xxxvi–xxxvii.
102 Jett (2018).
103 Manley (1994), 259–260.
104 Dweck (2007).
105 Dweck (2007).
106 Dweck (2007).
107 Banks (1988).
108 Trungpa (1993), 43.
109 Hanh (2008), 36.
110 Banks (1988).
111 Banks (1993), 5–7.
112 Hanh and Weare (2017), xxii-xxvii.

PART III
Multicultural Mindfulness for a Sustainable World

8
ENVIRONMENTAL LIBERATION EDUCATION

Guiding Purpose

Explain how Environmental Liberation Education is holistic action-reflection to

- Reduce bias, assimilation, segregation, and environmental destruction in education by integrating multicultural, mindfulness, and sustainability into academic activities.
- Empower educators and students by engaging core content with critical consciousness circles indoors and outdoors, on site and off, through big picture themes.
- Motivate subject engagement with local and global systems questions, cultural practices and stories, and scientific data through problem-solving projects.
- Apply Three Transformative Tools to structure, process, and assess academic engagement for inclusive humanization in a superdiverse-biodiverse world.

Provide

- Fresh examples showing the ease and joy of Environmental Liberation Education.
- Two Multicultural Mindfulness Activities and one journal question: *Nonverbal Communication Toothpick Game, Environmental Liberation Education Made Easy,* and *What's Environmental Liberation Education?*

Here's How I Explain it to My Students

It's the middle of a semester. My students and I discuss the field experience requirement in what we fondly call our circle of love. A female European American student, Ashlyn, raises a frequently asked question: How is it possible to do anything more than the basics in our stressed classrooms? She describes a fourth-grade classroom where she observes her hardworking mentor teacher struggling to get diverse students through state standards while trying to feel safe at school. The fourth graders are tasked with hitting test scores measured from an assimilation paradigm set in a segregated district. Nevada consistently finds itself at the bottom of the nation in K-12 education according to standardized curriculum results.[1] It's commonly believed that Nevada's teachers don't have the luxury for anything as optional or politically charged as multicultural education, let alone Environmental Liberation Education.

Super-Stressed

Working teachers tell my students they have no choice but to teach prescribed units in district-formatted lessons sequenced vertically. If any teacher gets out of line with core content progression, the school's trajectory is negatively impacted. Ashlyn reports that her mentor confessed to feeling "super-stressed" about completing district requirements while trying to mix in Social Emotional Learning (SEL). Ashlyn observes how her mentor gets through about half of the stipulated curriculum each week. "All she has time for is the basics, Dr. Rube."

Nevada teachers are told to teach reading, writing, and STEM (science, technology, engineering, and mathematics) standards geared to "English-oriented cultural patterns" and to meet industry demands in the state economy.[2] My education students ask valid questions: Don't we have to *choose* between state mandates and multicultural education since there isn't room for both? How is it possible to find room in jam-packed days – filled with paperwork, drills, and high-stakes bureaucracy – to activate *nine* multiple intelligences?[3] Isn't it too much to apply SEL *and* Culturally Relevant Education (CRE)?[4] Is it advisable to engage hot-button concepts – race, class, gender, identity, equity, climate change – with children? Does mindfulness breathwork really help with academics? On top of it all, how do we find time for Diversity Circles?

Spacetime Superpower: Diversity as a **Solution**

I answer these questions by explaining that Environmental Liberation Education empowers and integrates students and teachers. It's efficient because spacetime is our *superpower*. Teachers have the professional authority to work *with* diversity during academic engagement. Collaborating for unity in diversity doesn't create problems, it solves them. The real problem is that many educators don't deploy our collective superpower.

Instead, many educators operate in silos behind colorblind wishes. We fretfully try to marshal segregated students toward the assimilation standards we feel obliged to deliver in tiered sites. We convey prepackaged curriculum bundles, forgetting about our academic freedom to artfully design classroom space, time, materials, and learning environments into culturally responsive circles. We don't realize the connection between inclusive social-emotional health and holistic academic concentration.

Many credential programs don't train for antibias culture consciousness to calm social anxiety. Our programs don't fortify education students with cultural integration experiences in field placements. Education courses don't feature best practices to un-standardize, de-track, and diversify curriculum to professionalize future teachers with culture competence. Core standards in teacher education don't bridge environmental and mindfulness education to uplift knowledge with holistic humanization. Our training doesn't model multicultural-multiracial alliances. Coursework does not teach how to counteract cultural disaffection and divisions in education. Prospective teachers don't learn how to use non-defensive reconciliation practices for collaborations to advocate for better pay and academic freedom.

In part, because of this, our spacetime superpower lies dormant. But it's there inside the Diversity Circles available to us now. The Diversity Circles we cocreate awaken a transformative nucleus. In them, we collaborate on diversity through action-reflection to *de-stress* education with cultural creativity. This is the inward-outward peace process of Multicultural Mindfulness. Applying academic freedom unleashes teaching passion. Using big picture guides, such as the Approach-in-Dimension, the transformative teacher continually tailors a heartfelt philosophy of education to subjects and changing cultures, thereby engaging requirements holistically.

Our superpower is collectivizing to *enact* prosocial designs for subject engagement, such as implementing culturally responsive space, inclusive timing sequences, and diversity materials in high-expectations multimodal learning environments. We collect data points about our designs to assess equity in learning behaviors, such as prompt-and-response sequences or time-on-task. We use data feedback to improve designs with sustainability knowledge and skills. We analyze results to make culture-conscious decisions about the humanization goals that motivate teacher passion and student concentration.

Activating our teacher superpower is like saying no to getting drive-thru fast food alone in a car and saying yes to a lively home-cooked potluck with neighbors. While it seems easier to grab quick-order processed meals, it's actually healthier, tastier, and surprisingly more cost-effective and pleasurable to cook and share balanced meals with others. Healthful natural foods cooking and culture building *save net time* by avoiding long-term body-mind-soul medical problems from chemically processed foods, social alienation, and the destructive environmental footprint of industrialized foods.

The same is true in our classrooms. When we collaborate to engage subjects with body-mind-culture-environment holism activities, we set the stage for academic inclusion. We *relieve* test anxiety and defensive social stress as we *increase* hands-on activities to experience unity in nature. We develop the "broad networks of neurochemicals (dopamine, oxytocin) and the regions of the body (the vagus nerve)…for deep learning about the systems of life."[5]

We empower each other by embracing diversity with backwards design. When we approach requirements with culturally responsive questions, we shift from teachers doing the work of over-standardized education, to *students* doing the work of *integrative learning*. We reduce banking education that mirrors "oppressive society as a whole," in which, as Paulo Freire explains:

> (a) the teacher teaches and the students are taught; (b) the teacher knows everything and the students know nothing; (c) the teacher thinks and the students are thought about; (d) the teacher talks and the students listen – meekly; (e) the teacher disciplines and the students are disciplined; (f) the teacher chooses and enforces his choice, and the students comply."[6]

Instead, we interrupt the systemic inequities that weaken education with our teacher spacetime superpower. We facilitate real-world healing experiences with mixed-ability multicultural project teams. We bring diverse community supports and plants and animals into our projects. We do outdoor education when we can. We support student-led subject activities, such as nonviolent social justice teach-ins and Content Creation.

Global Inspiration

This is when I might bring up Finland. There *are* other places in the world with better education systems. Teachers in Finland instruct about 600 hours annually, whereas US teachers average 1,080. Finnish teachers use the extra hours in the school day for humanizing activities to detrack and "un-standardize."[7] National curriculum guides in Finland are slim, and students don't take standardized tests for advancement until getting into college. Teachers don't have to teach to the test. Instead, they spend time applying academic freedom to support students to make academic choices and engage differentiated curriculum. These best practices get results: Finland's students attain the world's top measures for academic achievement *and* equity. And, in full circle, teachers in Finland *love* their work, competing for limited spots in highly coveted teacher education programs that are tuition-free.[8]

The competition to become a teacher is so robust in Finland that it's easier to become a doctor or a lawyer than a teacher. Prospective teachers must complete master's degrees to earn credentials, entering employment highly prepared with subject expertise and collaboration skills. Pursuing humanization goals *with* students, Finnish teachers model cooperation through professional development, displaying how to alleviate academic anxiety with social-emotional academic learning. Finnish teachers don't have to scramble to comply with successive top-down orders. They have the liberty to nurture inclusion by synthesizing subjects into adaptive modalities that integrate student diversities into holistic education.[9]

I acknowledge that the US is no Finland. Our education system absorbs teachers into over-standardization and prefabricated mandates about what's deemed to be measurable. We are preoccupied with unreasonable teaching loads, loads of paperwork, siloed departments or grade levels, and relatively low pay. We've got globally unparalleled gun violence from a military-industrial complex that weaponizes society and schools. Our campuses have been segregated for centuries. It's true that US education is a hard nut to crack, culturally, racially, economically, and historically. In comparison, Finland doesn't have the racial diversity the US has, and it's a small country without a "colonialism settler-state" history.[10] Moreover, Finland's people aren't burdened with the cyclical history of an economy founded on plantation capitalism of racialized land-grabbing and slave and cheap labor.

But because the US and Finland are different doesn't mean that US teachers can't activate universal best practices now. US teachers *can* access our spacetime superpower that's available everywhere. We *can* collaborate for systemic change through education. We can collectively transform our institution's spacetime with inclusion experiences. Available to any US educator of any culture, subject, or level is an asset that's unparalleled in many parts of the world: The US has a system-wide multicultural-multiracial student body, which is the priceless asset of "deep diversity" in a changing world.[11]

Biodiversity and Superdiversity

I describe how biodiversity is a core concept in Environmental Liberation Education, encapsulating an ecological mindset that helps teachers reframe how we think about diversity. Biodiversity is "the variety of living species on Earth," and it expands the humanization goals that motivate our profession. Transformative teachers ask: How are humans, animals, insects, plants, bacteria, and fungi connected? How is the survival of each species dependent on the survival of other species? What are the "many species ... being threatened with extinction due to human activities...[putting] Earth's biodiversity at risk?"[12] Connecting humanity to biodiversity encourages teachers to reinterpret subjects. We shift away from the systemic divides that fracture and destroy, and we move toward academics for antibias-antiracist unity and sustainability.

We connect subjects to Earth by integrating arts and sciences *with* diverse ways of knowing. For example, we observe culturally responsive stewardship experiences, such as prescribed forest fires and ways to support medicinal plant life cycles. These deep diversity practices, demonstrated by various Indigenous communities for millennia, show how to protect Earth.[13] We care for biodiversity by integrating cultural practices into ecological activities during academic routines. We view Earth's biodiversity as both superseding and merging with human superdiversity.

> In nature, diversity can be observed both across and within species. This may superficially appear as unnecessary multiplicity, but upon closer examination, biologists have demonstrated that the enormous diversity of behavioral and morphological characteristics within a species provides it with a greater chance of surviving unanticipated environmental threats.[14]

We engage Environmental Liberation Education to transform substructure-superstructure inequities with equity ecosystems by learning *through* diversity for global resilience.

Global Citizenship

Environmental Liberation Education reduces banking education's dualities by acknowledging how global superdiversity impacts biodiversity complexly in regional lands now called the United States of America.

> The United States has more immigrants than any other country in the world. Today, more than 40 million people living in the US were born in another country, accounting for about one-fifth of the world's migrants. The population of immigrants is also very diverse, with just about every country in the world represented among US immigrants.[15]

US student demographics include a high percentage of the internationally born, along with historical diversity, including multiplicity among African Americans, Latinx, Asian and Pacific Americans, and Native Americans, the last of whom have practiced diverse ways of knowing to steward sun, land, sky, and water for thousands of years.[16] *Transformative* teachers develop culture competence with structural competence to engage subjects for global citizenship.

We teach how to responsibly use technology in an era of cyber ascendency, demographic flux, and culture conflict from displacement due to environmental crises and scarcities. We teach how to reduce consumption and redistribute resources to offset widening inequities. We do this work *humanely* because we recognize the irony of injustice and destruction that come from technological fixes themselves. Some technologies are so polluting, rapid-fire, and robotic that they alienate from the holistic relationships on the ground needed to heal *human-caused* problems.[17] Transformative teachers, thus, prepare students to be "multi-competent individuals."

We weave subjects into local and global proficiencies: "translanguaging," public health practices, and multicultural sustainability action.[18] We counteract nationalistic disciplinary assumptions. For instance, mainstream social science educators often start US history with 13 "colonies" in the 1600s, thereby defining citizenship within the Eurocentric conquest paradigm. However, when transformative teachers start US history with "land" four million years ago, and the cultivation of "corn" by diverse Indigenous women in the region approximately 12,000 years ago, citizenship opens to feminist perspectives, regional languages, and stewardship cultures for ecological thriving.[19] With simple changes like a date adjustment, transformative teachers facilitate academics for cross-cultural inclusion.[20] We see that teachers of all backgrounds and career stages have the capacity to make changes to reduce dehumanization. By reinterpreting subjects through systems analysis, we relate students to each other in diversity, thereby facilitating joyful justice activities during routines from a position of love.

Transformative Teaching Now

I invite education students to *be* transformative teachers now. We focus on what we *can* do about divisions and inequities in this present moment. For example, as field observers and assistants in local schools, our education students engage culturally responsive environmental education. Our students have assisted in sensory garden field trips with elementary students and conducted culturally responsive Earth Day stations outdoors about environmental stewardship, bilingual nature poetry, solar system physical education, and sustainability murals.

Our students have team taught activities to convert negative stereotypes into happiness experiences by relating the process of tasting an unfamiliar food cooked with different preparations to the process of reducing bias. Our students have team taught literacy stations reading aloud bilingual books about how Monarch butterfly migration from Canada through the US to Mexico relates to the migration of people between these countries. They have facilitated children to collaborate on colorful butterfly posters, write poetry in butterfly shapes, and fly like butterflies with parachute wings. Our students have helped plant native seeds and participated in green urban engineering projects, on site and off. Our Native American students have read bilingual books aloud about stewardship practices and facilitated cultural story sharing about medicinal plants. In these ways, our college students have changed mainstream academic space, time, materials, and learning environments by co-facilitating sustainable multicultural belonging experiences in real time.[21]

I challenge teacher preparation students to reflect: "How can something as simple as face-to-face circles facilitate cross-cultural curriculum engagement, compared to the cultural detachment of rows or online learning with eyes glued to slides, videos, or screens? How does breathwork with chimes or going outdoors prime the brain for academic concentration? How does sitting on the floor in a popcorn reading circle with nature examples and multicultural books about environmental science integrate human diversity into biodiversity ecosystems? How does lying down outdoors listening for Earth's heartbeat nourish inquiry science about nature's awe?[22] How does you designing exams from notes about the academic activities you led make our learning environment culturally responsive? How does you asking and answering questions of one other engage our diversity?"

I observe that *while* journaling about institutional norms and busy site conditions during field experiences, our students reflect on creative activities to meet state mandates *with* equity and sustainability criteria. I observe that our students help reduce the anxiety of compelling children in rows to fill in bubbles for lower-order objectives in standardized tests by assisting mentor teachers in hands-on activities.

These transformative teachers-in-training make use of the fact that school desks were unbolted decades ago to allow movement.[23] When permitted by master teachers, our students facilitate circle variations for multicultural interactions.[24] Guided by mentors, our students help with Socratic Seminars for reading comprehension. In this circle format, each child speaks five times for discussion flow. Children use positive reinforcement with phrases such as "I respectfully disagree" or "I really liked that idea, however...." For bigger groups, children form double circles – with an inside-talkers circle and an outside-researchers circle – where outside-ring *researchers* provide evidence to inside-ring *talkers*. Our students assist children in these circles to pose questions and discuss evidence-based answers, switching talkers and researchers for equity participation.[25]

These teachers-in-training take circle learning outdoors, integrating into green infrastructure and economic development projects on campus, such as observing solar panels on buildings and participating in reduction and recycling stations, greenhouse development, pollinator gardens, and green vocational education. When required to be inside, our students bring in nature examples and integrate green vocational education into content requirements. Rather than yield to the stress of perpetual catch-up or victimization mindsets, these education students co-lead change, weaving academic subjects into culturally responsive sustainability designs one teachable moment at a time.[26]

Student Cogen Diversity Circle:
Students create curriculum engagement with mindfulness, cultures, and nature activities, indoors and outdoors.

Question
- How do Earth food webs relate to human activities?

Activity
- Students visualize sustainability, reflecting on pollinator, seed, and plant ecosystems on school grounds for Earth Day.

Questions
- How do community gardens and greenhouses protect native seeds and plants in compromised environments? diverse peoples in harsh environments?
- How do people collect and distribute seeds justly and sustainably?

Activity
- Read native seeds book, Miss Maple's Seeds by Eliza Wheeler. Do sensory walk/journaling from the classroom to a greenhouse and a pollinator garden. Plant native seeds.

FIGURE 8.1 Student Cogen Diversity Circles in action. Photos by the author and Fe (fee) Danger.

MULTICULTURAL MINDFULNESS ACTIVITY

Nonverbal Communication Toothpick Game[27]

Outcome

- Apply culture-conscious nonverbal communication.
- Analyze body language during Culture-Conscious Listening.

Key Concepts

- **Antibias Communication Norms:** Non-defensive protocols, verbal and nonverbal: Noun/Pronoun-Use, Turn-Taking, Creative-Tension, Culture-Conscious Listening, and Academic Accuracy.
- **Culture-Conscious Listening:** Five steps, verbal and nonverbal, to welcome diversity: Culture-Conscious Breath, Pleasant Eye Contact, Compassionate Support, Brief Summary, and Antibias Question.
- **Nonverbal Communication Norms:** Body language, such as facial movements, eye contact, voice tone, and wordless cues. About 70% of a message is nonverbal. Norms vary across cultures, often linked to deep-seated community beliefs.[28]

Resources

- Natural wooden toothpicks, copies of Figure 6.8, writing implements, an example or symbol of nature, a place to meet indoors or outdoors.
- On strips of paper or notecards, write short nonverbal norm descriptions, such as "don't stand too close to the person who is speaking," "maintain eye contact without breaking it," "don't make eye contact," "touch the person on the arm when you're talking to the person," "hug your partner upon first encounter," "air kiss both cheeks upon first encounter," "interrupt your partner with a cool fact when the partner is speaking," "don't interrupt during partner's speech," "take long pauses between sentences as you're speaking," "smile and laugh often," "don't smile or laugh," "use hands vigorously," "keep hands folded," "walk while talking," "listen to music while talking," "kneel to eye level while talking," "do something productive while talking," "don't do anything while talking," "do things rather than talk," and "show things rather than talk."

Big-Picture Question

- What's antibias nonverbal communication?

Start

Whole group circle with Global Praxis Iceberg (Figure 6.8) distributed:

- **Explain:** This game is about recognizing how important aspects of culture are misunderstood.
- **View** Figure 6.8 and **list** a few examples from your education experience:

    1 Tip: Cultural *artifacts* and outcomes about suffering versus thriving observed at school.

2 Waterline: Cultural *practices* that engage suffering, thriving to thwart negative patterns and develop positive patterns through school activities.
3 Base: Cultural *beliefs*, emotions, and assumptions about suffering, thriving, and sustainability in systems, much of which is communicated unconsciously or nonverbally, to research at school.

- **Divide** participants into two-person partnerships.
- **Distribute** 20 toothpicks to each partnership, and a cultural norm card or two to each partner, kept confidential from each other (as in poker).
- **Instruct** each participant to follow the norm(s) stated on their card(s).

Middle

Partners:

- **Discuss a current academic topic** for two minutes; then switch partners.
- Whenever a partner violates a norm on the other person's card, they are to **hand over a toothpick** without saying why. One goal is to guess what's on the partner's cards based on the context of violations, so as not to repeat violations and accumulate toothpicks.
- After several discussion rounds, the game is over.
- **Everyone counts** acquired toothpicks. The more toothpicks each person has, the more unconsciously offensive that person was to the other's cultural norms.

Closing

Whole group circle:

- **Describe** nonverbal norms on each card.
- **Discuss**:

    1 How did it feel to tell someone to pick up a toothpick?
    2 How did it feel to acquire a toothpick?
    3 How difficult was it to discover a partner's nonverbal norms?

- To make the activity *Transformative*, **discuss**:

    1 What categories of norms are important to antibias respect?
    2 What culturally respectful body language changes can we make to facilitate *antibias* understanding during subject engagement?

- To make the activity *Social Action*, **discuss**: How do we use antibias nonverbal communication to connect a subject to cultural thriving in the real world?
- To make the activity *Environmental Liberation Education*, **discuss**:

    1 How do we integrate antibias nonverbal communication into academic engagement for sustainability? (Examples: Displaying seasonal nature inside the classroom, going on a silent school garden walk for subject observations).
    2 What nonverbal communication experiences for cultural thriving can be integrated into academic engagement for sustainability? (Examples: Authentically facilitated Native American dance circle about a subject, community gardening work session about a subject).

Transformative Teaching Fundamentals

Transformative teachers interlace multicultural, mindfulness, and environmental education into hourly and daily routines. We build on what highly effective teachers have been doing all along. Historically, good teachers of every cultural background and field of expertise, with any subject or set of students, have been applying a range of best practices to vitalize the humanization goals that energize education.[29] Some of these practices, the student-centered ones, can be called holistic education.[30] This is basic stuff. We are not reinventing the wheel. Excellent teachers have long used variations of the Three Transformative Tools explained in this book: We collaborate to include and motivate. We use social-emotional methods to adapt to change. We design and evaluate interdisciplinary activities with big picture rubrics.

Environmental Liberation Education integrates these best practices. It connects academics to mindful culturally responsive world healing. It uses *mindfulness* education to change suffering into true happiness with body-mind-culture-environment activities about interbeing, impermanence, and emptiness. It uses *multicultural* education to integrate diverse perspectives into academic engagement. It uses *environmental* education to cogenerate ecological stewardship now. Our synthesis questions intervene in mainstream education space, time, materials, and learning environments. We collaborate to un-standardize subjects with culturally creative circles, indoors with nature or outdoors. We make prosocial decisions with inclusion, equity, and sustainability criteria, checking results as we go. We model peace precepts to work through conflict during change, aware that our racially tracked and segregated schools need restorative justice.[31] We use backwards design to meet requirements and develop multicultural global citizenship.

Why Start with Culture-Conscious Listening?

The Three Transformative Tools – Diversity Circles, Multicultural Mindfulness, and Approach-in-Dimension – are holistically antibias and inclusively antiracist. Systemic inequities deceive us all. Hourly and daily, US teachers unintentionally deliver racially stratifying and ecologically damaging curriculum and knowledge. This is why Culture-Conscious Listening is the most important practice in this book. It is a core Multicultural Mindfulness practice because opportunities to listen are constant. Active listening grows present moment social-emotional trust. Cross-cultural collaborations for race-sensitive social justice depend on trust.

Culture-Conscious Listening – Culture-Conscious Breath, Pleasant Eye Contact, Compassionate Support, Brief Summary, and Antibias Questions – reveals evidence of racialized systems moment by moment. The five steps provide cultural context for Approach-in-Dimension planning and evaluation. Culturally contextualized stories and practices give meaning to humanization. Culture-Conscious Listening calms the amygdala and activates the vagus nerve to replace bias reactions with cultural respect. We use respectful listening to shift from "humanity-*over*-nature" thoughts and actions to "humanity-*through*-nature" collaborations from a position of love.[32]

Mainstream, Contributions, and Additive approaches to humanity in education don't facilitate structural change. For that, we use Transformative, Social Action, and Environmental Liberation Education approaches, which engage *listening* to cultures for both biases and community authenticity to understand how perceptions are shaped by systems. We use

> **Student Cogen Diversity Circle:**
> Question
> - How do viruses spread through superdiversity and biodiversity?
>
> Activity
> - Students cogenerate hands-on biology curriculum with mindfulness, cultures, and nature, replacing teacher talk with problem-solving activities.
> - Each student rubs a single color of lotion on hands, plays interactive pass-the-object games outdoors, and returns indoors for germ spread analysis.

FIGURE 8.2 Student Cogen Diversity Circle in action. Photo by the author.

Culture-Conscious Listening to counteract miscommunications and big emotions from the paradoxes of race-neutral and explicitly racist disinformation and cultural illiteracy. We develop Nonverbal Communication Norms together to prevent body language *faux pas*. We practice how to pause and calm fight, freeze, and flight emotions and defensive behaviors that fuel social conflicts.

Culture-Conscious Listening welcomes diversity and acknowledges cultural feelings, especially those triggered by politicized topics, such as critical race theory, bias accusations, and resource distributions. It assists people with cultural identities of privilege who may feel anger when asked to redistribute systemic benefits. It assists people with cultural identities of marginalization, who feel annoyed when asked to decipher social justice, represent a whole culture, explain stereotypes, describe racialized trauma, or define racism. Culture-Conscious Listening nurtures voice and supports transformative trailblazers who are otherwise silenced by fundamentalism and loud fears that hinder constructive dialogue.[33] Culture-Conscious Listening helps to reduce social anxiety from oppressor–oppressed dichotomies, making space for multicultural-multiracial alliances. Our collaborations meet subject requirements through multimodal arts and sciences activities, such as cultural journeys, dance, music, artwork, theater, teach-ins, meal sharing, play, and ecological projects, indoors and outdoors.

How are Transformative Teachers Essential to Diverse Student Success?

Apart from broad economic-social systems, teachers are the most important factor to student success within school.[34] Especially with at-risk students, teachers have more impact on

302 Multicultural Mindfulness for a Sustainable World

1. Diversity Circles:
Multicultural learning communities for critical consciousness through big picture academic engagement.
Question
How do we steward the Earth with cross-cultural respect?
Activity
Students practice compassion in Culture Conscious Listening circle outdoors, discussing Earth stories to prepare for science-based culturally relevant Earth protection activities.

Why get in a Circle?

2. Multicultural Mindfulness:
Inward-outward peace process, integrating body, mind, culture, and environment into social-emotional academic learning.
Question
How do we engage academics while protecting nature?
Activity
Circle-read diverse foods children's book, *Thank You, Omu* by Oge Mora, to inform culture-nature stories discussion during Culture Science, Technology, Engineering, Arts, Mathematics C-STEAM project outdoors.

3. Approach-in-Dimension:
Big picture design and assessment matrix to integrate professional passion, subject requirements, and site cultures into holistic education decisions.
Questions
- How do social animals, including humans, interact?
- How do social animals cooperate, defend, hurt, or assist the whole?
Activity
- Foster puppies from rescue shelter interact with student circle to discuss cultural stories about the impact of social animal behaviors on the environment.

FIGURE 8.3 Why get in a Circle? Photo on top left is by the author and Fe (fee) Danger, and the photo on bottom left is provided by Shutterstock. The photo on right was taken by the author.

academic achievement than any other aspect of education. We make about 1,500 decisions a day, before, during, and after academic activities. Teachers select cultures in curriculum and project teams. We curate perspectives in subject development, spotlight cultural contexts in space arrangements, sequence knowledge development with cultural topics and skills, select cultural ways of knowing represented in materials, and decide on community norms for learning environments.[35]

But there's a culture clash in US education. Most teachers are motivated to the profession by humanization goals, while administration focuses on economic efficiency goals. The US economy produces commodities and services from extraction, mechanization, and cyber industries rooted in corporatized systems that perpetuate consumption and accumulation disparities. Educators are immersed in these assimilation and segregation procedures. We rely on industry-produced merchandise to stock classrooms. We follow Eurocentric disciplinary norms, funneling youth into the culturally stratified substructure-superstructure cycles that finance education tiers with punitive evaluations.[36] Moreover, even as student diversity increases, teacher demographics remain mostly homogenous; European Americans comprise 80% of the profession.[37] On top of that, most teachers – lacking ethnic studies coursework, mindfulness education, and environmental education – haven't developed the culture competence or structural competence for holistic change.[38]

Even so, *good* teachers activate humanization by communicating subjects with passion and best practices.[39] *Good transformative* teachers address cultures in systems. We understand that assimilation and segregation systems dehumanize and spread extraction-consumption harm. That's why we are "critically conscious" teachers.[40] That's why we use culturally responsive practices to empower, integrate, and restore.

Transformative teachers facilitate humanization through subjects by featuring mindfulness of cultures in nature, such as through ecological breathwork and stewardship practices with sun, land, sky, and water.[41] In this way, we synthesize body-mind and culture-environment into academics. Multicultural Mindfulness practices calm fear, anxiety, and aggression from personal memories about painful cultural experiences. Metacognition about bias, especially with nature through the senses, can reduce suffering by improving mental health. As Dacher Keltner explains:

> The sounds of water activate the vagus nerve. Certain scents in nature calm our stress-related physiology. Many plants give off phytoncides, chemical compounds that reduce blood pressure and boost immune function. Encounters with images of nature lead to the activation of dopamine networks in the brain, which animate…exploration and wonder.[42]

Transformative teachers, thus, make up for the shortage of diversity, mindfulness, and environmental education in mainstream education. We weave body-mind-culture-environment into subjects *with* students for the well-being practices that sustain liberation.

Transformative teachers understand that the human brain perceives scarcity and territory from survival instincts. We recognize that over-standardized bureaucracy and insufficiently or unfairly distributed resources trigger defensiveness. Our amygdalae make emotional judgments from self-protective assumptions. These ego-bias constructions reinforce assumptions and stereotypes.[43] We also know that *environmental* breathwork calms the reptilian brain, moderating the heart rate and lowering blood pressure. That's why we facilitate Earth action-reflection during academic engagement. We bathe the emotional brain with ecological visualizations to relax nerves in the limbic system.[44] Transformative teachers nurture antibias-antiracist academic concentration with multiple ways of knowing, such as Traditional Ecological Knowledge, for integrative arts and sciences. We support diverse student success by engaging subjects with joyful justice projects for unity during "humanity-*through*-nature" activities.[45]

Why Develop Culture Competence?

To make antibias-antiracist changes, transformative teachers redefine "cultural competence" from status quo Contributions and Additive approaches with criteria from Transformative, Social Action, and Environmental Liberation Education.[46] We engage *culture competence* to reduce ten forms bias that affect education (Figure 3.1) and invite cultural joy. Like everyone, teachers have positive and negative reactions to events. We make decisions from assumptions, but because our determinations have power over students, teachers influence intergenerational economic-social patterns toward segregation or inclusion and toward assimilation or pluralism.[47] Culture competence, as defined in this book, is holistic cultural compassion. It is unity skills with the muscle of *critical consciousness* about cultural authenticity and structural conflict resolution. It includes action-reflection about one's own intersectional cultures in oppression *and* liberation systems to make inclusion decisions now. Culture competence is discerning when community practices dehumanize or humanize, and we choose to nurture the latter.[48]

Transformative teachers grow culture competence by developing healthy multicultural identities during professional practice. As we support the "psychic space" of diverse cultures navigating local *and* global realities, we get curious about community assets and intergenerational designs.[49] We incorporate ethnic studies, women's studies, other identity studies, and living cultural practices and stories into subject engagement. We advance community empathy, good will, curiosity, patience with ambiguity, social respect and trust, and cultural creativity during academics.[50] Thus, we deepen culture competence with structural competence to call out stereotypes and liberate from dehumanizing systems moment by moment.

Why Develop Structural Competence?

Transformative teachers grow culture competence with structural competence for breadth. Structural competence is about cultivating humanizing systems. It involves visualizing a global economic substructure-social superstructure that can cycle inequity *or* equity patterns.[51] Structural competence is systemic analysis that empowers change.

> [S]tructural competency pushes us to understand how "racialized assumptions and biases are historically embedded into the very DNA [of our systems], and shape interactions and outcomes long before the participants appear on the scene."[52]

Structural competence helps educators discern the skewed version of humanity from the US's stratified feedback loop.[53] We don't take bias personally; we recognize it systemically, and as such, we deal with it structurally. We see how the colorblind dream of individualism is shattered by for-profit investments in racialized divides that began with White supremacist land-grabbing, enslaved labor, and segregation. We see that, at all levels, US education ranks students and knowledge to fit the corporate extraction-consumption substructure-superstructure that dehumanizes, depletes the Earth, and produces global warming. This awareness gives us footholds for change.

Rather than blame or glorify individuals, transformative teachers use liberation philosophies to guide collective education decisions. We apply structural competence to subjects with holistic *designs*. We intervene in intergenerational Anglo-conformist economic-social cycles impacting nearly everything that happens at school. We recognize that educators are not responsible for injustices perpetrated by ancestors who constructed and enforced racial and gendered barriers to success, but we *are* responsible for what we *do* about the unjust structures we operate now. We detect "'new racism,' 'color-blind racism,' 'laissez-faire racism,' 'symbolic racism,' 'racial apathy,' or 'averse racism'" at school.[54] We dismantle "the iron cages"[55] of stratifying bureaucracy in which mainstream classrooms are situated.

Transformative teachers who choose Environmental Liberation Education develop structural competence through race-class-gender and mixed-ability project groups. We enact high academic expectations with "personal accountability" routines, using CRE methods to meet standards. We apply CRE "caring practices" through culture-conscious mentoring schedules, unity labs and games, and connecting diverse students to multicultural community supports during academic activities.[56] We "un-standardize" curriculum and "detrack" academics[57] with multilingual-multimodal cogeneration circles. We grow structural competence by integrating cultures, mindfulness, and nature into projects designed to reduce assimilation and segregation experiences at school. Then we assess for equity in subject mastery, prioritizing holistic criteria, such as to "Think Globally, Act Locally."[58]

How Can Educators Help Shift Consciousness?

Transformative teachers make decisions to reduce White superiority consciousness and double-consciousness. A premise of Environmental Liberation Education is that consciousness dichotomies fuel systemic inequities and social conflict in classrooms, labs, and meeting rooms. That's why transformative teachers develop holistic consciousness. We aim to reduce bias barriers to academic concentration. We develop culture competence to clear space for inclusion consciousness. We motivate *prosocial* subject engagement.

Superiority Consciousness

In the US, White inhabitants have unfair access to resources and institutional networks that direct racialized structural advantages to European Americans. These advantages fuel White superiority consciousness, which is a delusional cultural belief, centuries in the making. For instance, like other European American Founding Fathers who enslaved African peoples, Benjamin Franklin named White superiority consciousness by proclaiming a racial divide between the "lovely White" versus the "Blacks and Tawnys" as the split American identity.[59] Franklin's description of race is, of course, "an invented definition to categorize a group of people who share a particular physical trait, like skin color."[60] White superiority consciousness, then, is the ideology of Eurocentric dominance. It is a White supremacist idea that has been violently enforced to prop up the tiered US economy. Segregation permits enterprises to capitalize on the low cost of racially divided labor and commandeered resources. Racialized

306 Multicultural Mindfulness for a Sustainable World

1. Diversity Circles:
Joyful justice alliances to engage academics with sustainability experiences.
Question
How do we develop nonverbal culture competence?
Activity
Diverse students cogenerate nonverbal communication activity indoors to prepare for C-STEAM project outdoors.

2. Multicultural Mindfulness:
Antibias-antiracist peace process for global citizenship in a sustainable world.
Question
How do we apply big picture resilience themes to academics?
Activity
Diverse students cogenerate Environmental Liberation Education research game - Global Book Chain - on library floor, rotating stacks books about ecological themes to design C-STEAM activities outdoors.

3. Approach-in-Dimension:
Culturally relevant student-centered big picture academic design and evaluation matrix.
Question
How do students cogenerate reflective academics connected to world healing?
Activity
Student circles compete to design final exam, collaborating on higher order questions and multimodal answers to assess subject proficiency integrated into mindfulness, cultures, and nature.

Three Transformative Tools

FIGURE 8.4 Three Transformative Tools. The two photos on the left were taken by the author. The photo on the right was provided by Shutterstock.

profiteering from the extraction-consumption marketplace perpetuates corporatized wealth inequities that, in the short term, advantage White people but, in the long term, dehumanize everyone and destroy Earth.

Double-Consciousness

Described by W.E.B. Du Bois in 1909, double-consciousness is the bifurcated Black experience in the United States. It is a distortion of diversity. It is the devaluation of African Americans from European American prejudice anchored in White dominance over the US economic-social power hierarchy. In this arrangement, Black people constantly second-guess dehumanizing stereotypes about self-worth.

> It is a peculiar sensation, this double-consciousness, this sense of always looking at one's self through the eyes of others, of measuring one's soul by the tape of a world that looks on in amused contempt and pity. One ever feels his two-ness, – An American, a Negro; two souls, two thoughts, two unreconciled strivings; two warring ideals in one dark body, whose dogged strength alone keeps it from being torn asunder.[61]

Double-consciousness is acutely experienced by those ascribed to have Black "skin color" in the White supremacist logic of "colorism," which is "discrimination within an ethnic or racial group against individuals with darker skin in favor of those with lighter skin."[62] Double-consciousness is also suffered by all people of color within the overall US racialized caste system.[63]

Inclusion Consciousness

White superiority consciousness experienced by European Americans and double-consciousness experienced by people of color in the US dwell in assimilation and segregation ideologies, discriminatory practices, and institutional racism.[64] These beliefs and procedures are unsustainable because they artificially divide, enforced by hourly and daily bias and violence. For example, many students of color experience cultural dissonance in the dehumanizing conditions of the school-to-prison pipeline.[65] Many attend "intensely segregated minority schools," which, in step with the widening income gap, have further increased inequalities over time. For instance, segregated schools have tripled in number since 1988 in New York and California. Extremely segregated sites, serving a student body of less than 10% White students, are characterized by low expectations, uncertain funding, and treacherous environments.[66]

Further, segregated education is self-perpetuating. The students of color who graduate from high school, already dealing with "always looking at one's self through the eyes of others," are discouraged by complicated bureaucratic and financial transitions from enrolling in the segregated higher education system.[67] And once there, making it through college to graduate also means overcoming a new set of systemic barriers to success, such as byzantine procedures.[68] These difficulties prevent a diversified, highly qualified teacher pool from forming to help model *desegregation*, and the cycle continues.

Across almost all demographics, teacher credential programs have been experiencing declining enrollments.[69] Segregation not only racially homogenizes the waning profession with White domination but prevents a critical mass for multiracial collaboration to develop inclusion consciousness in education curriculum, outcomes, knowledge, communications, and interactions. Moreover, once employed, teachers of color are more likely to work in low-income segregated schools, where they're unfairly expected to operate Contributions or Additive diversity programs that, ironically, are evaluated according to Mainstream assimilation norms. Thus, academic evaluations, made by educators, most of whom are White, further divisive consciousness by administering "amused contempt and pity" to students and teachers of color and cultural ways of knowing. On the flip side, the evaluations confer unwarranted benefits and the over-valuation of White students and Eurocentric norms.[70]

Inclusion consciousness develops through shared purpose. Environmental Liberation Education's humanity-*through*-nature offers a unifier to remedy the superiority-versus-double-consciousness predicament that segregates.[71] It's an umbrella approach to guide decisions to move education space, time, materials, and learning environments toward holism. Prescient about a land condemned by warring consciousness, Du Bois cites a spiritual in *The Souls of Black Folk* about the woeful struggle against racialized dehumanization. The spiritual wraps human suffering with environmental consciousness:

> Unresting water, there never shall be rest
> Till the last moon droop and the last tide fail,
> And the fire of the end begin to burn in the west;
> And the heart shall be weary and wonder and cry like the sea,
> All life long crying without avail,
> As the water all night long is crying to me.[72]

The good news is that the heartache from superiority consciousness-versus-double-consciousness divisions is also the grist for liberating critical consciousness. The oppressed co-generate humanization from the sting of injustice.[73] Diversity Circles model how educators

Environmental Liberation Education:
- Action-reflection with mindfulness, cultures, and nature, indoors and outdoors, integrating academics into world healing experiences through cross-cultural collaborations, peace practices, and big picture design and assessment.

Question
- How do we observe, use, and protect water with culture

Activity
- Hazardous air from an active megafire keeps students indoors.
- Concentric circles unite intergenerational students into academic belonging through Indigenous environmental literature integrated in a C-STEAM activity.
- Inner-circle students develop literacy, touching nature words on a book.
- Students collaborate on art for public display about water, weaving yarn ecosystems colors onto regional megafire site branches.

FIGURE 8.5 Environmental Liberation Educaction. Photos created by Tim Ill.

and students gather to reinterpret assimilation education with holism practices, such as those outlined in the Multicultural Mindfulness tool. Then, guided by philosophical clarity about humanity, such as by the philosophies described in the Approach-in-Dimension tool, transformative teachers design and assess academics for inclusion consciousness. The Environmental Liberation Education philosophy is reparative. Educators who choose it do patient and compassionate work. We process anxiety and the growing pains of making changes to status quo consciousness with body-mind-culture-environment integrations to strengthen environmental consciousness.[74]

How Do Educators Apply Global Lessons to Professional Practice?

Transformative teaching happens in local collaborations across the world, illustrating best practices, and pitfalls to avoid, for systemic healing. Our activities develop diversity questions, share cultural practices, tell cross-cultural stories, and create sustainability projects for subjects from global experiences, such as in Chile, Finland, Brazil, and Minority-Serving Institutions (MSIs) in the United States, all profiled in this book. Global examples show why and how educators in classrooms, labs, and meeting rooms transform systems in different cultural contexts. Chile's privatization reform reveals the ideology of oppression in privatized education. The other cases display the ideology of liberation with transformative teachers connecting with one another and students for high-expectations equity academics.

Chile's privatization experiment demonstrates how *not* to reform. Chile's comprehensive education privatization disempowered and de-credentialed teachers. The policy diminished student support services, increased student debt, dumbed-down and eliminated fields of study, destabilized access to quality education in impoverished regions, and widened social-economic achievement gaps. By contrast, Finland's systemic investment in free public education has been relatively low-cost proportional to its government budget, yet it considerably improved teacher qualifications and student success through holistic programming. Finland's changes eliminated student debt, supported subject integrity, and raised education quality and equity throughout the country. Its reform *detracked* and *un-standardized* education to empower academic freedom and flexible offerings, raise academic achievement scores to the top of the world, and advance social justice outcomes for all students through universal access to high-quality education.[75]

Similar to Finland's prosocial transformation, liberation educators in Brazil and Chile, illustrated by Paulo Freire and Cecilia Vicuña, show community empowerment through culture circle critical consciousness methods. Such interdisciplinary social justice problem-solving, deepened through feminist environmental arts collaborations, demonstrates healing intersections between cultures, institutions, and Earth. Practicing in Santiago at the same time exiled Paulo Freire was writing *Pedagogy of the Oppressed* there, Vicuña's feminist works were produced in an artist collective, "*Tribu No*." Subsequently, during the Augusto Pinochet regime of privatized education in Chile, Vicuña was herself exiled from Chile, but she continued transformative work across the world.[76]

A seminal event in the 1950s sparked Vicuña's transformative drive. She was a young girl when she viewed a 500-year-old mummified child, *La Momia del Cerro del Plomo*, who had been sacrificed atop one of the highest mountains in the Andes at a spring that flows into the Pacific Ocean. The child was killed during a pre-colonial pre-capitalism epoch in accordance with water protection beliefs. As Vicuña declares in her "*Quipu* Womb" performance in Santiago in 2017, the child sacrifice was conducted to protect the *Mapocho* River, an intermittently brown body of water that today is polluted by industry waste from the global extraction-consumption economy.[77]

To honor this child's life with cultural environmental actions to reduce pollution in the *Mapocho* and restoring it as a wetland habitat, Vicuña created a 100-mile floating journey along the river. She used swaths of 9- to 24-foot-long brilliant red umbilical cords to depict the threads of suffering and vitality between children, mothers, and nature. She fashioned these giant *quipus* from wool to reflect energy transferences that the original *quipu* cords conveyed thousands of years previously. *Quipus* documented economic exchanges between various pre-colonial Andean communities. She investigated how *quipus* were used to disseminate the accounting of ecological resources during Indigenous commerce. She made connections between Indigenous *quipu* numeracy and how umbilical cords tie children and mothers to cultures and water on Earth as one. Vicuña used natural materials to depict womblike interbeing in the universe. Thus, Vicuña illustrates how to cogenerate knowledge with nature and cultures indoors and outdoors during environmental and social justice problem-solving unified by Mestiza environmental consciousness.[78]

In summary, global transformative examples illustrate best practices and unacceptable practices. The holistic student-centered practices that transformative teachers employ do triple-duty: We support diverse student well-being and success; we grow education's efficacy in intergenerational cross-cultural socialization toward equity and inclusion; we prepare graduates with subject skills aligned with a sustainability economy. Sharing multilingual, multiracial, multimodal data and integrating cultural and environmental knowledge into academic engagement, we reflect on oppression and take liberation action.

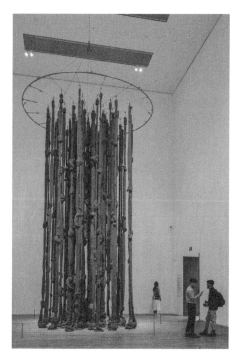

FIGURE 8.6 Cecilia Vicuña *Quipu Womb* installation.

In culture circles indoors with nature or outdoors, we observe the environment mindfully to protect the ecosystems in which we exist. Relating observations to global substructure-superstructure systems, we notice cultures within processes. We make antibias-antiracist interdisciplinary connections between cultures in the environment to sustain humanity with authenticity.

MULTICULTURAL MINDFULNESS ACTIVITY

Environmental Liberation Education Made Easy

Outcome

- Academic engagement through multimodal circle activities with cultures and nature, indoors and outdoors.

Key Concepts

- **Operating Principles for Ecological Systems:**[79] Carrying Capacity, Interdependence, Diversity, Change, Competition and Cooperation, Cycles, and Energy Flow (Chapter 6).
- **Environmental Consciousness Shifts in History:**[80]

    1 Hunter-Gatherer Age: Humanity-*in*-Nature
    2 Agricultural Age: Humanity-*with*-Nature
    3 Mechanistic Industrial Age: Humanity-*over*-Nature
    4 Information Solar Age: Humanity-*through*-Nature

Resources

- Breathwork bell and a safe outdoor location near classroom, lab, or meeting room (while extreme weather precludes the outdoors, some weather awakens the senses).

Big-Picture Question

- How do we engage academic space for cultural inclusion and sustainability experiences?

Start

- **Post and read aloud** two concepts: "Operating Principles for Ecological Systems" and "Environmental Consciousness Shifts in History" (above).

Two diverse project teams:

- **Split** participants into two discussion circles for one concept each. Ask each team to collaboratively write a one-sentence summary of the concept as if explaining to a child.
- **Instruct:** We are going outdoors to engage a required subject.

1. **Pack** required subject supplies and the sentences.
2. **Walk mindfully** to outside without talking.
3. **Practice box-breathing** (breathe-in 1-2-3-4, hold 1-2-3-4; breath-out 1-2-3-4, hold 1-2-3-4) with slow steps, aware of senses.
4. **Observe** changes in sights, sounds, smells, tastes, and touch in the transition from indoors to outdoors.

Middle

- Once at the designated outdoor location but before the required subject activity:

  1. **Form** a whole group circle.
  2. **Read** aloud the sentences.
  3. Ask students to individually **observe** one nature element: sun, earth, sky, or water.
  4. Ask students to take **four box-breathing cycles** while considering the element. (This breathwork starts and ends with chimes by a leader, who times by counting silently four box breathing cycles.)

- After breathwork, **do the required subject activity**.

Closing

- **Pack up** belongings when the required subject activity is complete.
- **Walk mindfully** to return indoors, aware of passing emotions and thoughts without judgment.
- Once indoors, **discuss a question**, such as the following:

  - What was the most important thing you learned about the required subject?
  - Did your academic concentration improve or diminish outdoors?
  - What was hard and what was joyful about doing school outdoors?
  - What ecological operating principles or environmental consciousness concepts did you observe outdoors?
  - How does sun, sky, earth, or water relate to the required subject?

Examples: Why Transformative Teaching is Easy and Fun

Education Students as Transformative Teachers

Education students illustrate that Environmental Liberation Education is easy and fun. The following examples happened in an MSI classroom of multicultural mixed-ability teacher education students. The first was led by two first-year European American females, and the second was led by a team with three Latinas and one European American female; both are examples of Student Cogens. The Cogens were assigned to apply transformative tools to design and conduct an approximately 30-minute Children's Literature teaching demonstration, "*Las Cebollas*" (The Onions), to improve the classroom with student-centered culture creation during academic engagement.[81]

Planning

Prior to their demonstrations, the Cogens met over snacks and music to plan how to reinterpret language arts, math, and science standards with a holistic diversity and sustainability lens. They were tasked to design and conduct a lesson to answer a big-picture question: How do we weave multicultural perspectives into curriculum requirements and increase cultural inclusion in environmental sustainability? This question prompts backwards design.

The teams brainstormed how to activate nine multiple intelligences in cognitive progressions with antibias-antiracist activities for unity about the "*Las Cebollas*" chapter in *Esperanza Rising* by Pam Muñoz Ryan. They followed a rubric with criteria to synthesize fifth-grade state requirements for reading, writing, math, and science. They had to find another book to compare to the assigned *Las Cebollas* chapter. One group selected *Return to Sender* by Julia Alvarez. The other group selected a graphic novel, *Measuring Up* by Lily LaMott and Ann Xu. One state standard that both Cogens targeted was, "Analyze how two or more texts address similar themes or topics in order to build knowledge or to compare the approaches the authors take."[82]

The Cogens used the Diversity Circles principle of Content Creation by handmaking content with onions. They applied the Equity Ecosystems principle by designing heterogeneous project-group activities. One Cogen engaged the Environmental Humanization principle by selecting a short video about an onion-processing plant that uses green technology. The other Cogen engaged Environmental Humanization by facilitating an activity with a living natural specimen about the onion plant life cycle.

Both Cogens planned to involve students in immigration topics to develop systemic analysis in an effort to transform the Additive approach of the course's required textbook, *Children's Literature Briefly*. The textbook's stand-alone diversity chapter, "Multicultural and International Books," portrays diversity as extra curriculum. The Cogens aimed to develop structural competence through justice-themed circle activities with nature indoors about immigration topics: citizenship exclusion and inclusion interracial conflicts versus alliances, how for-profit industries dehumanize migrant labor, Indigenous and immigrant experiences in a globalized world, and how to reduce bias.[83]

Demonstration #1

During the lesson, participating students formed three multicultural teams by hunting for name labels the partners made from onion skins and pre-distributed on station tables. The teams used Culture-Conscious Listening to compare *Esperanza Rising* to *Return to Sender* during a popcorn-passage read-aloud in English and Spanish. Participants threw a beach ball from table to table to prompt the next reader, discussing Spanish words as they arose.

Next, participants collaborated to fill in a handmade worksheet to match visuals with Spanish words. Native Spanish speakers mixed into each team were from different Latin American countries, and they laughed as they told stories to explain dialect variants for words, such as "in truth": "*de veras*," "*en serio*," and "*verdad que sí*."

Then participants walked mindfully to find three glass jars of different quantities of pickled pearl onions placed in far reaches of the classroom to do math calculations in an activity called "Pearl Onion Guesstimation."

When they returned to their stations, learners cut the "onion leather" that the demonstration partners had made to create clothes and hair for character-collages. Learners chatted while cutting paper doll dresses and writing book quotes onto the collages to combine visual and writing modalities in character analysis.

For closure, everyone viewed a video about an onion-processing plant, Gill's Onions in Oxnard, California, that generates 60% of its own energy and 75% less waste than other onion factories. After the viewing, participants left team tables to form a whole group circle to ask questions and discuss how Gill's Onions produces clean, renewable electric energy. They reviewed how the factory grinds 200,000 pounds of daily onion waste into a sludge that's processed into bio-gas that powers two 300-kilowatt fuel cells, with leftover waste used to feed livestock. Participants engaged critical consciousness, discussing how characters in the readings and video resist dehumanization and take humanization action. For instance, students observed how Marta, in *Esperanza Rising*, is portrayed as a Latinx female activist leader wearing pants and holding a "*Huelga*" (Strike) sign, fighting for human rights in her labor camp. Students compared Marta to Tyler in *Return to Sender*, who also agitates for immigrant rights. Students compared both characters to Gill's workers who make renewable onion sludge.

In summary, in 35 minutes, this Student Cogen models transformative teaching. They facilitate social-emotional learning through mixed-ability teams in stations and whole group circle discussion *with* cultures and nature. Participating students handle onions in several forms – raw onion name tags, pickled pearl onions, onions baked into leather, and fried onion rings – while talking about social justice and sustainability. Character-collages activate visual and kinesthetic modalities. Background songs in Spanish engage musical intelligence. Reading, conversation, and writing about the suffering and happiness of characters bring in emotional intelligence and bilingual skills. Walking mindfully to make calculations at the "Pearl Onion Guesstimation" stations, activates gross-motor kinesthetics and logical-mathematical intelligence.

Demonstration #2

At the start of the lesson, participating students formed two large multicultural circles. The teacher team asked the student teams to discuss least favorite foods, and some students named onions. The teachers explained that food is a cultural artifact and that the main characters in the two books for the lesson both have cross-cultural conflict experiences involving food as a metaphor for cultural bias.

Next, the two teams used Culture-Conscious Listening to compare *Esperanza Rising* to a summary of a graphic novel, *Measuring Up*, about an immigrant family from Taiwan who moves to Seattle. Then students took turns reading aloud a passage about onions in *Esperanza Rising* in English and Spanish. Then students acted out a scene from the passage by using forks to try to sweep up onion skins that the teachers had distributed on the two project tables, experiencing one reason why Esperanza might dislike onions.

Next, students stamped cut onions with paint onto paper to make flower designs while listening and talking about experiences with onions and onion flowers as Mexican American background music played.

Next, students observed the beauty of an onion specimen living in water in the flowering stage of its biennial growth cycle. Students noticed its delicate roots, the grace of the long plant neck above the bulb, its red color, and its drying flowers. One teacher explained that her mother cared for this specimen carefully to save seeds from its flowers to cultivate more onions after this plant, nearing its death, gets composted into dirt to nourish Earth.

Next, students debated and copied the names of stages in an onion life cycle from seed to death. Then students discussed different ways to prepare onions as a food and how different cultural preparations change its chemistry and flavor. Then students sampled pickled, raw, and grilled onion preparations used in Mexican American tacos.

For closure, students tallied most and least favorite onion preparations of the three. Then students calculated percentages of the preferences, finding a diversity of preferences from among student tastes. Then students discussed ways to respect one another's preferences and how diverse multimodal interactions with something specific can shift a generalized dislike into an affirmative like. All students during the lesson expressed that they ended up liking at least one onion preparation of the Mexican American culture. Students observed that

- There's diversity within single cultures.
- Onions change in life-cycle phases just as cultures change.
- Negative perceptions can be changed into positive perceptions with awareness of beauty in holism cycles and the stewardship involved in sustainability, and by experiencing cultural diversity viscerally.

In summary, this multiracial teacher team met state standards in English Language Arts by integrating multiracial perspectives and antibias activities into multiple intelligences engagement. They activated math and visual arts skills through cultural inclusion and diversity belonging experiences, wherein some students reduced bias on the spot. These students said they now liked something – a specific onion preparation as a representation of Mexican American culture – that they had previously thought they disliked. Participants experienced diversity in a cultural category, thereby gaining diversity awareness through literacy development.

Reflection

Reflection with philosophical transparency guides transformative accountability. After both demonstrations, in circle reflection using Approach-in-Dimension guideposts, the professor asked all participants to discuss the most important things they learned from the lesson and areas for improvement. Participants observed various ways the lessons were effective with antibias-antiracist and environmental education experiences. They noted how all the senses were activated while learning state standards, such as *seeing*, *smelling*, and *tasting* onions while *touching* smooth onion skin, sticky onion leather, and crunchy onion rings. They noted how they *heard* Spanish in song rhythms while native Spanish speakers echoed the rhythms during animated debates.

They also discussed missed opportunities. They found that demonstration #1 didn't activate Social Action or Environmental Liberation Education approaches because activities didn't involve students in applying knowledge to real-world action for change. However, lesson #2 did involve students in bias reduction changes. Students found that neither lesson included Multicultural Mindfulness *breathwork*. They found that Cogen #1 was not racially or gender-diverse (two White women), with no other apparent attributes of cultural diversity either (e.g., special needs, class, gender identity). They found that Cogen #2 was multiracially diverse but not gender-diverse. Students found that both demonstrations used some unsustainable materials because perishability factors prevent preservation in long-term unit storage boxes.

Reflection circles brainstormed how to improve. Students speculated that the demonstration #1 could have addressed restorative justice (Figure 4.6) by discussing the perspective shift in Tyler, a White protagonist in *Return to Sender*. Tyler had been fearful of Mexican immigrant farm laborers, labelling them as "aliens" and "extraterrestrials." However, by the end of the story, he takes action to support migrant rights. This action could be named and applied to a homework assignment or community project. Moreover, students concluded that for sustainability, both demonstrations could be improved by using unperishable onion skins for the artwork or dehydrated onions for smelling and tasting. Students thought that using scientific method steps, such as to observe, question, hypothesize, predict, test prediction, and iterate, with student-cared-for onion plants grown in the classroom over time could have deepened life-cycle understanding. Also, demonstrations could be improved by doing physical education onion games outdoors, looking for conditions to plant onions in campus dirt, or going on a field trip to a regional onion farm that sprouts onions, composts onion waste, and provides materials for biofuels. Furthermore, it was discussed that an activity about regional Indigenous onion stewardship would instruct about nutrition and medicinal plants with another cultural perspective. Finally, it was noted that Cogen partners should always be as diverse as possible.

In summary, these two Student Cogens demonstrate the joy of transformative teaching. The education students became transformative teachers during the demonstrations, integrating mind-body-culture-environment activities into state standards in reading and writing about realistic fiction through interdisciplinary arts, science, and math circle activities with nature and cultures indoors. They show how to reduce the assimilation standardization that homogenizes US curriculum and how to increase culturally creative intersectional activities about sustainability. With very little experience or subject expertise, these future teachers demonstrate that transformative teaching is easy and fun. We make cultural inclusion and ecology decisions about space, time, materials, and learning environments. We collaborate on big-picture backwards design for antibias social justice and environmental stewardship during subject engagement from a position of love. Then we reflect on humanization going forward.

Conclusion: Our Teachable Moment

As every seasoned educator knows, teachable moments can't be planned. But good teachers create designs to welcome them. The globalized world provides a continuum of teachable moments. Likewise, education, as an intergenerational institution, supplies examples of innovation. Approaches like Environmental Liberation Education support transformative teachers to facilitate diverse student success, multicultural education, and holistic sustainability. Environmental Liberation Educators collaborate on mindfulness peace practices to develop subjects and empower students with culturally responsive humanization. We engage integrative world healing in *this* moment.

I participated in one such moment at an event designed by a year-long Laboratory Diversity Circle. Our circle brought the campus community together in activities to answer the question, What's sustainability? We implemented hands-on projects involving a variety of fields, such as anthropology, biology, counseling, education, English, dental hygiene, geology, nursing, psychology, Spanish, social welfare, sociology, veterinary science, and visual and performing arts. During the year, we asked: What are we liberating from, and why? Are our liberation activities culturally responsive? Are they sustainable?

At this public event with about 450 participants, our table was run by six culturally and racially mixed student facilitators. The students guided participants through an environmental science clay activity. Participants made landscapes on medallions by rolling recycled clay with lodgepole pine branches carved by bark beetle larvae. Using methods explained and modeled by transformative teacher Candace Garlock, students stamped the rolled medallions with mindfulness phrases, such as "breathe," "Earth," and "joy."

At one point, a student explained to everyone at the table that she took the college's introduction to elementary education course on a lark, as an elective just before graduating in another major. But now she was hooked. This student wants to become an elementary school teacher.

To meet state standards, the education course she took requires 30 hours of field experience. The program coordinator, Julie Kauffman, transformed the requirement into a sister school partnership in a nearby public school for cultural congruence. The sister school enrolls mostly working-class students of color.

The student explained that, as a Latina, she personally identified with the children of color in her assigned classroom. She said she loved being a cultural role model for academic engagement. But she noticed that, like in almost every US school, most teachers at this school were White. She asked a difficult question, "Isn't this a problem? So many White teachers with so many students of color?"

There was an awkward pause. The European American education students at our table stared downward, busying their hands, looking uncomfortable. They were studying hard to become credentialed teachers, and there's nothing they can do about their skin color.

I chimed in with a happy smile, "We all have a place in diversity education! We're all cultural beings in diversity. We're all needed as antibias educators. Healing this racialized system involves culture conscious *teaming* for sustainability."

The White students looked up again, relieved. Their education professor had confidence that every teacher can *be* the change. I went on to explain how our teacher education program coordinator values diversity and intergenerational world healing. She mindfully administers our hands-on projects and does it with outdoor education as much as possible. I described how the coordinator designed the sister school relationship to deepen the field experience requirement with cultural connections. Not only do our diverse education students observe and assist in K-6th grade classrooms there, but we also *use* some course meeting times to leave campus to team teach diversity literacy, math, and environmental education stations at the school with cohorts of 60-70 elementary students at a time. Moreover, we host the children, many of whom live in families without college education, on campus to do science labs about nature, eat lunch together, and walk college grounds.

In this way, we engage local education systems holistically. We *collaborate* to include regional students and educators in multi-sector interactions. Diverse children of various ages, education students, experienced elementary school teachers, and college professors unite in culturally responsive subject engagement. We motivate education through the prosocial changes we make. We cogenerate antibias-antiracist education. Our intergenerational relationships involve *all* of us in supporting *inclusive* student success connected to the world.

In our teachable moment hand-making interdisciplinary art in a circle with recycled clay and nature stamping, we experienced how transformative teachers empower one another. We act and reflect about ecological knowledge *for* reciprocal wellness. We synthesize body, mind, culture, and environment while learning sustainability through diversity.[84]

What's the "New Social Order?"

Mexican American scholar George I. Sanchez concluded that the teacher is "the advance agent of a new social order."[85] Like other professionals in the substructure-superstructure network, teachers make decisions that influence social order. But what teachers do is *intergenerational*. We are cross-cultural cocreators. Preschool through graduate school, teachers make choices hourly and daily that either divide or support equity in the next generation. The knowledge we advance either connect diverse learners to the environment or ignore it.

Unintentionally, many US educators favor some cultures over others. Without meaning to, we deliver Anglo-conformist academics in segregated conditions. Many of our decisions are rote, falling in step with the bias systems we inhabit. Mainstream teachers unconsciously reproduce the race-class-gender-stratified and environmentally destructive economy that funds education. However, *transformative* teachers make clear-eyed decisions for humanity. We apply multicultural, mindfulness, and environmental activities to curriculum, outcomes, knowledge, communications, and interactions for sustainability experiences during routines. We engage local ecology projects and regional green economic developments with culturally relevant themes. We use a cultural *assets* lens to connect subjects to holistic outcomes.[86]

We engage systemic solutions. As we reinterpret academic requirements, we figure out how human superdiversity interacts with Earth biodiversity. Grace Lee Boggs put it well in *The Next American Revolution: Sustainable Activism for the Twenty-First Century*:

> Just imagine what our neighborhoods would be like if, instead of keeping our children isolated in classrooms for 12 years and more, we engaged them in community-building activities with the same audacity with which the Civil Rights Movement engaged them in desegregation activities 50 years ago! Just imagine how safe and lively our streets would be if, as a natural and normal part of the curriculum from K-12, school children were taking responsibility for maintaining neighborhood streets, planting community gardens, recycling waste, rehabbing houses, creating healthier school lunches, visiting and doing errands for the elderly, organizing neighborhood festivals, and painting public murals![87]

US educators commonly make routine decisions that are divorced from the real world. We wish for a colorblind dream but perpetuate racialized tiers. Our evaluations track students and rank cultures to maintain the racial achievement gap. However, *transformative* teachers integrate cultures, mindfulness, and nature into space, time, materials, and learning environment circles, on and off site.

Whether we like it or not, education is political.[88] Every school program or curriculum pushes an ideology. *Transformative* teachers collaborate to ascertain those ideologies, and if they exclude, harm, or destroy, we take restorative action for living cultural practices and ecological well-being. We recognize culture conflicts in motion. We notice racialized assumptions underneath race-neutral mission statements. We spot "humanity-*over*-nature" ideas in standards that ignore sun, earth, sky, and water, or detach diversity from humanity.[89] That's why transformative teachers reinterpret requirements with a transparent philosophy of education. The philosophy we support is about compassion. We respect life in economic, social, and environmental systems. Thich Nhat Hanh explains:

> Three Transformative Tools:
> - Diversity Circles – Multicultural collaborators change academic space, time, materials, and learning environments with justice and sustainability activities.
> - Multicultural Mindfulness - Body-mind-culture-environment integration practices, outdoors and indoors, for peace experiences during routines.
> - Approach-in-Dimension – Big picture design and evaluation rubric to realize humanization during subject engagement.
>
> Questions
> - Why keep the watershed clean?
> - How do diverse people together respect Indigenous cultures while participating in regional watershed stewardship?
>
> Activities
> - Diverse students create curriculum engagement with mindfulness, cultures, and nature along the watershed.
> - Race for Watershed Trash

FIGURE 8.7 Three Transformative Tools. Photos by Julie Kauffman and Ron Marston.

When we look at our planet, we see that humans are also made only of non-human elements. Looking into ourselves, into our body, we see that we are made of non-human elements: minerals, plants, and so on. If we remove all these non-human elements, the human race disappears. That is why to protect humanity, you must protect the non-human elements. That is the deepest kind of ecological teaching.[90]

What's Environmental Liberation Education Backwards Design?

Environmental Liberation Education backwards design counteracts systemic inequities. We engage and evaluate education with big-picture themes. We use three Diversity Circle strategies: *Sharing*, *Circle Questions*, and *Global Praxis*. During Sharing, we relate required subjects to social-emotional culture and nature practices and stories integrated into the arts and sciences. We pose Circle Questions to connect subjects to multicultural, mindfulness, and environmental evidence from Sharing. We answer questions to refresh ongoing Global Praxis in labs and field experiences. Then we use the Approach-in-Dimension to assess outcomes and adjust Diversity Circle activities with diversity, mindfulness, and sustainability themes. Backwards design thus creates a Multicultural Mindfulness feedback loop to unify a "reorientation of our consciousness."[91]

Environmental Liberation Education shifts superiority-versus-deficiency consciousness habits into inclusion consciousness. It restricts banking education. We reduce the bureaucratic burden of assimilation standardized into segregated sites by decreasing commoditization. We lessen the deluge of top-down curriculum and Anglo-conformist knowledge, such as prepackaged textbooks, proforma worksheets, bundled units, plastics materials, and high-stakes test schedules serving the stratified extraction-consumption economy that destroys Earth. We regulate the "act of depositing, in which the students are the depositories and the teacher is the depositor. Instead of communicating, the teacher issues communiques and makes deposits which the students patiently receive, memorize, and repeat."[92] Rather, Environmental Liberation Education increases cultural creativity for a sustainability economy, reconceptualizing academics for local and global citizenship. To prompt critical consciousness, we use horizontal designs like student-led teach-ins and service projects with diverse community supports.

Rather than suffering from too much volume and too little time, Environmental Liberation Educators are efficacy experts. We engage knowledge and comprehension objectives with application, analysis, synthesis, and evaluation activities during hands-on projects.[93] We retain the intention of banking education for technical skills and detailed subject knowledge, calibrating results with industry standards, but we reduce banking education's culturally negating ranks and exclusions. Our circles keep some of banking education's direct instruction for memorization and industry proficiencies, while prioritizing holistic high expectations.[94]

Be a Transformative Teacher Today

Life has always been dangerous for people of color in the United States, and now global warming threatens everyone. Systemic inequity and climate change are lethal bedfellows. Environmental destruction and pollution from an extraction-consumption economy mirror cultural imbalances and ruptures. Climate crises disproportionately impact people of color who tend to live in areas with inadequate infrastructure and support services. But climate change threatens the survival of *all* humans and biological life on Earth. We can try to run, but we can't hide from the environment, and we're all out of time.

Fortunately, we know what to do. Martin Luther King, Jr. called for direct action:

> I have been gravely disappointed with the white moderate…who is more devoted to order than to justice; who prefers the negative peace which is the absence of tension to a positive peace which is the presence of justice; who constantly says: "I agree with you in the goal you seek, but I cannot agree with your methods of direct action…"; who paternalistically feels that he can set the timetable for another man's freedom; who lives by the mythical concept of time.[95]

In the face of human-caused climate change, the *only* timetable for liberation is now. Violent extremism and *de facto* "subtle processes" of injustice must be resisted by antibias-antiracist practitioners across institutions. In education, this means that transformative teachers deploy our professional superpower to make inclusion and sustainability decisions. We change classroom, lab, and meeting room space, time, materials, and learning environments with cross-cultural compassion and ecologically sound experiences as our piece in the puzzle of systemic reform. We collaborate for cultural action because we don't "live by the mythical concept of time."[96]

In *How to be An Antiracist*, transformative educator Ibram X. Kendi entreats, "We know how to be racist. We know how to pretend to be not racist. Now let's know how to be antiracist."[97] Environmental Liberation Education's Three Transformative Tools help us be antiracist environmentalists together. In Diversity Circles of two or more participants, as diverse as possible, we practice Multicultural Mindfulness to integrate body-mind-culture-environment activities into requirements. Our peace process sprouts the seed of critical consciousness that germinates, like a lotus from mud, from harsh conditions.[98] Transformative teachers are highly qualified professionals who plan, implement, and evaluate *with* students in communities of care, using Approach-in-Dimension markers to guide humanization.

Transformative teachers weave multicultural, mindfulness, and environmental education into everyday practice. We team to connect academics to culturally responsive green projects, on site and off. We engage subjects to prepare superdiverse students individually and collectively for a sustainability economy in a biodiverse world. We use reconciliation methods to assuage anxiety about reparations to race, class, and gender schisms. We resolve fear-based conflicts with nonviolent critical consciousness.

Transformative teachers help break defensive habits that over-consume, divide cultures, and neglect local relationships. We connect academics and students to the environment through cultures to adjust to change and to create change. We act and reflect to redistribute and restore from a position of love. We grow culture competence with structural competence to nurture diversity belonging through joyful justice academics. As champions of Environmental Liberation Education, we *act* in compassion circles with nature and cultures, indoors and outdoors. We *reflect* in circles, developing curriculum and knowledge with deep diversity questions about holism. We refresh, design, apply, and assess sustainability anew because we're transformative teachers now.

TRANSFORMATIVE BREATHWORK AND JOURNAL

Journal Question: *What's Environmental Liberation Education?*

> In practicing mindful breathing, we become a real friend to our body, our emotions, our mind, and our perceptions. Only once we've developed a real friendship with ourselves can we effect some transformation within these different realms. If we want to reconcile with our family or with friends who have hurt us, we have to take care of ourselves first. If we're not capable of listening to ourselves, how can we listen to another person? If we don't know how to recognize our own suffering, it won't be possible to bring peace and harmony into our relationships.[99]
>
> –Thich Nhat Hanh

Breathwork

Wherever you are, take a mindful moment to relax. Use a timer chime if you like. Close or lid your eyes, taking several slow deep breaths, smiling slightly, noticing sensations: smells, sounds, touch, taste, and sight (if your eyes are open).

Now breathe while internally reciting the *gatha* below:

Breathing in, I calm my body.
Breathing out, I smile.
Dwelling in the present moment,
I know this is a liberation moment.[100]

Then:

> Breathing in ***What's Environmental Liberation Education?***
> Breathing out openness.

Repeat for as long as you like, or until the timer chimes.

Journal

Imagine we're in a Diversity Circle with the transformative practitioners cited in this book. We want to support superdiverse student success in a biodiverse world. Read our answers below. Reflect on your meditation. Briefly answer the journal question above in a way that's meaningful to you.

Paulo Freire

Liberation Education:

- Academic culture circles *with* the oppressed to use "dialectical thought [in which] world and action are intimately interdependent."
- The oppressed "perceive the reality of oppression not as a closed world from which there is no exit, but as a limiting situation which they can transform. This perception is a necessary but not sufficient condition of liberation; it must become the motivating force for liberation action.... The oppressed can overcome the contradiction in which they are caught only when this perception enlists them in the struggle to free themselves."
- Face-to-face *conscientização* – critical consciousness – in culture circles with community projects to alleviate real-world suffering.[101]

Cecilia Vicuña

Liberation Education:

- Collaborative feminist environmental arts education to intervene in for-profit economic substructure-social superstructure hierarchies that destroy Earth, cultures, and the sanctity between children and mothers.
- Holistic and ecological restoration to connect life to nature in the universe.
- Imaginative race-class-gender experiences to resist systemic oppression and grow intergenerational vitality with "virtual lines connecting the sacred places to the stars and the water sources on the peaks" to "spacetime on a cosmic scale."[102]

Sonia Nieto

Liberation Education:

- "'Worldmindedness' [to increase] the opportunities students have to become civically engaged on issues from human rights to environmental justice."
- Superseding "neoliberal microlevel policies [that] lead to a narrowing of the curriculum, an eroding of teacher autonomy and creativity."

- "A vision of literacy that is tied to power structures [to] motivate students to be active rather than passive learners."
- An approach to reduce "for-profit testing regimes" and "the pedagogy used with children living in poverty that consists primarily of asking questions, giving directions, making assignments, and monitoring seatwork."[103]

Django Paris and H. Samy Alim

Liberation Education:

- "Cultural, linguistic, and literate pluralism as part of schooling for racial justice and positive social transformation...about survival – a survival we want to sustain through education."
- "Changing the conditions under which we live and work by opening up new and revitalizing communities rooted in ways of being about education beyond 'the White gaze.' We want to create conditions where children of color can both survive and thrive."[104]

Micaela Rubalcava

Environmental Liberation Education:

- A holistic empowerment approach to reduce assimilation and segregation in mainstream education by increasing academic inclusion experiences.
- Critical consciousness circles to pose big-picture questions and engage subjects with cultures, mindfulness, and nature, indoors and outdoors, on site and off.
- Reshaping education space, time, materials, and learning environments with joyful justice sustainability activities.
- Action-reflection to connect core content to local and global healing, assisted with Three Transformative Tools: Diversity Circles, Multicultural Mindfulness, and Approach-in-Dimension.
- Culture-Conscious Listening for inclusive academic concentration and Global Praxis.
- Backwards design to change education's allegiance to corporatism with superdiversity-biodiversity questions for intergenerational Earth stewardship now.

Notes

1. Pak-Harvey (2018, January 17).
2. Gordon (1991), 249.
3. Gardner (1983).
4. Madden-Dent and Oliver (2021); Gay (2000); Ladson-Billings (1995).
5. Keltner (2023), 126.
6. Freire (1985), 59.
7. Sleeter and Carmona (2017).
8. Darling-Hammond (2010); Morgan (2014); Resnick (2013, April 9); Sahlberg (2015).
9. Darling-Hammond (2010); Morgan (2014); Resnick (2013, April 9); Sahlberg (2015).
10. Dunbar-Ortiz (2014), 14.
11. Porter (1995), 177.
12. National Geographic (2019).
13. Middleton (2018).
14. National Geographic (2019).
15. Budiman (2020, August 20).

16 Dunbar-Ortiz (2014); King (2018); Middleton (2018); Reese (2022, February 9–April 12); Takaki (all).
17 Gjelten (2015); Haraway (1991); Shaer (2018, March).
18 Valdés (2016), 79.
19 Boyd (1999); Dunbar-Ortiz (2014), 15, 5.
20 King (2018).
21 Julie Kauffman: 2022–2023 emails to the author, in Rubalcava (2001–2024).
22 Keltner (2023).
23 Cuban (1993).
24 Wink and Flores (1992).
25 Paideia (2018); Ross (2003); Rubalcava (2001–2024).
26 Rubalcava (2001–2024).
27 Adapted from Kristin Temme August 15, 2022 email to the author, in Rubalcava (2001–2024).
28 Hull (2016, May).
29 Darling-Hammond (all); Fried (2001); Rubalcava (2001–2024 [2005]).
30 Clark (all); Miller (1991, 1995); Nava (2001).
31 Banks (all); Clark (all); Bigelow and Swinehart (2014); Emdin (2016); Freire (1985); Hanh and Weare (2017); Gang (1991); Gay (2000); Ladson-Billings (1995); Sleeter and Carmona (2017); Sleeter and Zavala (2020); Urtubey (2023, June 20); Valenzuela (2016); Vicuña (2017, July 7).
32 Gang (1991), 79.
33 TMCC Joint Executive Board: *Declaration of TMCC Faculty, Staff, and Administration on Safety, Mutual Respect, and Civil Discourse*, November 10, 2021 email to the author, in Rubalcava (2001–2024).
34 Bethell, Newacheck, Hawes and Halfon (2014); Darling-Hammond (2006); Noguera (2017, 2018); Oakes and Lipton (2007); Sleeter (2001); Sleeter and Carmona (2017); Terada (2019, February 4).
35 Goldberg and Houser (2017, July 19); Cuban (2011, 2021); Lewis and Diamond (2015).
36 Reece (2022).
37 Ingersoll (all); Sleeter (all).
38 Sleeter (all).
39 Fried (2001); Rubalcava (2001–2024 [2005]); Spring (all); Gordon (all).
40 Valenzuela (2016).
41 Hanh and Weare (2017); Reese (2022, February 9–April 12).
42 Keltner (2023), 127.
43 Damasio (1994); Trungpa (1993), 37.
44 Keltner (2023).
45 Gang (1991), 79.
46 Howe and Lisi (2019), 271.
47 Banks, Banks and McGee (1989); Derman-Sparks (1989); DiAngelo (2018); Emdin (2016); Frankenberg, Garces and Hopkins (2016); Howe and Lisi (2019); Staats (2015, Winter); Perkins (2006).
48 Derman-Sparks (1989); Emdin (2016); Howe and Lisi (2019); Kendi (2019); Staats (2015, Winter); Rubalcava (2001–2024).
49 Emdin (2016), 23.
50 Howe and Lisi (2019), 272.
51 Ling-Chi Wang 1984 interview with the author at U.C. Berkeley.
52 Lewis and Diamond (2015), 173, citing Jonathan Metzl.
53 Barrera (1979); Bowles and Gintis (1976); Giroux (1983); Harman (1986, Summer); Williams (1973, November/December).
54 Lewis and Diamond (2015), 173, 8.
55 Takaki (1979), title.
56 Aronson and Laughter (2016); Gay (2000); Ladson-Billings (1995).
57 Sleeter and Carmona (2017), title; Lewis and Diamond (2015), 177, xix.
58 Clark (1991), 51.
59 Takaki (1993), 79.

60 Reynolds and Kendi (2021), 154.
61 Du Bois (1909), 3.
62 Reynolds and Kendi (2021), 154, 152.
63 Barrera (1979); Kendi (2019); Reese (2022, February 9–April 12); Wilkerson (2020).
64 Lewis and Diamond (2015).
65 Elias (2013); Ingersoll (2015).
66 Walter (2019, May 16).
67 Du Bois (1909), 3; Reece (2022).
68 Reece (2022).
69 Ingersoll and Smith (2003); Partelow, Spong, Brown and Johnson et al. (2017, September 14); Quinlan (2016, May 6).
70 Du Bois (1909), 3; Paris and Alim (2017).
71 Gang (1991), 79.
72 From Arthur Symons' "Of Our Spiritual Strivings," in Du Bois (1909).
73 Freire (1985).
74 Bigelow and Swinehart (2014); Gang (1991).
75 Arveseth (2014); Carnoy (1998); Darling-Hammond (2010); Guarda (2015); Hsieh and Urquiola (2006); Morgan (2014); Resnick (2013, April 9); Walker (2016, September 15); Claudia Heiss, Ximena Canelo-Pino, Ana Muñoz, César Peña, and Ivan Salinas 2017 Fulbright interviews/seminars, in Rubalcava (2001–2024).
76 Toledo and MacHugh (2022); Vicuña (2017, July 7).
77 Toledo and MacHugh (2022); Vicuña (2017, July 7).
78 Toledo and MacHugh (2022); Vicuña (2017, July 7).
79 Clark (1991), 44–48. See Chapter 2.
80 Gang (1991), 79. See Introduction.
81 Rubalcava (2001–2024).
82 Ford and Hardman, (2010, June 2), 16.
83 Young, Bryan, Jacobs and Tunnell (2020).
84 Rubalcava (2001–2024).
85 Au, Brown and Calderón (2016), 109.
86 Urtubey (2023, June 20).
87 Boggs and Kurashige (2012), 158.
88 Ling-Chi Wang 1984 interview with the author at U.C. Berkeley.
89 Gang (1991), 79.
90 Hanh and Weare (2017), xxiv.
91 Kendi (2019), 23.
92 Freire (1985), 58.
93 Bloom (1974).
94 Darling-Hammond (all); Lewis and Diamond (2015); Madden-Dent and Oliver (2021); Sleeter and Carmona (2017); Sleeter and Zavala (2020).
95 King (1964), 84–85.
96 King (1964), 84–85.
97 Kendi (2019), 11.
98 Freire (1985).
99 Hanh (2010), 36.
100 Hanh (2008), 36.
101 Freire (1985), 38, 34, 19.
102 Vicuña (2017, July 7), 22.
103 Nieto (2016), 202–219.
104 Paris and Alim (2017), 13.

GLOSSARY

Academic Faculty Diversity Circle (Chapter 5)

- Two or more teachers, as diverse as possible, collaborate to shape academic space, time, materials, and learning environments with multicultural, mindfulness, and environmental integration, engaging subjects holistically for diverse student success and world healing, indoors and outdoors, on site and off.

Academic Freedom (Chapter 7)

- An educator's fundamental freedom to pursue truth and express ideas without interference.

Administrative Faculty Diversity Circle (Chapter 5)

- Two or more administrators and non-teaching staff, as diverse as possible, collaborate to shape the institution with multicultural, mindfulness, and environmental integration for holistic education to support diverse student success and world healing, indoors and outdoors, on site and off.

Alaya (Chapter 2)

- *Sanskrit* for "home, as in Him*alaya*, 'abode of snow.'" A cultural interpretation of "basic goodness" to "open ourselves and join the rest of the world with a sense of tremendous generosity" during change.[1]
- Non-defensive breathwork with "complete openness" to mindfulness *of* interbeing, impermanence, and emptiness for "the fundamental unbiased ground of mind."[2]

Anglo-conformity (Chapter 3)

- An ideology that hides explicit race language with assimilation rhetoric about individualism to impose "English-oriented...cultural patterns as dominant and standard in American life."[3]

Antibias-antiracist (Chapter 3)

Someone who

- Acknowledges race as a "central axis" category in economic-social power systems, and implements "policy to reduce racial inequity." [4]
- Recognizes race-class-gender stereotypes and injustice systems, and makes cultural inclusion and social justice decisions about policy and practices.
- Develops culture competence with structural competence to reduce bias and increase inclusion actions from a position of love.

Antibias Communication Norms (Chapters 2 and 5)

- Non-defensive verbal and nonverbal protocols for Diversity Circles: (1) Noun/Pronoun-Use, (2) Turn-Taking, (3) Creative-Tension, (4) Culture-Conscious Listening, and (5) Academic Accuracy.

Approach-in-Dimension (Chapter 7)

- A rubric for academic freedom to plan and evaluate education with a transparent philosophy of humanity.
- A big picture matrix to make hourly and daily diversity decisions about space, time, materials, and learning environments for change.
- A guide with six approaches – Mainstream, Contributions, Additive, Transformative, Social Action, and Environmental Liberation Education; and five dimensions – curriculum, outcomes, knowledge, communications, and interactions.
- One of Three Transformative Tools for Environmental Liberation Education, the Approach-in-Dimension designs and assesses for holism.

Assimilation (Chapter 2)

- Enacting the ideology that "a racial group is … inferior, believing that a racial group can be changed for the better by acting like another racial group."[5]
- Actions and inactions that devalue diversity and inflict the dominant culture.

Backwards design (Chapters 5 and 8)

- Approaching a subject with holistic questions for culturally responsive development.
- Inquiry action-reflection to transform top-down subject objectives with horizontal integrations to replace over-standardized, stratified, and segregated education with culturally responsive, egalitarian, and high expectations holistic education.

Banking education (Chapter 8)

- Top-down assimilation education serving the extraction-consumption economy with dehumanizing standardization to commoditize, stratify, and segregate.

Big picture (Chapter 6)

- "Conceptual blueprint" for the "ecosystems context" to guide decisions to support the "organic nature of Planet Earth and all its systems, including cultural and knowledge systems." [6]

- Bird's-eye view to unify resistance to structural inequities and environmental destruction, and motivate joyful justice academic collaborations for healthy ecological systems.

Bias (Chapter 3)

- Categorizing likes and dislikes from positive or negative reactions and fight, freeze, or flight behaviors.
- Any feeling or belief from assumptions that results in and justifies divisive or unfair judgements or decisions, such as favoring or excluding.
- Ten forms of bias impact education: institutional, economic, explicit, implicit, familiarity, omission, tokenization, patronization, arm's-length, and projection.

Biodiversity (Chapter 2)

- "The variety of living species on Earth, including plants, animals, bacteria, and fungi" currently "at risk" due to "human activities."[7]

Breathwork (Chapters 1 and 6)

- Conscious breathing for body-mind wellbeing, prosocial behavior, and concentration.
- A mindfulness practice to calm fear and confusion from the amygdalae with prefrontal cortex and hippocampus exchanges.
- Practiced individually or collectively, standing, sitting, or lying down with a relaxed smile, inhaling through nose or mouth deep into the lungs, exhaling fully.
- Guided breathing, such as:
  - Box-breathing (*logical* modality):
    Breathe-in 1-2-3-4, hold 1-2-3-4. Breathe-out 1-2-3-4, hold 1-2-3-4.
  - Looking at a calming object (*visual* modality).
  - Closing eyes lightly and chanting or listening to sounds (*auditory-vocal* modality).
  - Placing hands on heart, belly, or ground (*kinesthetic* modality).
  - Closing eyes lightly and observing thoughts about future and past as "thinking" (*outward* modality).
  - Closing eyes lightly and observing inner-sensations and emotions as "feelings" (*inward* modality).

Breathwork bell (Chapter 1)

- An object for a pleasant sound to guide breathwork, such as a singing bowl, chimes, bell, cymbal, gong, drum, waterfilled jar, or ringtone.

Colorblind (Introduction, Chapters 1 and 3)

- The erroneous belief within systemic racism "that someone does not 'see race' and therefore is free from racial prejudice."[8]
- An idea linked to the individualistic American Dream about upward mobility.

Community Supports Diversity Circle (Chapter 5)

- Group of volunteers or aides, as diverse as possible, organized by an educator to assist academic inclusion and model holistic education with multicultural, mindfulness, and environmental activities to reinforce diverse student success and world healing, indoors and outdoors, on site and off.

Concept map (Chapter 3)

- Graphic organizer to document ideas for thesis development, e.g. Venn diagram, connected clouds, concentric circles.

Content Creation (Chapter 5)

- Collaborators cogenerate information, materials, works, and performances to reduce commoditized assimilation content and increase multicultural imagination.
- Action-research to deepen subjects with diverse ways of knowing, such as with interdisciplinary themes.
- One of 3 principles that distinguish Diversity Circles from mainstream learning communities.

Critical Consciousness (Chapters 2 and 5)

- Subject development through liberation education "culture circles" to "perceive social, political, and economic contradictions, and to take action against the oppressive elements of reality."[9]
- Academic engagement for humanization with 2 praxis stages about cultures and systems: (1) community "problem-posing" in "themes" with "decoding," and (2) taking "dialogical cultural action" for themed real-world solutions.[10]

Culture (Introduction, Chapters 1, 7, and 8)

- Authentic artifacts, practices, and beliefs of any group, impacted by basic human needs, power systems, and intergenerational cycles in micro and macro contexts.
- Communities that negotiate local and global experiences and intersections in systems.
- Group categories in flux within which individuals may identify with several, e.g. class, race, gender, ethnicity, language, national, regional, religious, political, age, and ability.

Culture competence (also known as "cultural competence") (Chapter 8)

- Holistic antibias-antiracist action and reflection about cultures and stereotypes in systems for cross-cultural compassion.

Culture consciousness (Chapter 5)

- Perceiving cultures and bias systems, including one's own cultures and biases, developed in "culture circles."[11]
- Awareness of the integrity of community artifacts, practices, and beliefs, and how cultures relate to dehumanization and humanization in systems and the environment.

Culture-Conscious Listening (Chapters 1 and 8)

- A Multicultural Mindfulness practice with 5 reflective breathwork steps:
    1. *Culture-Conscious Breath*: Breathe to perceive culture and bias.
    2. *Pleasant Eye Contact*: Use respectful body language for undistracted attention and cultural empathy.
    3. *Compassionate Support*: Convey patience during the talker's turn.

4 *Brief Summary*: Affirm and synopsize the speaker's information – content and tone – and ask, was that accurate?
5 *Antibias Question*: Pose an inclusion question.

Dehumanization (Chapters 2, 4, 5, and 8)

- Depriving an individual or group of basic rights, enforced by violent and discriminatory actions, such as forced relocation, labor, assimilation, segregation, and environmental destruction.
- A "distortion of the vocation of becoming more fully human," coerced by an "unjust order that engenders violence in the oppressors, which in turn dehumanizes the oppressed."[12]

Designated Committee Diversity Circle (Chapter 5)

- Two or more education participants, as diverse as possible, collaborate on a project about multicultural, mindfulness, and environmental integration, advancing holistic education for diverse student success and world healing, indoors and outdoors, on site and off.

Diversity Circles (Chapter 5)

- Liberation learning communities for holistic change with two or more participants, as diverse as possible.
- Critical consciousness collaborations to integrate multicultural, mindfulness, and environmental education into academic space, time, materials, and learning environments.
- Seven adaptable circles with three principles in five phases, Diversity Circles use three action-reflection strategies to humanize curriculum, outcomes, knowledge, communications, and interactions in education.
- One of Three Transformative Tools for Environmental Liberation Education, Diversity Circles organize for inclusion.

Double-Consciousness (Chapter 8)

- The bifurcated African American experience of second-guessing one's point of view due to prejudice, intentional or unintentional, from European Americans.
- The distortion of White supremacy and White superiority, enforced violently and institutionally through US systemic racism, which pits White people against people of color.
- Perpetual vigilance by people of color about identity from dehumanizing stereotypes and bias in US systemic racism.

8 forms of curriculum (Chapter 5)

1 Explicit – Official standards, subjects, knowledge, content, and materials.
2 Hidden – Unspoken standards, subjects, knowledge, content, and materials from cultural routines, networks, and patterns expressing economic-social systems.
3 Null – Removed or censored content, and materials.
4 Extra – Intermittent enrichment content and materials.
5 Required – Explicit curriculum assessed for achievement, often for high-stakes outcomes.
6 Recommended – Optional content and materials after hours.
7 Received – Partially or fully internalized content and materials.
8 Integrated – Interdisciplinary theme content and materials.

Environmental consciousness (Introduction, Chapters 6 and 8)

- Historical phases:

  1 Hunter-Gatherer Age – Humanity-*in*-Nature.
  2 Agricultural Age – Humanity-*with*-Nature.

3 Mechanistic Industrial Age – Humanity-*over*-Nature.
4 Information Solar Age – Humanity-*through*-Nature.[13]

- "Humanity-*through*-Nature" environmental consciousness:

  1 Awareness of Earth conditions in which all biological life, including humans, depend.
  2 Action-reflection to discontinue the human causes of climate change, reducing extraction-consumption productions that threaten all life on Earth, and increasing reuse, recycle, and restore cultural ecosystems.
  3 "Consciousness and world are simultaneous: consciousness neither precedes the world nor follows it."[14]

Environmental humanization (Chapters 2 and 5)

- Shifting self-concept from "humanity-over-nature" to "humanity-through-nature."[15]
- A citizenship identity that expands the humanization goals that motivate education with superdiversity and biodiversity.
- A collectivist identity to unify multicultural collaborations in sustainability projects – such as reducing, reusing, recycling, and restoring – during education routines.
- One of 3 principles that distinguish Diversity Circles from mainstream learning communities, and a capstone of Environmental Liberation Education.

Environmental Liberation Education (Chapter 8)

- Holistic empowerment education integrating multicultural, mindfulness, and sustainability themes into critical consciousness circles during academic engagement.
- Connecting subjects to cultures and world healing for student success with hands-on activities, indoors with nature and outdoors, on site and off.
- Using academic freedom hourly and daily to design, facilitate, and assess education space, time, materials, and learning environments to reduce bias with integrative social-emotional experiences.
- A big picture humanization philosophy of education with Three Transformative Tools: Diversity Circles for structure, Multicultural Mindfulness for process, and Approach-in-Dimension for planning and evaluation.

Equity Ecosystems (Chapter 5)

- Inclusion routines to develop structural competence in "community circles," "mediation circles," and "restorative circles" to humanize systems.[16]
- Diversity interactions to develop culture competence during holistic openers, core content engagement, and closures.
- One of 3 principles that distinguish Diversity Circles from mainstream learning communities.

Gatha (Chapters 1 and 6)

- Uplifting rhythmic verses, songs, or "small practice poems," vocalized self-reflectively or with others during mindfulness breathwork, daily peace activities, and meditative study.[17]

Global Praxis (Chapters 1, 5, and 6)

- One of three Diversity Circle strategies, along with Sharing and Circle Questions, to develop Environmental Liberation Education with labs and real-world experiences.
- Informed by Culture-Conscious Listening, Global Praxis is a Multicultural Mindfulness practice to connect subjects to the world, shifting from the "mechanistic-industrial age" to the "information-solar age" for an inclusive "global-ecocentric" economy.[18]

Growth Mindset

- A transformative approach that balances individual effort with collectivist action wherein "people believe their most basic abilities and qualities can be developed and cultivated through dedication and hard work. Brains and talent are just the starting point."[19]

Healthy multicultural identity (Chapters 1 and 7)

- Mindfulness of one's cultures in systems in a superdiverse-biodiverse world.
- Hourly and daily cross-cultural practices for sustainable "reverence for life," "true happiness," "true love," "loving speech and deep listening," and "nourishment and healing."[20]

Holistic education (Chapter 5)

- Integrative social-emotional academic learning for the whole-person – body, mind, culture – for peace and sustainability with mindfulness of systems and intergenerational cycles in a shared environment.

Humanization (Chapters 2, 4, 5, and 8)

- Restoring "humanity of both" oppressed and oppressors through "human solidarity," "speaking out" for cultural "choices" to "create and re-create" inclusive economic-social systems.[21]
- Healing suffering with mindfulness practices for sustainable "reverence for life," "true happiness," "true love," "loving speech and deep listening," and "nourishment and healing."[22]
- Expressing "voice that courageously and intelligently stands up against injustice and does so from a culturally and community-anchored standpoint."[23]

Integration (Chapters 3 and 5)

- Joining "formerly separated groups…to end the segregation of people in institutions and society."[24]

Laboratory Diversity Circle (Chapter 5)

- Campus culture learning community, as diverse as possible, to integrate academic programs during a year-long big picture theme for student-centered holistic education with creative interdisciplinary events connected to the world, indoors and outdoors, on site and off.

Liberation (Chapters 1, 2, 5, 6, and 8)

- Freedom to access and realize basic human needs supported by democratic regulations and social justice practices for diversity, inclusion, equity, and sustainability accountable to public good.
- Happiness – "Liberation and happiness are linked to each other; if there is liberation, there is happiness, and greater liberation brings greater happiness."[25]

Liberation Education (Introduction, Chapters 5, 6, and 7)

- Student-centered culture circles for academic engagement through critical consciousness to transform oppressor-oppressed dehumanization cycles into real-world humanization experiences.[26]

Mindfulness principles (Chapter 6)

- Mindfulness develops 3 principles to transform suffering into calm awareness for true happiness:
  1. Interbeing: Ecology and reciprocity of all things here and now.
  2. Impermanence: Change in all things here and now.
  3. Emptiness: Infinite spaciousness of all things here and now.

Multicultural Mindfulness (Chapter 6)

- Hourly and daily cultural respect practices to deepen subjects with joyful justice experiences, guided by impermanence, interbeing, and emptiness principles.
- Holistic action-reflection to integrate body-mind-culture-environment into academic concentration.
- Cultural awareness during change, such as to be present, be aware of others, observe evidence, relieve suffering, study deeply, understand compassionately, and transform inclusively.[27]
- One of Three Transformative Tools for Environmental Liberation Education, Multicultural Mindfulness is a peace process.

Neoliberal (Chapter 4)

- Ideology for materialistic individualism maintained through an under-regulated for-profit economy, not to be confused with "liberal" as in progressive politics.
- Enables corporatism while neglecting equity practices to manage capitalism with public good policies.

Nonverbal Communication Norms (Chapter 8)

- Body language and tone communicating emotions and beliefs through facial and hand movements, eye contact, voice pitch, wordless sounds, proximity, and objects.
- Essential to cultural respect since effective communication depends on nonverbal cues.

Nonviolent Direct Action (Chapters 5 and 6)

- 4 steps:
  1. "Collection of the facts" about perceived injustices.
  2. "Negotiation" about interpretation of facts.
  3. "Self-purification" in culture circles for nonviolent resolve during liberation.
  4. "Direct action" peace events for systemic justice.[28]

Oppression (Chapters 3, 4, 5, and 7)

- Unjust treatment in "dehumanization" systems operating stereotypes and biases to "manipulate" power through overt and covert violence and structures, such as "conquest," "divide and rule," and "cultural invasion."[29]
- Inflicting a "materialistic concept of existence" that views everything as objects for domination, such as "the earth, property, production, the relations of people, people themselves, time."[30]

Praxis (Chapters 3, 5, and 6)

- Liberation circles for "reflection and action upon the world in order to transform it" towards humanization.[31]
- Collective "cultural synthesis" to (a) observe "culture itself, as the preserver of the very structures by which it was formed," and (b) discern "myths" by coding domination structures and cogenerating themes for "dialogical cultural action" towards liberation.[32]

Pre-prejudice (Chapters 1 and 6)

- Ignorant and defensive impressions about cultures in childhood that harden into adult stereotypes and bias.

Race (Chapters 3, 5, and 7)

- A "sociohistorical construct" to categorize people "who share a particular physical trait, like skin color."[33]
- A "primary" or "central axis" category, "which cannot be subsumed under or reduced to some broader category or conception" due to economic and social experiences – imperialism, colonialism, land-stealing, slavery, genocide, *de jure* and *de facto* segregation, and systemic bias.[34]

Racialize (Chapters 5 and 8)

- To divide based on physical trait assumptions about appearances, specifically skin color, associated with economic-social systems.[35]
- To make racial in tone or character, explicitly or implicitly, mirroring the construction of race as a "central axis" category in contemporary cultures.[36]
- Though many people wish for a colorblind society, persistent stereotypes from historically racist systems necessitate race awareness to reveal disinformation and guide reparative justice.

Sangha (Introduction)

- A group of mindfulness practitioners engaged in the reconciliation of self and society for peace, practiced globally since at least 566 BCE.[37]
- *Sangha* members practice body-mind action-reflection *together* to strengthen compassion while working "for the benefit of others."[38]

Segregation (Chapters 2, 3, 4, and 5)

- "Discriminatory" policies and practices to separate groups, promoting the idea that some groups are "permanently inferior" to others.[39]

Socratic Circle (Chapter 5)

- Whole-group inquiry circle to develop subjects through evidence, answering questions posed by participants.
- When conducted face-to-face in culturally authentic settings, the method develops critical consciousness through dialectical, often uncomfortable, social-emotional discussions and research about economic and social contradictions and solutions.

Social emotional (hyphenated as an adjective) (Chapters 5 and 8)

- The term comes from "social and emotional learning (SEL)," which describes the process of developing self-awareness, self-control, and interpersonal skills for school, work, and life success.[40]

Spacetime (Chapters 2 and 8)

- An always-available, adaptable resource for educators to shape education space, time, materials, and learning environments.

- *Espaciotiempo* (spacetime) from Chilean poet, artist, and environmental educator Cecilia Vicuña. "We can simultaneously be time – and space – bound while completely free. I am constantly faced with that double capacity."[41]
- Cross-cultural, cross-national, and ecological existence – "the imaginary scale of the Americas united in the galaxy body…on the cosmic ladder [that] connects sacred places to stars…and water springs to mountain tops."[42]

Spacetime superpower (Chapters 2 and 8)

- Academic freedom to maneuver space, time, materials, and learning environments in classrooms, labs, meeting rooms, and sites during the "1,500 decisions" teachers make hourly and daily at school.[43]
- When deployed for holistic humanization, a teacher's spacetime superpower facilitates inclusive subject engagement with diversity, mindfulness, and sustainability activities.

Structural competence (aka "structural *competency*," originally from the medical field)[44] (Chapter 4)

- Critical consciousness about structural inequities that, in the United States, perpetuate patriarchal Anglo-conformist assimilation and segregation systems, impacting nearly everything that happens in education.
- Antibias-antiracist awareness of economic-social structures in education space, time, materials, and learning environments.
- Economic substructure and social superstructure awareness to guide educators as change agents for cultural inclusion in holistic education.

Student Cogen Diversity Circle (Chapter 5)

- Student Cohort subgroup, with 2 or more members as diverse as possible, collaborate to improve a classroom holistically with an academic activity involving multicultural, mindfulness, or environmental education for world healing, indoors and outdoors, on site and off.

Student Cohort Diversity Circle (Chapter 5)

- Co-enrolled students who engage academics with holistic themes about multicultural, mindfulness, or environmental education for diverse student success and world healing, indoors and outdoors, on site and off.

Substructure-Superstructure Model (Chapter 4)

- The superstructure is society, and the substructure is society's foundational economy.
- The model displays an institutional network with education as a core institution for educators to visualize the impact of hourly and daily decisions on substructure-superstructure cycles.
- The model shows how the economic substructure – the means of production and commerce – maintains and directs social institutions and cultural patterns; and how the social superstructure *reproduces* the substructure, unless participants act to *change* the outcomes that go into the substructure.

Superdiversity (Chapters 1, 2, and 8)

- World populations experiencing "mass migration" and intersecting cultures impacted by systems during climate change, irrespective of nation states.[45]
- Evolving cultures throughout the "movement of goods and capital," shaped by globalized for-profit corporations and technological developments that impact immigrants who negotiate "segmented

assimilation" patterns with "native minorities" and form worldwide oppression categories and liberation alliances.[46]
- Cultural responses to local events and "transnational population flows," defining humanity with planetary themes, wherein global citizens are "multi-competent individuals" with "translanguaging" and cross-cultural stewardship skills.[47]

Sustainability (Introduction, Chapters 5, 6, and 8)

- Stewardship for inclusive and equitable cultural, economic, and environmental systems to meet the needs of the current generation without compromising the needs of future generations on a planet that thrives on diversity.

3 Transformative Tools (Chapters 5, 6, and 7)

- Diversity Circles, Multicultural Mindfulness, and Approach-in-Dimension.
- Three resources - inclusion structure, peace process, humanization design/evaluation - for change during busy routines. These tools help educators make decisions to connect subjects and diverse students to cultures, mindfulness, and sustainability in real time.

Tonglen (Chapter 6)

- Counterintuitive breathwork for "sending and taking" to "reverse ego-clinging" by responding to suffering with healing actions.[48]
- The practitioner breathes-*in* discomfort, and breathes-*out* compassion, concentrating on one category at a time – friends, neutrals, and enemies – to reduce defensiveness and prompt compassion.

Traditional Ecological Knowledge (TEK) (aka "Native Ways of Knowing") (Chapter 2)

- Sustainability practices of diverse Indigenous communities to care for the planet regionally by protecting ecosystems and respecting sun, land, sky, and water.
- Cultural journeys about climate, flora, and fauna "creation" to act and reflect on lifecycles, mindful of past and future generations, adapting to changes "with equitable and inclusive systems of responsible land and water stewardship."[49]

Transformative teacher (Chapters 1, 2, 4, and 6)

A joyful justice educator who

- Collaborates on critical consciousness about systems to engage subjects and diverse students with big picture humanization activities.
- Connects academic routines to cultures to respond to and make real-world change mindfully.
- Facilitates holistic student success and professional empowerment with interdisciplinary questions about the economy, society, and environment during academic development.
- Integrates multicultural, mindfulness, and sustainability into antibias action-reflection circles during academics, indoors with nature or outdoors, on site and off.

True happiness (Chapters 6 and 7)

- Present moment mindfulness to reduce suffering and increase wellbeing compassionately with interbeing, impermanence, and emptiness awareness and action.

- Realizing that "the happiness and suffering of others are not separate from my own happiness and suffering… that happiness depends on my mental attitude and…practicing right livelihood so that I can help reduce the suffering of living beings on earth and stop contributing to global climate change."[50]

White superiority (Chapters 3 and 8)

- A bias mindset, conscious or unconscious, of White exceptionality, maintained by the unfair accumulation of resources and advantages to control racialized systems and dominate economic and social elements, such as land, labor, industry, law, citizenship, media, housing, and education.

White supremacy (Chapters 3 and 8)

- Violence and aggression to impose the ideology that White people are better than all others and should dominate and attempt to normalize the oppression of people of color.

Notes

1. Trungpa (1993), 12, 13.
2. Trungpa (1993), 11, 214.
3. Gordon (1991), 249.
4. Omi and Winant (1986), 61; Reynolds and Kendi (2021), 151.
5. Omi and Winant (1986), 61; Reynolds and Kendi (2021), 151.
6. Clark (2001), 69.
7. National Geographic (2019).
8. Reynolds and Kendi (2021), 151.
9. Freire (1985), 113, 19.
10. Freire (1985), 68, 103, 115, 158.
11. Freire (1985), 113.
12. Freire (1985), 28.
13. Gang (1991), 79.
14. Freire (1985), 69.
15. Gang (1991), 79.
16. Oliver (2023, June 21).
17. Hanh (2008), 5.
18. Gang (1991), 79.
19. Dweck (2007).
20. Hanh and Weare (2017), 316–318.
21. Freire (1985), 28, 31, 33.
22. Hanh and Weare (2017), 316–318.
23. Valenzuela (2016), 5.
24. Reynolds and Kendi (2021), 153.
25. Hanh (2006), 9.
26. Freire (1985).
27. Hanh (1998).
28. King (1964), 78.
29. Freire (1985), 28, 134, 137, 144, 150.
30. Freire (1985), 44.
31. Freire (1985), 36.
32. Freire (1985), 123, 182, 163, 158.
33. Reynolds and Kendi (2021), 154.
34. Lewis and Diamond (2015), 11; Omi and Winant (1986), 61–62.
35. Reynolds and Kendi (2021), 154.
36. Omi and Winant (1986), 61.

37 Buswell (2004), 933.
38 Trungpa (1993), 215.
39 Reynolds and Kendi (2021), 155.
40 Madden-Dent and Oliver (2021), 3.
41 Vicuña (2017, July 7), 22.
42 Vicuña (2017, July 7), 22.
43 Cuban (2021).
44 Lewis and Diamond (2015), 173.
45 Valdés (2016), 79.
46 Valdés (2016), 79; Suárez-Orozco and Michikyan (2016), 15.
47 Valdés (2016), 79.
48 Trungpa (1993), 224.
49 King (2018), x, 23; Reese (2022, February 9-April 12).
50 Hanh and Weare (2017), 316–317.

REFERENCES

Alexander, M. (2010). *The new Jim Crow: Mass incarceration in the age of colorblindness.* The New Press.

Anaissie, T., Cary, V., Clifford, D., Malarkey, T., & Wise, S. (2022). *Liberatory design: Your toolkit to design for equity.* The National Equity Project.

Angelo, T., Nilson, L., & Winkelmes, M. (2018). Modules 1A, 1B, and 1C: Course in effective teaching practices. In *Association of College and University Educators (ACUE) course at TMCC.* https://acue.org/

Ardoin, N.M., & Bowers, A.W. (2020). Early childhood environmental education: A systematic review of the research literature. *Educational Research Review, 31.* https://doi.org/10.1016/j.edurev.2020.100353

Arenas, A. (2004). Privatization and vouchers in Columbia and Chile. *International Review of Education,* 379–395. https://doi.org/10.1007/s11159-004-2629-z

Aronson, B. & Laughter, J. (2016). The theory and practice of Culturally Relevant Education: A synthesis of research across content areas. *Review of Educational Research 86,* 163–206.

Arveseth, L. (2014). Friedman's school choice theory: The Chilean education system. *All graduate plan B and other reports, Spring 1920 to Spring 2023* [Paper 386]. https://doi.org/10.26076/963d-dcf5

Assembly Bill No. 2542. (2020, September 30). California Racial Justice Act. Penal Code §745.

Au, W., Brown, A., & Calderón, D. (2016). *Reclaiming the multicultural roots of US curriculum: Communities of color and official knowledge in education.* Teachers College Press.

Aubrey, K. & Riley, A. (2016). *Understanding and using educational theories.* SAGE.

Banks, J.A. (1988). Approaches to multicultural curriculum reform. *Trotter Review, 3*(3). https://scholarworks.umb.edu/trotter_review/vol3/iss3/5

Banks, J.A. (1993). Multicultural education: Historical development, dimensions, and practice. *Review of Research in Education, 19,* 3–49. https://www.jstor.org/stable/1167339?origin=JSTOR-pdf

Banks, J.A. (2003). *Teaching strategies for ethnic studies.* Pearson.

Banks, J.A., C.A. Banks, & C. McGee (Eds.). (1989). *Multicultural education: Issues and perspectives.* Allyn and Bacon.

Banks, J.A., M. Suárez-Orozco, & M. Ben-Peretz (Eds.). (2016). *Global migration, diversity, and civic education: Improving policy and practice.* Teachers College Press.

Barnes, G., Crowe, E., & Schaefer, B. (2007). *The cost of teacher turnover in five school districts: A pilot study.* National Commission on Teaching and America's Future. https://files.eric.ed.gov/fulltext/ED497176.pdf

Barnett, S. (2020, May 6). Now is the time to invest in preschool education. Here's why. *Fortune.* https://fortune.com/2020/05/06/preschool-public-school-funding-coronavirus/

Barrera, M. (1979). *Race and class in the Southwest: A theory of racial inequality.* University of Notre Dame Press.

Bazin, M., Tamez, M., & Exploratorium Teacher Institute. (2002). *Math and science across cultures*. The New York Press.

Bell, L. (1991). Changing our ideas about ourselves: Group consciousness raising with elementary school girls as a means to empowerment. In C. Sleeter (Ed.), *Empowerment through Multicultural Education*, (pp. 229–249). State University of New York Press.

Bell, M., & Delacroix, J. (2019, Fall). Interview with Ned Blackhawk. A truer sense of our national identity. *Teaching Tolerance, 63*. https://www.learningforjustice.org/magazine/fall-2019/ned-blackhawk-qa-understanding-indigenous-enslavement

Berry, B., & Farris-Berg, K. (2016). Leadership for teaching and learning: How teacher-powered schools work and why they matter. *American Educator, 40*(2), 11–17.

Bertani, T., Carrol, L., Castle, M., Davies, K., Hurley, A., Joos, T., & Scanlon, C. (2010). *Culturally responsive classrooms: A toolkit for educators*. University of Pittsburgh.

Bethell, C., Newacheck, P., Hawes, E., & Halfon, N. (2014). Adverse childhood experiences: Assessing the impact on health and school engagement and the mitigating role of resilience. *Health Affairs, 12*, 33.

Bigelow, B., & Swinehart, T. (Eds.). (2014). *A people's curriculum for the earth: Teaching climate change and the environmental crisis*. Rethinking Schools.

Bizjak, T., Yoon-Hendricks, A., Reese, P., & Sullivan, M. (2018, December 4). Many of the dead in Camp Fire were disabled, elderly. Could they have been saved? *Sacramento Bee*. https://www.sacbee.com/news/california/fires/article222044970.html

Blake, D. (2018, March). Motivations and paths to becoming faculty at minority serving institutions. *Education Sciences*. https://www.mdpi.com/2227-7102/8/1/30

Bland, K. (2018, May 30). Blue eyes, brown eyes: What Jane Elliott's famous experiment says about race 50 years on. *The Republic*. https://www.azcentral.com

Block, G. (2016). UCLA sustainability committee guiding campus principles of sustainability. *UCLA Sustainability Charter*. University of California. https://www.sustain.ucla.edu/wp-content/uploads/UCLA-Sustainability-Charter.pdf

Bloom, B. (1974). *Taxonomy of educational objectives: The classification of educational goals*. David McKay Company, Inc.

Boff, L., & Boff, C. (1987). *Introducing liberation theology*. Orbis Books.

Boggs, G.L., & Kurashige, S. (2012). *The next American Revolution: Sustainable activism for the twenty-first century*. University of California Press.

Bond, B., Quintero, E., Casey, L., & Di Carlo, M. (2015). *The state of teacher diversity in American education*. Albert Shanker Institute.

Bourdieu, P. (1973). Cultural reproduction and social reproduction. In R. Brown (Ed.), *Knowledge, education, and social change* (Chapter 3). Routledge. https://doi.org/10.4324/9781351018142

Bouweraerts, P.K. (2015, March 12). Future student teachers partner with local school. *TMCC* [Website]. https://www.tmcc.edu/news/2015/03/future-student-teachers-partner-with-local-school

Bowles, S., & Gintis, H. (1976). *Schooling in capitalist America: Educational reform and the contradictions of economic life*. Haymarket Books.

Boyd, R. (1999). *Indians, fire, and the land in the Pacific Northwest*. Oregon State University Press.

Brannon, M. (2021, August 6). Greenville Rancheria health and tribal offices destroyed by Dixie Fire. *Redding Record Searchlight*. https://www.redding.com/story/news/local/fires/2021/08/06/greenville-rancheria-health-tribal-offices-destroyed-dixie-fire/5520722001/

Brill, M. (2018). *Dolores Huerta stands strong: The woman who demanded justice*. Ohio University Press.

Brown, B. (2018). *Dare to lead: Brave work. Tough conversations. Whole hearts*. Random House.

Budiman, A. (2020, August 20). Key findings about U.S. immigrants. *Pew Research Center*. https://www.pewresearch.org/fact-tank/2020/08/20/key-findings-about-u-s-immigrants/

Bullard, L., & Xin, X. (2012). *Earth day every day*. Millbrook Press.

Buswell, R. (Ed.). (2004). *Encyclopedia of Buddhism*. Thomson Gale.

Butler, J. (1989). Transforming the curriculum: Teaching about women of color. In J.A. Banks, C.A. Banks, & C. McGee (Eds.), *Multicultural education: Issues and perspectives*. Allyn and Bacon.

California State University. (2017, October 11). New grant funding will bolster CSU efforts to enhance diversity of teacher candidates [Press release]. https://www.calstate.edu/csu-system/news/Pages/New-Grant-Funding-Will-Bolster-CSU-Efforts-to-Enhance-Diversity-of-Teacher-Candidates.aspx

Campbell, D. (2000). *Choosing democracy: A practical guide to multicultural education*. Prentice Hall.

Carnoy, M. (1998). The theory and practice of Culturally Relevant Education: A synthesis of research across content areas *Comparative Education Review, 42*(3), pp. 309–337.

Chang, A., & Ifill, S. (2018, April 19). *A lesson in how to overcome implicit bias* [Radio broadcast]. National Public Radio. https://www.npr.org/sections/codeswitch/2018/04/19/604070231/a-lesson-in-how-to-overcome-implicit-bias

Child, B. (1998). *Boarding school seasons: American Indian families 1900–1940*. University of Nebraska Press.

Clair, M. (1994). Introduction to creative writing. In L. Fiol-Matta, & M. Chamberlain (Eds.), *Women of color and the multicultural curriculum: Transforming the college classroom* (pp. 251–259). The Feminist Press.

Clark, E. (1991). Environmental education as an integrative study. In R. Miller (Ed.), *New directions in education: Selections from Holistic Education Review* (pp. 38–52). Holistic Education Press.

Clark, E. (2001). *Designing and implementing an integrated curriculum: A student-centered approach*. Holistic Education Press.

Claybourn, C. (2023, February 22). Magnet vs. charter schools: Differences explained. *US News & World Report*. https://www.usnews.com/education/high-schools/articles/magnet-schools-vs-charter-schools-differences-explained

Coles, R., & Ford, G. (2010). *The story of Ruby Bridges*. Scholastic Paperback.

Crawford, J. (2008, January 8). Working the Quincy mill: African American lumber mill workers in Northern California 1926–1955. *BlackPast.org*. https://www.blackpast.org/african-american-history/working-quincy-mill-african-american-lumber-mill-workers-northern-california-1926-1955/

Cuauhtin, R.T., M. Zavala, C. Sleeter, & W. Au (Eds.). (2019). *Rethinking ethnic studies*. Rethinking Schools.

Cuban, L. (1993). *How teachers taught: Constancy and change in American classrooms 1890–1990 (Research on teaching)*. Teachers College Press.

Cuban, L. (2011, June 16). Jazz, basketball, and teacher decision-making. *Larry Cuban on school reform* (Website). https://larrycuban.wordpress.com/2011/06/16/jazz-basketball-and-teacher-decision-making/

Cuban, L. (2021, April 28). The complexity of teacher decision-making. *Larry Cuban on school reform* (Website). https://larrycuban.wordpress.com/2021/04/28/the-complexity-of-teacher-decision-making/

Damasio, A. (1994). *Descartes' error: Emotion, reason, and the human brain*. Putnam.

Darling-Hammond, L. (2006). *Powerful teacher education: Lessons from exemplary programs*. Jossey-Bass.

Darling-Hammond, L. (2010). Steady work. *Rethinking Schools, 24*(4). https://rethinkingschools.org/articles/steady-work-finland-builds-a-strong-teaching-and-learning-system/

Dastagir, A. (2018, May 28). As Starbucks trains on implicit bias, the author of "White fragility" gets real. *USA Today*. https://courageousconversation.com/as-starbucks-trains-on-implicit-bias-the-author-of-white-fragility-gets-real/

Daydí-Tolson, S. (2018). *Gabriela Mistral: 1889–1957* [Website]. Poetry Foundation. https://www.poetryfoundation.org/poets/gabriela-mistral

Derman-Sparks, L. (1989). *Anti-bias curriculum: Tools for empowering young children*. National Association for the Education of Young Children.

Deruy, E. (2017). Student diversity is up but teachers are mostly White. *AACTE in the News*. https://aacte.org/2013/03/student-diversity-is-up-but-teachers-are-mostly-white/

Desjardins, J. (2017, June 21). How copper riches helped shape Chile's economic story. *Visual Capitalist*. https://www.visualcapitalist.com/copper-shape-chile-economic-story/

DeVos, B. (2018, January 16). Prepared remarks from Secretary Betsy DeVos to the American Enterprise Institute. *US Department of Education*. https://content.govdelivery.com/accounts/USED/bulletins/1d38710

DiAngelo, R. (2018). White fragility. *International Journal of Critical Pedagogy, 3*(3), 54–70.

Diaz, K. (2018). Paulo Freire 1921–1997. *Internet Encyclopedia of Philosophy*. https://iep.utm.edu/freire/

Doig, B., & Groves, S. (2011). Japanese lesson study: Teacher professional development through communities of inquiry. *Mathematics Teacher Education and Development, 13*, 77–93.

Doll, B., Brehm, K., & Zucker, S. (2014). *Resilient classrooms: Creating healthy environments for learning* (2nd ed.). Guilford Press.

Drake, S.M., & Burns, R. (2004). *Meeting standards through integrated curriculum*. ASCD.

Du Bois, W.E.B. (1909). *The souls of Black folk: Essays and sketches*. A.C. McClurg & Co.

Dubin, J. (2017, Fall). Investing wisely in teacher preparation: A San Francisco residency program recruits and retains classroom talent. *American Educator, 41*(3), 31–40.

Dunbar-Ortiz, R. (2014). *An Indigenous people's history of the United States.* Beacon Press.

Dunnell, T. (2018). Sewell ghost town: The "city of stairs" sits high in the Andes above the world's largest underground copper mine. *Atlas Obscura.* https://www.atlasobscura.com/places/sewell-mining-town

Dweck, C.S. (2007). *Mindset: The New Psychology of Success.* Gildan Media Corp.

Eberhardt, J. (2019). *Biased: Uncovering prejudice that shapes what we see, think, do.* Viking.

Ebert, E., & Culyer, R. (2008). *School: An introduction to education.* Thomson Wadsworth.

Eckland, R. (2020, October 19). TMCC Voices: Micaela Rubalcava. *TMCC News* [Website]. https://www.tmcc.edu/news/2020/10/tmcc-voices-micaela-rubalcava

Editors. (2014, Fall). Restorative justice: What it is and what it is not. *Rethinking Schools, 29*(1).

Ehlers, K. (2023). *TMCC faculty* [Website]. https://faculty.tmcc.edu/kehlers/

Elias, J.L. (1975). The Paulo Freire literacy method: A critical evaluation. *McGill Journal of Education/Revue Des Sciences De l'éducation De McGill, 10*(002). https://mje.mcgill.ca/article/view/7044

Elias, M. (2013, Spring). The school-to-prison pipeline: Policies and practices that favor incarceration over education do us all a grave injustice. *Teaching Tolerance, 43.*

Ellison, K., & Freedberg, L. (2015, May 21). New California teaching credentials decline for tenth successive year. *EdSource.* https://edsource.org/2015/new-california-teaching-credentials-decline-for-10th-successive-year/80248

Ellison, S. (1998). *Taking the war out of our words: The art of powerful non-defensive communication.* Bay Tree.

Emdin, C. (2016). *White folks who teach in the hood…and the rest of y'all too: Reality pedagogy and urban education.* Beacon Press.

Englander, E. (2016). Understanding bullying behavior: What educators should know and can do. *American Educator, 40*(4), 24–29.

Espinoza, L., Turk, J., & Taylor, M. (2017). Pulling back the curtain: Enrollment and outcomes at minority serving institutions. *Center for policy research and strategy.* American Council on Education.

Ewing, E., & Hannah-Jones, N. (2018, November 29). *1A: The persistence of segregated schools* [Radio broadcast]. National Public Radio. https://the1a.org/segments/2018-11-29-the-persistence-of-segregated-schools/

Feather River Bulletin Staff. (2019, April 28). Achievement in supporting diversity earns research fellowship for Feather River College. *Feather River Bulletin* https://www.plumasnews.com/achievement-in-supporting-diversity-earns-research-fellowship-for-feather-river-college/

Felice, L., & Richardson, R. (1977). Effects of busing and school desegregation on majority and minority dropout rates. *Journal of Educational Research.* Vol. 70, pp. 242–246.

Ferlazzo, L. (2016, February 6). Response: How to practice restorative justice. *Education Week.* https://www.edweek.org/teaching-learning/opinion-response-how-to-practice-restorative-justice-in-schools/2016/02

Fiol-Matta, L. (1994a). Introduction. In L. Fiol-Matta, & M. Chamberlain (Eds.), *Women of color and the multicultural curriculum: Transforming the college classroom* (pp. 1–13). The Feminist Press.

Fiol-Matta, L. (1994b). Litmus tests for curriculum transformation. In L. Fiol-Matta, & M. Chamberlain (Eds.), *Women of color and the multicultural curriculum: Transforming the college classroom* (pp. 141–143). The Feminist Press.

Fiol-Matta, L., & M. Chamberlain (Eds.). (1994). *Women of color and the multicultural curriculum: Transforming the college classroom.* The Feminist Press.

Fleming, J. (1973). The nationalization of Chile's large copper companies in contemporary interstate relations. *Villanova Law Review,* 18 Vill.L.Rev. 593. https://digitalcommons.law.villanova.edu/vlr/vol18/iss4/2

Flores, A. (2017). *2017 fact sheet: Hispanic higher education and HSIs.* Hispanic Association of Colleges and Universities.

Ford, L., & D. Hardman (2010, June 2). *Nevada Academic Content Standards for English Language Arts & Literacy in History/Social Studies, Science, and Technical Subjects.* Nevada Department of Education. https://acrobat.adobe.com/id/urn:aaid:sc:us:dee4ece2-9388-4ca8-90b3-21c5a6315425

Frankenberg, E., L. Garces, & M. Hopkins (Eds.). (2016). *School integration matters: Research-based strategies to advance equity.* Teachers College Press.

Freire, P. (1985). *Pedagogy of the oppressed.* Continuum Publishing Company.

Fried, R. (2001). *The passionate teacher: A practical guide*. Beacon Press.
Friedman, M. (2007, January). Americans should be free to choose. *USA Today Magazine*.
Gandara, P. (2015). Fulfilling America's future: Latinas in the U.S. *The White House initiative on educational excellence for Hispanics*. http://escholarship.org/uc/item/6bt1m260
Gang, P. (1991). The global-ecocentric paradigm in education. In R. Miller (Ed.), *New directions in education: Selections from Holistic Education Review* (pp. 78–88). Holistic Education Press.
Gardner, H. (1983). *Frames of mind: The theory of multiple intelligences*. Basic Books.
Gasman, M., Samayoa, A., & Ginsberg, Alice. (2016). *A rich source for teachers of color and learning: Minority serving institutions*. University of Pennsylvania.
Gay, G. (2000). *Culturally responsive teaching: Theory, research, practice, and practice*. Teachers College Press.
Geri, L., & MacGregor, J. (1999, January). From innovation to reform: Reflections on case studies of 19 learning community initiatives. *ResearchGate*.
Giroux, H. (1983). *Theory and resistance in education: Towards a pedagogy for the opposition*. Bergin and Garvey.
Gjelten, T. (2015). *A nation of nations: A great American immigration story*. Simon & Shuster.
GLSEN. (2016). How educators address bias in school. *American Education*, *40*(4), 23.
Goldberg, G., & Houser, R. (2017, July 19). Battling decision fatigue. *Edutopia*. https://www.edutopia.org/blog/battling-decision-fatigue-gravity-goldberg-renee-houser
Goleman, D. (1995). *Emotional intelligence*. Bantam Books.
Goleman, D. (2022, June 21). *Emotional intelligence and social emotional learning* [Conference presentation]. Mindful SEAD Leadership Summit, Las Vegas, NV, United States.
Gordon, M. (1964). *Assimilation in American life: The role of race, religion and national origins*. Oxford University Press
Gordon, M. (1991). Assimilation in America: Theory and reality. In N.R. Yetman (Ed.), *Majority and minority: The dynamics of race and ethnicity in American life* (248–261). Allyn and Bacon.
Gramlish, J. (2023, April 6). Gun deaths among U.S. children and teens rose 50% in two years. *Pew Research Center*. https://www.pewresearch.org/short-reads/2023/04/06/gun-deaths-among-us-kids-rose-50-percent-in-two-years/
Grant, T., & G. Littlejohn (Eds.). (2001). *Teaching about climate change: Cool schools tackle global warming*. New Society Publishers.
Gray, L., & Taie, S. (2015). Public school teacher attrition and mobility in the first five years. *National Center for Education Statistics*. Department of Education.
Guarda, D. (2015). *The Finnish critical pedagogical interpretation between self-regulated learning and its transformative functions in a Finnish primary school* [Master's thesis, University of Oulu, Finland]. Ebook. https://eric.ed.gov/?id=ED556348
Guin, K. (2004). Chronic teacher turnover in urban elementary schools. *Policy Analysis Archives*, *12*(42). https://doi.org/10.14507/epaa.v12n42.2004
Gutierrez, G. (1973). *A theology of liberation*. Orbis Books.
Hall, G., Quinn, L., & Gollnick, D. (2008). *The joy of teaching: Making a difference in student learning*. Pearson.
Hanh, T.N. (1995). *Living Buddha, Living Christ*. Riverhead Books.
Hanh, T.N. (1998). *The heart of the Buddha's teaching: Transforming suffering into peace, joy, and liberation*. Broadway Books.
Hanh, T.N. (1999). *Going home: Jesus and Buddha as brothers*. Riverhead Books.
Hanh, T.N. (2002a). *Be free where you are*. Parallax Press.
Hanh, T.N. (2002b). *Friends on the path: Living spiritual communities*. Parallax Press.
Hanh, T.N. (2006). *Transformation and healing: Sutra on the four establishments of mindfulness*. Parallax Press.
Hanh, T.N. (2008). *Breath, you are alive! Sutra on the full awareness of breathing*. Parallax Press.
Hanh, T.N. (2010). *Reconciliation: Healing the inner child*. Parallax Press.
Hanh, T.N. (2014). *No mud, no lotus: The art of transforming suffering*. Parallax Press.
Hanh, T.N., & Weare, K. (2017). *Happy teachers change the world*. Parallax Press.
Haraway, D. (1991). A cyborg manifesto: Science, technology, and socialist-feminism in the late twentieth century. In *Simians, cyborgs and women: The reinvention of nature* (pp. 149–181). Routledge.
Hardin, G. (1968, December 13). The tragedy of the commons. *Science*, New Series, *162*(3859), 1243–1248. https://www.jstor.org/stable/1724745?origin=JSTOR-pdf

Harman, C. (1986, Summer). Base and superstructure. *International Socialism, Series 2*(32), 3–44. https://www.marxists.org/archive/harman/1986/xx/base-super.html

Heckman, J. (2020). *Invest in early childhood development, reduce deficits, strengthen the economy*. The Economics of Human Potential. https://heckmanequation.org/resource/invest-in-early-childhood-development-reduce-deficits-strengthen-the-economy/

Hernández, L. (2021, August 4). Dixie Fire tears through historic town of Greenville in Plumas County. *San Francisco Chronicle*. https://www.sfchronicle.com/bayarea/article/Dixie-Fire-tears-through-town-of-Greenville-in-16365252.php

hooks, b. (1994). *Teaching to transgress: Education as the practice of freedom*. Routledge.

Hotez, P. (2023). *The deadly rise of anti-science: A scientist's warning*, Johns Hopkins University Press.

Howe, W., & Lisi, P. (2019). *Becoming a multicultural educator: Developing awareness, gaining skills, and taking action* (3rd ed.). SAGE.

Hsieh, C., & Urquiola, M. (2006). The effects of generalized school choice on achievement and stratification: Evidence from Chile's voucher program. *Journal of Public Economics, 90*(8–9), 1477–1503. https://EconPapers.repec.org/RePEc:eee:pubeco:v:90:y:2006:i:8-9:p:1477-

Hu-DeHart, E. (1993). The history, development, and future of ethnic studies. *Phi Delta Kappa International, 75*(1) 50–54. https://www.jstor.org/stable/20405023?origin=JSTOR-pdf

Hull, R.H. (2016, May). The art of nonverbal communication in practice. *The Hearing Journal, 69*(5) 22–24. https://nvrc.org/the-art-of-nonverbal-communication-in-practice/

Iberlin, J., & Ruyle, M. (2017). *Cultivating mindfulness in the classroom*. Marzano Research.

Ingersoll, R. (2015). What do the national data tell us about minority teacher shortages? In Albert Shanker Institute (Eds.), *The state of teacher diversity in American education* (pp. 14–22). Albert Shanker Institute.

Ingersoll, R., & Smith, T. (2003). The wrong solution to the teacher shortage. *Education Leadership, 60*(8), 30–33.

Jett, T. (2018). Module 2G: Embracing diversity in your classroom. In *Association of College and University Educators (ACUE) course at TMCC*. https://acue.org/

Johnson, J., Musial, D., Hall, G., & Gollnick, D. (2017). *Foundations of American education: Becoming effective teachers in challenging times* (17th ed.). Pearson.

Kayes, P. (2006). New paradigms for diversifying faculty and staff in higher education: Uncovering cultural biases in the search and hiring process. *Multicultural Education, 14*(2), 65–69.

Keep Truckee Meadows Beautiful. (2019–2020). Warriors youth education program. *Annual Report*. https://www.ktmb.org/

Keltner, D. (2023). *Awe: The new science of everyday wonder and how it can transform your life*. Penguin Press.

Kendi, I.X. (2019). *How to be an antiracist*. One World.

Kiefer, B.Z. (2010). *Charlotte Huck's children's literature* (10th ed.) McGraw Hill.

Kim, V. (2022, April 6). *Reimagining change at a minority-serving institution* [Conference presentation]. Northern Nevada Summit, Reno, NV, United States.

Kimmerer, R.W. (2013). *Braiding Sweet Grass*. Milkweed Editions.

King, F. (2018). *The earth memory compass: Diné landscapes, and education in the twentieth century*. University of Kansas Press.

King, Jr., M.L. (1964). *Why we can't wait*. The New American Library.

Kleinrock, L. (2021). *Start here, start now: A guide to antibias and antiracist work in your school community*. Heinemann Publishing.

Kolbert, E. (2014). *The sixth extinction: An unnatural history*. Henry Holt and Company.

Kozol, J. (1991). *Savage inequalities: Children in America's schools*. Harper Perennial.

Kunhardt, P. (Director). (2018). *King of the wilderness* [Documentary]. HBO.

Ladson-Billings, G. (1995). Toward a theory of culturally relevant pedagogy. *American Educational Research Journal, 32*(3), 465–491. https://www.jstor.org/stable/1163320

Ladson-Billings, G., & Tate, W. (2006). Toward a critical race theory in education. In A.D. Dixson, C.K. Rousseau Anderson, & J.K. Donnor (Eds.), *Critical race theory in education: All God's children got a song* (pp. 47–68). Routledge.

Lardner, E. (2018, July 9–12). Plenary 1: Placing ourselves in context: Learning communities today [Conference presentation]. 20th Annual National Summer Institute on Learning Communities, Olympia, WA, Evergreen State College.

LeDoux, J. (1996). *The emotional brain: The mysterious underpinnings of emotional life* [Website]. https://motherhoodcommunity.com/what-part-of-brain-controls-emotions-and-how-does-chronic-stress-affect-the-brain/

LeFrancois, G. (2000). *Psychology for teaching*. Thompson Learning.

Letelier, O. (1976). *Chile: Economic freedom and political repression*. Transnational Institute 2015.

Lewis, A., & Diamond, J. (2015). *Despite the best intentions: How racial inequality thrives in good schools*. Oxford University Press.

Li, X., & Carroll, D. (2007). *Characteristics of minority-serving institutions and minority undergraduates enrolled in these institutions*. National Center for Education Statistics.

Libby, J. (2023, May 9). Earth Day: Honoring our precious planet. *TMCC News* [Website]. https://www.tmcc.edu/news/2023/05/earth-day-honoring-our-precious-planet

Lindstrom, C. (2020). *We are water protectors*. Roaring Brook Press.

Liu, R. (2016, September 27). The Chicago Boys now and then. *King's Review*. https://www.kingsreview.co.uk/essays/the-chicago-boys-now-and-then

Lonas, L. (2021, August 19). Wildfire burns across Sierra Nevada for first time in recorded history. *The Hill*. https://thehill.com/policy/energy-environment/568541-wildfire-burns-across-sierra-nevada-for-first-time-in-recorded/

Louisiana State Personnel Development Grant. (2010). Equitable classroom practices observation checklist. Adapted from *A Resource for Equitable Classroom Practice 2010*. Montgomery County Public Schools. https://www.montgomeryschoolsmd.org/departments/development/resources/ecp/ecp%20-%2008-13-10.pdf

Loveless, T. (2017, March 22). *2017 Brown Center report on American education: Race and school suspensions*. Brookings Institution. https://www.brookings.edu/articles/2017-brown-center-report-part-iii-race-and-school-suspensions/

Lynch, J. (1983). *The multicultural curriculum*. Batsford Academic and Educational, Ltd.

Madden-Dent, T., & Oliver, D. (2021). *Leading schools with social, emotional, and academic development (SEAD)*. IGI Global.

Madison, J. (2013, October 2). *The Black Eagle: Jane Elliot interview* [Radio broadcast]. SiriusXM Urban View.

Madison, J. (2018, September 13). *The Black Eagle: The Congressional Black Caucus Foundation legislative conference* [Radio broadcast]. SiriusXM Urban View.

Madison, J. (2020, December 3). *The Black Eagle: United Negro College Fund, Dr. Lomax interview* [Radio broadcast]. SiriusXM Urban View.

Maher, Michelle. (2005). The evolving meaning and influence of cohort membership. *Innovative Higher Education*, *30*(3), 195–211. https://doi.org/10.1007/s10755-005-6304-5

Malinowski, M. (2022, January 13). Chile's president-elect sounds the alarm amid economic boom. *Bloomberg.com*.

Manley, M. (1994). Developmental writing (ESL). In L. Fiol-Matta, & M. Chamberlain (Eds.), *Women of color and the multicultural curriculum: Transforming the college classroom* (pp. 259–262). The Feminist Press.

Marcetic, B. (2016, September 21). The murder of Orlando Letelier. *Jacobin.com*. https://jacobin.com/2016/09/orlando-letelier-pinochet-nixon-kissinger

Mascarenhas, M. (2020). *ESPM 15 - Society, environment, and culture* [Syllabus]. Department of Environmental Science, Policy, & Management, University of California, Berkeley.

Mascio, B. (2016, Summer). True teaching expertise: The weaving together of theory and practice. *American Educator*, *40*(2), 18–21.

Maslow, A.H. (1943). A theory of human motivation. *Psychological Review*, *50*(4), 370–396. https://doi.org/10.1037/h0054346

Maynard, M. (2021). *English 100* [Syllabus]. English Department, Truckee Meadows Community College.

Mcguire, J.M., Scott, S.S., & Shaw, S.F. (2006). Universal design and its applications in educational environments. *Remedial and Special Education*, *27*(3), 166–175. https://doi.org/10.1177/07419325060270030501

McIntosh, P. (1989, July/August). White privilege: Unpacking the invisible knapsack. *Peace and Freedom Magazine*, 10–12. https://psychology.umbc.edu/files/2016/10/White-Privilege_McIntosh-1989.pdf

Melhop, F. (2023). *Art 124: Printmaking* [Syllabus]. Fine Arts Program, Truckee Meadows Community College.

Menter, I., Eliot, D., Hulme, M., Lewin, J., & Lowden, K. (2011). *A guide to practitioner research in education*. SAGE.

Mercado, C.I. (2016). Teacher capacities for Latino and Latina youth. In A. Valenzuela (Ed.), *Growing critically conscious teachers* (pp. 24–38). Teachers College Press.

Merriam-Webster. (n.d.). American Dream. In *Merriam-Webster.com* [Thesaurus]. Retrieved September 1, 2023, from https://www.merriam-webster.com/thesaurus/american%20dream

Middleton Manning, B.R. (2018). *Upstream: Trust lands and power on the Feather River*. University of Arizona Press.

Miller, R. (Ed.). (1991). *New directions in education: Selections from Holistic Education Review*. Holistic Education Press.

Miller, R. (Ed.). (1995). *Educational freedom for a democratic society: A critique of national goals, standards, and curriculum*. Resource Center for Redesigning Education.

Morgan, H. (2014). Review of research: The education system in Finland: A success story other countries can emulate. *Childhood Education, 90*(6), 453–457. https://www.tandfonline.com/doi/abs/10.1080/00094056.2014.983013

Mountain Eagle (2023, August 11). *Indigenous spirituality* [Workshop presentation]. Truckee Meadows Community College.

Muñoz, C. (1989). *Youth, identity, and power: The Chicano movement*. Versobooks.

Museo de la Memoria y Los Derechos Humanos. (2017, July & August). *Cartelera: Seis Historias de Dictadura*. Santiago, Chile.

NASA Minority University Research and Education Project (2023–2024). https://msiexchange.nasa.gov/pdf/2023-2024%20MSI%20List.pdf

Natanson, H. (2023, March 6). Slavery was wrong and 5 other things some educators won't teach anymore. *The Washington Post*. https://www.washingtonpost.com/education/2023/03/06/slavery-was-wrong-5-other-things-educators-wont-teach-anymore/

National Association of Community College Teacher Education Programs (NACCTEP). (2023). *Member Profile* [Website]. https://www.nacctep.org/

National Geographic Society. (2019). Biodiversity. In *National Geographic Resource Library* [Encyclopedic entry]. https://education.nationalgeographic.org/resource/biodiversity/

National Head Start Association. (2019). *The head start model*. National Head Start Association.

National Native American Boarding School Healing Coalition (NABS). (2012). *U.S. Indian Boarding School History* [Website]. https://boardingschoolhealing.org/education/us-indian-boarding-school-history/

Nava, R. (2001). *Holistic education: Pedagogy of universal love*. The Foundation for Educational Renewal.

Neruda, P. (2023, September 6). Nothing but death. Retrieved from https://poets.org/poem/nothing-death

Nevada Pre-Kindergarten Standards Revised and Approved. (2010). *Building a foundation for school readiness and success, K-12 and beyond*. Nevada State Board of Education.

Niebuhr, G. (1999, October 16). A monk in exile dreams of return to Vietnam. *New York Times*. https://www.nytimes.com/1999/10/16/us/a-monk-in-exile-dreams-of-return-to-vietnam.html

Nieto, S. (2013). *Finding joy in teaching students of diverse backgrounds: Culturally responsive and socially just practices in U.S. classrooms*. Heinemann Publishing.

Nieto, S. (2016). Education in a globalized world. In J.A. Banks, M. Suárez-Orozco, & M. Ben-Peretz (Eds.), *Global migration, diversity, and civic education: Improving policy and practice* (pp. 202–222). Teachers College Press.

Noguera, P. (1998, June 12). Confronting the challenge of privatization in public education. *In Motion Magazine*. https://www.inmotionmagazine.com/pnpriv1.html

Noguera, P. (2017, April 16). What it takes: The debate over LA's charter expansion plan is an opportunity to devise ways to ensure all schools succeed. *In Motion Magazine*. https://inmotionmagazine.com/er17/pn17-what-it-takes.html

Noguera, P. (2018, March 7). *Here and Now: After Parkland, don't "turn our schools into prisons," says education activist* [Radio broadcast]. National Public Radio. https://www.wbur.org/hereandnow/2018/03/07/school-shootings-security

Nordell, J. (2021). *The end of bias: A beginning - the science and practice of overcoming unconscious bias*. Metropolitan Books.

Nyirenda, J. (1996). The relevance of Paulo Freire's contributions to education and development in present day Africa. *Africa Media Review, 10*(1), 1–20. https://n2t.net/ark:/85335/m5gm83074

Oakes, J., & Lipton, M. (2007). *Teaching to change the world*. McGraw Hill.

Obama, M. (2018). *Becoming*. Crown.

Ogay, T., & Edelmann, D. (2016). "Taking culture seriously": Implications for intercultural education and training. *European Journal of Teacher Education, 39*(3), 388–400. https://doi.org/10.1080/02619768.2016.1157160

Ogbu, J. (1982). Cultural discontinuities and schooling. *Anthropology and Education Quarterly, 3*(4), 290–307. https://doi.org/10.1525/aeq.1982.13.4.05x1505w

Oliver, D. (2023, June 21). *A.J. Crabill and student panel discuss student led restorative practices* [Conference presentation]. SEAD Summit, Las Vegas, NV, United States.

Olneck, M. (1990, February). The recurring dream: Symbolism and ideology in intercultural and multicultural education. *American Journal of Education, 98*(2), 147–174. https://doi.org/10.1086/443950

Omi, M., & Winant, H. (1986). *Racial formation in the United States: From the 1960s to the 1980s*. Routledge.

Orange, T. (2018). *There there*. Vintage Books.

Ormrod, J. (2000). *Educational psychology: Developing learners*. Prentice Hall.

Osta, K., & Vasquez, H. (2019, June 13). Don't talk about implicit bias without talking about structural racism. *National Equity Project* [Website]. https://medium.com/national-equity-project/implicit-bias-structural-racism-6c52cf0f4a92

Pabon, A., Sanderson, N., & Kharem, H. (2011). Minding the gap: Cultivating black male teachers in a time of crisis in urban schools. *The Journal of Negro Education, 80*(3), 358–367.

Paideia Active Learning. (2018). Socratic Seminars. https://www.paideia.org/our-approach/paideia-seminar/index

Pak-Harvey, A. (2018, January 17). Nevada ranks last in US for education, but officials upbeat. *Las Vegas Review-Journal*. https://www.reviewjournal.com/local/education/nevada-ranks-last-in-us-for-education-but-officials-upbeat/

Paris, D., & H.S. Alim (Eds.). (2017). *Culturally sustaining pedagogies: Teaching and learning for justice in a changing world*. Teacher College Press.

Parry, T. (1996, December). Will pursuit of higher quality sacrifice equal opportunity in education? An analysis of the education voucher system in Santiago. *Social Science Quarterly, 77*(4), 821–834.

Partelow, L., Spong, A., Brown, C., & Johnson, S. (2017, September 14). America needs more teachers of color and a more selective teaching profession. *Center for American Progress* [Report]. https://www.americanprogress.org/article/america-needs-teachers-color-selective-teaching-profession/

Perkins, J. (2006). *Let justice roll down*. Baker Books.

Petchauer, E., & Mawhinney, L. (2017). *Teacher education across minority-serving institutions: Programs, policies, and social justice*. Rutgers University Press.

Plimpton, G. (1916, October). The hornbook and its use in America. *Proceedings of the American Antiquarian Society* (pp. 264–272). https://www.americanantiquarian.org/proceedings/44806617.pdf

Porter, G. (1995). The White man's burden, revisited. In R. Miller (Ed.), *Educational freedom for a democratic society: A critique of national goals, standards, and curriculum* (pp. 170–188). Resource Center for Redesigning Education.

Prakash, M.S. (2013, July 16). Peaceful revolution? Gandhi's four paths to get there. *Yes! Magazine*. https://truthout.org/articles/peaceful-revolution-gandhis-four-paths-to-get-there/

Putman, S.M., & Rock, T. (2018). *Action research: Using strategic inquiry to improve teaching and learning*. SAGE.

Quinlan, C. (2016, May 6). Report shows there aren't enough teachers of color coming through traditional pipelines, think progress. *Center for American Progress*.

Rechtschaffen, D. (2016). *The mindful education workbook: Lessons for teaching mindfulness to students*. W.W. Norton & Company.

Reece, B. (2022). *Social justice and community college education*. Routledge.

Reese, D. (2022, February 9-April 12). *Supporting literacy and culturally responsive instruction for Native American students* [Webinar series]. Native Ways of Knowing. https://my.hcoe.net/event/native-ways-of-knowing-webinar-series/

ReShel, A. (2018). *Thich Nhat Hanh's 14 Principles of Engaged Buddhism* [Website]. https://uplift.love/thich-nhat-hanhs-14-principles-of-engaged-buddhism/

Resmovits, J., Kohli, S., & Poindexter, S. (2016, September 5). A closer look at test scores for English learners, magnet schools and charters. *Los Angeles Times*. https://www.latimes.com/local/education/la-me-standardized-test-snapshot-20160831-snap-story.html

Resnick, S. (2013, April 9). *History of education in Finland* [Website]. https://sites.miis.edu/sarahr/research-topics/the-education-system-of-finland/history-of-education-in-finland/

Reynolds, J., & Kendi, I.X. (2021). *Stamped (for kids): Racism, antiracism, and you*. Little, Brown, and Company.

Reynolds, P. (2021a). *Lifespan human development* [Syllabus]. Social Sciences Department, Truckee Meadows Community College.

Reynolds, T. (2021b). *Computer information technologies* [Syllabus]. Computer Technologies Department, Truckee Meadows Community College.

Ries, P. (1994). Understanding outcomes of curriculum transformation. In L. Fiol-Matta, & M. Chamberlain (Eds.), *Women of color and the multicultural curriculum: Transforming the college classroom* (pp. 37–49). The Feminist Press.

Roberts, S., & Pruitt, E. (2009). *Schools as professional learning communities: Collaborative activities and strategies for professional development*. Corwin Press.

Robertson, J. (2021). *Nibi Emosaaawdang the water walker*. Second Story Press.

Rome, D., & Martin, H. (2010, July 1). *Deep Listening* [Website] Lion's Roar. https://www.lionsroar.com/are-you-listening/

Ross, V. (2003). The Socratic method: What it is and how to use it in the classroom. *Speaking of teaching: Stanford University newsletter on teaching, 13*(1).

Rothstein, R. (2014, November 12). The racial achievement gap, segregated schools, and segregated neighborhoods - a Constitutional insult. *Race and social problems, 6*(4). https://www.epi.org/publication/the-racial-achievement-gap-segregated-schools-and-segregated-neighborhoods-a-constitutional-insult/

Rothstein, R. (2017). *The color of law: A forgotten history of how our government segregated America*. Liveright.

Rubalcava, M. (1965a). *Exhibit 1: Photograph of author at Mayfield School*. Head Start Program.

Rubalcava, M. (1965b). *Exhibit 2: Photograph of author in Head Start classroom*. Head Start Program.

Rubalcava, M. (1995). *Multicultural transformation: Historical development and three curriculum models* [Doctoral dissertation, University of California, Berkeley]. UMI Dissertation Services.

Rubalcava, M. (2001–2024). *Truckee Meadows Community College field notes* [Unpublished journal].

Rubalcava, M. (2005, May). Let kids come first. *Educational Leadership, 62*(8), 70–72. https://eric.ed.gov/?id=EJ725939

Rubalcava, M. (2020, Spring). *Heartfelt welcome statement* [Course assignment]. Social Science Department, Truckee Meadows Community College.

Sadker, D., Sadker, M., & Zittleman, K. (2008). *Teachers, school, and society*. McGraw-Hill.

Sahlberg, P. (2015). *Finnish lessons 2.0: What can the world learn from educational change in Finland?* (2nd ed.). Teachers College Press.

Salisbury, J. (2021). *Law 264 civil evidence* [Syllabus]. Paralegal/Law Program, Truckee Meadows Community College.

San Pedro, T.J. (2017). This stuff interests me: Re-centering Indigenous paradigms in colonizing school spaces. In D. Paris, & H.S. Alim (Eds.). *Culturally sustaining pedagogies: Teaching and learning for justice in a changing world*. Teacher College Press.

Sanders, W., Wright, P., & Horn, S. (1997, April). Teacher and classroom context effects on student achievement: Implication for teacher evaluation. *Journal of Personnel Evaluation in Education, 11*(1), 57–67.

Savage, G. (2017, September 6). New report brings facts to light on minority serving institutions. *Diverse: Issues in Higher Education*. https://www.diverseeducation.com/students/article/15101225/new-report-brings-facts-to-light-on-minority-serving-institutions

Schoorl, D. (2008). Finding aid for the Ethel Young papers, 1942–1992. *Center for Primary Research and Training (CFPRT)*. UCLA Library, Department of Special Collections, Manuscripts Division https://oac.cdlib.org/findaid/ark:/13030/kt6m3nf2bd/entire_text/

Shaer, M. (2018, March). The archaeology of wealth inequality: Researchers trace the inequality gap back more than 11,000 Years. *Smithsonian Magazine, 48*(4). https://www.smithsonianmag.com/history/archeology-wealth-inequality-180968072/

Sinarski, Jessica. (2022, June 21). *Light up the learning brain* [Conference presentation]. Mindful SEAD Leadership Summit, Las Vegas, NV, United States.

Sleeter, C.E. (1994, Spring). White racism. *Multicultural Education, 1*(4), 5–8.

Sleeter, C.E. (2001). Preparing teachers for culturally diverse schools: Research and the overwhelming presence of whiteness. *Journal of Teacher Education*, *52*(2), 94–106.

Sleeter, C.E. (2011). The academic and social value of ethnic studies. *National Education Association Research Department*. https://files.eric.ed.gov/fulltext/ED521869.pdf

Sleeter, C.E., & Carmona, J. (2017). *Un-standardizing curriculum: Multicultural teaching in the standards-based classroom* [Multicultural education series]. Teachers College Press.

Sleeter, C.E., & Zavala, M. (2020). *Transformative ethnic studies in schools: Curriculum, pedagogy, and research*. Teacher College Press.

Smith, A. (1776). *An inquiry into the nature and causes of the wealth of nations*. Liberty Classics.

Smith, B., MacGregor, J., Matthews, R., & Gabelnick, F. (2004). *Learning communities: Reforming undergraduate education*. Jossey-Bass.

Smith, D., & Tyler, N. (2006). *Introduction to special education: Making a difference*. Pearson.

Spring, J. (2000). *American education* (9th ed.). McGraw Hill.

Spring, J. (2014). *The American school: A global context* (9th ed.). McGraw Hill.

Staats, C. (2015, Winter). Understanding implicit bias. *American Educator*, *39*(4). https://www.aft.org/ae/winter2015-2016/staats

Strauss, V. (2016, December 21). To Trump's education pick, the U.S. public school system is a "dead end." *Washington Post*. https://www.washingtonpost.com/news/answer-sheet/wp/2016/12/21/to-trumps-education-pick-the-u-s-public-school-system-is-a-dead-end/

Strayhorn, T. (2021, October 1). *Intersectionality, belonging and student success: Putting it all together* [Conference presentation]. Southern Nevada Diversity Summit.

Suárez-Orozco, M.M., & Michikyan, M. (2016). Education for citizenship in the age of globalization and mass migration [Introduction]. In J.A. Banks, M. Suárez-Orozco, & M. Ben-Peretz (Eds.), *Global migration, diversity, and civic education: Improving policy and practice* (pp. 1–25). Teachers College Press.

Summers, J.K., & Smith, L.M. (2014). The role of social and intergenerational equity in making changes in human well-being sustainable. *Ambio*, *43*(6), 718–728. https://doi.org/10.1007/s13280-013-0483-6

Takaki, R. (1979). *Iron cages: Race and culture in nineteenth-century America*. Alfred A. Knopf.

Takaki, R. (1989). *Strangers from a different shore*. Little Brown and Company.

Takaki, R. (1993). *A different mirror: A history of multicultural America*. Little Brown and Company.

Teaching Tolerance. (2015). *Observing for equity* [Checklist]. Southern Poverty Law Center. https://www.learningforjustice.org/sites/default/files/general/Observing%20Equity.pdf

Teller, M. (2016). *The Black Lives Matter Reference Guide* [Website]. http://tinyURL.com/BLMRefGuide

Temming, M. (2021, April 14). STEM's racial, ethnic and gender gaps are still strikingly large. *Science News*. https://www.sciencenews.org/article/science-technology-math-race-ethnicity-gender-diversity-gap

Terada, Y. (2019, February 4). The research is in: Understanding a teacher's long-term impact. *Edutopia* [Website]. https://www.edutopia.org/article/understanding-teachers-long-term-impact/

Toledo, E., & MacHugh, K. (2022). Tejer y destejer en Cecilia Vicuña. *ALPHA: Revista de Artes, Letras y Filosofía*, *1*(11), 51–62. https://alpha.ulagos.cl/index.php/alpha/article/view/1059

Truckee Meadows Community College. (2018). *FREE Learning Community*. *TMCC* [Website]. https://www.tmcc.edu/free

Trungpa, C. (1993). *Training the mind: Cultivating loving-kindness*. Shambhala Press.

Tutu, D., & Tutu, M. (2014). *The book of forgiving: The fourfold path for healing ourselves and our world*. HarperOne.

United States Artists. (2019, October 8). *We can simultaneously be* [Artist's statement: Cecilia Vicuña]. https://www.unitedstatesartists.org/fellow/cecilia-vicuna

Upton, M. (2023, April 28). Levi Mullen circles his philosophy in new show. *Plumas News*. https://www.plumasnews.com/levi-mullen-circles-his-philosophy-in-new-show/

Urtubey, J. (2023, June 20). *Joyous and just education for all* [Conference presentation]. SEAD Summit.

US Department of Agriculture. (2019, June). *Nature's Benefits: Plumas National Forest*. https://www.fs.usda.gov/

Valdés, G. (2016). Language and immigrant integration in an age of mass migration. In J.A. Banks, M. Suárez-Orozco, & M. Ben-Peretz (Eds.), *Global migration, diversity, and civic education: Improving policy and practice* (pp. 77–104). Teachers College Press.

Valenzuela, A. (2016). True to our roots. In A. Valenzuela (Ed.), *Growing critically conscious teachers* (pp. 1–23). Teachers College Press.

Vedantam, S. (2023, March 13 & 14). *Revealing your unconscious Part I and II* [Audio podcast]. Hidden Brain Media. https://hiddenbrain.org/podcast/revealing-your-unconscious-part-1/& https://hiddenbrain.org/podcast/revealing-your-unconscious-part-2/

Vergou, A., & Willison, J. (2016). Relating social inclusion and environmental issues in botanic gardens. *Environmental Education Research*, 22(1), 21–42. https://www.tandfonline.com/doi/full/10.1080/13504622.2014.984161

Verschelden, C. (2017). *Bandwidth recovery: Helping students reclaim cognitive resources lost to poverty, racism, and social marginalization.* Stylus Publishing.

Vescio, V., Ross, D., & Adams, A. (2008, January). A review of research on the impact of professional learning communities on teaching practice and student learning. *Teaching and Teacher Education*, 24(1), 80–91. https://doi.org/10.1016/j.tate.2007.01.004

Vicuña, C. (2017, July 7). *Quipo Mapocho: Movimientos de Tierra: Arte y Naturaleza* [Art exhibit]. Museo Nacional Bellas Artes.

Vigil, J.D. (1988). The nexus of class, culture and gender in the education of Mexican American females. *The Broken Web: The Educational Experience of Hispanic American Women, editado por Teresa McKenna y Flora Ida Ortiz*, 70–106.

Walker, Timothy. (2016, September 15). Kindergarten naturally: Pine needles and crackling fires replace whiteboards and desks in Finland's forest classrooms. *The Atlantic*. https://www.theatlantic.com/education/archive/2016/09/kindergarten-naturally/500138/

Walter, A. (2019, May 16). *The Takeaway: School segregation is getting worse 65 years after Brown v. Board of Education* [Audio podcast]. National Public Radio. https://www.wbez.org/stories/podcast-2019-05-16-school-segregation-is-getting-worse-65-years-after-brown-v-board-of-education/bac7df0c-4bf9-4f72-abaa-204397667328

West, C. (1993). *Race matters*. Beacon Press.

Whalen, P., & Phelps, E. (2009). *The human amygdala*. Guilford Press.

Whitney, K. (2019, March 25). *Cecilia Vicuña* [Art exhibit]. UC Berkeley Art Museum and Pacific Film Archive (BAMPFA).

Wilkerson, I. (2020). *Caste: The origins of our discontents*. Random House.

Williams, R. (1973, November/December). Base and superstructure in Marxist cultural theory. *New Left Review*, I(82). https://newleftreview.org/issues/i82/articles/raymond-williams-base-and-superstructure-in-marxist-cultural-theory

Wink, J., & Flores, J. (1992). Induction programs for bilingual teachers: Addressing the needs of teachers in language minority education. In J. Flores (Ed.), *Chicanos in higher education* (pp. 73–80). The Journal of the Association of Mexican American Educators, Inc.

Woehr, C. (2021). *Diversity Training* [Workshop presentation]. Truckee Meadows Community College.

Wong, H., & Wong, R. (1998). *The first days of school: How to be an effective teacher*. Harry K. Wong Publications.

Yamamura, E., & Koth, K. (2018). *Place-based community engagement in higher education*. Stylus Publishing.

Young, T., Bryan, G, Jacobs, J., & Tunnell, M. (2020). *Children's literature briefly*. Pearson.

INDEX

Note: **Boldface** page references indicate glossary entries. *Italic* references indicate figures

academic freedom **326**; curriculum and instruction 59, 177–179; Finland 130, 152; learning communities 171; philosophy of humanity 12–13, 201; use in Approach-in-Dimension 26, 253, 257, 267, 271–272, 281; use in Multicultural Mindfulness 217; use of space, time, materials, and learning environments 5, 30, 55; *see also* spacetime superpower
academic integration *64*, 84, 115, 129, 152, 156, 175, 194, 221, 247
action-reflection 2, 11, 42, 54, 57, 65, 67, 72–73, 82, 84, 100–105, 156, 167–168, 185, 211, 216, 228, 235, 248–249, 257, 265, 293, *308*, 323
affirmative action 102, 166
African American migration to Quincy, California 79
Alaya (defined) 62, **326**
Alcatraz Island (Indigenous occupation) 22, 80
Alim, Samy 323
Allende, Salvador 138, 140–141, 155
Alvarez, Julia (*Return to Sender*) 313
Anglo-conformity *13*, 51, 57–58, 91, 93, *94*, *101*, 105, *106*, 108–110, 117, 120–122, *147*, 178, 180, 192, 222, 255, 265, 272–273, 283, **326**
Anishinaabe prophecy 40
antibias-antiracist 38, 90–124, *147*, 169, 203–204, 254, **327**
antibias brain 65, 66–67
antibias communication norms 73–75, *166*, 169, 182, 197, 298, **327**
anxiety 31, 33, 63, *116*, *154*, 176, 217, 222, 227, 246, 249n23, 262, 270, 284, 303, 309, 321; academic 294, 297; change 117; climate 66, 153; conflict 25; cultural 105; double-consciousness 105; math 243; parental 29; social 67–68, 104, 106, 119, 167, 217, 233, 242, 270, 272, 276, 292, 301; test 293
Approach-in-Dimension 252–288, **327**
aspects (ostensive and performative) 10
assimilation **327**
assimilation curriculum 12, 38, 103, 106, 110, 138, *179*, 180, 198

backwards design 2, *64*, 70, 75, *94*, 175, 178, 209, 244–246, 313, 319, 323, **327**
Ball, Teresa 23, 27–29, 43
banking education 4, *9*, *59*, 60, 145, *179*, 209, 218, 253, 255, 261, 266, 293, 295, 319–320, **327**
Banks, James A. 8–9, 12, 253, 263–267, 285
Bee Campus USA garden 30
bias 90–124, **328**; economic 93, 101–102; explicit 93, 102; familiarity 93, 103; history of 105–106; implicit 93, 97, 99–100, 102–105, 109, 119, 149, 155, 203, 227, 253; institutional 93, 100–102, 227; omission 93, 103–104; patronization 93, 104–105; projection 93, 105; ten forms, arm's-length 93–96, 104–105; tokenization 93, 104
big picture **327**
biodiversity 26–30, *53*, 77, 114, *234*, 266–268, 294, *301*, **328**
Blackhawk, Ned 83–84
Black Lives Matter 22
Black Panther Party 22, 37

Blanco, Rafael 79
Boric, Gabriel 22, 142
Bowles, Samuel 152
Brave New World mural *222*, 278, 280
Brazil 10, 23, 309
breathwork **328**
breathwork bell 33, 68, 311, **328**
Bridges, Ruby 234; William Frantz Elementary 234
Brown v. Board of Education (1954) 109, 115
Bullard, Lisa (*Earth Day Every Day*) 39, 209

Camp Fire 38, 77
Carmona, Judith 180
charter schools 144, 150–151
Chavez, Cesar 37, 73–74, 275, 277
Chicago Boys 140, 143, 155
Chicana-Mestiza 37–38
Chicano Studies 30, 74
Chile 8, 10, 27–29, 155; education system 125, 130–131, 138–143, 149–151, 309; student unrest 21–23
Chödrön, Pema 38
choice education 125, *146–148*, 150, 155
Clark, Edward 8–9, 86, 238
codification 205
colorblind 91–93, 97, 108–109, 115, 201–203, 261, 304, **328**; bias 31, 37, 103; hypocrisy *98*; ignorance 25, 44; individualism 57, *61*, 100–104, 133, 156, 175, 229, 247, 283; melting pot/salad bowl 126; policies 55, 166; racism 115; society wished for 7, 138, 167, 176, 195, 263, 270, 318
concept map 95, **329**
conscientização see critical consciousness
Content Creation 165, *166*, 169, 173–174, *174*, 182, 188, 197, *208*, 313, **329**
Covid-19 28, 202, 223, 278
critical consciousness 50–89, 163–215, **329**
cultural identity terms 7
Culturally Relevant Education (CRE) (sometimes "culturally responsive") 9, 47, 93, 292
cultural/multicultural identity 36, 64, *64*, 268, **329**, **332**; Healthy Multicultural Identity Quest 36–41, 259–260, *259*, 268, 270–271
culture 21–49, 252–288, 291–325; *see also* culture competence; Culture-Conscious Listening (defined); culture consciousness
culture circles 9, 23, 26, 30, 39, 54, 58, 82, 85, 126, 164–165, 181–183, 204, 211, 237, 255, 265, 322
culture competence (also known as "cultural competence") 291–325, **329**
Culture-Conscious Listening (defined) **329**
culture consciousness 32, 76, 78, 84, 115, 166, 175–176, 249, 270, 292, **329**; feminist 93

Culture Survey (provided) 6, 15
culture surveys (generally) 5, 42, 55
curriculum *see* eight forms of curriculum

DACA/DAPA (Deferred Action for Childhood Arrivals/Deferred Action for ParentalAccountability) 275
Danger, Fe (fee) *40*, *202*, *297*, *302*
De Anza College 30
de facto segregation 10, 100, 109, 129, 137
dehumanization **330**
desegregation 95, 98–99, 105, 115, *118*, 137, *147*, 153, 155, 192–193, 292, 307, 318; busing 137, 220
detracking 115, 130, 152, 192
Diamond, John B. 8, 99–100, 149
diversity baseline 5
Diversity Circles 153–215, **330**; Academic Faculty 42, *74*, 165, *166*, 169, 181, 198; Administrative Faculty *74*, 165–167, 169, 181, 198–200, **326**; Community Supports *74*, 165, *166*, 169, 181, **328**; Designated Committee *74*, 165, *166*, 169, 181, 273, **330**; Laboratory 42, *64*, *74*, 165, *166*, 169, *174–175*, 181, 185–186, 204, *206–207*, *222*, *239*, 244, *245*, 278, **332**; Student Cogen *74*, 165, *166*, 169, 181, *202*, *297*, *301*, 312–316, **335**; Student Cohort 35, *74*, 165–166, 169, 181, 197–199, **335**; three strategies (sharing, circle questions, global praxis) 67, 183, *185*, *209*, 239, 319
Dixie Fire 38–39, 77
Donahue, Rain *206*
double-consciousness 103, 105, 270, 305, 307–308, **330**
Drive-All-Blames-Into-One 230, *230*, 246
Dunbar-Ortiz, Roxanne 8, 43, 81

Earth Day 39, 205, *209*, 244, *245*, 264, 296
eight forms of curriculum (explicit, hidden, null, extra, required, recommended, received, integrated) *177*, 178, 267, **330**
El Teniente Mine 139–140
Emdin, Christopher 82, 181
English Language Learners (ELLs) 205
Environmental Consciousness 2, 10, *11*, 38–39, 58, 77, 98, 218, 222, 232, 243, 257, 308–312, **330**
Environmental Humanization 58, 84–86, 165, *166*, 172–174, *202*, *208*, 313; inquiry 169, 182, 197–199, **331**
Environmental Liberation Education 291–325, **331**
equity ecosystems *11*, *13*, 27, 94, *118*, 126, 151–157, 165, *166*, *173*, *175*, *208*, 221–222, 241, 277, 295, 313, **331**
equity education 125, *147*

espaciotiempo see spacetime
ethnic studies 194–196

Faculty for Radical Empowerment and Enlightenment (FREE) 30, 42–43, 186, 204–208, *222–223*, 278–279
farmworkers 73, 277; Afro-Brazilian 211
Feather River 76–78
Feather River College (FRC) 78–79
feedback loop 120, 127–129, 133, *136*, 144, 157, *173*, *175*, *185*, 241, 304, 319
fifteen hundred (1,500) daily decisions 12, 50, *128*, 253, 303
Finland 8–9, 130–131, 138, 151–152, 294, 309
Four-Rs (4-Rs) Antibias Practice 12, 24, 90, 112, *116*, 117, 246
Freire, Paulo 8–9, 37, 46, 58, 82–85, 116, 158, 164–165, *173*, 181–183, 191, 204–205, 211, 213n46, 237, 265, 293, 309, 322; exiled 23, 309; 45-day literacy program 23, 165, 211
Friedman, Milton 140, 143–144, 155
Fulbright-Hays Seminars Abroad Program 23, 27, 40

Gandhi, Mohandas K. 183, 234
Gang, Phil 9, 85
Garlock, Candace 207, *245*
gathas 34, 46, 85, 121, 157, 210, 230–231, 243, 248, 285, 321, **331**
generations: future 3; seven 184
GI Bill 34
Gill's Onions 314
Gintis, Herbert 152
global praxis (defined) **331**
Global Praxis Iceberg 240–241, 298
Goade, Michaela (*We are Water Protectors*) *3*, 278
Gordon, Milton 121
Great Basin Tribes ceremony 43, 205
Greenville Rancheria 39, 77–78
growth mindset 54, 57, 63–64, 104, 153, 189, 224, 245, 270, 284, **332**

Hall, Precious 38
Hammett, Julia 42
Hanh, Thich Nhat 8–9, 24, 38, 44–45, 82–83, 116–117, 158, 172, 211, 218, 222–224, 235–238, 248, 280, 285; exiled 236; with Martin Luther King, Jr. at news conference 235
Harlem Club 79
Head Start 34–37
healing pathways 232–239
High Desert State Prison 79
Hispanic Association of Colleges and Universities 191
holistic education 11, 13, 23, 27, 36, 54, 74, 82–83, 111, 130, 146, 151–152, 156–157, 163, 165, 168–169, 172, 181, 184, 198–200, 209, 241, 253, 260, 294, 300, *302*, **332**
homeschooling 144
homogeneity 106, 192, 195, 258, 262, 283
hooks, bell 8–9, 64, 83, 91, 114
Hornbook Ping Pong *207*
hornbooks 106–107, 206, *207*
Huerta, Delores 37, 73–74, 276–277
humanization **332**; goals 3, 9, 51–58, 61, 82, 84, 106, 152, 164, 171, 174, 208, 217, 252, 281, 293–294, 300, 303

Ill, Tim *3*, 222, 308
individualism and collectivism 76, 137, 141, 146, *147*, 164, 176, 180, 229, 233, 246, 266
individualized education plans (IEPs) 138, 220
integration **332**
invisible hand 102, 142–144
Itliong, Larry D. 74

Journals, Transformative Breathwork and (at the end of each chapter): How Do Anglo-Conformity and White Supremacy Impact My Classroom? 120; How do Diversity Circles reconcile the oppressor–oppressed conflict? 210; How is Global Praxis a verb and Environmental Humanization a noun? 84; What's a Transformative Teacher? 45; What's Environmental Liberation Education? 321; What's Multicultural Mindfulness? 247; What's the Approach-in-Dimension? 284; Why do Culture Conscious Listening? 157
"joyful and just" 2, 12, 23, 97, 118, 217, 233, 266

Kauffman, Julie 319
Keltner, Dacher 233–234, 303
Kendi, Ibram X. 66, 121, 280, 320
King, Jr., Martin Luther 1, 8–9, 44, 91, 172, 176, 182–183, 226–227, *235*, 236, 261, 320; with Thich Nhat Hanh at news conference 235
Kirkpatrick, Kate 222
Kleinrock, Liz 46
Krupka, Jenny *279*

Ladson-Billings, Gloria 47, 82
LaMott, Lily (*Measuring Up*) 313
Latin America 38, 183, 237, 313
learning communities 2, 9, 11, 86, 133, 163, *166*, 170–172, 178, 211, 220, 243, *302*
Learning Outcome Rubric Redesign 273–274, *274*
Letelier, Orlando 141; assassination 140–141, 155
Lewis, Amanda 8, 99–100, 149
liberation **332**; *see also* liberation education

liberation education **332**
liberation theology 183, 237
Lienlaf, Leonel (Mapuche poet) 158
liminality 196
Lindstrom, Carole (*We are Water Protectors*) *3*, 278
Lyon, Mary 59

magnet schools 115, 150–151
Maidu 39, 76–80
Mandela, Nelson 37
Mann, Horace 60
Mapuche 22, 158
Marston, Ron 319
Marvin Picollo School 198–200
mass incarceration 79, 83, 122, 137
Mayfield School 35–37
Medicaid/Medicare 34
Mendoza, Jean 43
mentorships 135, 152, 176, 189–192, 198, 200, 220
mindfulness principles (interbeing, impermanence, emptiness) **333**; *see also* Multicultural Mindfulness
Minority-Serving Institutions (MSIs) 8, 41, 190–192, 273, 309, 312
Mistral, Gabriela 74–75
Mount Holyoke 59
Mullen, Levi 78
Multicultural Mindfulness 216–251, **333**
Multicultural Mindfulness Activities: Choice Education versus Equity Education 146; Culture-Conscious Listening 33; Diversity Circle Now 14; Diversity Circle Recipe 185; Drive-All-Blames-Into-One 230, *230*; Environmental Liberation Education Made Easy 311; Five Diversity Circle Projects 168; 4-Rs Antibias Practice 112; Healthy Multicultural Identity Quest 258; Nonverbal Communication Toothpick Game 298; Reducing Arm's-Length Bias 94; Shaping Space for Interbeing 224; Split-Second Conflict Resolution 24; Structural Competence Imagination 134; Superdiverse Biodiverse Me Turtle 268, *269*; Un-biasing the Mind 62

National Black Farmers Association (NBFA) 135
neoliberalism 23, 121, 322, **333**
Neruda, Pablo 27
new social order 46, 122, 318
Nieto, Sandra 8, 322
Nobel Prize: Gabriela Mistral 74; Martin Luther King, Jr. 236; nomination of Thich Nhat Hanh 235; Pablo Neruda 27
No Dakota Access Pipeline (NoDAPL) *208*
nonverbal communication norms 298, 301, **333**

nonviolent direct action 9–10, 115, 119, 176, 183, 185, 234, **333**

Omi, Michael 122
opportunity hoarding 106, 148–149
oppression **333**
outdoor education 16n19, 36, 39, 42, 75–78, 82, 170, 199, 220, 293, 317

Paiute 76, *175*, 205; Newe-Numa (Shoshone Paiute) 39, 205; Numu (Northern Paiute) 39; Nuwu (Southern Paiute) 39
Paradise, California 28, 38, 77
Paris, Django 323
peace corners 71, 220
Pinochet, Augusto 140–143, 155, 309
Plumas Arts 79
Plumas Unified School District (PUSD) 76–80
Popol Vuh 277
praxis (defined) **333**
Predominantly White Institutions (PWIs) 41, 190–192
pre-prejudice **334**
Privatization ("choice") Theory 144
public education 9–10, 37, 60–61, 84, 130–131, 138, 141, 144, 146–152, 223–224, 245–246, 309

Quincy, California 38, 78–79
quipus 22; Cecilia Vicuña installation 309–310

race **334**
race-neutral policies 4, 10, 100–103, 115, 126, 149, 166, 175, 209, 265
racial achievement gap 91, 99–100, 111, 115, 122, 137, 166, 175, 192, 195, 220, 281, 318
racialize **334**
Racial Justice Act (RJA) 203
Reese, Debbie 43
Reno, Nevada 28, 39, 82, 198
reparative justice 102, 111–112, 233
research areas 8
restorative justice 26, *116*, 153, *154*, 156–158, 196, 221, 234–235, 238, 246, 249, 254, *259*, 284, 300, 316
Riverview High School 99–100, 149
Rothstein, Richard 133
Rubalcava, Micaela 47, 86, 122, 158, 211, 249, 286, 323
Rubalcava, Roberto 38
Ryan, Pam Muñoz (*Esperanza Rising*) 313

Sánchez, George I. 46, 121, 318
San Francisco Teacher Residency (SFTR) Program 190
sangha 11–12, 26, 164–167, 211, **334**
San Martín, Jose de 21–22

school-to-prison pipeline 138, 307
segregation **334**
shifts in history 11, 311
Sierra Valley 76
sixth extinction 77
slavery 23, 39, 81–83, 105, *147*, 194–195
Sleeter, Christine 8, 180–182
Smith, Adam 142–143; social emotional (hyphenated as an adjective) **334**; social-emotional learning (SEL) 9, 23, 30, 77, 151, 198, 249n23, 266, 292, 314
Socratic Circle 136, 168–170, **334**
Spacetime (defined) **334**
spacetime superpower 62, 69–73, 82, 292–294, **335**
Starlight Missionary Baptist Church 79
STEAM (science, technology, engineering, arts, and mathematics) 189, 191, *207*, 242, *245*, *297*, *302*, *306*, *308*; C-STEAM (culture, science, technology, engineering, arts, and mathematics) 43, 245
STEM (science, technology, engineering, and mathematics) 61, 138, 181, 202, 292
structural change 4, 10, 52, 151–153, 183, 237, 272, 300
structural competence (defined) **335**
substructure (economic) 125–160; *see also* substructure-superstructure model
substructure-superstructure model 29, *127–128*, *129–130*, 146, 159n7, **335**
superdiversity-biodiversity 30, 82, 94, 223, 323
superdiversity (defined) **335**
superstructure (social) 125–160; *see also* substructure-superstructure model
surveys *see* Culture Survey (provided), culture surveys (generally)
sustainability (defined) 3, **336**
Systemic Bias Taproot 100, *101*
systemic stratifications 66, 145, *179*

Takaki, Ronald 8, 23, 37, 44, 196
teachable moments 2, 26, 51, 75, 217, 297, 316–317
teacher paradox 51–52, 76, 188, 208
Tecuexe community 37–38
Thompson, Tommy (Wisconsin governor) 144
three mindfulness principles (interbeing, impermanence, and emptiness) 11, 86, 117, 163, 165, *166*, 172, 218, 232, 238

Three Transformative Tools (defined) **336**; *see also* Approach-in-Dimension; Diversity Circles; Multicultural Mindfulness
tonglen (defined) **336**
Traditional Ecological Knowledge (TEK) (aka "Native Ways of Knowing") 58, 195, **336**
transformative teacher (defined) **336**
transformative teaching theory 54
Troy Female Seminary 59
Truckee Meadows Community College (TMCC) 39, 70, 186, 198–201, 204, 206, 273, 275, 279
true happiness **336**
Trungpa, Chögyam 9, 84, 120, 157, 247–248, 284
turtle island 43, 245, 269

unbolting desks 209, 220
University of California, Berkeley 30, 37, 110
University of Chicago 140, 143, 155
Urtubey, Juliana 12, 189

VanWinkle, Marden *35–36*, 38
Vicuña, Cecilia 8–9, 69, 82, 309, *310*, 322; exiled 309
Vietnam 236
Vygotsky, Lev 199

Wašiw (Washoe) 39, 76, *175*, 205
Watershed Program (Sixth Grade) 76–77, 82
wealth gaps 37, 109
welcome statements 42, 201, 203–204, *273*, 274–280
White Fragility 105–106, 261–262
White privilege 37–38, 61, 105, *106*, 122, 195, 261, 276
White superiority 37, 92, 100, *101*, 103–105, *106*, 108, 111, 121–122, 145, 305–307, **337**; assimilation *147*; bias 57; norms 96; versus cultural deficiency 60
White supremacy 37, 46, 91, 100, *101*, 108, 111, 120 122, 176, 262, 270, **337**
Willard, Emma 59
Winant, Howard 122

Xin, Xiao (*Earth Day Every Day*) 39, 209
Xu, Ann (*Measuring Up*) 131

zone of proximal development 199